Once Upon a Time Lord

Once Upon a Time Lord

The Myths and Stories of
Doctor Who

Ivan Phillips

BLOOMSBURY ACADEMIC
LONDON · NEW YORK · OXFORD · NEW DELHI · SYDNEY

BLOOMSBURY ACADEMIC
Bloomsbury Publishing Plc
50 Bedford Square, London, WC1B 3DP, UK
1385 Broadway, New York, NY 10018, USA

BLOOMSBURY, BLOOMSBURY ACADEMIC and the Diana logo are trademarks
of Bloomsbury Publishing Plc

First published in Great Britain 2020
Reprinted 2020

Cover design: Charlotte Daniels
Cover images: Background © Cagatay Orhan / Unsplash Tardis © Alice in
Otherland / Getty Images

A catalogue record for this book is available from the British Library.

A catalog record for this book is available from the Library of Congress.

ISBN: HB: 978-1-7883-1888-4
PB: 978-1-7845-3267-3
ePDF: 978-1-7883-1646-0
eBook: 978-1-7883-1645-3

Series: Who Watching

Typeset by Newgen KnowledgeWorks Pvt. Ltd., Chennai, India
Printed and bound in Great Britain

To find out more about our authors and books visit www.bloomsbury.com
and sign up for our newsletters

For Mum,

in memory of Dad,

and with dimensionally transcendental love to Kate,

Molly, Grace and Eliza.

Contents

Figures

Acknowledgements

I would like to thank all those at Bloomsbury (and, initially, I.B. Tauris) who have ensured that this book didn't get lost in the space-time vortex, in particular my editors, Rebecca Barden and Philippa Brewster, my cover designer Charlotte Daniels, my original copy editor, Kate Reeves, and my project manager at Newgen, Kalyani. Thanks, too, to my many supportive, inspiring and endlessly knowledgeable colleagues at the University of Hertfordshire and beyond, and to my students, past, present, future: it's a pleasure learning with you. An earlier version of the lycanthropic musings in Chapter 3 of this book appears in Sam George and Bill Hughes' collection of essays *In the Company of Wolves: Werewolves, Wolves and Wild Children* (Manchester: Manchester University Press, 2020): thanks to Sam and Bill for permission to borrow from myself. Finally, thanks to my friends and family: without you, nothing would have been done, and nothing would have been worth doing. You remind me, as I keep moving, of all the people that I used to be.

Introduction: 'Quite a great spirit of adventure'

Defining terms: Myths, stories, *Doctor Who*

As the Doctor knows only too well, and as successive companions have quickly discovered, setting coordinates does not guarantee a destination. 'You don't steer the TARDIS,' Peter Capaldi's Time Lord tells Bill Potts (Pearl Mackie) in the opening scene of 'Smile' (2017), 'you negotiate with it. The still point between where you want to go and where you need to be, that's where she takes you.' A book that sets its coordinates as 'the myths and stories of *Doctor Who*' will likewise need to negotiate a still point between an apparently simple authorial intention and more complex critical needs. If 'story', for instance, is separated from 'myth' for anything other than rhetorical convenience, then it becomes necessary to clarify the distinction. The most straightforward definition of 'myth', after all, is 'story', from ancient Greek *muthos* and Latin *mythos*, but this brings with it an array of alternatives, including not only 'narrative' and 'plot' but also 'speech' and 'fable'. If the subject here is 'the myths and stories of *Doctor Who*', which myths are being referred to (or which sense of 'myth'), which stories (or sense of 'story') and, come to think of it, which *Doctor Who*?

Taking a pragmatic view, the notion of 'story' can be allowed to pass more or less unchallenged. *Doctor Who* is self-evidently preoccupied with storytelling – 'We're all stories in the end,' the Eleventh Doctor (Matt Smith) muses by the bedside of Amelia Pond (Caitlin Blackwood) towards the end of 'The Big Bang' (2010) – and it would serve little purpose here to get snarled up in a consideration of the relative dimensions of *story* and *plot*, *histoire* and *récit*, or *fabula* and *syuzhet*. This study is not, in the end, concerned with the finer discriminations of narratology. It is, however, concerned with understandings and applications of 'myth' as a viable categorical concept. A positioning of *Doctor Who* in relation to this over-familiar and much-contested term becomes, from this point of view, a matter of some significance. It is taken as read that, against any strict criterion of deep-rooted, shared and venerated origin stories ('the prime authority, or charter, for the religious institutions of each tribe, clan, or city', prescribes Robert Graves),[1] the series of tales woven around the character of the Doctor since his first appearance on BBC television on 23 November 1963 cannot qualify as a 'true' myth. It can, though, be seen to constitute a pseudo-myth, one that has drawn upon diverse narrative tropes with classical precursors. From this perspective *Doctor Who* seems to have a 'mythical method' akin to that identified by T. S. Eliot in James Joyce's *Ulysses* (1922), albeit much looser in its aims and methods – more open in its format, less coherent in its execution.[2] Joyce knew that his great mythopoeic anti-novel remained a novel: he knew, in other words, that it was *not* a myth. At the same time, he knew that it represented a radical critique and reinvention of the form it inhabited, of what (to apply Roland Barthes's distinct adaptation of the word) might be seen as the 'myth' of the realist novel. *Ulysses* achieved a subversive mythicization of Western life on a single day in 1904. *Doctor Who*, without the potential for a comparably unified vision or the impetus for a similarly uncompromising formal agenda, has nevertheless amounted to a mythicization of the cultural conditions out of which it is produced.

Using mythography to read *Doctor Who* is, in one sense, an intuitive response to a body of fantastic stories which must surely satisfy Joseph Campbell's definition of 'wonder tales'.[3] The field of study is far from clear-cut, however, presenting difficulties in terms of disputed boundaries, variable contexts and divergent understandings. Myth, mythology and their many cognates describe a landscape that is immense, slippery, unsettled. Neil Clarke, writing with specific reference to *Doctor Who*, describes the territory as 'riddled with ambiguities'.[4] Taking a broader view, Laurence Coupe asserts, 'Myth is paradigmatic, but there is no pure paradigm.'[5] Add to this the distinctive size, scope and disposition of *Doctor Who* itself, and the choice for anyone wanting to develop a workable mythography is stark: either settle on a single impure paradigm of myth and apply it with consistency, or allow for the possibility of an exploratory navigation between paradigms. I have chosen the second option, feeling that it is more suited to the temperament of the particular text, with its inherent contradictions, its sense of being at once infinite and intimate, continuous and disjointed, inventive and indebted, endlessly renewable yet essentially old-fashioned. Myth is a vast area of scholarly investigation and *Doctor Who* is a 'vast narrative'.[6] The opportunities for getting lost between the two are manifold. In attempting to refine my methodology I have resisted the temptation to place 'myth' *sous rature* in the Derridean manner, ~~myth~~ ('Since the word is inaccurate, it is crossed out. Since it is necessary, it remains legible'), but only just.[7] A brief overview of the history of writing on myth, necessarily partial, might be beneficial here.

The theorization of myth is old enough to have become mythical: 'There are no theories of myth itself,' writes Robert Segal, 'for there is no discipline of myth in itself.'[8] If it exists at all, then, the study of myth predates Euhemerus in the fourth century BC, with his rationalization of mythologies as the ornamented and fantastical reworkings of historical figures and events. And even if the *discipline* exists, some of its original exponents have raised the question of whether, by now, it should effectively be a discipline without a subject. Early social anthropologists like E. B. Tylor and Sir James Frazer believed that myth was the 'primitive' forerunner of science and as such was incompatible with a modern world view: in an advanced technoscientific age, myth simply should not exist. This would seem to anticipate more recent claims by, among others, Ivan Strenski, who has written that 'there is no such "thing" as myth. There may be the word "myth", but the word names numerous and conflicting "objects" of inquiry, not a "thing" with its name written on it.'[9]

Yet for a subject that does not exist, studied as part of an academic discipline that *should* no longer exist, myth has been a remarkably energetic area of scholarship, not least since the beginning of the twentieth century. The roll call of commentators who have written on myth in the last hundred years or so is prodigious, and the variety of approaches that they have taken to the subject scarcely less so. This variety is surely a vital sign (myth and the theorization of myth might exist after all!) but it is also a problem, since it requires ruthless selectivity, the acceptance of contradiction, a capacity for synthesis or, as seems most likely, all three. If the emotional-mystical ideas of myth proposed by Lucien Lévy-Bruhl are to be utilized alongside the cooler, more cerebral readings of Claude Lévi-Strauss, or the ideological analyses of Roland Barthes alongside the sacred schemas of Mircea Eliade, how are such contrasting viewpoints to be reconciled within a survey of storytelling in *Doctor Who*? Even a single writer can present starkly discrepant agendas, yet the early symbolic idealism of Ernst Cassirer is as resonant in the context of the Doctor's adventures as the politically brooding mythography of his later writings.

Of course, Strenski's denial of the existence of myth is not *really* consonant with the obsolescence predicted by Tylor and Frazer: it represents, in fact, a negation of their thesis. Where they contended that myth would wither away as an archaic irrelevance in the age of scientific apotheosis, Strenski implies that it is only within the technologized environment of modernity that its full suggestive power is understood:

> Myth is everything and nothing at the same time. It is *the* true story or a false one, revelation or deception, sacred or vulgar, real or fictional, symbol or tool, archetype or stereotype. It is either strongly structured and logical or emotional and pre-logical, traditional and primitive or part of contemporary ideology. Myth is about the gods, but often also the ancestors and sometimes certain men. It is 'Genesis' and 'General Strike', 'Twentieth Century' and 'Cowboy', 'Oedipus' and 'Frankenstein', 'Master Race' and 'Chosen People', 'Millennium' and 'Eternal Return'. 'Myth' translates *muthos*, but also *die Sage*, *die Mythe* or *lili'u*. It is both 'la *geste* d'Asdiwal' and 'le *mythe* de Sisyphe'. It is charter, recurring theme, character type, received idea, half-truth, tale or just a plain lie.[10]

Myth survives into the modern world because of its sheer promiscuity of significance, its adaptability to new conditions. Even a comparatively strait-laced account like that of G. S. Kirk makes this clear in its initial scoping of the topic, emphasizing the 'insistence on carrying quasi-mythical modes of thought, expression, and communication into a supposedly scientific age'.[11] It is here, in this quality of resilient, connotative plurality, that myth is seen most persuasively as a discourse suited to *Doctor Who*. Myth is mutable: it has not been rendered obsolete or meaningless by the demise of those ancient cultures into which its roots can be traced. On a much smaller scale, *Doctor Who* has survived its own mythic (or, more accurately, mythicized) origins, at the same time carrying them into its expanded present. The challenge is for criticism to acquire a similarly lithe durability.

In his contribution to Anthony Burdge, Jessica Burke and Kristine Larsen's *The Mythological Dimensions of Doctor Who*, Matt Hills brings two distinct readings into dialogue around the Russell T. Davies era.[12] The first of these (from cultural studies) is based on rationally formal principles derived largely from Lévi-Strauss; the second (from the TV industry) is founded on more emotionally and commercially attuned ideas of plot and character.[13] The tension that Hills negotiates is that between the intellectual objectivity (some would say 'aridity') of high theory and a more impressionistic (some would say 'populist') mode of enquiry. Within the domain of '*Doctor Who* studies',[14] this represents a stylistic conciliation of John Tulloch and Manuel Alvarado's high theorizing in the first book-length study of the series in 1983, and the accessibility that James Chapman set against it over twenty years later: 'The Doctor may have conquered Daleks, Cybermen and Ice Warriors, but would he survive an encounter with Foucault, Derrida or Deleuze?'[15] More importantly, it posits a correlation between myth as, in Bruce Lincoln's phrase, 'ideology in narrative form'[16] and myth as flourishing fantasy brand.

The aim in the present study is to take the hint from Hills, recognizing that a flexible approach is peculiarly suited to the subject matter. Barthes and Paul Ricoeur are, in many ways, the presiding critical spirits here, the former for his example as an interrogator of illusion, the latter for his advocacy of 'social imagination'.[17] Myth, for Barthes, is what 'transforms history into nature'; for Ricoeur, it is 'the bearer of other, *possible* worlds'.[18] If Barthes encourages us to read a text such as *Doctor Who* for its ideological taint, its inevitable complicity in the-way-things-are, Ricoeur tempts us to identify the utopian possibilities beyond this. In one of the earliest academic critiques of *Doctor Who*, John Fiske takes a Barthesian line to declare that 'popular art is not escapist, but mythic': in other words, it is an endorsement of everyday sociopolitical realities, not a liberation from them.[19] The more alien the alien worlds, the more monstrous the monsters, the more efficient the ideological reinforcement. The Doctor's exploits are depicted as a 'naturalizing force, denying the historicity of [their own] production and reception'.[20] Fiske's argument is well made, exemplary of its kind, and persuasive to a point, but it is itself a form of myth. As will become clear, I consider *Doctor Who* more than capable of satisfying the desire to discover 'just how a work of popular art can be other than reactionary'.[21]

Questions of canon: Keeping track (or trying to)

In the final years of its classic series *Doctor Who* showed an unusual degree of self-consciousness about its own mythological status and potential. The arrival of Andrew Cartmel as script editor towards the end of 1986 coincided with that of Sylvester McCoy as the Seventh Doctor and initiated a sequence of stories by new, young writers in which continual referencing of the show's history – a contentious element of *Doctor Who* throughout John Nathan-Turner's time as producer (1980–9) – was accompanied by both a heightened tendency to borrow from external mythologies and an intensified development of internal ones. 'The Curse of Fenric' (1989), with its mix of Hammer-style vampire eroticism, Lovecraftian monstrosity, Second World War techno-heroism and deep ideological unease, was typical in this respect. Not only did Ian Briggs's story exert imaginative pressure on a number of received mythic narratives (from the Viking invasions to English heroic wartime pastoral), but it also epitomized attempts after McCoy's first season to turn the Doctor himself into a less stable, more darkly perplexing kind of hero:

> FENRIC [IN SORIN'S BODY] The choice is yours, Time Lord. I shall kill you anyway, but if you would like the girl to live, kneel before me.
> ACE I believe in you, Professor.
> FENRIC/SORIN Kneel, if you want the girl to live!
> DOCTOR Kill her.

Calling his companion, Ace (Sophie Aldred), 'a social misfit' and 'an emotional cripple' is part of the Doctor's strategy to defeat Fenric, a necessary undermining of her faith in him, but it is still an act of cruelty. It restores something of the unease of the earliest *Doctor Who* stories, the first thirteen episodes from 'An Unearthly Child' to 'The Edge of Destruction', in which the volatility of the hero (William Hartnell) made him less than reliably heroic. This template for challenging behaviour on the Doctor's part has also been used in 'The Invasion of Time' (1978) and 'The God Complex' (2011), as well as in many of the Virgin novels (1991–7) and Big Finish audio dramas (1999–present).

Together with other stories of the period – Ben Aaronovitch's 'Remembrance of the Daleks' (1988) and 'Battlefield' (1989), Kevin Clarke's 'Silver Nemesis' (1988), Rona Munro's 'Survival' (1989) – 'The Curse of Fenric' represented an effort to recover a sense of the primal enigma of *Doctor Who*'s central character, what Tulloch and Alvarado had by then described as its 'hermeneutic code (the code of puzzles and mysteries)'.[22] Cartmel and his associates were not the first production team to give prominence to the perplexities of the Doctor's personality and to draw on prior mythologies in order to adjust the scope of the programme. They were, however, the most brazen in the attempt. They were also, crucially, the first to be informed by a fan sensibility. Not all of the new stable of creators had grown up watching *Doctor Who* from behind the sofa as children and then as dedicated enthusiasts into adulthood, but many of them had. The last three years of the classic series marked, in this respect, the point at which a complex merging of identities – fans, producers – began to take place. As a consequence, discourses of production and reception became ever more intricate, a situation intensified in the decade that followed as, following the final episode of 'Survival' on 6 December 1989, fans seized the means of mythic production. The quiet removal of the show from television – 'The BBC never publicly declared the demise of *Doctor Who*,' writes Miles Booy[23] – left a vacuum that was filled by the products of fan invention and aspiration.

How this mutation of the creative ecology affected the expanding mythology of *Doctor Who*, and the myths woven around it, will be a focus of the first chapter of this book. For now, it is worth noting the contrast between the official (and therefore public) condition of the show and the vitality of its continuing existence off-screen. Beyond McCoy's initially slapstick demeanour there had been a strategic deepening and darkening of the narrative that his portrayal embodied. Colin Baker's depiction of the Sixth Doctor had already emphasized elements of unpredictability and danger in the character but without, apparently, gaining the confidence of the core audience, the curiosity of a new one, or the respect and financial beneficence of BBC management. The popular success and longevity of Doctor Who seems, on the whole, to have been a source of bemusement to the organization that created it, but the loss of institutional support, exacerbated by a slow decline in ratings during the 1980s, was only one of the problems for the show. There was also the issue, as Chapman, Kim Newman, Jim Leach and others have observed, that the conceptual ambition of the later McCoy stories was undermined by a propensity to lose narrative coherence.[24] David Rafer, for instance, refers to 'Silver Nemesis' as 'a pretentious mish-mash' and 'The Curse of Fenric' suffered, in its broadcast version, from the need to edit it down to size, becoming a congested, occasionally brilliant riddle rather than the richly textured yarn that its novelization eventually revealed it to be.[25] As Booy writes, 'interpretation of the McCoy years necessarily became a search for some aborted level or hidden meaning'.[26] This might suggest that the attempt to extend the mythic scope of Doctor Who after a quarter of a century on TV screens was either a valiant failure or a fundamental miscalculation. In an important sense, though, it created the conditions from which – via Virgin Books, Big Finish and the TV movie of 1996 – the series would be regenerated by Russell T. Davies in the early years of this century. Moreover, in the cluttered, gapped, chaotic quality of some of the products of the 'Cartmel Masterplan' it is possible to discover the kind of evocative abundance that is almost definitive of classical myth.

However else it is defined, it is clear that a 'myth' is a cumulative and irregular mass of material that needs to be examined as a whole as well as in fragments. To form a mythic understanding of Doctor Who, every artefact contributing to its developing mythology must be available for study. With this in mind, the approach of the current book is comparable to that of Piers D. Britton in TARDISbound and Kevin S. Decker in Who Is Who?[27] In other words, a flexibly thematic arrangement is preferred to a more chronological one, with classic and new Who treated alongside each other and shown to be in dialogue. Similarly, although the public eminence and cultural reach of the television series mean that, inevitably, this will be the main focus of discussion, other manifestations of the mythology are a significant part of the story. This, of course, raises questions of canon and, tempting as it might have been to leave these for others to fail to answer, they have proven both difficult to avoid and extremely suggestive in relation to ideas of myth. 'Myth, after all,' Coupe has written, 'is inseparable from the idea of totality; yet myth has only ever been a gesture towards it.'[28]

The concept of a resolved canon is almost certainly incompatible with traditional understandings of myth and, in the context of *Doctor Who*, it is surely a fascinating chimera. Broadly speaking, when confronting the insoluble problem of canon, there is the pragmatic approach – 'the television series takes priority over what is said in the other media'[29] – and there are arguments. This book tends towards the latter, while keeping the television screen in constant view. Regrettably, however, its scope does not allow for extensive reflection on the offshoot dramas *K9 and Company* (1981), *The Sarah Jane Adventures* (2007–11), *Torchwood* (2006–11) and *Class* (2016).

Almost forty years ago, Tulloch and Alvarado supposed that the 'committed audience' would have 'an accumulated knowledge and clear memory of a programme's past'.[30] When that programme is as expanded and ramified as *Doctor Who*, however, the knowledgeable accumulation will inevitably include aporias and elisions, and the memory might only be clear in inverse proportion to its reliability. Towards the end of their study, Tulloch and Alvarado noted that the 'programme coherence' of *Doctor Who* was 'totally bound up with the mythology of two decades of adventure'.[31] Two decades have now become more than five decades and a concern for coherence is a fundamental aspect of 'brand management' for the regenerated television series.[32] It is a concern, though, that can never achieve more than a playful compromise with the contradictions of the mythology.

There are so many possible narrative tracks within *Doctor Who*, so many discursive practices and areas of disputed methodology, that the sensible strategy must be to set limits on any enquiry. Hills is explicit in making 'televised *Doctor Who* from 2005 onwards' the foundation of his *Triumph of a Time Lord*,[33] and both he and Andrew O'Day argue convincingly that 'new *Who*' can – and to some extent *should* – be separated from the 'classic' series in critical discussions, being the product of an entirely different ecology of creation and consumption. O'Day is right to suggest that, in terms of making general qualitative assessments of the old and the new, 'there is no comparison'.[34] From the perspective of an exploration of the mythology of *Doctor Who*, the idea of setting limits would risk an impoverishment of the analysis. It would also, I suspect, be impossible. The nature and success of the fiftieth anniversary celebrations in 2013 demonstrated not only a rich, vital interplay between classic and new *Who* but also an essential continuity which, in mythic terms, transcended half a century of wonderful incoherence.

'Inconsistency', Newman writes, 'was built into the format from the outset, to the eventual frustration of fans who like to hammer the whole series into some overarching design.'[35] Lans Parkin and Lars Pearson, at the start of their colossal and meticulous *Ahistory: An Unauthorized History of the Doctor Who Universe*, offer a disclaimer about the viability of their unifying project:

> Now, with dozens of new books, audios, comic strips, short stories and a new TV series, not to mention spin-offs, it is almost certainly impossible to keep track of every new *Doctor Who* story, let alone put them all in a coherent – never mind consistent – framework. References can contradict other references in the same story, let alone ones in stories written forty years later for a different medium by someone who wasn't even born the year the original writer died.[36]

Parkin has written elsewhere that, as far as the canon is concerned, this proliferation of material means that 'the problem for the twenty-first-century *Doctor Who* fan is not so much philosophical as logistic'.[37] Since no one can possibly know everything in the expanding mythos of *Doctor Who*, he proposes the importance of the 'personal canon', a concept that is 'the polar opposite of the normal use of the term, where canon is imposed by a central authority'.[38]

It might be argued that it is precisely this absence of a 'central authority' to settle questions of canonicity that justifies a claim for the mythic status of *Doctor Who*. As Britton and Decker have pointed out, the BBC – for all that it produces the television series and manages the global brand – has never put in place an official canonical framework like those that exist for such fictions as *Star Trek* and *Star Wars*.[39] Furthermore, just as there is no central authority for asserting the canon, there is no single figure, alive or dead, who can be identified as the originating author. *Doctor Who* was designed by committee, which means that – although Sydney Newman, Donald Wilson, C. E. Webber, Verity Lambert, Antony Coburn and a host of others have reasonable claims to be authors of the original series – none of them can be designated as its creator. Rather like Milman Parry detecting the multiple and historically disparate voices within the supposedly unified epics of a blind poet called Homer, the student or fan of *Doctor Who* must be aware of the patchwork plotting of its fictional territories.[40] A myth, in the loosest and most basic terms, is a story that is owned by nobody and, therefore, by everybody. The BBC owns the *Doctor Who* franchise but, as a quick search through fan fiction websites will demonstrate, it does not own the story.

Fear of getting it wrong: The Skinner–Hadoke paradigm

The comedian Frank Skinner, a self-proclaimed 'fanboy', has reported how he ignored his own inner voice of caution in order to realize a lifetime ambition by appearing as Perkins in Jamie Mathieson's story 'Mummy on the Orient Express' (2014). At the same time, he remembers dodging an after-show conversation with fellow comedian and *Doctor Who* aficionado Toby Hadoke because of a nervousness that he might reveal himself to be a fandom interloper:

> If I say I'm a fan, someone might ask me who was the third Cyberman from the left in *The Tenth Planet* [1966], and I'd struggle with that kind of information. Toby would know. He's probably interviewed the third Cyberman from the left.[41]

This expresses the kind of anxiety that might haunt any fan in conversation with other fans. It is one that can prove especially unsettling where fan enthusiasm and academic scruple converge, where fans who are also academics – fan-scholars or, as Henry Jenkins terms them, 'aca-fans' – try to reconcile the two sides of their engaged personality. Ian Bogost captures the situation well:

> One can like or dislike something, but we scholars, particularly of popular media, have a special obligation to explain something new about the works we discuss. There are plenty of fans of *The Wire* and *Mad Men* and *Halo* and *World of Warcraft* out there. The world

doesn't really need any more of them. What it does need is skeptics, and the scholarly role is fundamentally one of skepticism.[42]

The fan might be frightened of getting something wrong, the fan-scholar too, but the aca-fan is frightened of getting something wrong *and* being banal.

Hills's work on the complex relationship between the scholar-fan and the fan-scholar is important in this respect, noting how 'academic and fan identities are not always separable, and can be hybridised in a variety of ways'.[43] It is possible to go further and argue that these identities are *never* separable, always hybrid, and inevitably mythic. It is for this reason that the current book begins with a journey into the matrix of fandom and academia. To a large extent, the objective is to chart the uneven terrain where various tribes of expressive fan write into and across each other. Inevitably this involves finding a footing between academic and more popular, even populist, modes of discourse. Does this mean affording all sources the same degree of authority? There is, it can hardly be denied, a different set of pressures, expectations and allowances for the commercial writer than there is for the peer-reviewed academic writer, even the peer-reviewed academic *fan* writer. Just as the emotional investment of the latter might disrupt traditions of critical detachment, so the economic reliance of the former might undermine interpretive objectivity. An Amazon review of the DVD of 1979's 'The Creature from the Pit' is never going to be equivalent in methodology and analytical discernment to Fiske's essay on the story, but it will offer other perspectives, more recent ones, more direct, more 'authentic' from a fan standpoint. Evaluated in their own contexts, the different categories of commentary are able to cast an intriguing light on each other and therefore on *Doctor Who* itself.

Skinner has reported that, when he got the call to play Perkins, he was on a tour bus watching the third episode of 'The Sensorites' (1964). Some have suggested that it is proof of his fan credentials that he was watching this less-than-revered story from the first season of *Doctor Who*, but this is unfair as both an evaluation of 'The Sensorites' and an insinuation about the uncritical attitude of fans.[44] One of the distinguishing features of an established fandom is its disputatious criticality towards the thing it loves and, of course, those who jested at Skinner's choice of viewing are also fans, revealing a critical stance through their satire.

'The Sensorites' is an easy story to deride – too long, too slow, lacking a real sense of threat – but it is also a story that is notable for adding significantly to the developing series mythos. It features the first account of the Doctor's home planet, for instance, his granddaughter Susan (Carol Ann Ford) recalling how 'at night the sky is a burned orange, and the leaves on the trees are bright silver'. This nostalgic evocation is echoed by David Tennant's Tenth Doctor at the end of 'Gridlock' (2007), and in 'Planet of the Ood' (2008) it is hinted strongly that the Sensorites and the Ood are related species (see Figure 0.1 and Figure 0.2). This is more than a simple case of new *Who* 'fanwank': it is a recognition, via the gentle, exploited and sympathetic Ood, of the significance of the Sensorites as the first morally three-dimensional monsters in the series.[45] 'The Sensorites' is also noteworthy for its representation of a crucial shift in the relationship between the Doctor and his companions:

IAN There's one thing about it, Doctor. We're certainly different from when we started out with you.

SUSAN That's funny. Grandfather and I were talking about that just before you came in. How you've both changed.

Figure 0.1 The eponymous aliens of 'The Sensorites' (1964); ©BBC Worldwide.

Figure 0.2 The Ood first appear in 'The Impossible Planet' (2006); ©BBC Worldwide.

BARBARA Well, we've all changed.

SUSAN Have I?

BARBARA Yes.

DOCTOR Yes, it all started out as a mild curiosity in a junkyard, and now it's turned out to be quite a, quite a great spirit of adventure, don't you think?

This scene, emblematic of *Doctor Who* as a nascent mythology, is also emblematic of the attempt to understand that mythology, the many forms that it takes, the many voices that mingle around it.

This is not the first book to bring mythographical concepts to bear on *Doctor Who*. They feature recurrently in Tulloch and Alvarado's study, and more recently in Hills's *Triumph of a Time Lord* and in monographs by David Layton and Marcus Harmes. There are also myth-focused chapters in the collections edited by David Butler and by Ross Garner, Melissa Beattie and Una McCormack. To date, though, only Burdge, Burke and Larsen's lively rattle-bag has been dedicated solely to an analysis of the series from the viewpoint of mythology.[46]

Chapter 1 of this book is concerned with the ways in which institutional, academic and fan discourses contribute to mythological formations around *Doctor Who*. Chapter 2 discusses some of the internal mythologies of the show, exploring the balance between change and continuity across its long, untidy history, focusing especially on traditions of monster design and transmedia storytelling. In Chapter 3 the emphasis shifts from *intra*textuality to *inter*textuality, considering how the 'adaptive suppleness' identified by Harmes has been manifested in mythic borrowings from historical sources and the horror genre.[47] For the final chapter, world-building, hero myths and special effects provide a basis from which to take stock of *Doctor Who* as the Steven Moffat era ends and the Chris Chibnall era begins.

Chapter 1

Critics, fans and
mythologies of discourse

Writing about *Doctor Who*:
Difficult conversations and critical
projects

By the time *Doctor Who* returned to television screens on 26 March 2005, a lot of words had been published about the original series and its spin-offs. These were to be found in commercial non-fiction books (ranging from Terrance Dicks and Malcolm Hulke's *The Making of Doctor Who* in the 1970s to David Howe, Mark Stammers and Stephen Walker's series of reference texts in the 1990s), in fanzines and newsletters, and on the web.[1] The number of significant *academic* readings of the series, however, of critical-theoretical papers and books by professional scholars, could still be counted on the fingers of one Sontaran hand.[2] Since Tulloch and Alvarado's monograph in 1983, things had been quiet in those whispering corners of the academy where Arcalian, Prydonian and Patrex might seem like viable affiliations.

Tulloch and Fiske had both published journal articles in the period leading up to that first book-length study, and a few more were to follow. Even so, as the clock ticked down to the broadcast of 'Rose', any literature review on the topic of *Doctor Who* was going to be a relatively simple task, an excavation of what the traditional university-based academic might view as 'popular', 'mainstream', 'zeitgeist' or (most dubious of all) 'fan' sources, but with little need to engage with what the same academic would see as 'recognized authorities'. Beyond *The Unfolding Text*, the diligent researcher would need to become familiar with Tulloch and Henry Jenkins's *Science Fiction Audiences* (1995) and Piers Britton and Simon Barker's *Reading between Designs* (2003),[3] but otherwise the territory to be mapped might appear as sparse as a BBC quarry.

The field has grown since then in both fecundity and complexity. There would be little tolerance now for the kind of binaries assumed above, those easy oppositions between fan and academic, popular and esoteric, low-brow and high-brow, shallow and deep. The discourses of *Doctor Who*, of culture in general, are far more subtle and interwoven than such divisions suppose. This is partly due to the sheer quantity of material available, ensuring that everything is somehow in contact with everything else. It is also due to processes of mutual recognition and involvement, whereby professional academics have undertaken a sustained examination of the relationship between scholarly and fan activities, and fan communities have drawn increasingly on the activities of scholars. The fact that academic scholars are often participating members of these fan communities is suggestive of the ways in which distinctions have been elided. That said, it is reasonable to remark that the academy has been more willing to embrace fandom than vice versa.

Even where reviews are largely positive, as with those of Matt Hills's *Triumph of a Time Lord*, there is evident discomfort with the methods of the academy: 'persevere – it does get easier'.[4] The situation is not much improved when the work of professional academic critics is considered by their professional journalistic peers. Here is Robin Pierce, reviewing Decker's *Who Is Who?* for *Starburst Magazine*:

> Needless to say, it gets very heavy, very quickly. For example, when discussing the Doctor's homesickness in 2007's *Gridlock*, Professor Decker explains: 'While the Doctor exhibits melancholia for an actual place, existential phenomenology posits an analogous metaphysical homelessness that has the potential to affect anyone, even those of us who haven't locked the last members of our species in a time loop for eternity.' And while reeling from *that*, we're then treated to a quote from Simone de Beauvoir about how 'one may falsely assert oneself as being or assert oneself as nothingness'. Anyone?[5]

And this is Hywel Evans reviewing Hills's edited collection of essays, *New Dimensions of Doctor Who*, in *Doctor Who Magazine*:

> Get this: 'An unstated assumption guiding theories of intertextuality is that the viewing subject cognitively recognises and interprets intertextual references, thus casting them in the role of "amateur semiotician".' Well, if you say so, mate.[6]

Referring to Ross Garner's chapter 'Remembering Sarah Jane', this recalls Ian Briggs's importation of Tulloch and Alvarado's discussion of 'semiotic thickness' and 'auxiliary performance codes' into the pseudo-intellectual banter of an Iceworld guard in his script for 1987's 'Dragonfire'. Briggs also named many of the other characters in the story after media theorists (McLuhan, Bazin, Belazs, Kracauer, Arnheim, Pudovkin) and, in his subsequent novelization of the tale, took the satire further by having the Doctor groaning inwardly at the thought of a chat based around cultural studies: '*Semiotics?* The Doctor began to worry. This was going to be a very difficult conversation …'[7]

The stories told by 'fan-scholars' and 'scholar-fans' to stake their claims to the territory they share, the language used to tell these stories, can be revealing. Where James Chapman conspicuously dismisses 'the impenetrable critical language of high theory', Hills responds with an insistence that 'one person's "jargon" is another's useful vocabulary'.[8] He notes, furthermore, that linguistic obscurity is not the exclusive preserve of academic commentators:

> Fandom is often as guilty of this as academia. The word 'squee' probably doesn't mean much to non-fans, just as the word 'signifier' won't mean much to those who aren't already media students. So-called jargon is, in reality, just another cultural group's language that we don't want to spend time getting to grips with.[9]

In Barthesian terms, it is 'natural' for fans to use one common vocabulary and for academics to use another: one person's 'fanwank' is another person's 'strategic deployment of intertextuality for collective gratification'.

After a period of comparative inactivity, the academic presses have become very busy with *Doctor Who* in recent years. The machinery cranked into action with Kim Newman's pocket-sized BFI critical guide of 2005, closely followed by Chapman's *Inside the TARDIS* (2006). Reviewing the original edition of this for *The Independent*, Matthew Sweet argued that previous non-fiction on the series had

> existed principally to tell you what the acronym TARDIS stood for, and that Patrick Troughton played the central part [of the Second Doctor] in the style of 'a cosmic hobo' – whatever that was. The potential readership just wasn't ready to investigate the hermeneutic coding of William Hartnell's astrakhan hat.[10]

The corollary of this was that Chapman's history – 'unpretentious, readable, solidly authoritative and self-consciously anti-theoretical' – could be presented as a belated and critically conservative reiteration of material already published by fan-scholars in *Doctor Who Magazine* and elsewhere. Harsh as this is to Chapman, Sweet's supporting claim is persuasive: '*Doctor Who* is becoming more complicated and expansive by the day, and its effective analysis might require an author with a slightly more adventurous approach.' Read alongside Newman's entertainingly opinionated history, Chapman's detailed linear account suggests that a distinct academic manner, separable from that of fan-scholarship and informed by a sympathetic awareness of theory, has yet to be developed.

David Butler's edited collection *Time and Relative Dissertations in Space* (2007) can be seen, in this light, as a crucial publication. An overtly academic book, issued from a prestigious university press, it is a substantial volume (over three hundred pages), comprising seventeen chapters, plus an introduction and afterword. It features scholar-fans trying out various critical positions, but, more suggestively, it shows them mingling with (and often being indistinguishable from) fan-scholars. Of the nineteen contributors to the book, only around half were university-based at the time of publication, and at least seven were freelance authors. The afterword, taking the form of an autobiographical essay by novelist Paul Magrs, effectively returned the book to its own first causes, the business of storytelling: 'It is my job – as this writer/critic/reader/teacher thing I have made myself into – to pull and tease at these floating strands of fiction, and to ravel them up.'[11]

The trend towards a mingling of expert voices, exemplified by Lindy Orthia's *Doctor Who and Race* (2013), is far from absolute, and in some ways the partition of academic and non-academic remains firmly in place. The contributors to collections from academic publishers such as Cambridge Scholars, Open Court, Intellect and I.B. Tauris are almost all university lecturers, as are the writers of monographs from the same sources. Even so, the 'almost' is significant here, and it is notable that there is an occasional recognition of debt and influence between the authorial constituencies. So, the editors of *Impossible Worlds, Impossible Things* thank not only academics Matt Hills, Rebecca Williams and David Butler but also *Doctor Who* historian Andrew Pixley, *Doctor Who* writer Rob Shearman, and *Doctor Who* actor, writer and Dalek operator Barnaby Edwards. Hills, similarly, while thanking many fellow academics in *Triumph of a Time Lord*, makes a point of acknowledging prominent scholar-fans, recognizing 'the sheer brilliance of much fan commentary' in fanzines and blogs, and noting that the writing of authors such as Lawrence Miles and Tat Wood 'is frequently as illuminating as published academic critique, if not more so'.[12]

The key point here is that the years since 2005 have seen a profound transformation of the environment within which *Doctor Who* is examined. Plainly, this has been a direct result of the extraordinary success of the returned series. After all, where are the old oppositions between consumer and producer, spectator and participant, fan and critic, more radically entangled than in the contributions of the most famous and influential fans of all, Russell T. Davies, Steven Moffat and Chris Chibnall, David Tennant and Peter Capaldi? It would be reasonable to suggest, though, that changing cultural and economic contexts for both the BBC and UK universities have also been a significant influence. In 2002, writing about the mutual antipathy of fandom and academia, Hills commented, 'I can see no way that these institutional differences can be dissolved for as long as the university remains a residual site of cultural authority.'[13] Nearly twenty years on, such authority *is* being eroded by the effects of controversial university fees structures (outside Scotland, at least) and the rise of a distrustful audit regimen that is typified by the National Student Survey and governmental frameworks established to measure the 'excellence' of both research and teaching. As the fabled ivory tower of higher education becomes subject to escalating processes of accountability and marketization, a systematic disruption of the cultural authority of the university might be perceived. A similar destabilization is manifest in recent challenges to the status and institutional security of the BBC, its reputation as a public-service broadcaster waning in the aftermath of the Jimmy Savile scandal and assaults from successive governments.

The disturbance of two esteemed institutions crucial to the developing discourses of *Doctor Who* studies (the BBC and UK higher education), taken together with the rapid expansion of online platforms for analytical debate, content sharing and creative production, has been at least partially responsible for the narrowing divide between academia and fandom. This apparent hybridization of the critical culture, like the post-2005 *Doctor Who* phenomenon itself, has its origins in the creative and interpretive activities of fans and academic critics from the 1980s to the early years of the current century. If these activities are viewed as essentially mythical, associated with the telling of particular stories within particular communities, the formation of particular meanings around particular artefacts, and the uses of particular 'types of speech', then the present time is one in which the myths are being realigned.[14] The myth-makers – fans, critics, producers, performers – are discovering complex new identities for themselves, new interrelations. This amounts, in Barthes's model, to 'the relativization of the relations of writer, reader and observer (critic)', constituting a version of that 'social utopia' in which 'the Text' becomes all there is.[15] As the text unfolds, participation within it becomes an experience in which no one can attain the privileged status of 'judge, master, analyst, confessor, decoder'.[16] If fans and academics have traditionally had their own discrete disciplines, their own types of speech, their own outputs, these have become progressively implicated in each other, despite a residual wariness and tension. This emergent reciprocal association resembles the 'interdisciplinarity' that, according to Barthes,

> begins *effectively* (as opposed to the mere expression of a pious wish) when the solidarity of the old disciplines breaks down – perhaps even violently, via the jolts of fashion – in the interests of a new object and a new language.[17] (Emphasis in the original)

The 'shared, communal project' advocated by Hills is implicit in this, 'something cohesive, something cumulative' that is at once 'joined up' and open to engagement 'with a range of other texts, histories and concepts'.[18] A viable zone of activity in which enthusiasts are no longer 'writing across each other', this establishes a utopian realm in which fans are scholars and scholars are fans, and all are contributing to the ongoing project of creation, reception, understanding. Then again, every utopia contains its own dystopia and, more beguilingly, implies other possible utopias. Myths can be realigned but these alignments are only ever temporary, and perhaps illusory. As the narratives of fan-scholars and scholar-fans become increasingly interwoven, it might lead us to see ever more intricate and evocative patterns in the Castrovalvan tapestry of it all:

> PORTREEVE: With this tapestry and with patience, there's nothing one cannot achieve. Nothing, Doctor, in this world or in any other. The tapestry has the power to build and hold in space whole worlds of matter.[19]

The following sections of this chapter will consider some of the worlds that have become visible in the accumulated strands of critical mythology.

Fandom as a character: 'Most likely to fight back'

It is ironic that the television episode most self-consciously concerned with the cultural mythologies of *Doctor Who*'s fandom has never been popular within that fandom. 'Love & Monsters', written by Russell T. Davies and broadcast as part of the second season of the returned series in 2006 (David Tennant's first), elicits powerful responses of fondness or antipathy which are exemplified by fan commentaries posted to the online *Doctor Who Ratings Guide* at the time of its original broadcast. So, while Joe Ford describes it as 'the most daring, the most different episode we have had this year' and 'also one of the best', Ron Mallet declares that it 'represents everything I hate about the new series', characterizing it as 'cleve[r] dick television'.[20] Steve Cassidy is in agreement, and condemns the episode through association with unpopular stories from the original series:

> Not just the worst episode so far but the worst since the series came back. In fact it may well be a tussle with <u>Timelash</u> and <u>Time and the Rani</u> to the title of worst stinker of the last twenty years.[21]

Finn Clark also reads the story in relation to the extended text of *Doctor Who*, but he does so in order to highlight its achievement as a piece of engaged, reflexive mythography:

> This story adds so much to Doctor Who, both by bringing variety to the storytelling and by re-examining its mythology from the viewpoint of the ordinary people. A lovely piece of work.[22]

It is hard to believe that these comments are about the same story, although such extreme divergences are hardly unusual within fan communities. A more formal measure of the standing of 'Love & Monsters', at least among one subset of fans, is its position in the two *Doctor Who Magazine* polls that have taken place since its broadcast. In 2009 it came 153rd out of the 200 television stories to that date; in 2013 it was ranked 220th out of 241. Only one other new *Who* story in the 2009 poll ('Fear Her', 2006) and four in 2013 ('Fear Her', 'The Curse of the Black Spot', 'The Doctor, the Widow and the Wardrobe' (both 2011) and 'The Rings of Akhaten' (2013)) polled lower.[23]

Through the video diaries of a young transport manager called Elton Pope (Marc Warren), 'Love & Monsters' tells the tale of a ragbag crew of social misfits who are brought together through their shared obsession with the enigmatic and elusive figure of the Doctor. Showing how their lives change when they come under the influence of a sinister but absurd individual called Victor Kennedy (Peter Kay), the story is notable for being the first 'Doctor-lite' episode of the revived series. A narrative literalization of the hide-and-seek intimacy that exists between fans and the objects of their enthusiasm, this in itself might be seen as a cause of antipathy: after all, the putative star of the show is hardly in it! Subsequent Doctor-lite stories, however, have proved extremely popular, with 'Blink' (2007) ranking at 2nd in the polls of both 2009 and 2013, and 'Turn Left' coming in at 12th in the 2009 poll and 39th in 2013. Paul Cornell's double-episode story, 'Human Nature / The Family of Blood' (2007), although Tennant-heavy, can be thought of as Doctor-lite and has appeared in the top ten on both occasions. The Doctor-lite formula was not retained during Moffat's time as showrunner but, even so, there were stories in which the Doctor took on a subsidiary role to his companions – 'The Girl Who Waited' (2011), 'Flatline' (2014) – and these have also been well received.

Doctor-lite episodes are not, it should be noted, an invention of BBC Wales, with many broadcasts from the earliest days of the series being written to enable cast members to rest or take holidays. Since 2005 the strategy has been used primarily to ease the management of an intense production schedule; during the Hartnell era, when a season ran solidly for eight to ten months, it was a humane necessity. Clearly, though, the Doctor's reduced role in 'Love & Monsters' is not a significant reason for the story's dubious reputation among fans, especially since much of the thematic and narrative impetus for such an episode was derived from experiments with Doctor-lite and non-Doctor formats in the fan-written Virgin New Adventures novels of the 1990s. The fact that Rose Tyler (Billie Piper) also has a diminished presence in the episode, making it *companion*-lite as well as Doctor-lite, might be an issue, since the regulars are essentially replaced by a group of one-off characters who have only forty-five minutes to make an impression. Most other Doctor-lite tales have featured incumbent companions in central roles. Then again, 'Blink', not only the most popular story of its kind but also one of the most popular stories of all, shunts both the Doctor and Martha Jones (Freema Agyeman) into the margins while the one-off Sally Sparrow (Carey Mulligan) carries out her investigations. Strikingly, 'Revelation of the Daleks' (1985), always by some distance the most appreciated story of the Colin Baker years, is notable for the relatively peripheral roles played by both the Doctor and Peri Brown (Nicola Bryant) for much of its ninety-minute running time.

'Blink' introduced the Weeping Angels; 'Love & Monsters' gave us the Abzorbaloff (see Figures 1.1 and 1.2). This, almost certainly, is one cause of the story's generally poor standing among fans: not merely unlovable, its monster was felt to be an insult to the intelligence of viewers, embodying the errors of the story as a whole. Where the dark adult themes of 'Blink' were reinforced by a dark adult humour, many fans were affronted by what they perceived as the juvenile clowning of 'Love & Monsters'. The early scene in which the Doctor, Rose and a drooling, jagged-toothed alien are witnessed chasing each other back and forth at speed between multiple doors in a warehouse corridor has been cited as symptomatic in this respect. The sight, towards the end of the episode, of Elton being pursued by the tubby green, mohican-headed, jockstrap-wearing Abzorbaloff, played by comedian Peter Kay, has been similarly disparaged. Significantly, these two scenes feature

Figure 1.1 Sally Sparrow encounters the Weeping Angels in 'Blink' (2007); ©BBC Worldwide.

Figure 1.2 The Abzorbaloff is let loose in 'Love & Monsters' (2006); ©BBC Worldwide.

in a fan video on YouTube that has been edited to combine 'Love & Monsters' with the 'Yakety Sax' theme tune of *The Benny Hill Show*.[24]

The problem with 'Love & Monsters', at least as far as many long-term fans are concerned, is that it plays upon their shared vulnerabilities. In short, it brings back memories of the 'dodgy' monsters and tendency to 'send up' the show that are associated with the Graham Williams era of the late-1970s. There is an air of pantomime to the episode and the casting of Kay as Victor Kennedy/The Abzorbaloff – especially given his extravagant realization of the role – brings to mind Ian Levine's dismissal of the Williams years as 'a slap-stick *Fawlty Towers* in space'.[25] But then, there is far more to *Fawlty Towers* than slapstick, and there is far more to 'Love & Monsters' too. Whether or not the received view of *Doctor Who* under Williams is fair, it is important to understand it in its particular production context and with an awareness that, for all the pressures of the time (financial, moral, cultural, corporate), there was strategy as well as exigency in its outcomes. There was also, in terms of appeal to casual viewers, a fair level of success, with Williams averaging audiences of 9.4 million across his three seasons. For Davies, riding high on the wave of the outstanding critical and popular success of his first season as showrunner, 'Love & Monsters' represented a combination of industrial pragmatism, calculated risk, satirical knowingness and sheer creative hedonism. Just as Williams (and, briefly, his script editor Douglas Adams) knew that their comedic approach would be controversial, so Davies must have known that his yarn about a fat green alien from Clom would have the potential to aggravate the fan audience that he had been a part of since childhood. Some might question why the Hoix, for instance, an effective 'modern' monster, appears only fleetingly in the episode, being sidelined by the ludicrous and curiously 'old-fashioned' Abzorbaloff. But this, surely, is the point.

As is well known, the Abzorbaloff was designed by a fan, 9-year-old William Grantham, who won a competition on the long-running BBC children's television programme *Blue Peter*.[26] The appropriateness of this to an episode that is a love poem to the series and its fandom, as well as a satire on them, is clear. That the result should have caused such widespread discontent – Grantham was reported to be disappointed with the monster, Kay described his appearance as the biggest regret of his career and many fans reacted with hostility to the production as a whole – only adds to its suggestiveness as a metafictional artefact.[27]

Perversely, it ensures that 'Love & Monsters' has a good deal to tell us about the role of fans within the extended mythology of *Doctor Who*.

The working title for the story was 'I Love the Doctor', a direct gesture of intent, and it is significant that the final version should have shifted the emphasis towards monsters. In this sense, fandom and monstrosity are underlined as the core thematic elements within the tale, the Doctor being moved into the titular as well as the diegetic shadows. In his original drafts, Davies planned to extend Elton's backstory to include his witnessing of events from the original run of *Doctor Who*, such as the Skarasen emerging from the Thames in 'Terror of the Zygons' (1975). This version of events would have plotted Elton's life along the problematic 'real time' chronology of the series, with his third birthday coinciding with the Dalek occupation of Shoreditch in 1963 in 'Remembrance of the Daleks' (1988) and his mother's death, coincident with his first glimpse of the Doctor, being brought about by a lethal plastic daffodil from 'Terror of the Autons' (1971). The dating of UNIT[28] stories is notoriously tricky, but *if* the first story of Jon Pertwee's second season is taken to be contemporaneous with its broadcast, that would have made Elton eleven years old at the time of his mother's death, which seems plausible. Given that the Doctor he encounters at this point is the one played by David Tennant, the indication would be of a concurrence of the Tenth and Third incarnations, just as 'Remembrance of the Daleks' posits a synchronous presence of the First and Seventh. As things transpired, of course, this is strictly academic, since Elton's awareness of Doctor-related events in the final iteration of 'Love & Monsters' is confined to a selection from the revived series. This seems a pity, mythologically, as the initial concept would have revealed a long view of the serial narrative, making explicit a contiguity between the old and the new. It would, furthermore, have thrown the caricature of fan attitudes into sharper relief, demonstrating the conscious importation of traditional concerns within the renewed format. The reference here is not simply to myths of shoddy monsters and cheap jokes but to enduring arguments about whether fandom killed the thing it loved during the 1980s. Elton's observation of events from the classic series would, after all, have constituted a version of the kind of fan pleasuring that has often been blamed for driving away casual viewers.

Fans who enjoy 'Love & Monsters' tend to argue that, where the tendency under John Nathan-Turner was to appeal to fans through an obsessive ransacking of past content, Davies's inclination here is to risk the disaffection of those fans through a burlesque of their community and its attitudes. This is most obvious in the depiction of the small group that Elton joins, the self-reflexive nature of any mockery being hinted at in the 'good strong name' that he devises for them: 'Something like London Investigation 'n' Detective Agency. LINDA for short.' The same acronym had been used on the BBC children's television series *Why Don't You?* (1973–95) during Davies's time as a producer between 1985 and 1990, the 'L' in that case standing for 'Liverpool'. The members of LINDA in 'Love & Monsters' are a representative set of stereotypical fan characters: Elton, the nerdy lad; Ursula, the geeky girl (Shirley Henderson); Bliss, the would-be artist (Kathryn Drysdale); Mr Skinner, the would-be writer (Simon Greenall); and Bridget, the quietly damaged soul (Moya Brady). The stereotyping, as might be expected from a writer of Davies's deft control, exceeds its own limitations, refusing the stability of glib recognition. Although some have complained about the shallowness of the LINDA characters, they are presented with sympathy throughout, and their struggles to find identity and articulacy in relation to an understanding of the Doctor can be seen as emblematic of the series and its fans:

> BLISS What I'm trying to do is sum up the Doctor. What he means to us … What he could represent and what he should represent, and what he never won't represent, sort of thing.

The attempt by Bliss to explain her abstract art is comical, but it is also poignant.

LINDA meets, significantly, beneath an old library, a location gesturing towards the 'literaturisation' of fandom that Hills has referred to and that can be traced back at least as far as Terrance Dicks's description of *Doctor Who* as 'a very intellectual show'.[29] This might be at odds with Britton and Barker's later estimation that the programme 'can make no sustainable claim to possessing intellectual respectability', but it is consonant with Davies's statement that '*Doctor Who* made us clever'.[30] Toby Hadoke has talked of the series as 'a vocabulary-builder' and Booy concurs, referring to a 'generation of fans' who developed literacy through their encounters with the Target novelizations.[31] 'It is no coincidence', he writes, 'that at least one member of Elton's group is an aspirant author.'[32]

Beneath the pantomime of 'Love & Monsters', then, there is a fine weave of commentary on the various complex forms of a singular fandom. This becomes apparent in the opening moments of the story, when Elton's nerdiness is brought into conjunction with the distinctive enthusiasms of both *Doctor Who* fandom and televisual historiography: 'You can't imagine it: the Doctor's machine. The most beautiful sound in the world.' This reference to the noise of TARDIS dematerialization, cherished in fandom, iconic in the wider culture, links directly to the character's other sonic passion: the music of the Electric Light Orchestra (ELO).

Always popular but never fashionable, ELO acts as an index of 'cult' fervour. Three of the band's songs feature in the soundtrack to the episode, with the difference between diegetic and non-diegetic uses being clouded at times, so that it becomes tricky to tell whether the music is being played *by* the characters or *to* the audience, or both. An assumed barrier is thus tested, playfully, unobtrusively, the reassuring distance between worlds being reduced. Ultimately, this is the distance between fan and object, between viewing fan and depicted fan. That it is closed down through the jokey deployment of a perennially 'uncool' but successful band like ELO evokes Hills's discussion of his own 'oppositional' appreciation of Level 42 and Toto in *Fan Cultures*: 'I tend to value bands and programmes which lack obvious "credibility" but which nevertheless appeal to highly insular fan cognoscenti.'[33] The analogy with *Doctor Who*, and with the activities of LINDA, is clear, as is the irony of so many fans disliking a story that seems to unsettle the line between themselves and the object of their desires. The upshot is alienation and it is tempting to reach for Brecht's concept of *verfremdungseffekt*, defined in his essay on Chinese acting. Here there is little sense of a 'fourth wall' through which an audience can view the action from a comfortable distance. Instead, the performance of Elton's video diary 'expresses his awareness of being watched' so that 'the audience can no longer have the illusion of being the unseen spectator at an event which is really taking place'.[34] Kay's unrestrained performance – widely criticized, not least by himself – also seems to fit the bill.

The arrival of Victor Kennedy is an event which Elton recalls as a kind of Fall, marking the point at which LINDA loses its innocence: 'The golden age was gone.' Following Elton's confession of his feelings for

ELO, the five friends achieve a state of cohesion and happy mutuality, discovering sympathies beyond their interest in the Doctor. In the moment when their tribute band is halted by Kennedy in the midst of a spirited rendition of 'Don't Bring Me Down', the nature of their group, and the kind of fandom it represents, changes irreversibly. From being an informal, non-hierarchical coterie with a sense of exclusivity and specialness ('this little community. The select few') it becomes a formalized college with a sense of stern, directed specialism. 'You've forgotten your purpose in life,' Kennedy announces. 'You, with your band and your cakes and your blubbing and all the while he still exists: the Doctor.' As personified in their self-appointed new leader, this 'purpose' would seem to have the imperative force of a religious mission ('I am your salvation!') and both Hills and Booy have argued that the messianic Kennedy represents a particular form of fan mentality. For the former he 'stands in for bad, deviant fandom – seeking to control fellow fans and obsessively seeking the Doctor'; for the latter he symbolizes 'the bulldozer attitude of obnoxious fans'.[35] These convey an entirely plausible reading, but it is not the only one available.

The cane-carrying flamboyance and imperious, literally untouchable manner of Kennedy suggest a spoof theatrical impresario, perhaps reflecting a measure of self-satire in Davies's vision of the character. This being the case, the ghost of John Nathan-Turner might also be glimpsed. More than just a symbol of rogue fandom, Kennedy is representative of a particular kind of showrunner. He is not simply aware of 'fans', he has a relationship with them; he does not simply have a relationship with them, he is among them; he is not simply among them, he is of them; he is not simply of them, he is of them and empowered, with a clear aura of 'celebrity' and aloofness. As a character, Kennedy is a send-up not of producers like John Wiles (1965–6) and Innes Lloyd (1966–8), or even like Barry Letts (1969–74) and Philip Hinchcliffe (1974–7), but of such 'personalities' as JNT (1980–9) and RTD (2005–10), the only *Doctor Who* showrunners, prior to 'the Moff', who can be traced via Google using only abbreviations or nicknames.

Beyond interpretations of Kennedy as an image of perversely empowered fandom or the over-familiar-but-distant producer (he is touch-averse, after all), he can be seen as a figure of the scholar-fan, of the academic professional who is also a fan. He runs LINDA meetings as a classroom; his conduct is that of an authoritarian teacher and his presentation of research processes is couched in terms of schedules and outcomes:

> VICTOR Right then, homework. Using the Torchwood files, we're able to look at all the old databases in a completely new light. We're able to build up a more detailed profile of the Doctor. I've allocated tasks to each of you … I'd like you to complete your targets and meet back here this time next week, one step closer to catching the Doctor.

This speech is informed by the contemporary idiom of managerialized academia, replicating the dominant language of 'targets', 'actions' and 'reporting'. Kennedy comes across as a mixture of Gradgrindian pedagogue and scholarly systematizer, responding violently to looser or more 'human' approaches to the shared project of investigating the Doctor. When Elton freezes on being confronted in the flesh by his idolized quarry, Kennedy's response ('You stupid man!') is to threaten him with his cane. This elicits a spirited defence from another member of LINDA:

> URSULA Use that cane on him and you'll get one hell of a smack off me! And then a good kick. Is that completely understood, Mister Kennedy?
> VICTOR Duly noted: Ursula Blake, most likely to fight back.

The character's reaction, her resistance to Kennedy's autocracy, invites a reading of her name as knowingly allusive, recalling both Ursula Brangwen, the heroine of D. H. Lawrence's novels *The Rainbow* (1915) and *Women in Love* (1920), and the dissenting poet and artist William Blake. Creating a connection, however lightly and impishly, with mythologies of radical nonconformism, this casts Ursula as a representative of individualist, freethinking fandom, in opposition to the repressive, homogenizing version connoted by Kennedy.

The same assertion of independence is seen in Elton's denial of his 'training' following his aborted 'infiltration' of Jackie Tyler (Camille Coduri): 'It's shameful. We *used* that woman.' This rejection of Kennedy's system ('I don't care about Step 5!') is, in effect, a restatement of the original joy of the group. It is an attempt to restore the dynamic of LINDA as it had been when he first joined, and it is hard not to see this as a mock-heroic allegory of 'original' fandom yearning for the prelapsarian condition of innocence before fan-consultants, producer-fans and scholar-fans.

Ultimately, any victory for Elton and Ursula is brief and hollow, diminished by the revelation of the monstrosity that Kennedy has been masking. Disclosure that the members of LINDA have been incorporated one by one into the Abzorbaloff leads to a comedy chase and final confrontation. Continuing to exist as sentient faces in the green flesh of the alien from Clom, they are able, with the Doctor's intervention, to defeat the monster but only at the cost of their own extinction. Even the survival of Ursula within a paving slab can only be seen as a victory in the most bleakly ridiculous way. Enabling her to salvage, or be salvaged for, her relationship with Elton, Ursula's endurance is accompanied by a fellatio joke ('We've even got a bit of a love life') that some have found objectionable. In the context of the episode's metaphor of fandom, what does this say? That the purist romance of the authentic fan is a bizarre, delusional and perverse love affair, akin to someone having sex with a concrete slab?

Given the requirement for Davies to construct a story around a monster designed by a young fan, it is entirely appropriate that he should have written 'Love & Monsters' as an allegory of the fan experience, entirely predictable that it should have proved such a vexing contribution to that experience. The episode is marked by the recurrence of imagistic and linguistic tropes of intimacy and distance, exhibited in Kennedy's fretfulness about being touched: 'No, no, no, no, I don't shake hands. Back, back! I suffer from a skin complaint – exeema.' Kennedy claims to be untouchable but, in his modus operandi as the Abzorbaloff, he turns out to be irresistibly touchable. He needs to control physical contact in order to control his absorption of his victims, and it is a loss of this control that brings about his destruction. Elton, urged on by the Doctor, breaks his cane, which is revealed to have 'created a limitation field', preventing lethal indigestion: 'Now it's broken, it can't stop. The absorber is being absorbed.'

An oscillation between ideas of closeness and distance permeates 'Love & Monsters'. This is evident in the story's primary quest ('It felt like we were getting closer and closer to the Doctor') and the ways in which the doomed humans, lost in the swollen flesh of the Abzorbaloff, separated as part of the same monstrous body, maintain contact with each other: 'I'm here, Bridget,' calls Mr Skinner. 'It's all right. I'm close.' The image conjured here is grotesque, even horrific, but it is also oddly touching and, as rendered on screen, preposterous. It has its origins in the drawing of a 9-year-old fan, is scripted through the professional expertise of a forty-something fan, seems to lampoon the forms and behaviours of a wider fandom, is redolent of the supposed errors of a previous era of production, mixes registers of body horror and farce, and features an amplified performance from one of the most popular British comedians of his day: such a monster was always going to be tricky for fans to love.

Fandom as critique: Cultures and contributions

At the beginning of *Love and Monsters*, Booy remarks that fans of *Doctor Who* have sometimes 'loved' the programme 'in monstrous ways'.[36] There is evidence for this in both the hostility of many fans towards the episode from which he takes his title and the potential for reading its fan-designed monster as a metaphor of destructive fandom. 'Love & Monsters' might present a skewed view, but anyone researching commentaries on *Doctor Who* could be forgiven for wondering at times whether, with friends like these, it ever really needed Michael Grade. Fan-scholar Mark Campbell states in the original edition of his Pocket Essentials guide that it 'has always been shallow (it's one of its defining qualities)', intending this as a recommendation. Scholar-fans Britton and Barker take a similar tack, pointing to a general tendency to be 'narratively banal'.[37]

Britton's position might appear modified, his esteem for *Doctor Who* intensified, by the time of *TARDISbound* where, as sole author, he claims that it is 'capable of being rich and sophisticated, rewarding sustained or repeated engagement'.[38] Even so, his critical scrupulousness requires that such engagement involves a recognition of limitations: '[*Doctor Who*] is generally unsuited to charting ongoing moral or social formation, and may indeed be able to treat relatively few of the messy complexities of life.'[39] Pointing to a privileging of narrative and spectacle over characterization, these limitations suggest a basic triviality in *Doctor Who*. They reveal a tension, furthermore, between the instinctive reverence of the fan and the criticality that is often its flip side. As Hills comments, 'being a fan means being disappointed by the object of fandom as much as it means appreciating it'.[40] So, when Britton asks, 'Is *Doctor Who* any good?' and devotes a chapter to exploring possible answers, he is pondering a question that has been informing discussion far beyond (and long before it entered) the academic environment.

Effecting an inversion of the terms of Jonathan Swift's famous 'misanthropic' letter to Alexander Pope – 'I hate and detest that animal called man, although I heartily love John, Peter, Thomas, and so forth'[41] – fans tend to heartily love *Doctor Who* but hate and detest this story, that Doctor, this companion, those monsters, the latest redesign and so forth. The disapproval of fans is invariably provoked by some perceived lack or excess, some failure of the imperfect today in relation to an idealized yesterday. This, as Booy notes, can be the nostalgia of those who remember, or misremember, the experiences of their past ('the past was something desperately in need of recovery and it always seemed to be somehow better than the present'),[42] but it might also be a form of anemoia, the nostalgia of those who imagine the experiences of a past that they have inherited. An extreme form of this second-hand nostalgia is embodied in the character of Whizz Kid (Gian Sammarco) in 'The Greatest Show in the Galaxy' (1988–9). Bespectacled, tank-topped, BMX-riding and gibberingly enthusiastic about 'the show', Whizz Kid is a cartoon depiction of the fan as irritating geek and comes to an ironic end in the ring of the Psychic Circus where the tiny audience – a 1960s-styled mother, father and daughter, really the Gods of Ragnarok – judges him to be a tedious disappointment.

More than ten years into the revived series, the situation is more fraught than ever, since the 'gnawing feeling of disappointment' that Hills pinpoints as the 'defining emotion' of fannish idealism[43] is now available not only to middle-aged fans who grew up with the classic series but also to teenaged fans who grew up with Eccleston and Tennant. Just as the 18-year-old Kim Newman found himself cringing at the arrival of K9 in 1977, recalling his fear of the Macra a decade earlier, so today's 18-year-old might find the Pting of 'The Tsuranga Conundrum' (2018) risible when compared to the Vashta Nerada that had her hiding behind the sofa in 2008 during 'Silence in the Library' / 'Forest of the Dead'. Of course, disappointment is a sprightly emotion and it can travel in more than one direction, often at the same time. A 7-year-old thrilling to see the headlong rampage of Grand Marshall Skaldak (Spencer Wilding) through a Soviet submarine in 2013's 'Cold War' might be less than impressed by the slow, hissing menace of his fellow Ice Warriors (Bernard Bresslaw, Sonny Caldinez, Roger Jones, Michael Attwell, Tony Harwood) across the six episodes of their eponymous debut from 1967.[44] Meanwhile, there is no guarantee that someone who saw the original as a seven-year-old will have been thrilled by the CGI revelation towards the end of the Matt Smith story of what the Ice Warriors had kept hidden under their helmets for more than forty-five years.

The issue here would seem to be that although all *Doctor Who* fans are fans of *Doctor Who*, no two *Doctor Who* fans are fans of the same *Doctor Who*. This is, no doubt, a truism of the fan condition generally but because of the longevity and abundance of this particular text it becomes especially meaningful. If every fan is in love with a different version of *Doctor Who*, it follows that every fan is also carrying a set of powerful prejudices against those features which are perceived as disfiguring the object of their affection. Fandom is nothing if not romantic and, although romanticism is easily misread as something soft and uncritical, the reality tends to be rather more flinty and obdurate. Hills describes the basis of this frustrated reverence:

> The Doctor isn't in it (enough); it isn't serious (enough); it isn't science fictional (enough); it isn't British (enough); it doesn't have enough story; it has too much story; it assumes too much knowledge of continuity; it violates established continuity; and so on. Fan criticisms involve shaping an image of 'ideal' *Who*, a kind of Platonic essence of the series (which may never have been realised fully in any one story).[45]

If we approach *Doctor Who* from a mythographic perspective, this 'Platonic essence' becomes a crucial consideration, indicating as it does the forces at play across the narrative territories of the television series and its transmedia offshoots.

Tulloch has argued that fans will always strive for 'a unified interpretive position', working to become 'a cultural unit, an interpretive community'.[46] Writing with Alvarado, he goes on to assert that 'for long-term fans the endless unfolding of the show's mythology is pleasurable only if the continuity of *Doctor Who* as institution is upheld'.[47] The problem is, of course, that the unified interpretive position is a fantasy, questions of continuity (of the canon-in-motion) being the primary indicators of this. 'There *is*', as Tulloch notes ruefully, 'no neutral place where we can get access to the "real" interpretation of *Doctor Who*.'[48] Even so, in summoning the platonic phantom that haunts the interpretive community of fans, he draws attention to the mythic, almost mystic, urge that motivates fandom's most contrary behaviours. Newman, evoking a 'fannish industry' committed to resolving continuity problems, is more explicit on the pseudo-theological impetus behind the frequent disgruntlement of fans: '*Who* nit-picking boils down to a wish that the show was not a continually rewritten fiction but a body of obscured truth, to be treated like the *original* canon ... and sifted through for a definitive version.'[49] Fans know that there can be no definitive version but that does not stop them looking for one, especially as every fan holds a more or less hazy but nevertheless definitive *personal* version in their own head. Every fan is a maker and re-maker of myths.

One of the familiar traits of a myth, according to Segal, is the 'tenacity' of its 'adherents', their sense that it 'accomplishes something significant' for them. There is a 'weighty' quality about it that goes beyond 'the lighter functions of legend and folk tale'.[50] A lot might be said here about the finer discriminations of myth, legend and folk tale, and about equivocal definitions of significance and 'weight', but it must be conceded that a modern secular narrative like *Doctor Who* occupies a very different cultural space from the ancient mythologies that are the concern of Segal. The Doctor is not 'believed in' by fans in the same way that the Babylonians might have believed in Marduk's creation of the world out of Tiamat's sliced-up carcass, and the existence of the TARDIS is not credited by them in the same way that the existence of the World Tree, Yggdrasil, might have been credited by the Vikings. There is no sacred dimension to *Doctor Who* fandom, which is precisely why Davies was able to frolic so exuberantly with messianic tropes during his time as showrunner, notably in the conclusion to 'The Last of the Time Lords' (2007):

MARTHA I told a story, that's all. No weapons, just words. I did just what the Doctor said. I went across the continents, all on my own. And everywhere I went I found the people and I told them my story.

> I told them about the Doctor. And I told them to pass it, to spread
> the word so that everyone would know about the Doctor.
> THE MASTER Faith and hope – is that all?

There is no metaphysical belief demanded of even the most ardent fan, only – as Samuel Taylor Coleridge famously put it – 'that willing suspension of *dis*belief for the moment, which constitutes poetic faith' (my italics).[51] This poetic faith is a powerful and complex one and, like that of religious believers, it can be difficult to appreciate for those who are outside its influence or immune to its charms. It also has an affective intensity (it carries a 'weight', in other words) that even those who feel it most strongly often find themselves unable to articulate: 'I'm *Doctor Who*'s Number One victim. I don't know what it does to me but, by God, it does it well!'[52]

Here, as elsewhere, Moffat expresses the emotional involvement that he retains as a fan who has overseen the production of the primary object of his fandom. In part, at least, his excited utterance is a rhetorical feint because a basis of baffled, uncontrolled emotion would be unlikely to produce flagship television drama with global appeal in the twenty-first century. There no doubt needs to be an element of Keatsian 'negative capability' in the approach of the fan-showrunner ('when a man is capable of being in uncertainties, mysteries, doubts, without any irritable reaching after fact and reason'),[53] but the pressures of the role must also require the kind of analytical and dispassionately strategic approach that is almost the antithesis of stereotypical fan engagement. Between the unknowing affectiveness of 'I don't know what it does' and the knowing effectiveness of *actually making it do what it does* is the debate initiated by Tulloch and Jenkins's designation of fans as a 'powerless elite'.[54] This characterization has been challenged in relation to *Doctor Who* by Alan McKee and Hills and, indeed, has been modified by Jenkins himself.[55] Fans, as Tulloch noted from the outset, 'are far from being uncritical or sycophantic about their show'[56] and the stereotype of the gushing, undiscriminating 'fanatic' is rarely, if ever, encountered outside the realms of journalistic convenience. Furthermore, fans are instinctive narrators of their own analyses, they shape and share their readings, whether in the pages of the *TARDIS* fanzine or in costume at the Chicago TARDIS convention. These narrative and performative instincts have a marked prominence in the context of a revived TV series that has been, to an unusually large extent, the creation of fans of the original show.

The extraordinary success of new *Doctor Who* makes it harder than ever to sustain a persuasive argument for the 'powerless' side of the initial Tulloch–Jenkins equation. Even so, a case might be made for claiming that the 'elite' aspect is more noticeable now than at any time in the show's history. The otherwise welcome ascendancy of a small cadre of fans to prominent roles in the revived series means that those fans – the vast majority of them, obviously – who are not able to write, produce or star in the series might be expected to feel an escalation in their own sense of powerlessness. This would suggest a profound new split in the culture, the 'powerless' and the 'elite' becoming two distinct species of fan, but it is far from clear that this is actually how things stand. Apart from anything else, as McKee and Booy have shown, the blurring of the lines between consumption and production in *Doctor Who* has been happening since at least as far back as the mid-1980s, gaining momentum during the 'wilderness years' of the 1990s when it was fans who seized the creative initiative and kept the text unfolding.

Brigid Cherry draws attention to the use of the term 'the Not-We' by the *Doctor Who* fan community, especially in its online formations, to describe casual viewers and those who might not watch the series regularly or, indeed, at all.[57] The label is appropriate because it refers to the designation of outsiders by the Deva Lokan tribe of the Kinda in the 1982 story of that name. There is a self-mythologizing wit in this, fandom casting itself in the character of a people notable for their quietism, mystic unity and attitude of calm apartness. The Kinda, largely derived by writer Christopher Bailey from aspects of Buddhist teaching, are a tribe at one with their paradisal environment. They communicate with each other through telepathy and with the Not-We through the voices of the elderly blind 'wise woman' Panna (Mary Morris) and her young apprentice Karuna (Sarah Prince). In the latter instance, the communication is kept to a minimum and it is quickly apparent that the Kinda, pacific as they are, feel a degree of superiority over their colonial visitors and would rather have nothing to do with them.

The fundamental differences between the Kinda and the trespassers are stressed throughout the story, as when Karuna 'translates' for the rebellious male Aris (Adrian Mills) in his confrontation with Panna. The danger posed by Aris is announced by his development of orality, something usually restricted to the women of the tribe, and very few of those. This is reflected tellingly, and amusingly, in Panna's reaction to the Doctor when she learns that he has accompanied Todd (Nerys Hughes), the only woman among the Not-We, whose presence has been requested:

KARUNA There is another.
PANNA What other?
DOCTOR Hello.
PANNA A man!
KARUNA He was with her.
PANNA Impossible. Was he present when you opened the box?
DOCTOR Yes. Most enlightening!
PANNA What's he babbling about? No male can open the Box of Jhana without being driven out of his mind. It is well known. Unless ... Is he an idiot?
KARUNA *Are* you an idiot?
DOCTOR Well, I suppose I must be. I have been called one many times.
PANNA Keep silent, idiot.

As the solitary woman, Todd is also the only member of the expedition who has remained sane. The Box of Jhana, a small wooden casket presented to the Not-We by the Kinda and opened by the Doctor under threat of instant execution from the unhinged acting commander, Hindle (Simon Rouse), is at once a kind of MacGuffin and a floating signifier. Apart from a grimacing tribal puppet that springs from it as the Doctor releases the catch, the audience never sees the contents of the box and, in a narrative sense, like Marsellus Wallace's briefcase in *Pulp Fiction*, it can be considered as containing both nothing and everything. Suggestively, in the Pāli language, *Jhāna* (Sanskrit: *Dhyāna*) is a state of profound awareness, stillness, absorption and total concentration.

In essence, an influential section of the *Doctor Who* fan community has self-identified with a pseudo-hippy community from the classic run of the series that is notable for its quiet unity, sophisticated simplicity and reflex deferral to the wise authority of its womenfolk. A parodic inversion of perceived ideas of fandom is clear to see. That the Kinda are also vulnerable to colonization and susceptible to possession by evil forces in the form of the serpentine Mara is likewise indicative of a shared and sardonic introspection. Half-serious fan discourse around a sense of 'We' and 'Not-We' creates a peculiar tension between romanticism – fandom as a kind of noble, utopian savagery – and wry self-deprecation. The capacity for 'Kinda' to frame such a richly contradictory and symbolic fan consciousness can be traced through the shifting narrative of the story's own reputation. At the time of its first broadcast, 'Kinda' was not well received by fans (it finished bottom of the Season Nineteen survey in *Doctor Who Monthly*, for instance) but is now one of the most highly regarded stories of the 1980s.[58] Given that the close attention paid to 'Kinda' within *The Unfolding Text* would, at the time, have been unlikely to garner the approval of fans, this might also amount to a satire on the origins of the academic *Doctor Who* community, its tendency to concentrate on stories that fandom might prefer to spend less time on. Other than Fiske, for example, how many viewers in the early 1980s would have felt that David Fisher's 'The Creature from the Pit' (1979) warranted over thirty pages of analysis?[59] As noted previously in relation to both the inherent disappointment of fandom and the persistence of its enthusiasm, the *Doctor Who* experience is, fundamentally, an emotional one. This is consistent with the affective impulse that Lucien Lévy-Bruhl and Ernst Cassirer see as core to the myth-function in societies.[60] It also has parallels with the cultural readings of early media theorists such as Marshall McLuhan and Walter Ong, both of whom make use of figures and narratives from ancient mythology in their attempts to probe the effects of communication technologies. Given their mutual Catholicism, this is largely a case of inscribing a mythology of media effects within the framework of a pervasive theology. The essence of this, for McLuhan, is the 'miraculous' recreation of individual consciousness through its involvement with the external environment. The primal narrative, in other words, 'the drama of ordinary human perception', is a 'poetic process' resulting in 'the magic casement opening on the secrets of created being'.[61] If this seems rather overblown as a way of reading the mythic impulses of *Doctor Who* and its fandom, it nevertheless invokes the kinds of language the series has typically adopted and adapted, whether starkly oppositional (as in the classic era, where Good tended to battle Evil) or apocalyptic (as in the revived franchise, where the Skaro Degradations, the Horde of Travesties and the Nightmare Child accompany the Could've-Been-King, with his army of Meanwhiles and

Neverweres, into the Final Sanction at the End of Time): 'Knowledge of the creative process in art, science, and cognition shows the way to earthly paradise, or complete madness: the abyss or the top of mount purgatory.'[62] This might be the collapse of Heaven into Hell embodied – or, more accurately, disembodied – by Omega in 'The Three Doctors' (1972–3) or the day of reckoning anticipated by the Eleventh Doctor at Trenzalore ('The Name of the Doctor', 'The Time of the Doctor' (both 2013)). If it seems to be some distance from the lived experience of fans, it nevertheless reflects the rhetorical extremes to which they can be provoked by the programme they adore.

The Aristotelian entelechy that haunts *Doctor Who* fandom, the expectation of some epitomic version of the Time Lord's tale, is typical of the absolutism that the literary theorist Kenneth Burke associated with the mythic drive.[63] It is also a version of 'the mythical method' that Eliot discovered in James Joyce's *Ulysses*, that amounted to 'a way of controlling, of ordering, of giving a shape and a significance to the immense panorama of futility and anarchy which is contemporary history'.[64] It is unlikely that the elitist Eliot would admit any parallel between *Ulysses* and a mass media text like *Doctor Who*, and it would take a brave critic to argue for equivalence between the wanderings of Leopold Bloom and those of the Doctor. Even so, it is worth recalling that Eliot had a consistent (if disdainful) fascination with popular culture, one that is manifested both thematically and formally in his poetry, and that the text on which he based his reading of modernity's absorption of classical mythology is one of the most profoundly vernacular works in literature. There is nothing incongruous, then, in discovering a version of the mythical method at work in *Doctor Who*. The apparent urge among fans to, in Newman's terms, 'hammer' its ramified and often contradictory narratives 'into some overarching design' can be seen to bear a clear resemblance to Eliot's emphasis on the canonical coherence of 'tradition'. Such a vitalist desire is inevitably frustrated, for *Who* fans as for Old Possum, and this can lead to paranoia, prejudice and reactionary attitudes. Hostile responses in areas of *Doctor Who* fandom to, first, the revelation of Missy (Michelle Gomez) as a female incarnation of the Master (2014) and, then, the casting of Jodie Whittaker as a female Doctor (2017) have, in this respect, some surprising links with Eliot's often noxious political views, expressed most disturbingly in *After Strange Gods* (1934). It would be foolish to claim direct analogies between a minority of *Doctor Who* fans getting hissy about Missy on the internet and a leading cultural figure like Eliot publishing anti-Semitic comments in the context of the mid-1930s. There is, however, a comparable mythographic impulse in evidence.

As Coupe makes clear, 'myth' for Eliot is synonymous with 'tradition', his urge being to stabilize an uncertain present through the perceived solidity of the past. For *Doctor Who* fans, a similar urge would seem to be widespread, at least among those who grew up with (or have subsequently enjoyed) the classic series. For fans who are engaged closely with over fifty years of the series and its adjuncts, there is a tendency to feel that its continuation depends on 'the historical sense' that, for Eliot, appreciates 'not only the pastness of the past, but of its presence'.⁶⁵ This encourages a valorization of the original run of the series as constituting 'an ideal order', its component parts standing as 'existing monuments' that must be respected if 'conformity between the old and the new' is to be assured and the power of *Doctor Who* maintained.⁶⁶ Within Eliot's absolutist view of tradition, the historically sensitive writer is compelled 'to write not merely with his own generation in his bones, but with a feeling that the whole of the literature of Europe from Homer and within it the whole of the literature of his own country has a simultaneous existence and composes a simultaneous order'.⁶⁷ On a much smaller scale, the absolutist view of *Doctor Who* expects every Moffat, Davies or Chibnall to achieve order by feeling the 'simultaneous existence' of classic-series writers such as Terry Nation, Robert Holmes and 'Uncle Terrance' Dicks. Whether this channelling of tradition extends beyond Brian Hayles and Malcolm Hulke to include Ian Briggs and Marc Platt – writers of *Doctor Who* during the years of (arguably) enriched mythology but diminishing audience – is perhaps a moot point. And what of less-venerated contributors such as Pip and Jane Baker?

Here we begin to drift away from mythography into the realms of canonical debate, the discourse of golden ages: 'Golden ages are times – usually in the fans' past, often transmitted before they were fans – when communication between producers, fans and audiences is perceived as transparent and true.'⁶⁸ The mythology of golden ages is implicit within the mythology of canons. Both are individual whims masquerading as collective understandings. In the context of new *Who*, the situation is unusually complicated, with fandom now firmly embedded in the structures and processes of production. Even the toughest critic of his work would find it hard to furnish evidence that Steven Moffat wrote with anything other than a feeling that the whole of the history of *Doctor Who* (and the weight of expectation that comes with it) was in his bones. Does this, then, equate to a golden age? His own stories and the seasons he oversaw were increasingly willing not only to reference *Doctor Who*'s past but also to incorporate it through significant plot devices. This was most apparent in the anniversary episodes of 2013 – featuring the return of Karn and its Sisterhood, of the Zygons, UNIT and the Time Lords, the adaptation of classic-series footage to support cameo appearances by past Doctors, and so on – but it was also prevalent throughout the narratives of the Capaldi era. For fans craving what Tulloch and Jenkins call 'the accurate historical *continuity* of the series',[69] this should have been highly satisfying, but commentaries suggest that this was not always the case. Mentioning Metebelis III in Neil Cross's 'Hide' (2013) is one thing; getting the lead actor to pronounce it correctly is something else.

The irony of Eliot's mythical method as a way of fixing tradition within the fabric of the present is that it is essentially atemporal: an assertion of history as the primary pattern for modernity functions by denying the very sequence that produces history in the first place. In effect, history is depicted as simultaneous, the idea of tradition stalling in a spatial architecture of asserted eternal values. Eliot offers an account of mythology that relegates its founding principle – its etymological essence, *story* – to a bonding agent for apparently transcendent images. His vision is approximated in the scenario that introduces 'The Wedding of River Song' (2011), Earth history converging within the frozen moment of 5.02 pm on 22 April 2011. Featuring cameo roles for both Winston Churchill (Ian McNeice) and Charles Dickens (Simon Callow), the episode is far from earnest in its representation of historical collapse. Nevertheless, it insinuates a degree of satire. This seems to target the 'perpetual present' that some theorists (notably Fredric Jameson) have identified as a characteristic of postmodernism. The phenomenon is generally associated, however, with a form of 'historical amnesia', with the kind of rootless forgetting that Eliot set out to oppose, rather than with the confused over-remembering enacted in 'The Wedding of River Song'.[70] That the unsettling burlesque of the story is haunted by the Silence, memory-resistant monstrosities who have been influencing human history from its beginning, adds a further element of narrative richness. The revelation in 'A Good Man Goes to War' (2011) and 'The Time of the Doctor' that the Silence are a religious order affiliated to the Church of the Papal Mainframe brings into this epic of remembrance and forgetting an intimation of the high church sympathies at the heart of Eliot's historical outlook. The same ecclesiological sources are evident in the Monks of 'Extremis', 'The Pyramid at the End of the World' and 'The Lie of the Land' (2017).

The canon of *Doctor Who* long ago outgrew any official limits. Fans who post their fictions or videos online, don costumes to attend London Comic Con or deliver scholarly readings at conferences or in print are engaged in acts of revision, renewal and re-enactment that are analogous to those undertaken by successive production regimes. The shared enterprise of direct, passionate involvement in the work can be viewed as a secular adaptation of the ceremonials associated with myth in studies from Frazer's *The Golden Bough* onwards. Such ritual re-creation, in the writings of Mircea Eliade, is fundamental to the continuation of a culture:

> It is a living world – inhabited and used by creatures of flesh and blood, subject to the law of becoming, of old age and death. Hence it requires a periodical repairing, a renewing, a strengthening. But the only way to renew the World is to repeat what the immortals did in *illo tempore*, is to reiterate the creation.[71]

Every new telling of the *Doctor Who* tale returns, in a sense, to the original telling of the *Doctor Who* tale. The myth is renewed not simply with every new incarnation of the main character or redesign of the Cybermen but with every fan who dresses as her favourite Doctor or acts out a scene in the playground. As Segal writes, summarizing Eliade, 'To hear, to read, and especially to re-enact a myth is magically to return to the time when the myth took place.'[72] This sees myth as a kind of 'magic carpet' or time machine, which in many ways is what *Doctor Who* has always been to its multifarious fans. Unlike Eliade's transport of mythic delight, that of *Doctor Who* fans – like the TARDIS itself – travels into the future as well as the past, although it might not always seem that way.

Chapter 2
Doctor Who as mythology

On mythic identities: Flying carpets and silly robots

In her 1994 Reith Lectures, Marina Warner stated that 'every telling of a myth is a part of that myth; there is no Ur-version, no authentic prototype, no true account'.[1] Myths are metamorphic – formally, thematically, ideologically – so no version of any myth is 'truer' than any other. If we accept Warner's view, it seems to follow that there is no point in searching for the mythic essence of *Doctor Who*, since there can be no such thing. The broadcast version of 'An Unearthly Child' (1963) is no more authentic than the pilot episode that it replaced or the Terrance Dicks novelization that followed eighteen years later. Is it, though, more authentic than the very different foundation tale that replaced it in the early pages of David Whitaker's 1964 novel adaptation of 'The Daleks' (1963–4), the story that succeeded it on screen? And is it a truer reflection of the myth than other episodes or stories from the television series, including those like 'The Space Pirates' (1969), 'Time and the Rani' (1987) and 'Fear Her' (2006), that have often been disparaged by fans? Taking the argument to its logical conclusion, 'An Unearthly Child' is no truer in mythical terms than a fan fiction posted online or scribbled in the back of a school exercise book in the early 1980s.

Warner's rejection of an authentic, fixed and primal mythic account tends to undermine the concept of a stable, knowable corpus to which such an account could belong. In this respect, her approach is at odds with the totalizing instinct that characterizes fan activity and that shapes critical debates about the *Doctor Who* canon, whether these take place within, beyond or across academic environments. Then again, canon and mythology are not the same thing; they might even be opposites. Warner's fluid sense of how versions of a myth run into and through each other means that her reading is not actually incompatible with that of Fredric Jameson, whose notion of 'universal history' proposes the complex coherence of 'a single great collective story'.[2] Although this unitary narrative is the sustained amalgamation of all the stories ever told, not just the stories told within a specific, identifiable body of fiction, it nevertheless offers a compelling way of considering the extended narrative of *Doctor Who*. From Jameson's standpoint its many stories, the endlessly ramifying iterations across time, space and media, can be seen as 'vital episodes in a single vast unfinished plot'.[3] The important qualification to be made in this respect is that the vast plot is not just unfinished but *unfinishable*: like the digressive ironies and generic transformations of Laurence Sterne's *Tristram Shandy* (1759–67), the story of the Doctor – as Ood Sigma observes in the closing moments of 'The End of Time, Part 2' (2010) – never ends.

The juxtaposition of Sterne's cock-and-bull story and the BBC's 'quirky science fiction serial' is not as gratuitous as it might at first appear.[4] Both are narratives that, by most critical and commercial criteria, should never have worked. Samuel Johnson's well-known deprecation of *Tristram Shandy* – 'Nothing odd will do long'[5] – points towards an eccentricity that is shared by *Doctor Who*, notably in the lack of a secure teleology, the proliferating excess of story and the resistance to generic definition. Here, for example, in a scene from David Fisher's 'The Stones of Blood' (1978), the conversation between the Fourth Doctor (Tom Baker) and Professor Amelia Rumford (Beatrix Lehmann) shifts between pseudo-technological seriousness, existential gravity and comic levity:

> DOCTOR There you are. Now, if [the Ogri] should break through, run as if something very nasty were after you, because something very nasty will be after you.
> RUMFORD Yeah, but what about you?
> DOCTOR Don't worry about me. I'll be doing plenty of that in any case.
> RUMFORD Yes, but how will you get back?
> DOCTOR You just switch on for thirty seconds, say, every half hour.

RUMFORD If you think that'll work.

DOCTOR Well, of course it'll work and even if it doesn't work, what does it matter? You know what they say about hyperspace.

RUMFORD No.

DOCTOR They say it's a theoretical absurdity, and that's something I've always wanted to be lost in.

As they work with K9 (John Leeson) to construct a ramshackle hyperspace projection device in the living room of Rumford's cottage, the Doctor and his archaeologist friend resemble Uncle Toby and Corporal Trim working in the grounds of Shandy Hall to reconstruct the Siege of Namur in model form. Disparagers of the Graham Williams era would see such a scene as a travesty of the paradigmatic *Doctor Who* mode, but it is more typical than they might like to admit and seems very close, tonally, to the more knockabout elements of the post-2005 series.

David Butler has observed that, from the earliest discussions about its format, purpose and intended audience, '*Doctor Who* was a programme with an identity crisis, but [that] this crisis would result in a genuine strength'.[6] Such a 'confused identity' is hardly surprising for a series extemporized in its origins, then maintained by successive creative teams over a period of more than half a century. The 'strategy of periodic renewal' noted by Chapman is analogous to the process of continuous mythical retelling described by Warner, albeit across a much shorter span of time.[7] Where Warner introduces myths by referencing the 'continuous enterprise' of reiteration through which they assert their immutable significance while undergoing endless 'contingency, changes and transitoriness', *Doctor Who* is defined by Tulloch and Alvarado in relation to a '*continuity* of professional concern' offset by 'a *variety* of signatures' (emphasis in the original).[8] In other words, with no requirement to sustain an ur-version of the myth, all makers of *Doctor Who* have been concerned with making a successful *part* of that myth, one that *makes it differently*.

Clearly, there are elements of the *Doctor Who* mythology – Britton calls them 'structuring *icons*'[9] – that are *sine quibus non*: the Doctor, his ability to regenerate, the TARDIS as his vehicle, its fixed erroneous form as a police box, the fact that it is bigger on the inside, its capacity to traverse both time and space, the sound of its arrival and departure, the coming and going of companions, the periodic return of enemies such as the Daleks and the Cybermen. For all its well-attested 'lack of genre purity',[10] its tendency to slide between science fiction, horror, comedy and period drama by way of soap opera, psychological thriller and picaresque fantasy, often intermingling several of these modes within a single story, there remains a quality that is unmistakably *Doctor Who*. This quality, a distinct brand identity, is realized with a coherence that belies the improvisation of the programme's origins, the stresses and strains of its long history, the variability of its outputs. At the same time, because there is no pure condition of *Doctor Who*, the resilience of perhaps the most pervasive of the 'folk theories' noted by Butler is assured. *Doctor Who* does indeed have 'a format that can apparently go anywhere and tell any kind of story'.[11]

The previous chapter ended with a reference to Eliade's treatment of myth as a form of magic carpet. If we direct the flight of that metaphor towards Darko Suvin's groundbreaking study of 1979, *Metamorphoses of Science Fiction*, we find it used to a strikingly different end. For Suvin, the magic carpet is a 'stock folktale accessory', a 'wish-fulfilling element' that 'evades the empirical law of physical gravity'.[12] In effect, it is an emblem of the incompatibility of the folk tale with science fiction and, by association, of the fairy-tale, fantasy and traditional understandings of myth. Suvin's typology of science fiction insists on a balance of estrangement and rational cognition, the absence of which in folk-tale traditions is appraised in a sentence of oxymoronic sharpness: 'Anything is possible in a folktale,' Suvin writes, 'because a folktale is manifestly impossible.'[13] The same might be said about *Doctor Who* and, regardless of whether a challenge is made to Suvin's categories, it is worth testing the assumption, dominant throughout its history, that the extended tale of the Doctor is an example of science fiction.

It should be recalled here that, in the initial development of the series at the BBC from early 1962, the designation of 'science fiction' was not always welcomed. Butler overstates the case slightly when he writes that 'as far as the official line tended to go, *Doctor Who* was categorically *not* science fiction',[14] but the commissioning of successive reports into the state and status of the genre is indicative not only of a properly methodical approach to programme development but also of an institutional unease with such a popular contemporary form. The exclusive emphasis in these reports on *literary* science fiction is, in this respect, significant. Some of the criteria proposed in the reports ('do not include Bug-Eyed Monsters', 'never Tin Robots', no elaborate or exotic settings) is both significant and, in retrospect, richly ironic, as is the assessment of time-travel themes as being 'indigestible stuff for the audience'.[15]

Suvin's delineation of science fiction refuses any meaningful correlation between the genre he is championing and those other traditions with which it has often been associated. Linked with myth, folklore, fantasy and fairy tale through its defiance of naturalistic modes of storytelling, science fiction is seen by Suvin as distinct from (and superior to) these other manifestations of supra-realist narration. Advocating 'that the critic be a Darwinist and not a medicine-man', he asserts that 'where the myth claims to explain once and for all the essence of phenomena, SF [science fiction] first posits them as problems and then explores where they lead'.[16] *Doctor Who*, playing freely, at times subversively, across the categories of fantastical narrative styles, posits many problems and explores their leads but somehow allows us to be fairly respectable Darwinists and utterly disreputable medicine-men at the same time. Tulloch and Alvarado recognized this in the early 1980s when they asserted that 'tensions and contradictions within SF texts were founding principles of the genre', a genre that 'was never either simply "bourgeois" or "subversive"'.[17] This can account, at least in part, for the discrepancy between those who see *Doctor Who* as an essentially conservative myth and those who argue for its more progressive and socially interrogative tendencies.

Ample evidence can be found to corroborate both readings and, of course, they are not mutually exclusive. Alan McKee discovered this through his primary research into the perceived politics of *Doctor Who*, with one of his interviewees commenting, 'It's kept incredibly vague … A conservative will see the Doctor as conservative. A liberal will see the Doctor as liberal. A socialist will see the Doctor as socialist. An anarchist will see the Doctor as an anarchist.'[18] More specifically, in relation to Robert Holmes's 'The Sun Makers' (1977):

> The interesting thing about [it] is that although it purports to be a political satire, it doesn't actually take a political stance at all. Left-wing viewers watch it as a parody of capitalism gone mad; right wing

viewers watch it as a parody of bureaucracy gone mad. It's neither and both at the same time.[19]

Neither and both at the same time: a particular property of *Doctor Who* is its capacity to hold contradictions in a state of equilibrium. This comes close to the mythic ideal of Claude Lévi-Strauss, in which structures resolve cultural contradictions, but it should be borne in mind that the patterns traced in books such as *The Raw and the Cooked* and *Myth and Meaning* are relational rather than narrative.[20] Lévi-Strauss is not at all concerned with myth *as storytelling*, and Hills has already shown how his emphatically logical approach is an uneasy fit with the emotionally inflected matter of *Doctor Who*, especially in the post-2005 series.[21]

Although no official announcement was ever made by the BBC to confirm that the series had ended with 'Survival', as far as most viewers were concerned it vanished from sight for sixteen years apart from a fleeting reappearance in 1996 (with Paul McGann as the Eighth Doctor) and a scattering of repeats, mostly on satellite and cable channels. Out of sight was out of mind, but the myth was continuing in those marginal spaces of cultural production where only the devoted would think to look: in the pages of the Virgin novels, in independent video productions by Dreamtime Media, Reeltime Pictures and BBV, in the Big Finish audio dramas and, very occasionally, on BBC radio and BBC online, and eventually in the BBC Books range of novels. In a vital sense (adopting Ricoeur's terminology) the 'social imagination' of *Doctor Who* persisted and, indeed, expanded and diversified through the years of apparent hiatus. When, finally, the programme returned to BBC television it had behind it not only the quarter century of the original series and its spin-offs but also the dense, complex inheritance of activities that had taken place between 1989 and 2005.

Following the announcement in September 2003 that the BBC would be reviving *Doctor Who*, Russell T. Davies stated that his aim was 'to write a full-blooded drama which embraces the Doctor Who heritage, at the same time as introducing the character to a modern audience'.[22] Given the success of the reboot, it is easy to forget the extent to which excitement about the new series was mingled with anxiety. Writing in *The Observer*, Rachel Cooke, attributing her career in journalism to a childhood idolization of Sarah Jane Smith, reflected on her disappointment when rewatching Chris Boucher's 'The Robots of Death' (1977) – 'How slow the whole thing seems, how silly the robots look' – and expressed serious misgivings about the imminent regeneration:

> Perhaps, then, Russell T's Doctor will find an audience. But these viewers must be young, they must know nothing of Gallifrey or Exxilon or Karn; they must see the autons and the daleks with new eyes. Anyone with precious memories – obsessive fans excepted – is probably done for so far as the timelord's [*sic*] ninth incarnation goes. Then again, as The Robots of Death forcefully reminded me, the past is not always what you think, and little is to be gained by wallowing in it.[23]

Tellingly, both Gallifrey and Karn have now featured in twenty-first-century *Doctor Who*, Exxilon has been namechecked and the art deco design of the mechanical servitors in 'The Robots of Death' has been referenced in that of the Host in the 2007 Christmas special 'Voyage of the Damned'. The 'precious memories' of those fans who grew up with the classic series are helping to form the precious memories of those who are viewing the new series.

Ancient mythologies, because of that ancientness, and because of the sacred aspect that is assumed for them, can seem to float free (dangerously so, in some cases) of the messy matter of history, giving them an air of natural, transcendent permanence. *Doctor Who*, as a new mythology, secular, authored and knowable in its context, a context that is at least partly industrial, economic and sociopolitical, must be understood in its historical situation. 'Myths have a historicity of their own,' Ricoeur remarks, and this is evident in a nascent myth like *Doctor Who*, old in television terms, a renovated heirloom to those who watch it, but newborn in the total span of storytelling.[24] Such a myth is subject, for the time being at least, to a form of collective total recall, whereby both its beginnings and its latest ends exist in living memory, comprehended (extant or not) across a range of media forms, from online streaming services to the BBC Written Archives Centre in Berkshire. No individual can know everything, but everyone knows something, and many know much.

The historical proximity and personal intimacy of the *Doctor Who* myth means that its successful revival was always going to require an adroit synthesis of nostalgia and newness. Ricoeur would have been optimistic: 'Nothing travels more extensively and effectively than myth,' he wrote, arguing for its 'capacity to emigrate and develop within new cultural frameworks'.[25] Making his pitch for the revival, though, Davies took no chances:

> The fiction of the Doctor has got 40 years of back-story. Which we'll ignore. Except for the good bits. He's a Time Lord, he's got a Tardis, he's got two hearts, a sonic screwdriver, and he's 900 years old. And, contracts pending, there's an old enemy called the Daleks.[26]

As a fan, Davies knew all too well the impact of an excessive concern with internal continuity. As a canny professional, he knew the importance of *showing* that he knew this and he made sure that the tone and language of his pitch were emphatically those of a confident, contemporary maker of cutting-edge popular television drama rather than those of a lifelong *Doctor Who* fan: 'The rest of the series' continuity is absolutely irrelevant. I don't care that in 1973 he used gadget X to escape from planet Y.'[27] Significantly, Davies framed the revival in explicitly mythical terms, but this was myth as innovation: 'The important thing is, this mythology is discovered, as new, by Rose.' Five years later, facing questions about continuity in relation to his own appointment as showrunner, Moffat would offer a response tilted beautifully towards the sarcastic side of ironic: 'Having taken the precaution of having memorised every single event in *Doctor Who*'s history, it's fairly easy for me to keep continuity because I remember it all.'[28] Interestingly, Moffat proved himself to be both more disposed than Davies to dust off aspects of the classic series and more willing to court controversy in his remaking of them.

The remainder of this chapter will explore contradictions and confluences between the classic series, the new series and those acts of storytelling that have taken place around the edges of these. Because monsters, identified as being of particular importance in the revived series, are both emblematic of the particular mythology of *Doctor Who* and indexical of the processes of change and continuity within it, they will provide the initial focus of discussion.[29] Attention will then turn to the flow of the television series into other media forms across two generations of storytelling.

Remaking the monsters: Nostalgia and novelty

Among the 'good bits' that Davies built into his new mythology of *Doctor Who* were several of the classic monsters.[30] Christopher Eccleston's season as the Ninth Doctor began with the Autons and the Nestene Consciousness and went on to include the Daleks twice. Subsequent seasons under Davies featured returns for the Cybermen, the Macra, the Sontarans and many more Daleks. During Moffat's tenure as showrunner, returning monsters included the Silurians, the Great Intelligence, the Ice Warriors, the Zygons, and more Autons, Cybermen and Daleks. In addition, both Davies and Moffat took the creative liberty of bringing classic monsters together, whether in a spectacular showdown ('Doomsday' (2006)) or as part of an improbable alliance ('The Pandorica Opens' (2010)). Such carnivals of monstrosity are an official validation of the extended narrative of *Doctor Who*, emphasizing the unity of its mythology while scratching an itch that most fans have experienced at some time or other.

The ease with which four Daleks defeated an army of Cybermen at Canary Wharf in 'Doomsday' was not enjoyed by all viewers, but the manifest wish-fulfilment remains compelling:

> CYBERMAN Our species are similar, though your design is inelegant.
> DALEK Daleks have no concept of elegance.
> CYBERMAN This is obvious.

The thrill of the Doctor's most lethal enemies engaging in banter (all voiced by Nicholas Briggs) might strike some as a dubious one, reviving debates about the impact of a certain kind of comedy on the *Doctor Who* myth.[31] Traditions of humour will be considered in the next chapter but, regardless of whether monsters trading mutually provocative wisecracks is seen as conduct unbecoming, it can hardly be denied that Davies's script for 'Doomsday' flouts the conventions of deadpan mechanical belligerence in style:

> CYBERLEADER Daleks, be warned. You have declared war upon the Cybermen.
> BLACK DALEK This is not war. This is pest control.

CYBERLEADER We have five million Cybermen. How many are you?

BLACK DALEK Four.

CYBERLEADER You would destroy the Cybermen with four Daleks?

BLACK DALEK We would destroy the Cybermen with one Dalek. You are superior in only one respect.

CYBERLEADER What is that?

BLACK DALEK You are better at dying.

Although it never aspires to this kind of Wilde-and-Whistler-in-the-playground raillery, the coalition of creatures surrounding Matt Smith's Doctor as he is dragged towards the Pandorica constitutes a similar moment of fan-pleasuring. An alliance of enemies rather than a face-off, with mentions of the Drahvins, Draconians and Terileptils (and, in an acknowledgement of extra-televisual mythology, the Chelonians), its cost-effective pageant of recent costumes was suitably impressive, amounting to an intra-diegetic *Doctor Who* exhibition.

When redesigning classic monsters for new *Who* the concern, as noted by Britton, has been for 'responsible modernisation'. Aiming for a balance of homage and revision, the 'double encoding' that Linda Hutcheon sees as a feature of postmodernism,[32] production teams have presented returning monsters as recognizable 'upgrades' of their predecessors. A complicating factor has been the diegetic continuity that links, for instance, the Daleks that first appeared on screen in 1963 to those that have trundled or flown into view since 2005. *Doctor Who* is not being *retold* in the twenty-first century; it is being *continued*, which raises (or at least implies) the question of how Daleks that can now 'fly like bastards'[33] were ever the subject of long-running jokes about stairs. The answer, of course, is the advancement of special effects techniques in the years since the classic series, but this is not an explanation that makes sense within the storyworld. The Fourth Doctor's taunt towards the end of the second episode of 'Destiny of the Daleks' (1979) – 'If you're supposed to be the superior race of the universe, why don't you try climbing after us?' – has been a target of fan indignation over the years, but it is even more problematic now that armies of Daleks can fly in lethal formation. Then again, this particular continuity issue is not a new one, since Daleks were seen to levitate to memorable effect in 'Remembrance of the Daleks' in 1988 and had been taking to the air as far back as the *Dalek* annuals and *TV 21* comic strips (and the Cadet sweet cigarette cards) of the mid-1960s.

As Moffat has pointed out, the format of *Doctor Who* contains a ready solution to these apparent internal contradictions: 'In the end, a television series which embraces both the ideas of parallel universes and the concept of changing time can't have any continuity errors.'[34] Paul Cornell is more direct:

> Not giving a toss about how it all fits together is one of *Doctor Who*'s oldest, proudest traditions, a strength of the series ... It's allowed infinite change, and never left the show crunched into a corner after all the dramatic options had already been done. Terrible continuity equals infinitely flexible format.[35]

Cornell goes on to refuse the idea that there is any fatal conflict inherent in such flexibility:

> That doesn't mean we lose the lovely thought that *Doctor Who* is all one big story. It's one big and very complex story, that rewrites and contradicts itself. That was always the case. Only now it does it with purpose, rather than by accident.

This 'purpose' is illustrated in Moffat's two-part story 'The Magician's Apprentice' / 'The Witch's Familiar' (2015), in which his prison-planet scenario from 'Asylum of the Daleks' (2012) becomes the basis for a renascent Dalek culture on a born-again Skaro, designs from throughout the history of *Doctor Who* coexisting on screen. The sight of the original silver Daleks mixing with the Davies-era bronze Daleks in a city that, both inside and out, is modelled on that discovered by the TARDIS crew in 'The Dead Planet' (1963) imparts a playful confidence about the creative potential of continuity. This impression is intensified by Capaldi's Doctor wearing check trousers reminiscent of those worn by William Hartnell and Patrick Troughton, as well as by the presence of Davros (Julian Bleach), the Dalek Supreme from 'The Stolen Earth' / 'Journey's End' (2008) and the Special Weapons Dalek from 'Remembrance of the Daleks' (1988). In effect, Moffat's sleight-of-narrative-hand brings together the most physically restricted Daleks in the series' history (those first encountered by Hartnell could not function beyond the metal floors of their city) and the most physically liberated ones, with neither being diminished by the association. A half-century-plus of relatively venial incongruities is resolved.

An earlier, less mischievous but comparably deft response to the challenges of legacy can be found in Tom MacRae's scripts for 'Rise of the Cybermen' / 'Age of Steel' (2006), episodes that introduced the Cybermen to the revived series. Situating the metal monsters on a parallel contemporary Earth, MacRae circumvents the muddled continuity of the classic Cybermen by giving them a new beginning rather than a belated renewal. These Cybermen, created by the CEO of Cybus Industries, John Lumic (Roger Lloyd Pack), cannot contradict the Cybermen whose origins on Mondas are explored by Marc Platt in his Big Finish audio drama *Spare Parts* (2002) – which, ironically, is a direct influence on MacRae's story – because they have nothing at all to do with them. 'It's happening again,' says David Tennant's Doctor as he gets his first view of the Lumic Cybermen, but it's happening again *differently*: he might have 'seen them before', but not quite like this.

Seeing the Cybermen differently is hardly a new experience for the viewer of *Doctor Who*: the classic Cybermen were habitually remodelled, from the soft-faced, human-handed cyborgs of 'The Tenth Planet' in 1966 to their glass-jawed counterparts in the 1980s. The frequent redesign of their appearance has proved less problematic, though, than the continuous replotting of their narrative provenance and function. A familiar element of messiness has now developed around the timeline of the revived-series Cybermen, with it being unclear at times whether the narrative is still following the peregrinations of the Lumic upgrades or whether we are back in the ambit of the original tin soldiers. The Cybus Industries logo has been absent from the design of the Cybermen from 'A Good Man Goes to War' (2011) onwards, implying the latter, but there has been no overt confirmation of this. Neil Gaiman, in fact, talking about the redesign of the Cybermen for his 'Nightmare in Silver' (2013), has speculated on miscegenation between the Mondas/Telos and Lumic versions:

> My theory is [that] the Cybus Cybermen were sent to Victorian days and zapped off into time and space at the end of 'The Next Doctor'. They met a bunch of the Mondasian/Telosian Cybermen, and there was some cross-breeding and interchange of technology, which is

why you then get the ones that look like, but actually aren't, the Cybus Cybermen. And then I thought well, they're going to keep upgrading themselves – my computer doesn't look like it did five or ten years ago, definitely not 15 years ago. It's going to be faster and it's going to be better.[36]

The Cybermen created from human remains by Missy in Moffat's 'Dark Water' / 'Death in Heaven' (2014), flying like the Iron Man-style suits that they so closely resemble, are apparently unconnected with those seen in 'Nightmare in Silver' and seem to denote yet another foundation myth. That they look identical to the fast-moving infiltrators of Hedgewick's World of Wonders is, presumably, more to do with the extra-diegetic constraints of time and money than intra-diegetic consistency of pedigree. If such murkiness of lineage seems preferable to the manic plaiting of narrative strands that characterized 1985's 'Attack of the Cybermen', then Moffat's composition of a creation tale for the Mondasian Cybermen in 'World Enough and Time' / 'The Doctor Falls' (2017) begins to look like a bold but hazardous enterprise. A 'genesis of the Cybermen', as John Simm's Master quips, it is effectively a prequel to both 'The Tenth Planet' (1966) and 'Dark Water' / 'Death in Heaven', drawing on Platt's *Spare Parts* at the same time as it disregards it.

A drawback of the Cybermen as returning monsters, presumably because of their inherent lack of individuality, is that they have often been used as an 'easy' popular invader, a generic rent-a-baddie. This became clear in the two-and-a-bit years between Hartnell's swansong and the debut of UNIT in 1968's 'The Invasion', when they featured in no fewer than five stories, amounting to twenty-six episodes. During this period they underwent three major redesigns, with peripheral details being tweaked along the way. After 'The Invasion', they would not be seen again until Tom Baker's debut season in 1975 (apart from fleeting cameos in 1969's 'The War Games' and 1973's 'Carnival of Monsters'). Another seven years would pass until their return in the Peter Davison story 'Earthshock', after which there would be a further three Cyber-stories before the end of the classic series. How many of these narratives, typically of the base-under-siege variety, actually required the Cybermen *specifically* to be the adversarial monsters is debatable. Certainly, in terms of 'The Five Doctors' (1983), scripted by Terrance Dicks, their role seems to have been to make up the numbers at the twentieth-anniversary party and to provide a high metallic body count, not least when pulverized by the Raston Warrior Robot. (Then again, they fare no worse than the story's lone Dalek, which is tricked into shooting itself, and the bedraggled Yeti, which seems to be jolted by a rockfall into remembering that it shouldn't be able to move at all without the controlling presence of the Great Intelligence.)

Some fans have bemoaned a similar treatment of the Cybermen in the revived series, particularly in stories such as 'Closing Time' (2011) and 'Death in Heaven', the last of which sees them reduced to a massed army of spear carriers. When Missy has them performing a synchronized slow aerobics session in a graveyard (see Figure 2.1) – 'Look at Mummy! Raise your arms. Lower your arms. Raise your right. Lower your right. Turn on the spot' – it might be considered that the humiliating downgrade is complete.

After this, the heroism of a resurrected Danny Pink (Samuel Anderson), overriding his cyber-conditioning to protect Clara Oswald (Jenna Coleman) and save the world, and of a similarly converted but indomitable Brigadier Alistair Gordon Lethbridge-Stewart, rescuing his daughter Kate (Jemma Redgrave) in her plummet from the presidential plane, can seem to add insult to injury. The last of these struck a clanging note for many fans, who felt that its gratuitous plot

Figure 2.1 The Cybermen work out in a graveyard in 'Death in Heaven' (2014); ©BBC Worldwide.

twist represented not only a diminishment of the Cybermen but also a betrayal of the legacy of the Brigadier and, crucially, an affront to the memory of the actor who had portrayed him for forty years, Nicholas Courtney. What was intended as tribute was taken as defilement. This was by no means a universal response – the comments thread on a *CULTBOX* posting about this 'unbearably poignant' season finale is violently mixed, for instance[37] – but there was enough controversy to expose the sensitivities of inheritance and the dangers of exploring the narrative limits of nostalgia.

'We're not in the business of being nostalgic,' Moffat commented when he took over *Doctor Who*; 'we're making nostalgia for the future.'[38] This chimes with Davies, and also with Ricoeur's insistence on the mutability of myths, his view being that they 'are not unchanging and unchanged antiques which are simply delivered out of the past in some naked, original state'.[39] Importantly, the focus here is on those ancient, often anonymous mythologies that span centuries or millennia. Ricoeur's reflections on 'the necessity of critical discrimination between liberating and destructive modes of reinterpretation'[40] has a very different import in the context of stories, characters and creatures created within living memory by known authors contributing to an ongoing narrative.

The divided motivation of the fan-producer was evident when Davies brought back classic-series monsters such as the Autons and the Macra. The first of these, included in the comeback story 'Rose', were presented as an example of respectful continuity. The sight of mannequins smashing their way out of shop window displays was an explicit reference to the famously nightmarish scene from Jon Pertwee's launch adventure as the Third Doctor, 'Spearhead from Space' (1970). A nod to the fandom of which he is a part,[41] Davies's use of the Autons also signalled his singular position as a fan, linking his risky enterprise of resurrecting *Doctor Who* with a story that had marked a crucial and uncertain transition in its original run. 'Spearhead from Space' introduced a new Doctor and a new companion (scientist Liz Shaw, played by Caroline John). It also saw the establishment by Derrick Sherwin (briefly in the role of producer) and Terrance Dicks (as script editor) of a new narrative template, the hero exiled to twentieth-century Earth, working reluctantly as the unpaid Scientific Advisor to the United Nations Intelligence Taskforce. Most prominently, it saw the transition from monochrome to colour. 'Rose', equally, introduced a new Doctor, a new companion, a new production team and a new narrative template. There was no comparable colour shift but there was the emergence of *Doctor Who* into a radically different media environment from that of 1963–89.

The decision to represent the Nestene of 'Rose' as a burbling fiery soufflé rather than the foaming giant squid of 'Spearhead from Space' was noted by some as a violation of continuity (see Figure 2.2). Unsurprisingly, views were polarized on this, from the admiring – 'the wonders of CGI render the Nestene Consciousness as a truly terrifying creature' – to the dismissive – 'I'm not so enamored of the Nestene Consciousness, however, which is portrayed as a CGI lava face'.[42] In these reactions, fans are often more focused on the technique of the representation than the outcome: 'The Nestene consciousness was pretty bad. For goodness sake, computer special effects without Peter Jackson's bank balance are worse than any amount of hand puppets and full body suits. Lets [*sic*] hope they don't digitise the daleks.'[43] That would *never* do … The irony here, of course, is that the decision to recreate the Nestene using computer graphics was almost certainly informed by a desire to avoid the perils of physical realization that had vexed classic *Who*, at least in popular memory and especially in relation

Figure 2.2 The Doctor (Christopher Eccleston) addresses the Nestene Consciousness in 'Rose' (2005); ©BBC Worldwide.

to large-scale monstrosities. Fan responses to the Nestene's makeover from 'an octopoidal mass of tentacles' to a 'molten living plastic vat' suggest ways in which redesign can exhibit the contradictions between continuity and variation.[44] Fans who approve of the change – 'certainly an improvement from the squid like creature we first saw' – are at odds with those who feel, like one blogger, that the metamorphosis 'from Octopus to Blob is a big stretch'.[45] A more extreme anxiety is contained in the question asked by another fan: 'What happened to the Nestene's true squid-like form?'[46] Here there is an essentialist notion of the mythology, a sense that there is a 'true' representation, distinct from issues of realism.

Intriguingly, an overview of the Nestene myth as it has been shaped across the media landscapes of *Doctor Who* indicates that the concept of the giant squid might owe more to non-televisual than televisual accounts of the alien intelligence. The prevailing impression of floundering green tentacles, rooted in the televised version of 'Spearhead from Space', is duplicated in accounts provided by Terrance Dicks in his Target novelizations of the first two Auton stories. Both *Doctor Who and the Auton Invasion* (1974) and *Doctor Who and the Terror of the Autons* (1975) describe the manifested Nestene Consciousness as a 'many-tentacled monster, something between spider, crab and octopus', referring to 'a single huge eye glar[ing] at them, blazing with alien intelligence and deadly hatred'.[47] The second novel adds an adjective ('deadly') and a comma; otherwise the descriptions, showing characteristic Dicksian economy, are identical. The cover art and interior illustrations for the novels, by Chris Achilleos, Andrew Skilleter, Alun Hood and Alan Willow, tend to follow the prose sketches provided by Dicks, offering a further authentication of the cephalopodic idea of the Nestene (see Figure 2.3).

Adopted for the trilogy of BBV productions in the late 1990s – *Auton* (1997), *Auton 2: Sentinel* (1998) and *Auton 3* (1999) – it was also endorsed by Craig Hinton in his BBC Books novel of 2004, *Synthespians™*, which echoes and enhances Dicks's description:

> Clasped around the aerial, an enormous creature writhed and undulated. It must have been tens of miles across, a greeny-yellow cross between a spider, a crab and an octopus, its single baleful eye looking through the plexiglass dome at the millions of terrified

Figure 2.3 Alan Willow's illustration of the Nestene (detail) from Terrance Dicks's *Doctor Who and the Terror of the Autons* (1975); ©Alan Willow, ©BBC Worldwide. Coloured in by the current author as a child.

inhabitants. All the while, it flickered in and out of existence, its tentacles and claws and tendrils grasping and feeling.[48]

Perhaps the vague spidery flickering between two satellite dishes at the climax of 'Terror of the Autons' (1971) is tending towards another tentacular manifestation. It remains, however, what one fan, approving of the 'Rose' adaptation, describes as a 'white video effects blob'.[49] The tenacity of the spider-crab-octopus image must be seen as testament to the combined power of first impressions and mythic extension. That such extension has taken place through licensed, fan-created narratives must lend weight to McKee's contention that it is fandom which ultimately defines canon.[50] It is worth noting that the Consciousness as it is depicted in 'Rose', described by the Doctor as 'a living plastic creature', is much closer to Robert Holmes's original conception than the widespread impression of an enormous mass of tentacles: 'The Nestene itself I thought of as a plasticky, swirling mass, a glob of pure instinct which spawns the Autons.'[51]

If the Nestene evolution suggests, like those of the Daleks and the Cybermen, that the continuity of monstrousness in *Doctor Who* is 'a custom more honour'd in the breach than the observance', the same might be said of other classic-series aliens that have returned since 2005. Taking Hamlet at his word, this means that monsters from the Troughton era such as the Macra and the Great Intelligence are respected more by being adapted for modern audiences and contexts than they would be by being reinstated in their primal condition. Not all fans were pleased by the treatment of the Macra in 'Gridlock' (2007) and others will have felt dismayed that the return of the Great Intelligence in 'The Snowmen' (2012), 'The Bells of Saint John' and 'The Name of the Doctor' (both 2013) did not also mark the return of the Yeti. For some, these are poor tokens of continuity: they show that the price paid for ensuring that nostalgia stays relevant is a diminished sense of the distinctiveness and richness of inherited mythology. The requirement to modernize in order to secure such an inheritance is also acknowledged, however, as in this fan blog responding to rumours of the Yeti's possible return in early 2012:

It's hard to watch much of the early *Doctor Who* without the nostalgia that helps you to overlook how horribly cheesy and bad most of it was. Some of the most awkward parts of the modern series involve classic creatures. When *Doctor Who* steps away from the old series, while still staying true to the character and heart of the show, you see the story soar like in 'Blink' or 'The Girl in the Fireplace'. The lore of the show is set by the past, but these are new stories.[52]

Referencing two of Moffat's Davies-era stories, this supplies a context for the new monsters brought in to serve the Great Intelligence (Ian McKellen initially, then Richard E. Grant).

The Snowmen, the Spoonheads and the Whispermen are, in very different ways, reactions against a too-easy restoration of the popular shaggy robots introduced to the series in 1967 by writers Henry Lincoln and Mervyn Haisman. Like the Sea Devils and the giant maggots, the Yeti seem to rank highly in the nostalgic recollections of those who grew up with *Doctor Who* in the late 1960s and early 1970s. Also like the Sea Devils and the giant maggots, though, their affective power seems to be closely linked to their physical environment: the Sea Devils rising from the waves, the maggots writhing in a Welsh mine, the Yeti shambling through the London Underground. Their debut appearance in the Tibetan landscape (actually the Nant Ffrancon Pass in Snowdonia) of 'The Abominable Snowmen' (1967) is less well remembered and it is the unsettling juxtapositions of their relocation that have most vividly influenced their reputation as classic *Who* monsters. Yeti are supposed (in legend, at least) to inhabit the Himalayas, not the Piccadilly line. Moving them into an eerily deserted and dormant version of modern London's subterranean transport system places an emphasis on other strange aspects of their constitution: that they are ostensibly mammals but actually robots, that they appear to be wild nature but are controlled culture, that they are brutally clawed but now armed with hi-tech web guns. It is this compounded incongruity that led to Pertwee's famous quip about 'coming home and finding a Yeti sitting on your loo in Tooting Bec' (although, ironically, this was one threat that the Third Doctor never encountered).[53] Similarly, when the Eleventh Doctor offers a biscuit tin decorated with the London Underground map to the Great Intelligence in 'The Snowmen', this is Moffat drawing on the preposterousness of the established myth to play a timey-wimey game with the continuity. 'I do not understand these markings,' says the Intelligence, demonstrating that the Yeti, the Det-sen Monastery and the tube-line between Covent Garden and Holborn are all in its future.[54]

Considered too huggable in their original design, the Yeti were made more fiercely bestial and unkempt for their visit to London in 'The Web of Fear'. This, together with their alienating presentation in a familiar and iconic environment, no doubt intensified the fear factor for children watching in early 1968. The reputation of the monster was consolidated through Target novelizations by Dicks in the 1970s, introducing those who had not seen the two television serials (and who seemed unlikely ever to do so, given erasures from the BBC archive and the rarity of *Who* repeats at the time) to enormously powerful creatures with yellow fangs, slashing claws and fiery red eyes. Developments in both physical and digital special effects techniques during the almost twenty years since the Yeti's last screen appearance, in the Reeltime video spin-off *Downtime* (1995), along with the increase in institutional belief and budget, would have enabled Moffat to realize a convincing return for the robotic beasts. In the event, he opted to replace them with new servant-monsters. Whether the titular Snowmen of the 2012 Christmas special are able to evade the kind of shortcomings that have been suggested for the Yeti is questionable: fanged and ferocious they might be, but they are perhaps too uniform and cartoon-like in their design to entirely translate the tubby amiability of a Raymond Briggs-style snowman into the stuff of nightmares. Their remembered monstrosity is hardly enhanced by association with Olaf from Disney's *Frozen*, whose rise to celebrity took place less than a year later. It is possible, of course, that an uneasy mix of the cute and the chilling was an intended effect, a slanted critique of, and homage to, the Abominable Snowmen of 1967.

The Spoonheads that followed in 'The Bells of Saint John', parasitic Wi-Fi robots sent out by Miss Kizlet (Celia Imrie) to harvest people into the Great Intelligence's data-cloud, are undoubtedly disconcerting, embodying the anxieties of the smartphone age, but they have generally been seen as not-quite-successful monsters in a not-quite-successful story. The Whisper Men of 'The Name of the Doctor', on the other hand, have been well received and it is worth imagining how they might have compared to the Yeti as monstrous stalkers of the deserted London Underground. Certainly, these pale, eyeless spectres with blackened, sharp-toothed mouths and the sartorial elegance and deportment of Victorian funeral directors are a disturbing creation. Their whispering obsessive intonation of darkly portentous nursery rhymes is especially unsettling:

> Do you hear the Whisper Men? The Whisper Men are near.
> If you hear the Whisper Men, then turn away your ear.
> Do not hear the Whisper Men, whatever else you do.
> For once you've heard the Whisper Men, they'll stop and look at you.

This at once sets the Whisper Men apart from the Yeti but also establishes a curious parallel, given that – although they can make articulate sounds – they are still not open to dialogue. The ritualistic rhythm of their one-way communication is more frightening, or more *artfully* frightening, than the brutish roars of the Yeti, especially as it links to the cadences and phrasings of childhood. Likewise, the slow processional progress of the Whisper Men is both comparable to, and distinct from, the shambling gait of the Yeti: where the latter can now appear clumsy or even comical, the former is understatedly sinister.

By a curious coincidence, the return of the Great Intelligence to *Doctor Who* was closely followed by the return of four missing episodes of 'The Web of Fear' to the BBC archives in October 2013. The almost immediate release of this legendary story (minus the still missing third episode) via iTunes download and Virgin Media's on-demand service, and four months later as a DVD, enabled the Yeti to be reassessed. The elation of classic-series devotees was not always matched by the approval of more recent fans – 'My wife laughed at clips of Yeti in news stories,' lamented Kevin Mahoney[55] – and even some old-school fans seemed disappointed: 'As monsters go, the Yeti are reasonable opponents … not especially scary.'[56]

Such acknowledgement that the Yeti might not be quite as effective as popular remembrance envisaged them to be might seem to ratify Moffat's thinking on other monsters from *Doctor Who*'s initial run. His reluctance to bring back the Ice Warriors in the face of Mark Gatiss's entreaties is well known, related to his suspicion that 'they were maybe the default condition for what people thought of as rubbish *Doctor Who* monsters'.[57] Specifying their lumbering slowness, Moffat's criticism is equally applicable to the Yeti and, although the aristocratic Martian militarists have intellect and language, he notes their vocal limitations, commenting that they 'spoke in a way that meant you couldn't hear a word they said'. Consequently, when persistence won the day and Gatiss was able to realize his ambition of restoring the Ice Warriors to the screen after an absence of nearly forty years, it was in a form that emphasized not only their strength but also their speed, agility and ability to enunciate clearly. This is typical of a pattern within adaptations of classic monsters, one that was established in the Eccleston season. The combination of physical robustness and kinetic swiftness in the monsters has effectively replicated the visual slickness and narrative pace of new *Who*.

The Daleks, adhering to Raymond Cusick's original design, were given an armoured sturdiness, aerial mobility (far beyond that seen in 1988's 'Remembrance of the Daleks') and the capacity for speed. These modifications, representing a trade-off between nostalgia and enhancement, have been examined by Britton, as have comparable changes made to the basic templates of the Cybermen and the Sontarans. Britton makes it clear that processes of 'responsible modernisation' in the design of monsters are as conceptual as they are visual. Arguably, the forms of the Cybermen and Sontarans as they were revised under the purview of Davies were intended to correct the noted errors of their final appearances in the classic series. Shifting to an idiom that placed emphasis on the Cybermen as steel rather than silver implied a critique of the shambolic 'Silver Nemesis' (1988), a celebration of the show's silver anniversary that bundled the emotionless tin soldiers into a plot that was never meant to contain them and in which they struggled to shine, despite the heightened sparkle of their appearance. Likewise, the insistence by Davies on the diminutive stature of the Sontarans for their return in 'The Sontaran Strategem' / 'The Poison Sky' (2008) rectified the unfortunate elongation of the clone warriors in 'The Two Doctors' (1985), where they were shown to be as tall as they were militaristically inept.

Along with increased robustness, the Daleks' armoured travel machines were now seen to have independently rotating sections, allowing for optimum flexibility in battle. They were also able to dissolve bullets and neutralize other forms of enemy firepower, including those of satirical derision: not only could they now overcome stairs, they were also able to rid themselves of minor eye-stalk obstructions ('My vision is *not* impaired,' one Dalek declares to the paint-gun-wielding Wilfred Mott in 2008's 'The Stolen Earth') and make murderous use of the sucker-like appendages that had for many years been mocked as 'sink plungers'. An equivalent process of practical and aesthetic muscularization was evident in the redesign of other returning monsters. The previously 'soft' bodies of the Cybermen were replaced by shells of solid metal, although – in keeping with the decision to stress a one-off 'tinning' of the conscious brain over the gradual scientific augmentation of the body – other ways were found to highlight their organic essence. These ranged from the ribbons of tissue threaded through the Cybus Industry exoskeletons to the mummified face that gurns at Amy Pond (Karen Gillan) from the bodiless, unlocked head of the Cyberman left guarding the Pandorica.

The coherent vacuum-formed designs of the new-series Cyber-suits (prior to 2017's 'World Enough and Time') avoid the more Heath Robinson aspects of earlier versions: the headlamps of those from 'The Tenth Planet', the practice golf balls and washing-machine tubing of those from 'The Moonbase' and 'Tomb of the Cybermen' (both 1967). This change reflects the advances made in physical effects and costuming, as well as increases in the programme budget and the evolution of production values in reaction to the more challenging expectations of twenty-first-century audiences. (The large visible rip in the costume of one awakened Telosian in 'Tomb of the Cybermen', for instance, would no longer be able to make it to the screen.) It also, however, suggests the influence of cultural trends related to the representation of the body. This has been primarily, and problematically, the *male* body and it is no surprise that the majority of post-2005 Cybermen have the sculpted approximation of defined pectoral and abdominal muscles, in line with the fashionable 'male model' look of the day. Britton, drawing on Cynthia Fuchs (who herself draws on Donna Haraway), makes the point that 'cyborgs always trouble gender norms' and refers to both the 'evident genital lack' of the Cybermen and the femininity of their voices prior to the 1980s.[58] This argument is broadly persuasive but needs to be offset by the hyper-masculine depictions in new *Who*, with Cyber-voices being as low as they have been since they apparently broke in 'Earthshock' (1982). The situation is complicated further by the blatant eroticization of Lisa Hallett (Caroline Chikezie), the partially converted girlfriend of Ianto Jones (Gareth David-Lloyd) in the 'Cyberwoman' episode of spin-off series *Torchwood*, broadcast in 2006. A more overtly gendered and sexualized cyborg would be hard to imagine. (The later revelation of Ianto's own fluid sexuality adds a further retrospective edginess to the Cyber-erotic encounter.)

The muscular styling of the new Cybermen is emulated in the blue Sontaran battle armour that has replaced the quilted silver-black uniform of 1974 to 1985 (and the coppery red jumpsuits of 1994's 'Shakedown', the non-Doctor video drama that was subsequently expanded into a Doctor-featuring novel). Redesign of both the Ice Warriors and the Zygons has, likewise, emphasized bulk, both races now looking more powerfully built than in their classic-series outings. The Ice Warriors were always hulking creatures, but their build from 'Cold War' onwards is marked by an inversion of proportions, replacing the rounded torso and wide hips of their original form with wide shoulders and a more streamlined waist. This has given them the upturned triangular shape associated with the physique of the bodybuilder from Charles Atlas onwards. By contrast, the original Zygons had a slim upper body and spindly limbs, emphasizing the disproportionately vast dome of their heads and their unnerving resemblance to human foetuses. The new *Who* Zygons are undeniably impressive but, in gaining mass, have lost something of their inaugural creepiness, their faces no longer quite so grotesquely shrunken and baleful in the context of their oversized heads.

Even as they have grown in physical bulk, the monsters have typically gained in pace and agility. This has been most marked in the bullet-time velocity of the Cybermen in 'Nightmare in Silver' and in the lurking naked terrorism of Skaldak in 'Cold War', hiding in the walls like the Xenomorph in Ridley Scott's *Alien* (1979). It is tempting to read an allegorical connection between this well-built, accelerated form of monstrosity and Paul Virilio's concept of 'dromology'.[59] For Virilio there is a direct correlation between technologically enhanced speed and power; the drive to quicken the tempo of the monsters in *Doctor Who* would seem to reflect a similar mythic logic. This is evident not only in the turbocharged attack of several returning monsters but also in the fleetness of new creations, in particular the *modi operandi* of the Weeping Angels and the Silence, both of which can be upon their victims in the blink of an eye or the turning of a back.

Formal and functional alterations to the representation of established monsters are chancy. Apparently minor changes can be contentious, even within an apparently successful redesign. Graham Kibble-White, for example, praising the quality of the Ice Warrior reimagining for

'Cold War', nevertheless laments the loss of the fur that had originally sprouted from the gaps in the creatures' armour. He also takes issue with the 'taboo' revelation of the Martian beneath the mask, describing the exposed face as 'a not especially memorable CGI tortoise'.[60] There is a danger of anticlimax in showing the face (and long-fingered hands) of a monster that has been concealed from full view for half a century. Allowing the Doctor to 'look into the eyes' of an Ice Warrior for the first time is a daring moment of narrative possibility (it is how Gatiss finally sold the return to Moffat) but it translates decades of imaginative speculation among fans into a moment of official determination. The question of whether the Ice Warriors' reptilian outer shell is their organic body or a technological augmentation, made unclear from the outset by the rift between Brian Hayles's script for 'The Ice Warriors' (1967) and Martin Baugh's design, is here given resolution.

In a wry account of eleventh-hour changes between script and screen, *Doctor Who Magazine* has recalled how the concept that Hayles devised originally was for a technologically augmented Viking-style warrior. This is a concept that remains as verbal traces in both the broadcast script ('This headpiece is no warrior's tin-hat. It's a highly sophisticated space helmet!') and in the author's own 1976 novelization, with the Britannicus Base crew discovering in the glacier 'the massive figure of an armoured man, which looked like a monument to some ancient king'.[61] However, Innes Lloyd as producer and Derek Martinus as director considered that the cyborg-warrior idea was too near to the Cybermen and instructed Baugh to carry out a radical redesign. In the event, diegetic logic failed to keep pace with the drive for variety: 'It becomes quite distracting that at no point does anyone [in the story] see fit to remark that Varga is not in fact a tall Scandinavian with a couple of diodes stuck to his head, but a flipping great scaly green space monster with Lego hands.'[62] By the time the Martian warriors made their second appearance on screen in 'The Seeds of Death' (1968), the introduction of a variant design for the ruling Ice Lords – in this instance, Alan Bennion's Slaar – restored something of the original Viking concept. The incidental anomaly of 'reptiles who thrive in sub-zero temperatures' has, however, remained.[63]

Interestingly, Hayles's original script for a follow-up to 'The Ice Warriors' was a foundation story, 'The Lords of the Red Planet', which revealed that the species was engineered by an earlier race of reptilian

Martians, the Gandorans. Dropped from Patrick Troughton's second season to make way for 'The Seeds of Death', it was eventually adapted by John Dorney as a Big Finish audio drama in 2013. Clarifying that a cyborg constitution is intrinsic to the Ice Warriors, it also demonstrates how decisions taken in such disparate areas as commissioning and design can alter the course of an extended narrative. In the case of the Ice Warriors, powerful ambiguities are seen to have been generated through pragmatic and often pressurized choices within production. In effect, a different story (more detailed, arguably richer, but less enigmatic) has been consumed by those who have gone beyond the dominant broadcast sources. Readers of Craig Hinton's Virgin novel *GodEngine* (1996), for example, are less likely than others to be either surprised or provoked by the eponymous ruler of Mark Gatiss's 'The Empress of Mars' (2017, see Figure 2.4), as are any Big Finish aficionados who have noted Dorney's conversion of Hayles's original Gandoran tyrant, Zaadur, from male to female.

Novelizing his first Ice Warrior tale almost a decade after its transmission (and a year after adapting his third, 'The Curse of Peladon', in which the Martians startled in their role as benign and noble allies), Hayles took the opportunity to stress the disturbing ambiguity of their organic-technological physicality:

Figure 2.4 Iraxxa takes control in 'Empress of Mars' (2017); ©BBC Worldwide.

The so-called armour of the helmet head and massive body was in fact tough, and reptilian in substance – but unlike animal eyes, its hard glass-covered eye sockets revealed no emotion. Only a vaguely flickering light illuminated their dark depths.

Like the eyes, the creature's ears looked mechanical in design – electronic, as the Doctor had said. But the mouth was different: mobile, leathery, lizard-like.[64]

In this context, the unmasking of Skaldak in confrontation with the Doctor in 'Cold War', dramatic in itself, can be seen as giving too much information to the audience, sacrificing some of the 'hermeneutic code' of uncertainty that Tulloch and Alvarado consider essential to the success of *Doctor Who* on television.[65]

A comparable case of excess can be found in the substantive redesign of the Daleks during the tenure of Matt Smith. Appearing initially in their disguised state as Bracewell's Ironsides, the Daleks in 2010's 'Victory of the Daleks' (also written by Gatiss) achieve a khaki quintessence of the squat, armoured, tank-like solidity that the new-series design embodies, their usual bellicosity subsumed within a performance as patriotic, tea-serving defenders of Britain. That they are supplanted ruthlessly by the 'New Paradigm' Daleks – tall, shiny, brightly coloured, gravel-voiced – suggests an attempt to stretch *Doctor Who*'s most distinctive mould, continuing the impulse towards enlargement that has dominated the approach to redesign since 2005 (see Figure 2.5). Unlike the outsized Sontarans of 'The Two Doctors', these outsized Daleks are well made but, despite harking back to the two Amicus films of the 1960s, these 'purebred' mutations proved divisive among fans. Given their marginality from 'Asylum of the Daleks' (2012) onwards, and conspicuous absence from the dustbin jamboree of 'The Magician's Apprentice' / 'The Witch's Familiar', it would seem that they are now considered a rare failure of revived *Doctor Who*. This is almost certainly because they represent *too much* Dalek, too big, too bright, too colourful, as Moffat implied in an interview at the Doctor Who Festival in London in November 2015:

When I looked at them in person I thought 'My god, the new Daleks are awesome. They're so huge and powerful – they're brilliant.' But

Figure 2.5 The 'New Paradigm' Daleks meet their predecessors in 'Victory of the Daleks' (2010); ©BBC Worldwide.

> I learned a grave lesson, which is that when you put them on screen, of course, they don't look bigger, they just make all the other Daleks look smaller.[66]

This semiotic overload of Dalek-ness hints that, in the context of modern mass-media mythologies, there is a point at which strategies of successful innovation bring about their own collapse.

If Skaro's New Paradigm represents the disappointed limitations of monstrous expansion, their antithesis would seem to be the Silurians, restyled for 'The Hungry Earth' / 'Cold Blood' (2010) as part of the same season as 'Victory of the Daleks'. On first learning that the prehistoric lizard race (originally seen in 1970's 'The Silurians', then in 1984's 'Warriors of the Deep') were to return to the series, Millennium FX assumed that the requirement would be for an enhanced version of the classic design. Neill Gorton's initial concept work, including an impressive head-and-neck maquette, represented a faithful upgrade of Gerald Abouaf's 40-year-old Silurian mask. As Chris Chibnall developed his scripts for the long-awaited return, however, Gorton found himself responding to a very different vision of the Earth's aboriginal aliens, one requiring the human to be discernible within the reptile.

Retaining the triple crest of their antecedents, the new Silurians were actually closer in design principle to the Draconians of 'Frontier in Space' (1973), with heavy masks replaced by subtle and supple prosthetics, enabling actors to perform facially, using eyes, mouths, even nostrils. Fish mouths and false eyes (including the flashing third eye, a weapon that also acted as a convenient indicator of speech) were gone, as were clawed hands and feet. The equivocal morality of Chibnall's tale could thus be conveyed as an aspect of performed dialogue and physiognomic expressiveness as well as a feature of heightened narrative incident. Moreover, the cultured complexity of *Homo reptilia* was represented through their clothing and the richly ornamented environment of their underground city.

The classic *Who* Silurians wore no clothing at all, while their Sea Devil cousins – due to director Michael Briant's unease at their nudity – were shrouded in surprisingly effective 'string vests'. These would be replaced by far less successful samurai-style outfits, complete with visually and physically cumbersome helmets, for their return in the 1980s. Strikingly, aspects of both the meshed fabric and the samurai styling were incorporated within the new Silurian costume design, showing an elegance of response to the challenge of balancing renewal with reverence. This, together with the wit and nuance of Neve McIntosh's dual performance as sisters Alaya and Restac, would lead to her subsequent casting as the Silurian-Victorian sleuth Madame Vastra, leader of the recurring Paternoster Gang from 'A Good Man Goes to War' (2011) onwards. The attitude of respectful change within classic monster redesign, enabling a revitalization of the established mythology of *Doctor Who*, is thus embodied in the figure of its first lesbian reptile humanoid (see Figure 2.6).

Transmedia traditions: Of fishmen, fanfic and sweet cigarettes

Towards the end of the fiftieth-anniversary mini-episode 'The Night of the Doctor', as Paul McGann's Time Lord prepares to drink the long draught prepared for him by the Sisterhood of Karn to trigger his reluctant regeneration into a 'warrior', he raises the chalice in valedictory

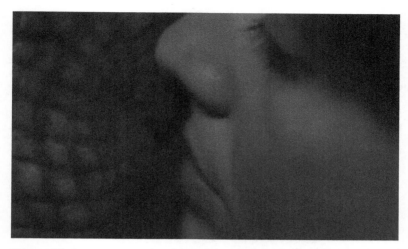

Figure 2.6 Same sex, different species. Madame Vastra (Neve McIntosh) and Jenny Flint (Catrin Stewart) kiss in 'Deep Breath' (2014); ©BBC Worldwide.

tribute to past companions. The roll call might have caused puzzlement to some audience members on first viewing, in particular those whose engagement with *Doctor Who* had been primarily through the TV series, whether classic or new:

DOCTOR Will it hurt?
OHILA Yes.
DOCTOR Good. Charley, C'rizz, Lucie, Tamsin, Molly, friends, companions I've known, I salute you. And Cass, I apologise. Physician, heal thyself.

The identity of Cass is clear enough: she is the young woman (Emma Campbell-Jones) apparently killed in the mini-episode itself when her damaged gunship smashes into Karn because of her refusal to be rescued by the Doctor, supposing him to have blood on his hands from the Time War. The other names, however, are less obvious, being companions from the Big Finish series of Eighth Doctor audio dramas, specifically Charley Pollard, C'rizz the Eutermesan, Lucie Miller, Tamsin Drew and Molly O'Sullivan. The last four of these, like Cass, were killed in the course of their adventures with the Doctor. The fate of Charley is less certain, complicated as it is by a series of kinks in her narrative timeline. Kinky narratives have become the stock-in-trade of Steven Moffat, both in *Doctor Who* and *Sherlock* (2010 onwards). His overt referencing of companions from outside the BBC television series shows not only a respectful awareness of McGann's contribution to the accumulated mythos of *Doctor Who* through the audio dramas but also an official recognition of the cross-platform or transmedia exchanges that typify the 'convergence culture' described by Henry Jenkins.[67] In effect, it is a gesture of mythopoeic inclusivity, like the mention of Chelonians in 'The Pandorica Opens' (2010). In such moments, Moffat signals a formal affinity with aspects of the Doctor's story as it has been developed beyond the parent programme. This at least tests Tulloch and Alvarado's assertion that the primary auratic power remains with televised *Doctor Who* rather than with any of its 'home-made secondary texts'[68] (not least because 'The Night of the Doctor' was made available through the BBC iPlayer online streaming service and YouTube rather than through the broadcast network).

Noticeably, among the companions referred to in 'The Night of the Doctor' there are none who have origins in the Eighth Doctor Adventures series of novels published by BBC Books from 1997 to 2005. There is no mention of Sam Jones, Fitz Kreiner or Compassion, each of whom could more than hold their own with Charley Pollard in terms of narrative kinkiness. (Compassion, for example, initially a human called Laura Tobin, is eventually reborn as a TARDIS.) Nor does McGann's Doctor mention Anji Kapoor (who, given ambiguities and inconsistencies in the writing of her character, might be viewed as ethnically kinky) or Trix Macmillan and Sabbath (who are, to say the least, ethically kinky). Miranda Dawkins, daughter of the ruthless and assassinated Time Lord Emperor, brought up in Derbyshire in the 1980s and adopted by the Doctor, is similarly missing from the list, despite the fact that she, like C'rizz, Lucie, Tamsin and Molly, dies during the course of their adventures together.

So, Moffat's scripting of a contiguity between televisual and extra-televisual narratives is restricted to those developed by Big Finish. Just as it has been argued that the Virgin New Adventures novels were a continuation of the later Target novelizations rather than the later television series (Ben Aaronovitch's novelization of 'Remembrance of the Daleks' rather than the broadcast version of his tale), so it might be speculated that Moffat associates his *Doctor Who* more with the

Big Finish output than with the BBC Books Eighth Doctor series.[69] The situation is knottier than this, though, given that several of the Eighth Doctor Adventures have been adapted for Big Finish, and that the implications of intensified transmedia storytelling within culture generally are still being worked through. Jenkins has noted that it is still early days for this 'emerging concept', although it has precursors at least as far back as Tolkien's reflections on 'sub-creation' in his 1939 essay 'On Fairy Stories'.[70] In an oft-cited definition, Jenkins describes it as

> a process where integral elements of a fiction get dispersed systematically across multiple delivery channels for the purpose of creating a unified and coordinated entertainment experience. Ideally, each medium makes its own unique contribution to the unfolding of the story.[71]

The elements of *Doctor Who* as a fiction are never integrated but the experience of them as a vast narrative rarely feels less than unified, or at least *unifying* (even when divisive), and somehow coordinated (even when chaotic). They enact the kind of 'radical intertextuality' that Jenkins sees as differentiating the merely 'multimodal' from the genuinely transmedia.

Doctor Who does more than simply repeat its story (or stories) in different media forms, even when apparently carrying out a 'straight' adaptation from, say, television broadcast to novelization. The variant modes of *Doctor Who* borrow from each other in terms of narrative content, and the borrowing is sometimes close, but there is always an element of transformation to assist 'additive comprehension'.[72] The audio soundtrack CD of the lost 1964 Hartnell tale 'Marco Polo', released in 2003, included not only linking narrations from William Russell (who played Ian Chesterton on screen) but also a map of Cathay at the time of the adventure; rereleased as part of the series *The Lost TV Episodes* in 2010, it also gained a set of interviews. These might be viewed simply as practical apparatus to support understanding or as extraneous contextual padding to embellish the product, but they also offer enrichment of the mythos, in line with the affordances and audiences of the different media. Such strategies for licensed narrative and market enlargement do not, in themselves, distinguish *Doctor Who* from other popular fictional franchises, such as *Buffy the Vampire*

Slayer (WB, 1997–2001; UPN, 2003). When regarded as part of the wider creative and subcreative ecology, though, a more divergent set of conditions and activities becomes apparent.

The origins and history of *Doctor Who*, as already discussed, mean that it has been unusually open to the storytelling potential of expansion and dispersal across multiple platforms, evolving into a profuse example of what Hills terms 'hyperdiegesis'.[73] Moffat's referencing of the Big Finish companions as part of the fiftieth-anniversary celebrations amounts to a high-profile endorsement of a transmedia identity that has been apparent from the beginning. The wedding of Stacy Townsend and Ssard, for example, in Gary Russell's novel *Placebo Effect* (1998), is doubly remarkable for presenting not only the union of human and Ice Warrior but also the transfer of those characters from one medium in the hyperdiegesis (the *Radio Times* comic strip) to another (the BBC Eighth Doctor Adventures). Such cross-species marriages are utopian in their implications but might be expected to involve a degree of cultural awkwardness.

This awkwardness is captured well in Davies's reference to 'that idiot equation, the dull $e = mc^2$ of fandom: canon = telly'.[74] The critical edge of this seems especially keen given that Davies implicates himself directly in the equation, having 'forged' the pre-eminence of the television series as part of his own attitude as a fan. This mythic bias is unsettled somewhat by Davies's contribution of a novel, *Damaged Goods* (1996), to the Virgin New Adventures range. One of only three novels published by Davies to date (the others being his 2018 novelization of 'Rose' and that of his 1991 young adult science fiction series for BBC1, *Dark Season*), this signifies at least a partial challenge to the supremacy of televised *Doctor Who*. A product of the 1990s broadcast screen hiatus, which forced a reversal of the traditional hierarchy, *Damaged Goods* is now recognized as Davies's rehearsal for the series revival nearly a decade later. Not only does it take place on a British council estate and feature a family called Tyler (as do several other fictions by Davies), but it also situates the domestic at the heart of its dark fantasy and privileges the emotional dimensions of plot. Intriguingly, while he has acknowledged the links between *Damaged Goods* and the 2005 revival, Davies notes the necessary limitations of transfer. Having taken full advantage of the potential for adult themes in *Damaged Goods*, he resisted moves to have the novel, with its tale of alien-contaminated street drugs, published to the official *Doctor Who* website as a promotional tie-in with the new family-orientated series:

> There were already enough 'GAY SEX' headlines around because of my sheer involvement with the project. To invite the headline '*Doctor Who* showrunner writes plots in which cocaine explodes in your head!' would have been terribly, terribly misleading, and it would have been damaging.[75]

Paul Clarke, for the online 'Discontinuity Guide', makes the same point in stronger terms:

> Without the need to aim for a family audience, *Damaged Goods* is nasty, showcasing the grinding misery often associated with a working class life in Thatcher's Britain, and with a plot that revolves around drug abuse, squalid unprotected sex in isolated public gathering points, and some of the most grisly deaths in any of the New Adventures.[76]

Nevertheless, Davies's novel was a presence when 'Rose' began *Doctor Who*'s successful return to television, having already been incorporated discreetly within the set for the flat of *Who*-loving Vince Tyler (Craig Kelly) in Davies's Channel 4 series *Queer as Folk* (1999).[77] In 2015 it underwent a further remediation, being released as a full-cast audio drama by Big Finish.

In the audio-adapted version, some details from the original story have been changed, notably those which are most liable to prove controversial. The featured narcotic, for example, is now a substance called SMILE rather than cocaine, and the sexual activity between Chris Cwej and David Daniels is toned down. Considerations of audience and brand management were far more of a constraining factor a decade into the revived global franchise than they were back in the relatively carefree days of the mid-1990s when, the TV movie notwithstanding, *Doctor Who* was off-radar. The minor but marked variations between *Damaged Goods* the novel and *Damaged Goods* the audio drama are significant, however, in returning us to those frequently asked questions about the canon and, beyond the canon, the mythology. Most obviously, is either version of Davies's story canonical and, if so, which one? More interestingly, how might such questioning of canonicity in relation to the cumulative intricacies of transmediation provide a basis for understanding *Doctor Who* as a mythology?

Questions of canonical conflict were raised early in the life of the renewed television series, specifically in response to screen adaptations of stories which had already been told in alternative formats. Rob Shearman's 'Dalek' (2005), shown as the sixth episode of Season 1, introduced Skaro's most famous mutations to a brand-new audience through an adaptation of his Big Finish audio drama, *Jubilee* (2003), a story which had featured the Sixth Doctor. Moffat expanded his Ninth Doctor story for the 2006 *Doctor Who Annual* – ' "What I Did on My Christmas Holidays" by Sally Sparrow' – into the TV episode 'Blink' (2007). Most dramatically, Paul Cornell adapted his 1995 novel, *Human Nature*, a well-regarded Seventh Doctor tale for the New Adventures series, into the Tenth Doctor episodes 'Human Nature' and 'The Family of Blood' (2007). It was in reply to fan unrest about how an adventure could be experienced by two Doctors independently that Cornell wrote his blog post arguing that 'in *Doctor Who* there is no such thing as "canon" '.[78] Belief in this 'canon', he claims, is a form of metaphysical delusion that tends towards 'bullying', manifesting as a will to power:

> You're yelling a battle cry, not stating the truth. Because there is no truth here to find. There was never and now cannot be any authority to rule on matters of canonicity in a tale that has allowed, or at the very least accepted, the rewriting of its own continuity. And you're using the fact that discussions of canonicity are all about authority to try to assume an authority that you do not have.

This 'allowance' or 'acceptance' of rewritten continuity – of perpetual contradiction – is the narrative device of the Last Great Time War, a recurrent point of reference within new *Who* that 'puts all historical events up for grabs': 'Nothing necessarily happened like we think it did.' This is more than an expedient dodge by an author writing in the context of a multipart work for which 'there is no authorial authority' and 'no council of Bishops'. Cornell's argument, using the taxonomy of scriptural studies, allows for both the pleasures of 'ecumenical' discussion of canon and the excitements of an 'infinitely flexible format'. It is here that the constraining, circular disputes of canonicity begin to give way to the liberating idiosyncrasies of mythography. The coinciding narrative premises of Steve Lyons's Big Finish story *The Fires of Vulcan* (2000) and James Moran's TV story 'The Fires of Pompeii' (2007) – the Seventh and Tenth Doctors are both in Pompeii in the hours preceding the eruption of Vesuvius – cease to be a problem. Not even the Seventh Doctor's *dual* presence – he returns to Pompeii's 'Volcano Day' in Lloyd Rose's BBC Books novel *The Algebra of Ice* (2004) – is enough to trigger a canonical version of the Blinovitch Limitation Effect.[79]

Strikingly, when adapted for television, both *Human Nature* and ' "What I Did on My Christmas Holidays" by Sally Sparrow' were boosted by the addition of new monsters, the Scarecrows and the Weeping Angels, respectively, in line with one of the brand values of the revived series. As seen in the preceding section of this chapter, the representation of monstrosity is revealing when appraising *Doctor Who* as a mythology. This is the case not only when the evolution of classic monsters within the new series is studied but also when classic monsters are studied at their point of origin. The situation can be especially intriguing when the monsters in question are 'one-offs' of the television series who nevertheless transferred to other media forms at an early stage of the myth. The first *Dr Who Annual*, published in 1966, offers four examples, with stories featuring the Voord from Terry Nation's 'The Keys of Marinus' (1964, see Figure 2.7), the eponymous telepaths from Peter R. Newman's 'The Sensorites' (1964, see Figure 0.1), and the Zarbi and Menoptera from Bill Strutton's 'The Web Planet' (1965).

'The Fishmen of Kandalinga' from the *Dr Who Annual* tells a tale of the Doctor's arrival on the aquatic planet of the title and his close encounter with a ragtag band of Voord who have escaped from Marinus following their defeat by the Arbitan forces (presumed by the Doctor to be named after the erstwhile Keeper of the Conscience). Attempting to engineer the watery environment of Kandalinga to suit their needs, the Voord have enslaved the indigenous fishmen, whom they both exploit as a workforce and eat as a food source (see Figure 2.8).

In time the Voord plan to annihilate the fishmen entirely, their ultimate aim being to return to Marinus to wreak revenge. Since the Doctor is captured by the Voord and spends much of the story in their presence, he is able to observe them in rather more detail than in his previously televised skirmish with them. In 'The Keys of Marinus' the Voord appear in only the first and last of six episodes and, because the Doctor spends

Figure 2.7 Susan (Carol Ann Ford) is unaware of a Voord in 'The Keys of Marinus' (April–May 1964); ©BBC Worldwide.

little on-screen time with them, they remain enigmatic. Here they are drawn in greater detail, but whether they gain in mythic impact in the process is debatable. Discovered to be telepathic and hypersensitive to noise, the Voord seem ill-suited to the sonic brutalities of war and as near to the Sensorites as to their dagger-wielding televisual counterparts. Their leader's casual disclosure of a primary weakness to a potential enemy also suggests a lack of martial nous: 'And also, you must speak much lower than you do. Your normal loud harsh noises are able to do much harm to the sensitive structures of my people.'

The sensitive structures of another race are the focus of two other stories in the first annual. Set on Vortis, both 'The Lair of Zarbi Supremo' and 'The Lost Ones' feature the Doctor becoming involved in adventures with the Menoptera and their *bêtes noires* the Zarbi. The Menoptera of the first story seem consistent in manners and motivation with those

Figure 2.8 The Doctor spits out his food in 'The Fishmen of Kandalinga', featured in the first *Dr Who Annual* (1966); ©World Distributors / BBC Worldwide.

seen on television, but there is a more callous and belligerent character to their actions in 'The Lost Ones'. They plan, for instance, to dissect the Doctor while he is still alive, believing him to be one of an alien species that has been attacking them. Correspondingly, the Zarbi are represented in 'The Lair of Zarbi Supremo' as harmless drones when not controlled by a malevolent intelligence, in this case the eponymous Supremo rather than the Animus of 'The Web Planet'. By contrast, 'The Lost Ones' utilizes them as background antagonists, apparently driven by an evolved queen of their own species (she appears briefly in 'The Lair of Zarbi Supremo') to drive the Menoptera into lunar exile in a distant but unspecified past.

The appeal of these stories and their often awkward incorporation of material from the TV series is that they present a view of *Doctor Who* mythology in its earliest phase of development, with nothing settled and brand management at a minimum. Even the fact that 'The Lair of Zarbi Supremo' was written by the series' first story editor, David Whitaker, does little to stabilize the mythic framework. Authorship was not credited in the book, or in most subsequent annuals (until the *Doctor Who Yearbook* of 1992), so it is possible that Whitaker penned other stories in the inaugural edition; some have suggested, in fact, that he wrote them all. Whether or not this is the case (and, given the variability of style and quality, it seems unlikely), the most noticeable aspect of these texts is their incoherence, both in relation to each other and the 'home' television series. This is at its starkest in the portrayals of the Doctor himself – or 'Dr Who', as he is invariably termed. 'The Lair of Zarbi Supremo' evidently takes place after the televised events of 'The Web Planet', the Doctor remembering Vortis and its insectoid inhabitants. He is travelling alone, however, which – bearing in mind the crowded nature of the TARDIS in its early years – makes the story difficult to place in any timeline. 'The Lost Ones' is more puzzling. Positioned after 'The Lair of Zarbi Supremo' in the annual, it seems to chronicle the Doctor's earliest visit to Vortis.

This makes it strange that, by the time of his subsequent visit in the company of Ian, Barbara and Vicky, his memory of Vortis, the Menoptera and the Zarbi should have been erased entirely. His amnesia is even more surprising when it is noted that the *TV Comic* story, 'On the Web Planet' (1965), in which he visits Vortis with the canonically tricky companions John and Gillian, only makes chronological sense if placed between 'The Lost Ones' and 'The Web Planet'. Then again, there is a Flann O'Brien-ish footnote in 'The Lost Ones' that is gnomic enough to suggest that pretty much anything might or might not be the case: 'Dr Who is prevaricating because, of course, he did not come from Earth.'

Or, as we would be told forty-five years later (initially by River Song in 'The Big Bang'), 'Rule One: The Doctor lies.'

These kinds of inconsistency so early in *Doctor Who*'s history might be taken as signs of its essentially improvised diegesis, the varied myth-makers of its initial period weaving free-form patterns around a structure knocked together from the notes and proposals of assorted BBC employees. (Even the spelling of Menoptera was unstable: originally containing the second 'e', it appeared as 'Menoptra' in the production documents for the TV serial but had changed back again by the time Strutton delivered the novelization of his script.)[80] *The Dr Who Annual*, in transferring a nascent narrative to a new medium through the efforts of (mostly) staff writers and freelance artists with little or no knowledge of that narrative, was bound to contain inconsistencies.

The presence of Zarbi, Menoptera, Voord and Sensorites within the pages of the 1966 *Dr Who Annual* demonstrates the rich potential for transmedia storytelling inherent in the franchise from the start. The stories that feature them are far from being classics, even of their kind, but they are revealing experiments, prefiguring more sophisticated things to come. Whether they are canonical is hardly important: they are, like all stories in the annuals and other spin-off productions, part of the matter of *Doctor Who*. It is notable that these stories were the last ones to feature monsters taken from the TV series in twenty years of the World Distributors annuals, although Cybermen and Yeti would appear on the cover of the 1969 edition and the Master (not a monster but prone to monstrosity) would be included in the 1974 publication, and again in those from 1983 to 1986.

The Sensorites, beyond their kinship to the Ood, have never travelled far beyond their initial appearances. The Zarbi, Menoptera and Voord, on the other hand, have been restored to the *Doctor Who* mythos through supplementary narratives in graphic and audio formats. As mentioned, the Menoptera and Zarbi appeared in a *TV Comic* strip that began only a week after the final episode of 'The Web Planet' was aired.[81] After this story, and the tales included in *The Dr Who Annual*, the denizens of Vortis would not appear again until the 1990s (apart from a brief Keller Machine-induced hallucination of a Zarbi in 1971's 'The Mind of Evil'). Warwick Gray's comic strip for the *Doctor Who Yearbook 1995*, 'The Naked Flame', showed the Fourth Doctor and Sarah Jane Smith taking on Vursus, a renegade Menoptera, as he threatened to disrupt a golden age of life on Vortis. A year later, Christopher Bulis's novel for the Virgin Missing Adventures range, *Twilight of the Gods*, told of events involving the Second Doctor, Jamie and Victoria. Since the return of *Doctor Who* to television, Daniel O'Mahony's audio drama for Big Finish, *Return to the Web Planet* (2007), has taken the Fifth Doctor and Nyssa to Vortis, while the first instalment in the IDW comic book series *Prisoners of Time* (2013), by Scott and David Tipton, has revealed what happened when the Doctor, Ian, Barbara and Vicki came up against an infestation of Zarbi in the London Underground.[82]

The transmedia existence of the Voord has been even more prodigious. Their framing role in 'The Keys of Marinus' as sinister but mysterious villains – men in black rubber suits and full-face masks, violent, creeping, perhaps (retrospectively, at least) a little 'BDSM' in their aura – means that they are left as a kind of menacing blank presence in the narrative. Described as 'eel-like' in the initial script and as 'a rival race as sinister as the Daleks' in the *Radio Times* billing, the story as broadcast never specifies their nature, beyond illustrating that there is something beneath the rubber.[83] (A damaged Voord suit, voided of its occupant by the acid seas of Marinus, is discovered on the glass beach by the TARDIS crew soon after their arrival.) They have a named leader, Yartek, but whether they are a distinct species, a mafia-like organization, a terrorist militia or even a rogue law enforcement agency is unclear. The back-cover blurb on the 1980 Target novelization by Philip Hinchcliffe describes them as 'sub-human', the adaptation equating their 'protective suit' with their 'skin' and hinting at a machine-like homicidal efficiency ('a Class I Voord Assault Trooper, programmed to kill enemy life-forms on sight!'). Fan-orientated reference guides of the 1970s and 1980s maintain the ambiguity: Dicks and Hulke's *The Making of Doctor Who* calls the Voord 'alien' (but to whom?) and Jean-Marc Lofficier's *The Doctor Who Programme Guide* defines them, helpfully, as 'Inhabitants of the planet MARINUS'. Lesley Standring's entry for *The Doctor Who Illustrated A–Z* is perhaps definitively indefinite: 'Vicious featureless creatures clad in acid-resistant suits.'[84]

The Voord, then, based on their negligible but somehow haunting role as the brute phantoms of the televised Marinus, became a dark *tabula rasa*. The blank space they occupy within the panoply of the Doctor's monsters has proved recurrently tantalizing since 1964, leading to elaborations that have, at times, stretched the hyperdiegetic fabric of *Doctor Who* to its limits. With the Daleks, in fact, the Voord were the first monsters to be subjected to a transmedia reworking. *Doctor Who and the Daleks*, a story in two parts related across a set of fifty collectible cards included in packets of Cadet sweet cigarettes, seems to have been marketed a month or so before *The Dalek Book* in 1964 and is therefore the earliest example of the mythology extending beyond its foundational medium.[85] In it, the Doctor stumbles across a war between the Voord and the Daleks on Marinus, the conflict subsequently relocating to Earth. Necessarily written with an almost Twitter-like concision (and tendency towards typos), the story, with vibrantly eccentric illustrations by Richard Jennings, adds little to our knowledge of the Voord. It does, however, supply a number of elements that are picked up in later, more substantial narratives. These include the first sightings of both flying Daleks and the original Dalek Emperor, complete with the golden dome that would mark its appearances in *TV 21* comic strips and on television in 'Remembrance of the Daleks'. Furthermore, the second half of the card series, in which the action moves to Skaro, seems to anticipate key plot points of the new *Who* episodes 'Dalek' and 'Asylum of the Daleks'. Including a lone Dalek that refuses to speak to anyone but the Doctor, it also features a desperate plea to him from the Dalek Emperor that he save the Daleks from their own worst excesses (in this case, 'a super machine brain that is greater than anything ever devised in the whole universe'). The Daleks' eager ingestion, in the preceding half of the story, of 'a certain type of mushroom, which was used by Inca Priests' and which causes them to 'shout with excitement' as their 'brain power' increases, is not a narrative paradigm that is likely to be repeated any time soon. Similarly, their penchant for emotional displays, including 'a cry of dismay' and 'squeals of wonder and terror', not to mention a 'banquet held in [the Doctor's] honour' (see Figure 2.9), seems peculiarly *un*-Dalek when divorced from the strategic deviousness of similar behaviour in televised stories such as 'The Power of the Daleks' (1966) and 'Victory of the Daleks' (2010). Even so, from the perspectives of mythic evolution and canonical debate, the *Doctor Who and the Daleks* card story is a curiously prophetic aberration.

The Voord, in the sweet cigarette cards and, arguably, in 'The Fishmen of Kandalinga', serve as a form of generic, adaptable monster, for all that the Chief Voord in the former tale is granted a degree of moral ambiguity and self-sacrificing honour. It is therefore appropriate, if surprising, that they should have become fused, at one point, with a more celebrated monster that has been similarly vulnerable to exploitation as generic baddies-of-the-week. In Grant Morrison's comic strip 'The World Shapers', which ran in *Doctor Who Monthly* from August to October 1987, the Voord are shown to be an early form of Cybermen, Marinus becoming Mondas. This, whatever other audacious syntheses it might achieve, conflates the *Who* myth-set of Terry Nation with that of Kit Pedler and Gerry Davis. Paul Cornell, working with the artist Neil Edwards in his *Four Doctors* comic series (2015), goes further, crafting a scenario in which the Voord-shaped hole is potentially filled by a race that, during the 1980s, threatened to become the generic pompous-bureaucrats-of-the-week. Following a pact between the Voord and the Time Lords to join the Last Great Time War against the Daleks (recalling the set-up for the Cadet card story), a disaffected version of the Twelfth Doctor seeks not only to establish himself as their leader but also to engineer them into a new race of Time Lords.

The mythology of the Voord has evolved most satisfyingly within the Big Finish audio dramas *Domain of the Voord* (2014) and *Beachhead* (2015), written by Andrew Smith and Nicholas Briggs, respectively. The first of these, in particular, is noteworthy for articulating a coherent cultural identity for the species, one that builds on previous iterations to establish them as essentially colonial, conquering worlds and converting

Figure 2.9 The Doctor dines with the enemy in the Cadet Sweets *Doctor Who and the Daleks* story cards (1964); ©Richard Jennings, ©BBC Worldwide.

their inhabitants (again, a kinship with Cybermen is implied). The black suits are explained as being fused with the body of the wearer, impossible to remove, ritualized as corporeal emblems of maturity and loyalty. They also prolong lifespan and bestow the psychic abilities referred to in 'The Fishmen of Kandalinga', although the debilitating sonic hypersensitivity displayed in that story is conveniently forgotten. The genocidal mania that seemed to drive the Voord on Kandalinga has also been left behind, replaced here by a more strategic attitude to conquest.

So, what does a consideration of the transmedia antics of the earliest *Doctor Who* monsters tell us about questions of mythology and canon? Put bluntly, it tells us that the mythology is too big to be resolved into a canon but that an inquisitiveness about canon can be enlightening when studying paradoxes of the mythology. This might seem obvious, but it is worth remembering that, from its beginnings, the *Doctor Who* story has greatly exceeded the screen with which it is predominantly associated and that, more importantly, this quality of narrative surplus invariably short-circuits discussions of canon. The reasons for this are twofold and most easily exposed by recognizing the problems intrinsic to a privileging of the televised programme. In essence, even those stories that would be most widely accepted as canonical across the history of *Doctor Who* (those that were originally broadcast on television as part of a regular sequence of self-contained seasons) are

1. riddled with mutual contradictions, often of a substantial and long-standing nature; and
2. informed by elements (usually unacknowledged, sometimes almost certainly unconscious) from stories that are widely considered to be of dubious canonicity.

Faced with the intractability of the canon question, it would be reasonable to respond in a similar way to the Eleventh Doctor when faced with the anomaly of 'Roman' Rory Williams (Arthur Darvill) in 'The Pandorica Opens':

RORY But I don't understand. Why am I here?
DOCTOR Because you are. The universe is big. It's vast and complicated and ridiculous.

Why do fans and academics, and those hybrids produced from the convergence of the twain, continue to obsess about the *Doctor Who* canon? Because they do. *Doctor Who* is big, vast, complicated, ridiculous. On this basis, Britton's appeal to the 'vast narrative' concept of Pat Harrigan and Noah Wardrip-Fruin seems not just eminently sensible but, perhaps, the only viable way forward. A massive, complex, ridiculous 'skein of texts' with no ultimate authoritative source of adjudication is never going to discover a settled form, especially when it is in a state of continuous enlargement and revision.[86]

The 'seismic shift' in understandings of fandom that Hills reported a decade ago, triggered by the growth of a narrative context in which 'the world's longest-running TV science fiction series doesn't need TV', has only intensified.[87] This is seen most explicitly in the radically altered status of computer games within the hyperdiegesis. From *Doctor Who: The First Adventure* (1983) to *Doctor Who: Legacy* (2013) a transition can be seen from haphazard, hurried and largely disregarded spin-offs to carefully engineered and seriously appraised tie-ins.[88]

One prominent theorization of computer games, and of interactive media generally, is suggestive in relation to issues of canon and myth in *Doctor Who*. Lev Manovich notes that 'the narrative shell of a [computer] game' often 'masks a simple algorithm', the surface features of story concealing, or distracting from, the underlying operations of data. Beyond this, he asserts a 'symbiotic relationship' between algorithms and data structures and records the usefulness, but also the limitations, of any straightforward distinction between 'passive' data and 'active' algorithm. In the same way, he draws attention to the complex association between the 'natural enemies' of database and narrative.[89] Interestingly, Manovich's survey of the subject veers restlessly between the literal-technical and the metaphorical-critical. For this reason, it is useful for the student of *Doctor Who*, offering analogues for canon and mythology as related but distinct ways of 'mak[ing] meaning out of the world'. The temptation is to equate canon with database and mythology with narrative, the first pairing concerned with organizing a stable 'list of items', the second with creating a more dynamic 'trajectory' of items. However, this might be a category error: database, after all, 'refuses to order [the] list', whereas narrative, even at its most experimental, is all about shaping the list into a sequence. This being the case, narrative begins to resemble more closely the fixed plotting of the canon, with database approximating the available myth-kitty. Ultimately, although Manovich's theory offers a tractable mechanism for working through definitions and distinctions, there is no algorithm to determine the nature of mythology, any more than there is an algorithm to decide the canon. Both dream of an impossible wholeness.

This returns us to Britton's 'structuring icons', those elements that remain whenever the dream of wholeness is broken. As adaptable as they are recognizable, these icons within the mythological database of *Doctor Who* are highly susceptible to what might be characterized as a benign virus, a bug that causes data to move, unnoticed, between formats. As Parkin has noted, for instance, the Target novelizations of the 1970s, for many years the only means by which fans were able to access the past of their beloved television series, furnished the mythology with several of its key components. This occurred, simultaneously, at the levels of lexis and narrative. So, the naming of the 'time rotor' in the TARDIS, the appellation of the 'chameleon circuit', the designation of the Sontarans as a clone race: these are all accepted facts of the canon that originated in the Target novels.[90] Booy reminds us, likewise, that the first mention of a 'timewar' is to be found in a comic strip from the early 1980s.[91] This is not 'the Last Great Time War' of the new series (or not explicitly so), but the notion of a 'time war' surely does strange things to ideas of chronological sequence. It is hard to think of one time war being separable, in any meaningful way, from others. In a similar way, it is hard to think of one source of *Who* mythology being separable from others, especially since the more formalized and sophisticated transmedia expansion that began during the off-screen years of the 1990s. This established the foundations for what Booy refers to as 'the new mix-and-match aesthetic provided by the dissolution of canonical boundaries'.[92] Tellingly, it was the only new *broadcast* outing for the Doctor during that decade, the TV movie of 1996, scripted by Matthew Jacobs, that encapsulated this accretion of the franchise and pointed to the need for a more nuanced attitude to change, continuity and canon. As Jonathan Morris remarks, 'Jacobs alone seems to have appreciated that an important – no, *essential* – part of the appeal of *Doctor Who* is that it is *all one big story*, set in a fictional universe that has been nurtured and developed since 1963.'[93] This recalls the purposeful rewritings and contradictions of Cornell's 'big and very complex story'.[94] When a big story has purpose, it will be prone to that dream of contained, canonical wholeness; when it is vast, complicated, ridiculous, it will find that dream deferred endlessly through the sheer profusion of mythology.

Ultimately, as McKee has argued, any preoccupation with canonicity begins and ends with the fans.[95] The BBC as an institution is as unconcerned with establishing an 'official' story for the Doctor as it has ever been, having recognized from the start that mutability and ambiguity are fundamental to the show's character, embodied in its title. 'Doctor Who?' asked the *Radio Times* on 21 November 1963, two days before the first broadcast. 'That's just the point. Nobody knows ...' Nearly fifty years later, the same question – a question that is also an identity and, to some, a name – was repeated insistently and to minatory effect by the living, severed head of Dorium Moldovar (Simon Fisher-Becker) in the closing scene of 'The Wedding of River Song':

> The first question, the question that must never be answered, hidden in plain sight. The question you've been running from all your life. Doctor Who? Doctor Who? Doctor Who!

The Eleventh Doctor walked away from both Dorium and 'the question', setting up a tease (a reset of the original tease) that would still be a tease by the end of 'The Name of the Doctor', nineteen months later. The tease would only be resolved (teasingly, of course) through Clara's address to the Time Lords at the end of 'The Time of the Doctor' on Christmas Day 2013:

> You've been asking a question, and it's time someone told you you've been getting it wrong. His name. His name is the Doctor. All the name he needs. Everything you need to know about him.

The name of the Doctor is, like the canon of *Doctor Who*, a distraction – an amusing distraction, passionately engaging from time to time, but still a distraction. For casual viewers it is likely to be of only peripheral interest, but for fans it holds the periodic and sometimes obsessional fascination of the unsolvable puzzle. It is the ultimate floating signifier, drifting into view with apparently deep meaning at regular intervals, both the essence of the myth and of absolutely nothing at all. Every fan knows, as an instinct, that if the Doctor was ever named *Doctor Who* would be finished. In this respect, they are waiting for Godot and would have it no other way.

The notion of the canon must, it seems, be similarly deferred, and in the same spirit of occasionally abrasive playfulness. Just as the production error of revealing the Doctor's name to be Theta Sigma in 'The Armageddon Factor' (1979) was resolved into a student nickname by the succeeding production team ('The Happiness Patrol' (1988)) and then, via Big Finish, into an alternative timeline in which the Doctor never left Gallifrey (*Forever* (2011)), so any canonical settling will be prevented through the turbulence of addition, revision, difference. The canon 'is produced discursively', as McKee claims, through fan activity, and can only ever be 'provisional'.[96] Making sense of the scattered, gapped, contradictory story is a defining activity for many fans. Not all of them are concerned to determine the status of 'The Fishmen of Kandalinga' or its relationship to 'The Keys of Marinus' or *Domain of the Voord*. Nor do they all fret about the implications of John Peel's Terry Nation-endorsed retconning of the last four classic-series Dalek stories in his 1997 Eighth Doctor Adventure for BBC Books, *War of the Daleks*. And few lose sleep over whether or not it really *is* a retcon. But all fans (and most regular viewers) need to come to some adequate personal understanding of the relationship of the new series to the old.

The increasingly intimate involvement of fans with the reception of *Doctor Who* is a correlative of the increasingly powerful involvement of fans with the production of *Doctor Who*. Whether they are Moffat writing 'The Day of the Doctor' or a 12-year-old posting her first YouTube trailer or fanfic, knitting an Adipose or a Fourth Doctor scarf, attending Chicago TARDIS dressed as Jamie McCrimmon or a Weeping Angel, the result is a performed variation on G. S. Kirk's reflection that myths

> will be varied in some degree on virtually every occasion of telling, and the variations will be determined by the whim, the ambition or the particular thematic repertoire of the individual teller, as well as by the receptivity and special requirements of the particular audience. Themes will be suppressed, added, transposed, or replaced by other apparently equivalent themes. Admittedly these changes will often be minor, and they will not utterly transform the appearance and possible implication of a myth over a length of time.[97]

In this context, a vast fictional universe like that of *Doctor Who*, one that contradicts itself endlessly without ever losing its basic sense of coherence, begins to look like an ideal form of myth. Moreover, as its storytelling procedures become progressively transmediated, it takes on the formal qualities of myth in the digital age when, more than ever, and in spite of fortified brand management, the canon is seen to be discursive, fluid, shaped and reshaped by fans who are all, to a greater or lesser extent, interpreters and producers.

This does not mean that questions of canon go away, but they do become more complex, perhaps more absurd. Can the curious but cack-handed mash-up of *Doctor Who* and *Eastenders* (BBC, 1985– present), 'Dimensions in Time', broadcast for the *Children in Need* telethon between 26 and 27 November 1993, ever be considered canonical? A decent case could be made on the grounds that it was produced and co-written for the BBC by John Nathan-Turner, that it was shown on peak-time television to audiences in excess of thirteen million, that it constitutes a multi-Doctor, monster-packed celebration (some would say desecration) coinciding with the thirtieth anniversary of the show. Even so, the point is moot.

Regardless of whether the Cadet cigarette cards or 'Dimensions in Time' is canonical, they are part of the *Doctor Who* mythology. Playing off heartfelt personal preferences and prejudices is a pastime as old as fandom itself, one that must always veer towards debates about quality, but this has little real impact on the wilder, looser, more anarchic phenomenon that is the subject of this book. No amount of fan scorn will erase 'Timelash' (1985) from the unfolding text or dislodge it from a commonly held sense of the official canon. On the other hand, a fanfic that describes the Doctor and Rory 'fuck[ing] themselves into a state of bliss' in the Time Lord's 'utterly massive' bedroom on board the TARDIS – something that in no realistic sense is ever likely to be accepted as canonical – must still be thought of as part of the mythos.[98]

It is in the mythos, rather than in some durable sense of canon, that the most powerful, utopian but also potentially unsettling meanings of *Doctor Who* are to be found. In February 1985 a ten-minute sketch, scripted by Eric Saward and supported by Nathan-Turner (who insisted that performers should be in character throughout), was broadcast on BBC1. 'A Fix with Sontarans', featuring Colin Baker as the Doctor and Janet Fielding as a version of Tegan Jovanka at odds with her own continuity, aired earlier on the same evening as Part Two of that other tall-Sontaran story 'The Two Doctors'. It enabled 8-year-old Gareth Jenkins to fulfil a dream and it ended in a way that now seems chilling:

> TEGAN Doctor, look at the screen. It's monstrous!
> DOCTOR It's revolting!
> *[On the scanner is the close-up, gurgling face of Jimmy Savile. The Doctor opens the doors to the TARDIS and Savile enters to loud applause.]*
> SAVILE Ah! A-ha! The good Doctor! *[He shakes the Doctor's hand.]* And the lovely, lovely lady. Allow me … [He kisses Tegan's hand.][99]

What could the canon do with this, other than reject it? Even so, the *Doctor Who* mythology has to allow for its own inevitable entanglement within a network of other mythologies, accepting the fact that this will sometimes require the Doctor to come face-to-face with genuinely scary monsters.

Chapter 3

Doctor Who and mythology

Representing history: 'In an area of human thought'

One of the most curious episodes of *Doctor Who* was broadcast in June 1965, towards the end of the programme's second season. 'Journey into Terror', the fourth of the six parts comprising the story usually known as 'The Chase', shows the First Doctor (William Hartnell) and his companions, Ian (William Russell), Barbara (Jacqueline Hill) and Vicki (Maureen O'Brien), arriving in the entrance hall of what appears to be a deserted old house, dark and classically spooky. They are fleeing from the Daleks through time and space, but the iconic monsters they encounter in this strangely familiar setting are a more motley mix than anticipated, including Dracula (Malcolm Rogers), Frankenstein's Monster (John Maxim) and the ghostly Grey Lady (Roslyn De Winter). The fifteen minutes of screen time spent in the haunted house are never likely to be held up as top-notch *Who*, but 'Journey into Terror', despite its shambolic oddness, marks a significant moment in the show's history.

What makes 'Journey into Terror' notable is its explicit preoccupation with the act of storytelling, specifically its own act of storytelling, the narrative conditions in which the TARDIS crew find themselves. Like a sketch to rehearse the scenario of Peter Ling's celebrated story 'The Mind Robber' three years later, Terry Nation's script features not only characters taken from pre-existing fictions but also debates among the regulars about what this might mean:

> DOCTOR This house is exactly what you would expect in a nightmare. Yes, we're in a world of dreams. Creaking doors, thunder and lightning, monsters and all the things that go bumpety-bumpety in the night.
>
> IAN With one vital difference, Doctor. This house is real. It exists.
>
> DOCTOR Yes, yes, it exists in the dark recesses of the human mind. Millions of people secretly believing. Think of the immense power of all these people, combined together, makes this place become a reality.
>
> IAN Then we're safe.
>
> DOCTOR Safe? What on earth do you mean, dear boy?
>
> IAN But the Daleks can't touch us here? Not in the human mind.
>
> DOCTOR You know, I believe you're right. Yes! The Daleks can never land here!

The Daleks *do* land there, of course (see Figure 3.1), and when this leads Ian to question the Doctor's 'theory', the latter responds by restating it – 'We were lodged for a period in an area of human thought' – before resorting to evasive rudeness: 'Oh, I don't want to enter into it. A discussion with him! Oh!' The uncertain ontology of the location had been deliberated ahead of filming by Verity Lambert in a letter to the story's director, Richard Martin. Expressing concerns about the disruptive possibilities of Nation's metafictional interlude, Lambert, as producer, wrote of her fears that this might jeopardize the established 'realism' of the series, its 'kind of illogical "reality" '.[1]

The haunted house remains a mystery to the Doctor and his companions but is explained to viewers through a lingering close-up on an empty ticket booth following the departure of the TARDIS. It seems that the Gothic tormentors of the pursuing Daleks are the presumably robotic stars of an abandoned future tourist attraction, 'FRANKENSTEINS [*sic*] HOUSE OF HORRORS', part of the 'Festival of Ghana 1996' which has been portentously 'Cancelled by Peking'. The android constitution of the characters literalizes their artifice, their presence as mechanisms within the narrative. In John Peel's novelization of 'The Chase', published more than twenty years after the original

Figure 3.1 Dracula greets a Dalek in 'Journey into Terror' (1965); ©BBC Worldwide.

broadcast, the Doctor's 'theory' is expanded and the Festival of Ghana becomes the Battersea Funfair, 'Closed for Repairs'.[2]

Ghana or Battersea, what these revelations achieve – in terms proposed by Tsvetan Todorov in his influential study of the fantastic[3] – is a shift of the action away from the marvellous (where strangeness remains strange) and into the uncanny (where strangeness is finally explicable). The insistence on at least a semblance of positivist justification, Lambert's 'illogical "reality"', means that even the most fantastical *Doctor Who* locations and stories are never quite permitted to reach the condition of true fantasy as defined by Rosemary Jackson: 'Unlike marvellous secondary worlds, which construct alternative realities, the shady worlds of the fantastic construct nothing. They are empty, emptying, dissolving.'[4]

It is interesting that Peel rephrases the Doctor's dismissal of Ian's objections to show a clearer cause of his irritation: 'I don't want to enter into it. A discussion with him!' becomes 'I refuse to argue with a closed mind, Chesterton!' The difference here is subtle but important. In the televised version, the Doctor waves Ian away because he seems to be losing the argument; in the novel, he is infuriated by the teacher's refusal to entertain a concept that exceeds his own rational limitations. The Doctor might be awry in his explanation but he is, at least, showing a willingness to accept the kind of 'alternative realities' described by Jackson.

A version of the Festival of Ghana moment forms the climax of the 2006 story 'The Girl in the Fireplace', with the mystery of the clockwork androids' obsessive pursuit of Jeanne Antoinette Poisson (Sophia Myles) across time and space being solved through the disclosure that their derelict spaceship is the SS *Madame de Pompadour*. Intriguingly, on this occasion, the Doctor is shown to be content to live with uncertainty ('We'll probably never know'), attributing the actions of the droids to 'massive damage in the computer memory banks' and leaving it at that. For the television viewers, the narrative is resolved, as it was for those watching 'Journey into Terror'. Here, though, while the more complex explanation, the diegetic actuality, is again provided for the audience alone, the 'simpler' or 'logical' one is that endorsed by the Doctor.

Scripted by Steven Moffat, 'The Girl in the Fireplace' is an example of 'the pseudo-historical' in *Doctor Who*, a story in which a depicted period of history 'has either been invaded by a science-fictional presence before the Doctor shows up … or turns out to be a fabrication'.[5] The haunted house section of 'Journey into Terror' is an early example of the second of these variations and can be seen as a key moment in the development of the pseudo-historical category. Crucially, it paves the way for Dennis Spooner's 'The Time Meddler' (1965), the story that follows 'The Chase' and that has often been seen as initiating the shift from 'the pure historical'. It does not represent, or even try to represent, history. It does, however, represent the ways in which mass culture has represented history.

It is worth considering Raymond Cusick's designs for the haunted house at this point. The fireplace in the entrance hall recalls that of Georges Méliès's 1899 film *Le Diable au Convent*, a link to the theatrical-magical traditions of early cinema that is also a starkly aberrant signifier within an architecture designated by the Doctor as Central European. The staircase is similarly anomalous, fusing a number of historical registers, most noticeably by fixing a quartet of life-sized, quasi-Grecian statues at regular intervals on the quasi-Gothic banisters. Uncannily prescient of the Weeping Angels in new *Who*, these figures, female but somehow androgynous, hold bowls of tumbling smoke on their heads and seem eccentrically at odds with the more familiar trappings of the location, the tapestries, candelabras, suits of armour. Thick with shadows and cobwebs, this setting is a generic composite of architectural or, more accurately, filmic styles and, like its inhabitants, it owes a good deal to the Universal horror films of the 1930s and 1940s. The staircase recalls that depicted in the meeting between Renfield and the Count in Tod Browning's *Dracula* (1931), where weirdness was connoted not by incongruous classical statuary but by fauna not normally found in Transylvania (most famously an armadillo, but also a possum and a Jerusalem cricket). The laboratory in which the Doctor and Ian find the Monster is similarly indebted to Universal, in this case James Whale's *Frankenstein* (1931). Although restrictions of resource, production schedule and screen time mean that it lacks the scale and spectacle conjured by Whale's designers Charles D. Hall and Ken Strickfaden, it replicates their designed collision of medievalism and futurism, keeping the mad scientist in the medieval attic.

It is the setting of this brief pastiche that makes it interesting rather than the camp presence of its twitchily pathetic Dracula, incoherent Grey Lady and Dalek-bashing Monster (listed erroneously in the credits as 'Frankenstein'). Paying a kind of tribute to the stars of screen horror Boris Karloff and Bela Lugosi, it retains only a ghost of their literary source texts. Somewhere in the frenzied shrieking of the Grey Lady it is possible to hear the distant voice of the novelist Ann Radcliffe, that most metacritical celebrant of the high Gothic mode in the English novel, but on its surface this is just a divertingly bizarre sketch on the dawn of the horror talkies. Strikingly, when *Doctor Who* returned to horror influences in the 1970s, in Pertwee-era stories such as 'The Dæmons' (1971) and during the Hinchcliffe–Holmes years of Tom Baker's Doctor, it was to the lurid operatics of Hammer Films that it would turn, not the creaky monochromatic unease of Universal Pictures. Its own transition to colour by this time means that such an intertextual conversion is hardly surprising, as does the fact that the era of Karloff and Lugosi was already beginning to recede into a cherished but mannered distance. What can be traced to 'Journey into Terror', though, is not simply a recycling of horror tropes and narratives but a particular slant on depictions of the past.

The founding educational remit of *Doctor Who* – 'each story will have a strong informational core based on fact'[6] – resulted in some of the strongest tales of the programme's first season, including John Lucarotti's 'Marco Polo' and 'The Aztecs' (both 1964). These stories benefitted from the BBC's established expertise in producing historical drama, not least through access to its ample store of props and costumes. From a practical (i.e., budgetary) point of view, the pure historicals held a considerable appeal for the production team. It should be noted, too, as Chapman has demonstrated, that in contrast to the received view of these stories, they tended to be just as popular as the science fiction tales with which they alternated.[7] Even so, the narrative constraints placed on them meant that writers had little room for manoeuvre, being expected to simply vary the ways in which the TARDIS crew could become separated from each other as inert agents within historical events. 'Doctor Who is an observer,' as David Whitaker insisted in 1964, a sincere objective in the earliest days of the TV series but a progressively difficult position for a hero to be in or a writer to imagine.[8] As a result, the didactic detail of Lucarotti's scripts gave way to the more comedic approaches of Dennis Spooner and Donald Cotton. By the time of 'The Chase' there were signs that the initial Reithian impulse – humanist, edifying, inherently conservative – was being tested and dispersed. It is notable that Whitaker's 'The Crusade' (1965), just two stories before 'The Chase', exhibits a starkly revisionist stance on history, presenting Richard, *Coeur-de-Lion*, as a jaded and petulant despot (played by Julian Glover), and his nemesis, the Sultan Saladin (Bernard Kay), as sympathetic, if dangerous.

Looking like a relic from the past, or like a fantasy version of a relic from the past, the haunted house of 'The Chase' turns out to be a relic from a fantasy version of the future (a future which is now our past). In Jean Baudrillard's terms, it is a third-order simulation which '*plays at being* an appearance' and 'masks the *absence* of a basic reality' (emphases in the original).[9] The imagined features of a non-specific medieval history are brought together to construct the location for a brief, flimsy amusement that – when studied from the vantage point of the new millennium – seems to endorse Umberto Eco's view that 'the work of the twentieth-century mass media' was 'the rediscovery of the Middle Ages'.[10] Invoking, however crudely, the architectural and literary foundations of the cinematic horror tales of the early 1900s, it offers a reminder that the Gothic has never been a straightforwardly nostalgic mode, that it was born out of modernity and has always been implicated in the technological moment. After all, Mary Shelley's *Frankenstein* (1818) has claims to be the first science fiction novel, as well as a kind of ghost story, and Bram Stoker's *Dracula* (1897) is, among other things, a tale of emergent mass media and the youth culture that adopts it. Eco again: 'People started dreaming of the Middle Ages from the very beginning of the modern era.'[11]

With its compact theme park of the mock-medieval, 'Journey into Terror' initiates a certain kind of scenario in *Doctor Who*. It is, for all its ragged brevity, an important prototype for many later, more extensive, more successful stories. Not a historical story in itself, it nevertheless has the material trappings of a historical story, the hollow signifiers of a version of *pastness*. Emptied of historical referents, these result in an ahistorical simulacrum of the historical that, at the time of broadcast, had not been seen in *Doctor Who* but would be seen again, on many occasions. It is appropriate that when, towards the end of the episode, the Doctor insists on his interpretation of events to Ian, Hartnell fumbles his lines: 'I am convinced that that house was neither tame – *time* – nor space. We were lost in a period – in an area of human thought.' Such 'billyfluffs' are legendary, but here it is almost as if the actor is struggling with the concept as much as the words: he says 'lost', for instance, while William Russell returns to the scripted 'lodged', and he tries to insert the historicizing 'period' in place of the more nebulous but spatializing 'area', enacting the very conundrum that the character is attempting to resolve.

The paradigm tested in the haunted house emerges fully fledged in the abandoned monastery of 'The Time Meddler'. These imaginary locations become material metaphors for the shift from a hard-line position encapsulated in the First Doctor's admonitions of Barbara in 'The Aztecs' ('You can't rewrite history, not one line!') and Vicki in 'The Crusade' ('History must run its course') to a more flexible approach in which, to quote Daniel O'Mahony, 'History is now up for grabs.'[12] Although O'Mahony supports the idea that this less austere attitude to history was boosted decisively by 'The Time Meddler', he sees early indications of the change in the 'almost disposable sequence' on board the *Mary Celeste* in the third episode of 'The Chase'.[13] Chapman refers to the same sequence when he describes 'the irreverent attitude to history that was increasingly affecting the series'.[14] It is true that attributing the mystery of the abandoned merchant sailing vessel, found drifting off the Azores in December 1872, to a flying visit from a Dalek assassination squad constitutes a primal moment of pseudo-history in *Doctor Who*. The Universal interlude in the subsequent episode, however, represents a more substantial shaping of things to come.

Broadcast between 'The Crusade' and 'The Chase', Glyn John's 'The Space Museum' (1965) had already given signs that the programme's attitude to time was changing. Faced with a menacing cabinet display of himself and his companions, aware that the TARDIS has 'jumped a time track', the Doctor indicates (albeit in the context of a science fiction story) that historical events might, after all, be meddled with: 'What we are doing now is taking a glimpse into the future, or what might be or could be the future. All that leads up to it, is still yet to come.' More than forty years before Moffat's 'Blink' (2007), this articulates a mythology of temporal mutability, with chronological causation and experience being presented as 'a big ball of wibbly-wobbly, timey-wimey stuff'. Such post-Einsteinian suppleness does not, in itself, release writers of *Doctor Who*, or the characters they write about, from a requirement not to meddle with what the original notes for the series describe as 'the best factual information' available.[15] It does, however, give recognition that, as Matthew Kilburn states, 'for most *Doctor Who* writers their imagination [is] more valuable than research in libraries'.[16] The issue here is the relationship between historical events and their representation, the dialectic of occurrence and mediation that runs through the discourse of history itself. 'History', as Robert Rosenstone has noted, 'does not exist until it is created.'[17]

Before 'The Chase', whenever history provided the narrative context for *Doctor Who*, it was played straight, even when – as in 'The Romans' (1965) – it was also played for laughs. After 'The Chase', it would be approached in a more impious and experimental spirit. If this spirit would be informed, in part at least, by the Gothic, it would be the Gothic as a disruptively modern, or postmodern, style. 'Journey into Terror' marks the point at which the series began to exhibit what Fred Botting sees as the Gothic's 'challenge to modernity's assumptions, meanings, exclusions and suppressions', the reflexivity through which, as Jim Leach writes, 'every story generates a long list of influences and allusions, pointing to [an] affinity with postmodernist theories that stress the tendency towards pastiche'.[18] Despite the fact that the fictional premise of the programme was thickened from the start with the kind of playful and excessive elements associated with postmodernism (visual eclecticism, conceptual oddity, tonal variation) it had not, in its first eighteen months, given free rein to these, or to the possibilities that they implied. Across sixteen tales, five of them historicals of varying 'purity', *Doctor Who* had been testing its own limits. Trying out a variety of science fiction modes in alternation with a variety of approaches to historical drama, it had appeared settled in little but the resolve to keep the two genres apart. As Barbara and Ian swap a Dalek time capsule for a London bus at the end of 'The Chase', perhaps their real journey with the Doctor has been from a sober and earnest, modernist-inflected social idealism to a condition resembling postmodernist consciousness.

Postmodernism is a notoriously slippery idea, of course, with its value as a critical category being widely contested. From its apotheosis in the 1980s and 1990s, it has become an increasingly marginal and strangely old-fashioned area of discourse since the start of the twenty-first century, tainted by the Sokal hoax of 1996 and undermined by a range of counter-jargons (metamodernism, post-postmodernism, digimodernism, hypermodernism) which can hardly be considered an improvement. It has, however, provided a framework within which *Doctor Who* has been examined by several of its most incisive critics. In relation to the present discussion, Alec Charles's polemical contribution to *Time and Relative Dissertations in Space* is especially pertinent, reading into the classic series the kind of postmodernism – 'a paradigm of ideological and ontological conservatism' – targeted by such Marxist critics as Fredric Jameson, Terry Eagleton and Alex Callinicos. Charles argues that an impulse towards 'postcolonial nostalgia' in classic-era *Doctor Who*, tantamount to an aestheticizing (even fetishizing) of the past, resulted in 'the junking of history'. The claim is, in essence, that the programme, across a period of twenty-six years, depicted history with the history taken out.[19]

Far from what Sydney Newman and Co. intended, the ahistoricism that Charles alleges is perhaps the inevitable outcome of what they instigated, given the cultural context of the post-war, post-imperial BBC. The case is persuasively presented and it has clear mythographic justification. It aligns, for instance, with Eliade's argument that the transcendence of history is a primary function of myth, his admiring assertion of the 'continual present' of primitive cultures having direct correspondence with Jameson's more pessimistic diagnosis of the 'perpetual present' of postmodernism.[20] Likewise, it resembles Clifford Geertz's claim that the detached academicism practised by Claude Lévi-Strauss results in the deletion of history.[21] Both Eliade and Lévi-Strauss have been censured for the ideological connotations of their mythic strategies (Eliade most dramatically, given his association with the far-right Iron Guard in his native Romania during the 1930s), and the argument put forward by Charles effects a comparable indictment of what he sees as 'an ideology of anachronism'. This is congruent with charges made about the conservatism of *Doctor Who* and its lead character in texts spanning John Fiske in 1983 and Lorna Jowett in 2017.[22] If the series underwent a conspicuous postmodernist turn during the second half of its second season, becoming a subtly different kind of mythology, this has done little to rescue it from ideological suspicion.

'The Time Meddler' is quintessentially postmodernist in its playful disrespect for history, hierarchies and serious intent, its mixing of styles and registers, its often sharply self-referential dialogue:

DOCTOR You know as well as I do the golden rule about space and time travelling: never, never interfere with the course of history!
MONK Who says so? Doctor, it's more fun my way!

In this exchange with Peter Butterworth's Monk (apart from Susan, the first member of the Doctor's own race to be seen in the series), it is possible to hear a sly rejection of Newman's original strictures on the programme's 'basis of teaching'. The 'time meddler', we realize, is not just the Monk, it is *Doctor Who* itself, a serial that began with solemn intent but that has now discovered the confidence to be facetious. The Monk is shown to be recklessly childish in his desire to manipulate historical events, but he is also allowed to be charming in his resistance to the idea of a grand chronological narrative. More than a decade before the publication of Jean-François Lyotard's *The Postmodern Condition* (1979), the character gives expression to the idea that history has no fixed pattern of progression, no imperative sequence or moral structure. Challenged by the Doctor to explain his scheme of 'mischief' and 'deliberate destruction', the Monk replies that his aim is to 'improve things':

MONK Well, for instance, Harold, King Harold – I know he'd be a good
king. There wouldn't be all those wars in Europe, those claims over
France went on for years and years. With peace the people would
be able to better themselves. With a few hints and tips from me
they'd be able to have jet airliners by 1320! Shakespeare would be
able to put *Hamlet* on television.

DOCTOR He'd do what?

MONK The play – *Hamlet* – on television.

DOCTOR Oh, yes, quite so, yes, of course, I do know the medium.

The Doctor knows the medium. He is intimate with it, *inside it*, and is
heard to invoke it as both an explanatory metaphor and a metafictional
device in the very first episode of the series: 'By showing an enormous
building on your television screen, you can do what seemed impossible.'
Here, however, he acknowledges it as an emblem of the Monk's frivolous
and dangerous rejection of temporal fixity: 'He's utterly irresponsible. He
wants to destroy the whole pattern of world history.' That there is a
pattern to destroy is not, it seems, in doubt, and even as recently as
'The Lie of the Land' (2017) Peter Capaldi's Doctor has been heard to
assert that there is such a thing as 'the *true* history of the world'.

In confrontation with the Monk, the Doctor assumes the role of a
traditionalist, defending an austere historical linearity. This is a role he
will continue to play in the series, declaring his faith in history's often
brutal workings midway through the following season as he justifies his
'abandonment' of the young servant Anne Chaplet (Annette Robertson)
on the eve of the St Bartholomew's Day massacre:

History sometimes gives us a terrible shock, and that is because we
don't fully understand. Why should we? After all, we're all too small
to realize its final pattern. Therefore, don't try and judge from where
you stand.

An acquiescence in his own negative incapability, this appeal to
an unknowable 'final pattern' comes close to an avowal of intrinsic
teleology and deterministic quietism. The Doctor is not always so
passive in formulating a relationship to historical processes, but it is
intriguing to note how the award-winning 'Rosa' episode of 2018 sees
such passivity being transformed into a crucial form of action, the Doctor

and her companions looking on as Rosa Parks (Vinette Robinson) is arrested for refusing to give up her seat on board a racially segregated bus in 1950s Alabama.[23] Vinay Patel's 'Demons of the Punjab', an episode from the same season, also culminates in a refusal to intervene in traumatic historical events, in this case the partition of India in 1947.[24]

Even as the Doctor begins to radiate something of the Monk's appeal to 'fun' through successive post-Hartnell regenerations, direct interference with the progress of history, or histories, remains problematic. Consider, for example, his questioning of his 'right' to affect events in 'Genesis of the Daleks' (1975) or his reaction to Rose's intervention in her own familial timeline in 'Father's Day' (2005). It might even be argued that this is the fundamental enigma of the Doctor: his relationship to time and the incidents that time contains. From this perspective, *Doctor Who* is a narrative about our own complex and insoluble position in time, our responsibility towards (and agency within) historical events. One of the compelling paradoxes of the Doctor is his capacity to insist on the unassailable sequence of history at the same time as he challenges it through acts of open rebellion. Only on rare occasions does the strain of this contradiction lead to a loss of composure, as in the climax to 'The Waters of Mars' (2009).

By using a gramophone (futuristic in 1066, old-fashioned by 1965) to fill the air around an eleventh-century Northumbrian monastery with plainsong, by bringing wristwatches and tea within the purview of a Saxon village, the Monk reveals his idea of fun to be a version of the postmodern imagination described by Richard Kearney as 'a flexible hermeneutic which construes history as an open-ended drama of narratives'.[25] This would be a fair description of *Doctor Who*'s own mythic basis, condensed within the opening scenes of the story as Vicki, child of the future, inspects the ormolu clock in the TARDIS console room and Steven Taylor (Peter Purves), pilot of the future, stowed away after his narrow escape from Mechanus, stumbles in from the living quarters clutching a toy panda. The incongruity of this scenario combines nostalgia and futurism in an already familiar strangeness. Like the Doctor's Edwardian clothing and the police box exterior of the TARDIS, it signals an intrinsic incompatibility with the notion of a unified historical sequence, 'a breakdown of the temporal order of things' that – in David Harvey's reading of postmodernity – results in 'a peculiar treatment of the past'.[26] This means an eschewal of simple progression and a plundering of history as a creative resource. For Kearney, this is continuous history giving way to 'history as collage'.[27] For Charles, it marks a drift into 'historical *mélange*'.[28]

That a television fiction about time travel (especially one so obviously rooted in the tradition of H. G. Wells) should take on characteristics of historical *mélange* is hardly surprising. Nor should this, in itself, guarantee that postmodern discourse will furnish appropriate tools for the job of interpretation. *Doctor Who*, though, has a particular disposition in relation to time, history and the collocation of prior materials. This means that it both exceeds any generic category into which it is placed and takes on something of the environment in which it is created and received, increasingly jumping its own time-tracks through DVD and audio releases, digital channel repeats and online streaming. This is why, writing about the series in studiedly postmodernist terms, Hills describes time travel as inherently metaphorical of modern life: 'In the here-and-now in which the show is made, we are all everyday time-travellers.'[29] Naturally enough, Hills refers closely here to the critique set out by Charles but, being concerned almost exclusively with post-2005 *Doctor Who*, he tends to circumvent the negativity of that argument around culpable historical amnesia in the classic series, focusing instead on the more socially alert, critically revisionist mythology of the regenerated format. Explicitly, Charles claims that the Russell T. Davies revival marks a belated reaction against 'the stagnant decadence of postcolonial nostalgia in which the [classic] series had been steeped'.[30] It is no challenge to find dubious history and cringe-making stereotypes in the original programme (Robert Holmes's 1977 story 'The Talons of Weng-Chiang', wonderful in so many ways, is culpable in this respect). It would be reductive, though, to see only new *Who* as uneasy with received, settled and 'correct' narratives of history, places, people.

'Journey into Terror' is a blundering episode in an uneven and not-much-loved story. It is also, however, a strangely groundbreaking episode in a story that is hectic with experiments and format changes. Caught between two tales that profoundly test the conception of time as a plot device ('The Space Museum', 'The Time Meddler'), it posits a model of history not as something to be studied and represented 'truthfully' but as a rich exploratory pageant, yielding narratives that comprise a form of secular mystery play. This is the sense of history implicit in Hayden White's claim that 'historical discourse wages everything on the true, while fictional discourse is interested in the real – which it approaches by way of an effort to fill out the domain of the possible or imaginable'.[31] This separation of 'the true' from 'the real' in the representation of historical material recalls Samuel Taylor Coleridge's famous distinction between 'the fancy' and 'the imagination, or esemplastic power' within poetic creation. The first of these is defined by Coleridge as 'no other than a mode of memory emancipated from the order of time and space', whereas the latter (derived from Schelling's concept of *Ineinsbildung*) means 'to shape into one'.[32] In this idealist binary vision, fancy is seen as inferior because it is too closely bound to 'the ordinary memory', having 'no other counters to play with but fixities and definites': where the fancy is 'aggregative and associative', concerned with 'objects' that are 'essentially fixed and dead', the 'vital' imagination has 'shaping or modifying power'.

During its second season, *Doctor Who* went through a radical shift in its treatment of history, moving away from an ostensibly factual depiction to one that was open to imaginative transformation. For all that an easy conflation of Coleridgean aesthetics with the ironical practices of postmodernism would be a serious category error, in this much at least there is a compelling association: they disdain a closed, mechanistic approach to sources in favour of one that is playful and open. This is not to argue that, following 'The Space Museum', 'The Chase' and 'The Time Meddler', valueless anarchy is the dominant mode – that 'anything goes', in Lyotard's terms, or, as Kearney has it, 'all is one and everything is everything else'.[33] It is, rather, to note an increased willingness to admit the 'synthetic and magical power' of the imagination into the processing of historical material.[34] At heart, this is about viewing 'old and familiar objects' with a 'sense of novelty and freshness'.[35] More loftily, it brings about a utopian politics at the level of storytelling, shaping a mythology that 'dissolves, diffuses, dissipates, in order to re-create', aspiring to 'the balance or reconciliation of opposite or discordant qualities' as it 'struggles to idealize and to unify'.[36] The kind of story tested briefly, tentatively, in 'Journey into Terror' was to be developed soon through bigger, more complex, more wholehearted stories such as 'The Celestial Toymaker' (1966) and 'The Mind Robber' (1968). Predictive of a certain kind of creative license in *Doctor Who*, the fantastical aspects of these stories might have jarred with some viewers upon first broadcast, but they also prepared the way for a wide range of later stories. The empty white environment of the first episode of 'The Mind Robber' was to be repeated in 'Warriors' Gate' (1980), another tale that mixed historical and fictional references in its design of something ineffably, wonderfully strange. The Matrix scenes in 'The Deadly Assassin' (1976), and those in the final two instalments of 'The Trial of a Time Lord' (1986), are similarly indebted to 'The Mind Robber', as is the nightmare encounter of Tegan (Janet Fielding) with Dukkha, Anatta and Annica (Jeff Stewart, Anna Wing, Roger Milner) in 1982's 'Kinda'.

The kind of fantastical filtering of historic and fictive sources seen in 'Journey into Terror', 'The Celestial Toymaker' and 'The Mind Robber' has continued to be impactful, with stylistic traces evident in several post-2005 episodes, most noticeably in Moffat-era tales such as 'Amy's Choice' (2010), 'Night Terrors' (2011) and 'Heaven Sent' (2015). These are stories that, using Todorov's terminology again, depend upon a sustained 'hesitation' between the uncanny and the marvellous.[37] It is interesting to note, though, that an explanation tilting the narrative towards the uncanny is usually provided: the Dream Lord (Toby Jones) is conjured from a grain of warmed-up psychic pollen; a child with powerfully manifest nightmares turns out to be a scared infant alien with heightened empathy and psychic sensibilities; the torturing castle haunted by the Veil (Jami Reid-Quarrell) turns out to be a trap set by the Time Lords and located in the Doctor's Confession Dial. This is not always the case: the source of the menacing 'Silence will fall' voice in 'The Pandorica Opens' (2010) is never revealed, nor is the identity of the Curator (Tom Baker) in 'The Day of the Doctor' (2013) ever confirmed.

When Siegfried Kracauer relates the 'uneasy' feeling of audiences confronted with the 'irrevocable staginess' of historical representation on screen, he points to something that is both crucial and weirdly liberating for *Doctor Who*.[38] History is *always* a pageant, a costume drama, 'an artificial creation radically shut off from the space-time continuum of the living'.[39] It is either being lived or it is being re-created, and the etymological coincidence with recreation is, of course, no coincidence at all. History – the moment it *becomes* history – is interpretation. The point might even be stretched to contend that all history is a form of pseudo-history, an approximation of what it purports to be. This is as true of Herodotus writing his account of the Battle of Thermopylae as it is of Frank Miller drawing on the same events for his comic series *300*

(1998) or of Zack Snyder adapting this for cinema (2006). It is as true of Lucarotti scripting 'The Reign of Terror' (1964) or Andy Lane writing his Virgin Missing Adventure *The Empire of Glass* (1995) as it is of Thomas Carlyle writing *The French Revolution* (1837) or Eric Hobsbawm writing *The Age of Revolution* (1962). If this sounds both self-evident and facile – and if it risks slipping into the historical amnesia and amoral relativism for which postmodernism has so often been castigated – it is important to emphasize that such a recognition is not incompatible with an insistence that some history is more meticulous, accurate and 'historical' than other history. It is not to deny that some history is 'better' than other history, any more than the hesitation of these inverted commas constitutes such a denial. It does, however, render claims of any particular history's objective accuracy more problematic, requiring (but not always receiving) a critically alert and sceptical attitude to the accompanying ideological narratives, an acute alertness to the politics of retrospection. It also throws doubt on the idea that any history is free from nostalgia.

History is an unbound volume of latently instructive, frequently romanticized, potentially highly dangerous stories, but it is also a junkyard (like that in which the TARDIS is first discovered), a museum, an archive, an exhibition, a theme park, a satirical review. The writers and designers of *Doctor Who* have made extensive use of it as a resource but rarely, at least from 'The Time Meddler' onwards, without an ironic challenge to the narratives that it provides. In this sense, even the most frivolous uses of historical matter, those that encourage a reassuringly conservative reading, can be provocative of a less settled consciousness. The flippancy of the Doctor's visit to Leonardo da Vinci during 'City of Death' (1979), for example, is more troubled and disruptive of historical romanticism than is often appreciated. Even the thumbscrew scene – 'If there's one thing I can't stand, it's being tortured by someone with cold hands' – is as disturbing as it is silly or, perhaps more accurately, disturbing in its silliness. The camped-up interchange between the captured Doctor and Julian Glover's charmingly hostile Tancredi is played for laughs (emphasized by the taciturn buffoonery of the guard, played by Peter Halliday) but it is, nevertheless, an intensely sinister encounter. One of Scaroth of the Jagaroth's temporally splintered selves threatens to 'confiscate' the Doctor's tongue and crush the bones of his hand. Beyond this, he is intent on rewriting history, preventing the human race from being created in order to save himself and his own long-dead species. The desperate, repeated phrase in which he articulates this aim is peculiarly chilling: 'The centuries that divide me shall be undone.' Themes of torture, genocide and the disposability of human life – the disposability of *history* – are threaded through Douglas Adams's deft, witty dialogue and exemplified by the sadistic killing of Professor Kerensky (David Graham) at the end of the third episode.

When the Doctor scrawls 'THIS IS A FAKE' in squeaky black marker pen on the back of the six 'new' *Mona Lisa* panels, he scrawls doubt, playfully but explicitly, across the received narratives of Western culture. Significantly, Leonardo himself never appears on screen in the story: he is a physical absence, present only at the level of dialogue. That the Doctor, before returning to twentieth-century Paris, should leave his friend a hurried note, mirror-written in Leonardo's own favoured mode, is another historical reference that effectively erases itself, since the code is unlikely, surely, to present much of an obstacle to one of the great race of the Jagaroth. You can't rewrite history. But you can write histories that show history being rewritten. And you can show the rewriting to be susceptible to rewriting: 'Sorry about the mess on the panels. Just paint over, there's a good chap. See you earlier.'

A similarly absurdist treatment of history can be found in the scenario of the Eleventh Doctor story 'The Wedding of River Song', in which the clocks have stopped and Earth's timeline has contracted into a single moment. 'All of history is happening at once,' as Winston Churchill, the Holy Roman Emperor, observes to his bearded Soothsayer, having returned to Buckingham Senate on his personal mammoth following a meeting with Cleopatra in Gaul. Meanwhile, picnickers in Hyde Park are pestered for scraps by pterodactyls and Charles Dickens is quizzed by Sian Williams and Bill Turnbull on *BBC Breakfast* about his upcoming Christmas Special ('it involves ghosts, and the past, the present and future, all at the same time').

The Soothsayer is, it turns out, the Doctor, the epicentre of a temporal disorder that stems from his reluctant avoidance of the fixed point of his death. The motif of stopped clocks that acts as a synecdoche for this looks like a realization of the first clause of W. H. Auden's 'Funeral Blues'. This becomes more compelling when the original version of the poem, published in 1936 as part of Auden and Christopher Isherwood's play *The Ascent of F6*, is considered. Retaining the first eight lines of the original version, the revised text, published two years later and made famous by Mike Newell's *Four Weddings and a Funeral* (1994), is markedly different from its longer, lesser-known, bleaker predecessor. Recited following the death of the character Sir James Ransom, it refers (not without irony) to a lost leader, which might bring to mind either the Doctor as he features at the start of 'The Wedding of River Song' or the teleological simplicity of History itself – history, that is, with a capital 'h'. That Ransom is a representative of the Colonial Office adds further resonance to this reading, associating both the hero and the heroic stability of traditional 'knowable' history with imperialist and patrician models of culture.[40] The Doctor is a rebel, we remember, but he is also an aristocrat: 'He's Robin Hood,' as Moffat has said, 'a slumming-it toff'.[41] In 'The Wedding of River Song', to allude to another well-known twentieth-century poem, W. B. Yeats's 'The Second Coming' (1919), he is discovered at a centre that cannot hold, mere anarchy being loosed upon the world. The Lord of Time, disguised in rags, a holy prisoner in the manner of John the Baptist, is called to predict the future: 'Time isn't just frozen, it's disintegrating. It will spread and spread and all of reality will simply fall apart.' This is the Doctor talking to Amy, but it sounds uncannily like one of those opponents of postmodernism, railing against the deleterious effects of relativism.

In this context the significance of the Silence, calling themselves 'the sentinels of history', becomes apparent. These pin-striped, skeletal, finger-pointing ghouls, creeping in the shadows of human history, forgotten as soon as seen, remembered only as marks inscribed on the medium of the skin, begin to look like an embodiment of historical process. The moral ambivalence of their feud with the Doctor reproduces the tensions between competing views of history: he is our alluring hero, they are the monstrous 'baddies', yet they seem to be attempting to protect the Universe from his harmful impact. The complexity of the Doctor's relationship with history is the main narrative driver here, along with the complexity of *Doctor Who*'s relationship with history. Where the diegetic shades into the extra-diegetic, the difficult questions posed in 'The Time Meddler' and elsewhere are still being probed. Since the Hartnell years, the pure historical has (with the kinky exception of 1982's 'Black Orchid') vanished from the TV series, although its tradition has continued within novels, audio dramas and computer games.

White's discussion of history and fiction begins by invoking Michel de Certeau's succinct and powerful claim that 'fiction is the repressed of historical discourse'.[42] If this is the case, then the particular history of history (or of historical representation) within *Doctor Who* can be seen to have a distinctly political aspect. The continual 'mixing of the types' encouraged by its format, along with the consequent 'inversion of generic hierarchies', means that it is ideally situated to assume the characteristics of what White calls 'an art worthy of serving the political needs of our time'.[43] If this seems like a bold or even rash statement for a mythology that has so often (and with justification) been targeted for its sociocultural conservatism, the implications of its often eccentric relationship with the epoch in which it has been created need to be considered. In this context, allegations of 'campness' and of technological belatedness are also relevant, regardless of whether or not they are valid, because they suggest a condition of being ever so slightly but forever out of step with whatever the creative mainstream might be. Consciously or not, and however playfully, this points to a disruptive critical stance, one that is at least partially analogous to White's position on the decriers of postmodernism:

> So the anti-postmodernist handwringers are wrong when they say that the postmodernists are 'against' history, objectivity, rules, methods, and so on. What we postmodernists are against is a professional historiography, in service to state apparatuses that have turned against their own citizens, with its epistemically pinched, ideologically sterile, and superannuated notions of objectivity – a historiography which, in cutting itself off from the resources of *poiesis* (invention) and artistic writing, also severed its ties to what was most creative in the real sciences it sought halfheartedly to emulate.[44]

There is something in the expansive *poiesis* of *Doctor Who* and its spin-offs that (often in spite of itself) resists the 'pinched', the 'sterile', the 'superannuated'. Just as White challenges some versions of 'professional historiography' on the grounds of political petrification, so the myths and stories of *Doctor Who* constitute a challenge to some professionalized versions of genre, narrative and representation. This is most evident in the adaptations from prior myths and stories, notably those derived from the discourses of history. Crucial to this are the processes and patterns of world-building that *Doctor Who* has developed since 1963, and the ethical unease that has been tracked through the lives of its eponymous hero. These will be the focus of the final chapter in this book but there is time, before we get there, for a brief, ghostly interlude and some reflections on Gothic monstrosity.

Themes of haunting: Ghosts in the time machine

Whatever else it might be, history is a haunting. It frequently appears as a ghost. The most renowned example is Marx's 'spectre of communism', but there are other manifestations, most of them less obviously motivated and energized by the winds of historical change, but motivated by them nonetheless: Banquo's ghost, Marley's ghost, the resurrected corpse of *Frankenstein*, the tick-tock accusation of Edgar Allan Poe's 'The Tell-Tale Heart' (1843), the electrical haunting of Rudyard Kipling's 'Wireless' (1902). Jacques Derrida summoned Marx's revolutionary spectre when he came to reflect on the collapse of the Soviet Union in the late 1980s and its subsequent dissolution in 1991.[45] He also, however, invoked the spirit of the elder Hamlet in Shakespeare's most famous play (*c.*1600), specifically through his son's claim that 'the time is out of joint'. An enigmatic phrase, this carries a sense of time having been injured or damaged, slipped from its socket; for a *Doctor Who* fan, it has an appealingly 'wibbly-wobbly, timey-wimey' resonance. This is the mysterious intangibility of time imagined in material form through metaphor.

Hamlet's description of time gone awry brings to mind a scene in the first episode of 'City of Death'. Following a temporal disturbance, Romana (Lalla Ward) retrieves the discarded portrait that a bad-tempered artist has been sketching of her in Le Notre Dame Brasserie. It shows her in Dalí-esque mode, with the face of a clock:

DOCTOR For a portrait of a Time Lady, that's not at all a bad likeness.
ROMANA That's extraordinary.
DOCTOR Yes, isn't it.
ROMANA I wonder why he did it like that? The face of the clock is fractured.
DOCTOR Ha. Almost like a crack in time.

Describing the disturbance they have experienced, the Doctor comments that 'it's as if time jumped a groove for a second'. In *Hamlet*, the injury inflicted upon time through Claudius's murder of his brother is also an injury inflicted upon the body politic; here, the body is considerably larger than Denmark.

Later in 'City of Death', as the Doctor tries to hail a taxi from Scarlioni's chateau to the Louvre, he cries out with comical exasperation, 'Is no one interested in history?' The apparently glib complaint contains an existential desperation, since his anxiety is for history as a volatile, unpredictable and revered process rather than as a basis for costume drama and shallow conceptions of heritage. As Scaroth has accepted the erasure of humanity and its history (a history he has shaped from the beginning) as a trivial consequence of saving his own species, the race against time is, in this case, literal. The Doctor's plea, light-hearted as it seems, is in sympathy with the reflexive line of historical discourse typified by Rosenstone: 'Surely, I am not the only one to wonder if those we teach or the population at large truly know or care about history.'[46] Seen in this context, the struggle to defeat Scaroth (accomplished by an uppercut from the boorish private detective Duggan) becomes analogous to the struggle to retain the idea of grand historical narrative, 'that larger History, that web of connections to the past that holds a culture together'.[47]

In trying to hold together established history, the Doctor, as a Lord of Time, takes on the stabilizing role that he has always tended to have in the television series. Given the scale of the threatened disruption on this occasion, the narrative imperative is clear. Scaroth's plan, after all, is reliant on a temporal paradox of epic proportions: in going back in time to prevent his own death and that of his species, he will prevent the creation of the human race and therefore of the timeline within which he nurtured them to the point at which they had sufficient technical competency to enable him to go back in time to prevent his own death and that of his species. Such challenges are in addition to the wider complication that his plan is running in parallel with the comparable nurture-and-monitor schemes of the Dæmons, the Fendahl, the Silence and Light.[48] When it comes to fault lines of this kind in both the immediate and the extended diegesis, the viewer (the fan in particular, who is most likely to notice such things) is required to perform an act of faith, akin to that of Rosenstone's historian: 'Perhaps history is dead in the way God is dead. Or, at the most, alive only to believers.'[49] The believer in relation to any mythology is someone who accepts the hero's expertise, regardless of narrative contradictions or uncertainty:

> DOCTOR I can't let you fool about with time.
> SCARLIONI/SCAROTH What else do *you* ever do?
> DOCTOR Ah, well, I'm a professional. I know what I'm doing. I also know what *you're* doing.

The Doctor's professionalism (as seen most clearly, perhaps, whenever he finds himself with a 'proper job', whether as Scientific Advisor to UNIT, caretaker at Coal Hill School, or President of the High Council of the Time Lords of Gallifrey) is improvisatory rather than designed. In Lévi-Strauss's terms, he is a 'bricoleur' rather than an 'engineer', although, like the latter, he resists 'the constraints imposed by a[ny] particular state of civilisation'. His affinity for bricolage positions the Doctor as mythical rather than scientific in his character and agency, and yet his refusal of limits seems to collapse or resolve the binary opposition.[50] This is surely vital to his appeal as a hero.

'City of Death' is not, in any conventional sense, a ghost story. Most obviously, it lacks ghosts. Even so, it can offer a way of thinking about the meaning of ghosts and the ghostly within the *Doctor Who* mythos, implying a correspondence with the key concept that emerges from Derrida's speculations on the Marxian spectre, that of 'hauntology': the haunting of the present by the past's failed futures. Scaroth of the Jagaroth is, ultimately, a form of spectre, a self-haunting phantasm splintered throughout the human story just as the theme of history is splintered throughout *Doctor Who*. His influence on the development of 'this puny race of humans', creating them in order to destroy them, threading himself like an invisible, barely tangible stitch through their possible pasts and futures, means that he effectively prefigures Derrida's punning creation of *hauntologie* out of its homophone *ontologie*.

In *Specters of Marx*, Derrida's response to the apparent demise of communism is to open up a line of questioning about the importance of embodied presence within the ideological systems of the West: can something be acknowledged as 'real' even when it has no fixed, determined or discoverable material existence in the present? This is typically abstruse but its essence is clear enough, the ontological 'is' being implicated in the hauntological 'might be' or 'might *have* been'.

That the temporal, spatial and material dimensions are equally entailed by the formulation is intensely suggestive in the context of *Doctor Who*, a mythology that proposed from the outset a capacity to travel 'through time, through space, and through matter'.[51] Materialization and dematerialization are, after all, the signature operations of the TARDIS: it enters the material realm and departs from it, repeatedly, making it as much a ghost-ship as a spaceship. Its dimensional transcendentalism, bigger on the inside, means that, even in its material form, it rejects the restrictions of material laws. Furthermore, as a time-space vessel, it performs the preoccupations of hauntology, defined by Mark Fisher as having 'two dimensions':

> The first refers to that which is (in actuality is) *no longer*, but which is still effective as a virtuality (the traumatic 'compulsion to repeat', a structure that repeats, a fatal pattern). The second refers to that which (in actuality) has *not yet* happened, but which is *already* effective in the virtual (an attractor, an anticipation shaping current behavior).[52]

Pamela McCallum is more concise, commenting that 'Derrida positions time within an unstable interaction of past, present, and future'.[53] This unstable interaction is where Scaroth's ambitions reach their apotheosis, and it is where ghosts become manifest and the Doctor (as he phrases it in 1975's 'Pyramids of Mars') 'walks in eternity'.

The TARDIS is spectral. Caught in a moment of formalized nostalgia through its external appearance, it is haunted by memories of the police box that have, over the years, merged into memories of the TARDIS itself. A ghost in machine form, shown to be somehow sentient as early as 'The Edge of Destruction' (1964), it has a mysterious 'soul' that has become foregrounded in the revived television series. Accessed in times of crisis – literally the *deus ex machina* in several stories of the Davies era, where it is used to provide a plot resolution – it is depicted as a glowing, plasmatic energy and, in 'The Doctor's Wife' (2011), takes possession of a woman called Idris (Suranne Jones) in order to communicate in humanoid form. Sometimes referred to as the Matrix of the TARDIS, or identified as the Eye of Harmony, this intelligent essence is apparently connected to (or even permanently integrated with) the technological core of Time Lord culture on Gallifrey. The TARDIS fascinates as an aspect of the developed mythology through its sheer fantastical refusal of fixed categories. Here and there, now and then, big and small, organic and inorganic: the TARDIS unsettles all of these classifications, and more besides. Fixity and flux. Presence and absence. Material and immaterial. Just like a ghost.

Ghosts, in structuralist terms, inhabit the anomalous zone between poles of fixed meaning: they cannot be contained within stable categories. Dead but somehow alive, absent but present, immaterial but materialized, they signify temporal instances yet exist outside time; they appear in spatial locations but have no spatial existence. They are 'traces', to use Derrida's terminology, enacting a key concept within hauntology through their demonstration that being is not the same as presence. This quality, 'the spectrality effect',[54] is recognizable in the absent-presence of Scaroth, broken in space but integrated across time, dead but held suspended in a version of life, manifested as human but manifestly non-human, the spirit of old European charm haunted by genocidal cosmic monstrosity. Attempting to fulfil his ancient stratagem in the cellars of a château in the heart of Paris, a city thickened with historical traces, Scaroth is a fatal version of the ideologically haunted processes of history. Indeed, with his violently obsessive, monocular vision, he partakes of the mythic mock-heroism of Joyce's Citizen in the Cyclops episode of *Ulysses*.

Where ghosts or ghostly occurrences are featured in *Doctor Who*, it is frequently within scenarios that encourage either a questioning of the generic constructions of narrative ('Journey into Terror' (1966)), a challenging of facile notions of historical cause and effect ('Day of the Daleks' (1972)) or a more or less revisionist reading of a specific epoch ('Hide' (2013)). In the final years of the classic series, when its own mythologies were being recalibrated, this resulted in Marc Platt's 'Ghost Light' (1989), another story featuring no actual ghosts but depicting the human race as haunted by the absent-presence of an advanced and ancient alien power. In this case, the threat is posed by Josiah Smith (Ian Hogg), the apparent owner of Gabriel Chase mansion in Perivale in 1883. Smith, it transpires, has evolved from the survey agent of an expeditionary spaceship that had been involved in cataloguing the species of the planet many millennia previously. Keeping the leader of the expedition, Light, in a state of prolonged hibernation, Smith also imprisons the ever-evolving Control and retains the educated 'sample'

Neanderthal, Nimrod (Carl Forgione), as a manservant. As Smith approaches his ultimate evolutionary form as a Victorian gentleman, discarding the grotesque animated husks of his previous selves in the cellar of the mansion, he plans to use the connections of the affably insane explorer Redvers Fenn-Cooper (Michael Cochrane) to gain murderous access to Queen Victoria. Meanwhile, Light (John Hallam) is set free by Sylvester McCoy's Doctor and Sharon Duce's Control and, taking the form of an irritated angel, begins to contemplate ridding the Earth of the evolutionary chaos in which he now finds it. Also at large in Gabriel Chase are Gwendoline (Katharine Schlesinger), supposedly Smith's niece; the icy housekeeper, Mrs Pritchard (Sylvia Sims); the anti-Darwinian clergyman, Revd Ernest Matthews (John Nettleton); and – revived from storage in a specimen drawer – the policeman, Inspector Mackenzie (Frank Windsor).

'Ghost Light' is quite a party and it becomes, at times, as hectic and confused as Light discovers the Earth to be after his thousands of years of sleep. Even so, it is a remarkable story, using its late-Victorian suburban setting to take on a number of myths of modernity, satirizing both Darwinism (its advocate, Smith, is a self-creating fascistic monster) and those who oppose it (the pompous Matthews ends up transformed into an ape, immobilized and holding a banana in a display case). The ethereal Light, cheaply realized on screen and hammily performed, becomes sublimely Miltonic, a close cousin of Blake's Orc, in Platt's novelization: 'Robed in liquid gold and silver, with skin shimmering, it had the noble and terrible beauty of a seraph, fallen to Earth from its place beside the Throne.'[55] Light is the principal source of the story's spectrality, giving some illumination to the themes of evolution, entropy, belief, knowledge, power and humanity that permeate the claustrophobic atmosphere of Gabriel Chase like a ghost.

The Doctor's companion, Ace (Sophie Aldred), a native of Perivale, is indeed haunted within this tale, troubled by her recollection of a visit to the mansion that will take place in a hundred years' time. Then, disturbed by the firebombing of her Asian friend Manisha's family home by 'white kids', and sensing a lingering spirit of something evil in the deserted mansion, the teenage Dorothy sets fire to it. In 'Ghost Light', the Doctor – in the manipulative manner of his seventh incarnation – returns Ace to the scene of her earlier (but yet to occur) trauma in order to exorcise her angry demons. Caught in a paradoxical relation to linear chronology and experience, Ace is haunted by her personal past in a national past that becomes her temporary present, a present disrupted by her awareness of its provisional future and threatened by the destructive potential of a prehistoric past. This is complicated. It is restless, contradictory, self-enfolding, even self-indulgent, and it demonstrates vividly why 'Ghost Light' – the final story produced in the original run of *Doctor Who* – has been recognized as an important precursor of both the Virgin New Adventures novels and the twenty-first-century television series. It also indicates why it might be described as an exemplary parable of Derridean hauntology.

Ace's experiences in 'Ghost Light', and in other stories of that brief, valedictory season (notably 'The Curse of Fenric' and 'Survival'), enable her to develop as a morally complex character, one who comprehends and challenges the Doctor like no previous companion. This development is due, fundamentally, to a gradual, partial and uncomfortable revelation of the events that haunt her and the instincts that tempt her. There is, for instance, a queasy uncertainty in Ace's feelings about the attack on Manisha's home, one that is most evident between the lines of the novelized story. In the opening pages of this, in a scene that is not part of the televised version, the 14-year-old Dorothy recalls with fury the 'hatred' with which Manisha, 'her best friend', had looked at her following the attack. She is clear in her attribution of the racist abuse to 'the animals [who] always hung around the back alleys on the estate'. Later, though, in the preceding century, raging at the Doctor for bringing her back to the site of her past-and-future arson, she says the following:

> When I lived here in Perivale, me and my best mate, we dossed around together. We'd out-dare each other on things – skiving off, stupid things. Then they burnt out Manisha's flat: white kids firebombed it and I didn't care any more.[56]

There is a semantic jolt here: who is this 'best mate'? The beginning of the novel is explicit in designating this role to Manisha and there is no reason to think that this is not another reference to Ace's Asian friend, but the sudden switch from 'we' to 'they' seems agitated, troubled, perhaps evasive, as if there was another best friend whose 'out-daring' perhaps escalated to an act that has haunted Ace's conscience ever since. She has, as we know, a violent streak, encapsulated in her reliance on Nitro-9 and dramatized through her animalistic conversion in the following story, Rona Munro's 'Survival'. And she is, after all, a 'white kid'.

This is the shadow of a doubt, no more than that: a ghost. Elsewhere, in Nigel Robinson's novel *Timewyrm: Apocalypse* (1991) and Paul Cornell's *Timewyrm: Revelation* (1992), Ace's righteous anger at the treatment of the Purkayastha family is consistent and without ambiguity. But there are so many conflicting messages around Ace and her extended story that it would hardly be unreasonable to speculate that her fury at the bigotry of some of her peers – her ferocious tolerance and idealism as she travels with the Doctor – might be rooted in a regretted personal lapse. The nature of her departure from the Doctor and her ultimate fate have never been resolved, with a number of different versions presented across audio and prose media. Her surname, too, has been subject to a slippage in continuity: originally intended to be Gale, in line with the *The Wizard of Oz*, it was subsequently given as McShane in several New Adventures novels and Big Finish dramas, before returning to Gale in the BBC Past Doctor Adventures, finally settling to the doubled-up Gale McShane in the course of that series. The outcome of the attack on the Purkayastha family home is similarly in narrative flux, with some sources indicating that Manisha was shaken but unharmed, others that she was badly injured and others that she was killed. The haunting of Ace's tale by divergent possibilities can make her resemble – incongruously, and across disparate texts – a version of John Dowell in Roger Poole's deconstructive reading of Ford Madox Ford's *The Good Soldier* (1915). If Ace is not an unreliable narrator, as Poole alleges Dowell to be, she has at least been unreliably narrated.[57]

The title of 'Ghost Light' refers to the angelic nemesis that lies dormant within the ancient survey ship beneath Gabriel Chase, but it also evokes the ghost lights that are left to illuminate the stages of empty theatres. Thought by some to be as much a provision for thespian phantoms as a concession to health and safety, these (like the atmospheric will-o'-the-wisp or St Elmo's Fire) have been linked with supernatural phenomena. Crucially, though, they are the eerie products of technology. Derrida is emphatic in his association of hauntology with technological conditions, Fisher noting that it is 'proper to the time of "techno-tele-discursivity," techno-tele-iconicity," "simulacra," and "synthetic images"' rather than 'something rarefied'.[58] This epitomizes the theoretical jargon shunned by Chapman and yet it is hard to ignore its relevance to *Doctor Who*, where the trope of haunting has invariably had both a techno-cultural provenance and a scientific, or pseudo-scientific, explanation.

Ghosts are everywhere in *Doctor Who* but they are never revealed, or allowed, to be supernatural in origin. The Grey Lady of 'Journey into Terror' is discovered by the audience to be a robot (and, presumably, also a projection, since she walks through Ian at one point). The Doctor, meanwhile, is content to stick to his metafictional theory that she, like everything else in the haunted house, is a collective virtual rendering of dark human fantasies. Other ghosts-that-are-not-ghosts include the would-be assassins of Sir Reginald Styles in 'Day of the Daleks' and the 'man in armour' linked to the disappearance of scientists in 'The Time Warrior' (1973–4). In both cases, these apparitions are signs of temporal disturbance, the Sontaran Lynx (Kevin Lindsay) being a haunting from the Earth's past and the band of human guerillas a visitation from its future. They represent, in other words, the 'no longer' and the 'not yet' of Derrida's spectral theory. 'None of your clanking chains and chilly fingers,' as the Doctor comments in 'Day of the Daleks', 'but ghosts nonetheless.' Other cases of spectrality in *Doctor Who* place emphasis on the present–absent nexus of hauntology through their testing of the line between materiality and immateriality. Most obviously, the Phantom Piper of Jamie McCrimmon (Frazer Hines) in 1967's 'The Moonbase' turns out to be a very-much-embodied Cyberman; in 'Army of Ghosts', nearly twenty years later, the titular apparitions are revealed to be 'footprints' of the Cybus Industries brand of the same silver giants as they attempt to cross between alternative versions of the Earth.

The prevalence of ghosts and the ghost-like in new *Who* has been noticeable. This might seem surprising in a period of rapid technological advance and supposedly secular, rational values. The Gothic, though, has always been technologically engaged in its backward glances and is a sensibility distinctly attuned to the processes of the modern.[59] Moreover, the digital culture of disembodied information constitutes a particular challenge to notions of presence and absence, its constant and pervasive mediation of experience placing a particular strain on understandings of spatial and temporal location, knowledge, intelligence and, ultimately, life and death. It is no coincidence, surely, that the age of video conferencing, internet memes, cloud computing and online gaming is also the age of *Game of Thrones* (HBO, 2011–19), countless fairy-tale reboots (both family- and adult-orientated) and the exponential rise of the Marvel and DC superhero franchises. More ominously, the techno-scientific rationalism of contemporary capitalist culture has been accompanied by an intensification of tribalized and often lethally reactionary world views, producing both the bellicose atavism of Islamic State in the Middle East and the 'crusading' pugnacity of far-right political movements in Europe and the United States.

Derrida's hauntological writings are politico-economic in substance rather than mythopoeic, and they are far removed from the anthropological traditions of E. B. Tylor and J. G. Frazer. Even so, the shaping spirit of all mythologies, whether ancient or modern, whether channelled through the interpreting framework of a Jessie Weston or a Roland Barthes, is directed towards the containment of current anxieties.[60] The ways in which popular narratives of the past thirty years sublimate the economic and political circumstances of the age are therefore essential. In *Specters of Marx*, Derrida identifies ten 'plagues' of global capitalism, including an intensified unease about immigration, tensions between market protectionism and free trade, the grotesque foreign debt of developing countries, the unchecked escalation of a black market arms trade and the growth of dangerously unstable 'phantom states'. The mythic replication of such troubled phenomena, explicit or otherwise, can be traced in contradiction to prevailing idealist narratives of liberal democracy. Representing the haunted mood of twenty-first-century life, this renders the pervasiveness of the ghostly in post-2005 *Doctor Who* rather less surprising than it might at first appear.

The hauntological features of the relaunched series became more prominent during the Moffat years, with their conscious accenting of Gothic fantasy and fairy-tale concepts. This trait had been evident in Moffat's memorably creepy contributions to the Davies era – the Empty Child, the Clockwork Droids, the Weeping Angels, the Vashta Nerada – but it was consolidated in his own time as showrunner. His two most celebrated monsters, the Weeping Angels and the Silence, are potently spectral in both their appearance and comportment, sharing a quality of eerie cognitive elusiveness: creatures that can only move when unseen, creatures that can only be remembered while in view. This resembles the 'supernatural and paradoxical phenomenality' described by Derrida, its 'tangible intangibility'.[61] Even the intertextual haunting of these monsters (their designs resembling, respectively, the grave angels of nineteenth-century cemeteries and the skeletal trauma of Edvard Munch's 1893 artwork *The Scream*) means that they, like the corpse-like Monks of 'Extremis', 'The Pyramid at the End of the World' and 'The Lie of the Land' (all 2017), shimmer with the ghosts of cultural recollection. Moffat's tendency to give his monsters catchphrases ('Are you my mummy?', 'Hey, who turned out the light?'), or to associate them with anxious *leitmotifs* ('Don't blink!'), ensures that they will haunt viewers long after the credits have rolled.

This is not a new strategy in *Doctor Who*: its original monsters were given 'Exterminate!', after all, and Davies oversaw the introduction of 'Delete! Delete!' for the new generation of Cybermen. Children of the 1970s, meanwhile, might still recall the playground intonations of 'Contact has been made' following the broadcast of 'The Invisible Enemy' (1977). Nor are such mottos confined to monsters: the classic series gave us 'Reverse the polarity of the neutron flow' and 'Would you like a jelly baby?' while the new series offers up 'Fantastic!', 'Alons-y!' and 'Geronimo!' The use of ominous, repetitive phrases by Moffat, however, has a melancholy intensity that is most clearly seen in the dying moments of Miss Evangelista (Talulah Riley) towards the end of 'Silence in the Library' (2008). As the lights in her communicator flicker out one by one to show the fading of her consciousness within the neural relay – 'Don't tell the others, they'll only laugh … Don't tell the others, they'll only laugh …' – the 'afterimage' of her existence starts 'looping' in the technology. The result is like something out of Samuel Beckett: 'I can't think. I don't know. I, I, I, I scream. Ice cream. Ice cream. Ice cream …' That Miss Evangelista gives up the ghost via an electronic circuit (and returns as corrupted data shrouded in Victorian mourning dress in the succeeding episode) makes manifest a connection between technological cause and supernatural effect that is an essential implication of Derrida's *Specters of Marx*.

This connection is dramatized in several stories from the first series of revived *Who*. In 'The Unquiet Dead' (2005) the incorporeal Gelth, their bodies lost in the Last Great Time War, inhabit the relatively new gas supply of Cardiff in 1869, using the pipes as a network through which to travel.[62] Described by the celebrity guest star of the story, Charles Dickens (Simon Callow), as 'ghosts that are not ghosts', the Gelth are both spectral and physical, wraiths and zombies, flowing between presence and absence. As is usually the case in *Doctor Who*, ghostly creatures become the catalyst for a debate between supernatural and rational viewpoints, the Doctor (and Dickens) representing the latter. In essence, this is a debate – producing, in narrative terms, a Todorovian hesitation – between mythical and scientific conceptions or, perhaps more satisfactorily, between metaphysical and scientific mythologies. That the Gelth should lurk in the gas pipes, part of the technological infrastructure of the emergent Welsh town, is richly resonant. Cardiff grew rapidly following the building of its docks and subsequent arrival of the railway in the 1830s, but it was not awarded city status until 1902 and did not become the capital city of Wales until 1955. The Doctor and Rose visit at a time of burgeoning civic development, in other words, with their adventure forming a correlative to the extra-diegetic tale of new *Who*'s association with Cardiff through its production by BBC Wales. Hills makes the case that 'Welshness is not semiotically and symbolically important to the narratives of *Doctor Who*', noting that the 'burden of representation' in this respect was devolved to *Torchwood*, but this is a case when a South Glamorgan provenance can be seen as vitally inscribed at the level of story.[63] Gatiss's tale of funeral parlours and the walking dead is ghosted by a cultural awareness that is at least partly economic and political. If, as Hills claims, 'the Doctor's implicit home, 2005–9, is surely England's capital city', then 'The Unquiet Dead' is a spectre that drifts behind the series' primarily 'metropolitan, London-centric routines'.[64](More recently, under Chris Chibnall, these routines have been relocated to Sheffield.)[65]

Significantly, 'The Unquiet Dead' introduces the idea that Cardiff is built on a rift in time and space, making it important as a source of both energy and instability. The Rift is notable for being the first of several phenomena or technologies in new *Who* associated with the interface between different or opposing places, dimensions or states of being. The crack in Amy Pond's wall is the most obvious of these but there are others: the Untempered Schism of 'The Sound of Drums' (2007) and 'The End of Time' (2010), the wormholes of 'Planet of the Dead' (2009) and 'Hide', the Confession Dial of 'Heaven Sent' (2015), other rifts associated with Mount Vesuvius ('The Fires of Pompeii' (2008)) and the Medusa Cascade ('The Stolen Earth' / 'Journey's End' (2008)). This is not to say that such gateways did not feature in the classic series. The 'time fissure' of 'Image of the Fendahl' (1977), for example, is linked with ghostly activities. The 'time-space tunnel' accessed through an Egyptian sarcophagus in 'Pyramids of Mars' betokens a similarly haunted technology. Tellingly, it is a ghost – that of Ianto Jones – which closes the Cardiff Rift in the *Torchwood* radio drama, 'The House of the Dead' (2011).

A rift is a gap, split, fracture: it implies damage and, in this case, acts as a reminder of Derrida's fixation on Hamlet's diagnosis of temporal dislocation: 'The time is out of joint.' For the Danish prince, this is a result of his father's death but, in another story from the Eccleston season, a similar rupture is caused by Rose's attempt to *stop* her father from dying. In Paul Cornell's 'Father's Day' the Doctor agrees, reluctantly, to take his companion back to 1987 to comfort her father as he dies in the street following a hit-and-run accident. She is unable, however, to let him die and, instead, intervenes to prevent the accident from taking place. As a consequence, time is 'wounded' and gigantic bat-like creatures, Reapers, appear and begin erasing humanity from history. The Doctor's description of the damage in medical terms – the Reapers are 'like bacteria, taking advantage', 'they've come to sterilize the wound, by consuming everything inside' – calls to mind Marcellus's line from *Hamlet* ('There is something rotten in the state of Denmark') and perhaps also, by association, Antonio's speech about 'the corruption of the times' from the opening of John Webster's *The Duchess of Malfi* (1612–13). 'Father's Day' is not a revenge tragedy but there is an air of the Jacobean or Elizabethan macabre about the scenes of demonic Reapers scraping and scratching at the fabric of the suburban church within which the Doctor, Rose and a party of wedding guests – including Rose's infant self and her parents, Pete and Jackie Tyler (Shaun Dingwall, Camille Coduri) – have taken refuge. And, just as the courtly 'domestics' of revenge dramas have effects far beyond the walls of the palaces within which they take place, so Rose's actions threaten to bring about an apocalypse.

The political dimensions of *Hamlet* or *The Duchess of Malfi* are inextricable from the personal intrigues that drive their narratives. In 'Father's Day', politics is less obviously an aspect of the tale, but there is enough social detail in the depiction of late-1980s aspirational life to suggest that the satirical edge of the Virgin novels, and of the Sylvester McCoy era that preceded them on TV, has been carried over by Cornell and Davies. The humorous nostalgia of breeze-block mobile phones and tower-block flats bursting with (in Jackie's words) 'cut-price detergents, tonic water, Betamax tapes' and other 'rubbish' evokes the milieu of John Sullivan's long-running sitcom *Only Fools and Horses* (BBC, 1981–2003). As critiques of Thatcherism go, this could seem rather light and affectionate if it were not for the grim allegorical potential of a scenario that presents a gathering of dressed-up, nervous, working-class Londoners hiding in a late-Victorian church as history dies and the world ends around them.[66] Guided only by a drifting, damaged, increasingly desperate aristocrat, supposedly the last of his kind ('My people would have stopped this. But they're all gone. And now I'm going the same way'), they are forced to sit and wait while the shrill, avenging shadows gather beyond the stained-glass windows. The church that was built to save their souls now stands as the place where their souls will be lost.

The spectral theme of 'Father's Day', quite apart from the fact that Rose meets a kind of antemortem ghost of her dad, an infant prefiguring of her future boyfriend, Mickey Smith (Noel Clarke), and an incunabular version of herself, is provided through the depiction of technology. The TARDIS interior, for instance, is lost as a result of the damage to time, the Doctor throwing open the doors of his ship with confidence, only to be confronted with an empty cupboard, the inside smaller than the outside. Here the police box is, as Ian Chesterton put it all those years ago, 'just a police box', but it is a police box haunted by the cultural icon that it has become. No one – not the Doctor, not the viewer – looks at a police box and thinks 'police box' anymore. This is the diegesis determining the extra-diegesis, an intertextual role reversal that is also an act of semiotic takeover.

A similar process of imbrication, the fictional narrative intersecting with its own cultural resources, is evident in the representation of telephones. Beyond the comic contrast of Stuart's dad's 'brick' and Rose's (now outmoded) smartphone, there is the looping utterance that comes though all phones in the story as another symptom of the temporal wounding: 'Watson, come here! I need you!' This, as the Doctor recognizes, is the voice of Alexander Graham Bell, calling for his assistant Thomas Watson in what is reputed to have been the first communication by telephone. So, the technology is haunted by its origins. Except, of course, that this is a *representation* of those origins, and an erroneous one at that: the words spoken by Bell are generally thought to have been 'Watson, come here! I want you!' The lapse from 'want' to 'need' – a single syllable, trivial in narrative terms and of no mythic significance – is a minor and largely imperceptible fault that shows the broadcast version of the story being marked by its processes of production, its *own* origins. The historical line was written correctly in Cornell's script and originally recorded accurately, only drifting slightly when rerecorded to correct an overly hammy Scots accent.[67]

The spectrality of the Bell–Watson reference is intensified if its unsettled biographical and commercial contexts are noted. Firstly, the long-held designation of Bell as the inventor of the telephone is now a matter of dispute, with the claims of Antonio Meucci to this accomplishment having been upheld by the US House of Representatives in 2002, and a rival claim by Elisha Gray also being credited by many. More than a case of variant histories, this controversy is ghosted by competing allegations of professional skullduggery (did Bell 'steal' Meucci's work and/or interfere with the processes of the US Patent Office, to which Gray applied on the same day in 1874?) and social inequity (financial hardship prevented Meucci from applying for a patent and he died before legal action against Gray could be completed in 1889).[68] The peculiarly eerie resonance of Bell's summons to Watson is further increased by knowledge of the less-than-scientific attitude of the latter to some elements of the invention.

Watson, a spiritualist and occultist, was a member of the Society for Psychical Research and referred to electricity as 'that occult force', considering the operations of the telephone as analogous to those of a spirit medium.[69] While he did the work of constructing Bell's devices, he also did much to invest the technology with an air of mystic ineffability. Erik Davis has referred to the telephone as 'the ultimate animist technology', exploring both the existential and political dimensions of 'the telephonic uncanny'.[70] Despite its ubiquity in the twenty-first century, the telephone continues to possess a 'spectral ambiguity', unsettling notions of presence and absence, self and other, here and there, now and then, even life and death:

Does it talk, do we talk through it, or are those vibrations only the ghosts of ourselves? When we pick up a receiver and hear no dial tone, why do we say that the line is 'dead'? … Or think of the outgoing messages we leave on our answering machines. 'I am not here right now,' we say, which of course begs the inevitable question: If we are not there, then who is speaking? Such an apparently trivial question becomes palpably eerie to anyone who has reached the answering machine of the recently deceased and heard the chipper message of the dead.[71]

It might seem extravagant to read so much into a single misquoted phrase within 'Father's Day', but – given its mood, its mode, its themes – it is hard to believe that such contextual reflections did not, in some way, inform Cornell's writing of the story.

As the first series of new *Who* went into production, social media was beginning to emerge and Apple Inc.'s first iPhone was being developed (to be released in 2007). A story set in the earliest days of home computing and mobile telephony, unfolding amidst the stalled ritual intimacy of a wedding, with the tragedy of one family escalating rapidly into a quiet global catastrophe, seems all the more powerful as the temporal wound that motivates it begins to leak the mythic moment of the first electrical speech. The TV audience, on the verge of an age of trolls, vloggers and Facebook memorials, hears a simulated ghost in the background of an eccentric new drama that is also, strangely, rather old.

A key scene in 'Father's Day' is mirrored in the Capaldi episode 'Before the Flood' (2015), the second part of the tale begun in 'Under the Lake'. Where, in the 2005 story, the Doctor and Rose watch their slightly earlier selves as they wait for Pete Tyler's fatal accident to take place, in the 2015 story the Doctor and marine biologist Mason Bennett (Arsher Ali) watch their slightly earlier selves as they take part in events that will lead to the killings of Tivolian undertaker Albar Prentis (Paul Kaye) and Bennett's adored military colleague, Alice O'Donnell (Morven Christie), by the supposedly deceased warlord the Fisher King (Neil Fingleton, Peter Serafinowicz). Where the wounding of time in 'Father's Day' turns upon Rose's attempt to prevent her dad's death, in the later story, written by Toby Whithouse, the haunting of one time period (1980) by another (2119), and vice versa, is something that the Doctor is unable to prevent. Where the haunting of 'Father's Day' is signified by the Reapers (and by the repetitive crackle of the words from Bell), in 'Before the Flood' it is represented by the black-eyed ghosts that the Fisher King has transmitted across the centuries to summon his armada to conquer the Earth.

Ostensibly a traditional base-under-siege story, with the crew of the underwater mining facility the Drum under attack from ghosts that seem to have a connection to the small abandoned spacecraft discovered in the ruins of a flooded town, 'Under the Lake' / 'Before the Flood' is a more complicated tale than it first appears to be. In particular, it places strain on many of the same concepts as 'Father's Day', especially those concerned with ontology, causation and time. The ghosts of the tale, with their scorched eye sockets, are in some ways generically typical: they walk through walls, rise up through floors, are transparent and only come out at 'night' (an artificial state in the subaquatic environment). In other ways, though, they are aberrant, being able to handle heavy implements as weapons and intoning constantly, silently, as they stalk the crew. Notable for being the closest to literal ghosts in the series' history, they are given a rationalization, but this remains vague and they are never revealed to be anything other than the disembodied spirits of the dead. This contrasts markedly with the Gelth-possessed corpses of 'The Unquiet Dead', the Ice Governess (voiced by Juliet Cadzow) created by the Great Intelligence in 'The Snowmen' and the Witch of the Well in 'Hide', revealed to be the time-travel pioneer Hila Tacorian (Kemi-Bo Jacobs).

The first ghost encountered in 'Under the Lake' is that of Prentis, who had died 139 years earlier, the second that of Jonathan Moran (Colin McFarlane), the Drum's captain, killed by a blast from the mystery spacecraft's engines in the opening scene of the story. As other characters die, either in 1980 or 2119, they join the predatory phantom crew in the later age. Conceptually, the ghosts inhabit Whithouse's intricate yarn as harbingers of temporal, spatial and existential disturbance, forerunners of confused categorical boundaries. This is made clear at the threshold between the two halves of the story. The first part ends with a cliffhanger that is, almost literally, a 'suspended enigma', to use the term favoured by Tulloch and Alvarado.[72] Clara, having remained in the Drum in the twenty-second century while the Doctor traces the source of the ghosts back to 1980 in the TARDIS, is confronted suddenly by the sight of a new ghost drifting outside the base: that of the Doctor (see Figure 3.2). The second part of the story begins with the Doctor in the TARDIS, addressing the audience directly in a playful explanation of the bootstrap paradox, a popular premise in science fiction since Robert A. Heinlein's 1941 story 'By His Bootstraps'.[73] Here the Doctor speculates on a visit

Figure 3.2 The Doctor (Peter Capaldi) haunts the Drum at the end of 'Under the Lake' (2015); ©BBC Worldwide.

to eighteenth-century Germany to visit Beethoven: 'No one's heard of him, not even his family.' The composer 'literally doesn't exist', he *will* never exist, but the music does, so: 'Who really composed Beethoven's Fifth?'

It is possible that 'Under the Lake' / 'Before the Flood' constitute two of the most spectral *Doctor Who* episodes ever. In relation to hauntology, they fit the bill perfectly, their mythic structure being suffused with narratives of late-capitalist economics and Cold War politics. Richard Pritchard (Steve Robertson), representing Vector Petroleum, the company with mining rights to the oil reservoir beneath the Drum, is as obnoxious a characterization of corporate interest as the series has produced, with none of the charm of a Tobias Vaughn (Kevin Stoney, 'The Invasion' (1968)) or the redeeming humanity of Strackman Lux (Steve Pemberton, 'Silence in the Library' / 'Forest of the Dead' (2008)). He is the first crew member to be killed after Moran and few of his colleagues appear to miss him as he returns to prey upon them as a dumbly muttering ghost. Pritchard's priorities and motivations are understood through his obsession with the flooded town beyond the Drum, built as it is on the potential for vast profits. The town itself, though, is a clue to the haunted mythology he occupies. Visited by the Doctor, Bennett and O'Donnell in the hours before it is flooded by the destruction of the nearby dam, this is revealed to be a ghost village, an uninhabited military simulacrum of a Soviet Russian town from, as the Doctor calls it, 'the height of the Cold War'. Hollow, echoing and concealing a brutal monster, the town is a grim correlative of the ghost-infested submarine complex that will succeed it.

Tellingly, in a story full of misunderstandings, bad-tempered exchanges and troubled silences (not just the blank mouthings of the ghosts but the words not spoken by Bennett to O'Donnell, or by the Doctor to Bennett and Clara), it is the sign language of the deaf crewmember Cass (Sophie Stone), translated by her interpreter Tim Lunn (Zaqi Ismail), that provides a trusted line of communication through the two episodes. Cass is the only member of the crew not to be given a full name (is Cass her personal or family name?), making her seem less formed, defined, settled as a character, more spectral perhaps, with an ironic hint of the mythical Cassandra, whose ears heard the future but whose prophecies were never heard. Cass is recognized as the leader upon Pritchard's death (and arguably before that, certainly by the Doctor) and, with her voice 'ghosted' through that of another, she comes to embody a new spirit of empathy, connection and openness after the defeat of the Fisher King. Prompted by the grieving Bennett, Lunn signs his feelings to Cass for the first time and the two acknowledge that they are in love with each other.

In 'Under the Lake' the Doctor moves from a repeated rational refusal to believe in ghosts ('They're not ghosts') to a state of scientific enthusiasm for the empirical fact of ghosts:

> They're not holograms, they're not Flesh Avatars, they're not Autons, they're not digital copies bouncing around the Nethersphere. No, these people are literally, actually, dead. Wow. This is – it's amazing! I've never actually met a proper ghost.

Ultimately, the ontology of the ghosts hardly matters. What they are is less important than what they mean, what they are *doing* in the story. As Northrop Frye wrote of the spectre that was to give Derrida his hauntological starting point, 'The appearance of a ghost in *Hamlet* presents the hypothesis "let there be a ghost in *Hamlet*". It has nothing to do with whether ghosts exist or not, or whether Shakespeare or his audience thought they did.'[74] Ghosts in *Doctor Who*, like the ghost in *Hamlet*, invariably indicate that 'the time is out of joint', that there is 'something rotten', that understandings are in a process of transformation or collapse. In essence, these are epistemological understandings – of what it is to live (and die), to know, to communicate, to act – and the pressure placed upon them is reflective of the kind of paradigm shift described by Thomas Kuhn and Michel Foucault.[75]

An emphasis on spectral themes entails a questioning of 'the order of things', expressed particularly in the responses of the principal characters, both the Doctor himself and his companions. An exchange from 'Hide' is powerful in this respect, arising from Clara's increasingly distressed witness of the Doctor's casual checking off of 'the entire life cycle of Earth, birth to death' as he investigates the Caliburn Ghast. This leads her to reflect on the significance of her life and that of her planet on a scale adjusted to match the almost infinite perspective of the Doctor:

CLARA To you, I haven't been born yet, and to you I've been dead one hundred billion years. Is my body out there somewhere, in the ground?
DOCTOR Yes, I suppose it is.
CLARA But here we are, talking. So I am a ghost. To you, I'm a ghost. We're all ghosts to you. We must be nothing.
DOCTOR No. No. You're not that.
CLARA Then what are we? What can we possibly be?
DOCTOR You are the only mystery worth solving.

An earlier scene, between the Doctor and the reticent, melancholy Professor Palmer (Dougray Scott), is similarly expressive of a troubled empathy for human experience, again turning a literal reference to ghosts into a metaphorical appeal to the concept of haunting:

DOCTOR Yes, but how does that man, that war hero, end up here in a lonely old house, looking for ghosts?
PALMER Because I killed, and I caused to have killed. I sent young men and women to their deaths, but here I am, still alive and it does tend to haunt you. Living, after so much of the other thing.

Such dialogue, suggestive of richly complex relationships, might be thought by some to be exclusive to post-2005 *Doctor Who*, but it is consistent in tone with other examples from throughout the history of the series. It explains the thrill, beyond any mere kick of intertextual recognition, that can be had from hearing the words of the First Doctor (from the third episode of the first ever story) in the mouth of the Twelfth Doctor in the beautifully spectral 'Listen' (2014): 'Fear makes companions of us all.'

Another Capaldi-era ghost story, this time penned by Moffat, 'Listen' is a meditation on loneliness which uses fear of the dark as its inscrutable monster. It has some parallels with Davies's 'Midnight' (2008) and Gatiss's 'Night Terrors' (2011) but is a uniquely subtle and unsettling episode. Focusing on a nightmare that the Doctor posits everybody to have at some point – waking in the dark sensing that something is there with you, swinging your feet from the bed and feeling the sudden grasping of a hand around your ankle – the story draws on both the monster-under-the-bed apprehensions of childhood and debates within modernity about the limits of empiricism. The Doctor starts the episode in a mode of question-conjecture-experiment enquiry and ends it in reluctant acceptance of unknowing following Clara's urgent instruction: 'Don't look where we are. Take off, and promise me you will never look where we've been.'

What Clara does not want him to discover is the origin of his nightmare, the fact that it is the return of a repressed memory from his Gallifreyan childhood. Upset and unhappy, seeking solitude away from 'the other boys', he has been sleeping in an outhouse and, woken by his future self calling to Clara from the TARDIS, is about to investigate when she grabs his ankle in panic from under the bed: 'It's okay. This is just a dream.' The Doctor, believing that his ship has tapped into Clara's subconscious to access the coordinates for the recurring dream, has in fact travelled back down his own timeline, to his own beginnings. He has, unwittingly, become the catalyst in a narrative that links the isolation of his infant self with that of the infant Rupert 'Danny' Pink, lonely in a children's home, and that of Orson Pink, apparently a descendant of Danny and a time-travel pioneer from twenty-second-century Earth, who has been left trapped and alone at 'the end of everything' following a miscalculated time-shot. Whether the monsters that haunt young Danny, or that lurk outside Orson's capsule, or that shadow the Doctor throughout his many lives, are real or not is, for once, less important than their provocation to self-knowledge and a sympathy for others. As Clara realizes, the barn in which the Doctor sought refuge as a child is the same barn in which he will face his greatest fears in the closing days of the Last Great Time War, the barn to which he will carry the Moment in 'The Day of the Doctor'.

Perhaps the most hauntological aspect of 'Listen' is its central premise, the Doctor's claim about the universality of the ankle-grabbing nightmare. In an early exchange with Clara, the Doctor takes it for granted that 'the exact same nightmare' is experienced by 'everybody'. Clara's response to the question of whether *she* has experienced it is, however, ambiguous: 'Okay, yeah, probably. Yes. But everyone dreams about something under the bed.' Variations on a theme, then, but not necessarily a precise match. Does this matter? The Doctor's projection of his own nightmare onto everybody else, his pursuit of an investigation that is possibly or even probably based on a false premise, means that 'Listen' is imbued with a properly Gothic spirit of uncertainty. Just as the period of scientific advance from the mid-1700s in Europe coincided with a renaissance of the fantastical (we might think of John Polidori, soon to write *The Vampyre: A Tale* (1819),[76] completing his medical thesis on nightmares and sleepwalking in Edinburgh in 1815), so the Doctor's examination of a dream sees rational process being destabilized by the inexplicable. Haunted by the ghost of the knowable, he finds himself stranded at the literal limits of knowledge, speculating on the unfathomable:

> CLARA What are we doing?
> DOCTOR Waiting.
> CLARA For what? For who? If everybody in the universe is dead, then there's nobody out there.
> DOCTOR That's one way of looking at it.
> CLARA What's the other?
> DOCTOR That's a hell of a lot of ghosts.

Or a hell of a lot of memories.

In the end, spectral themes provide a way into the recognition and testing of those 'mythic binaries' discussed by Hills, binaries that are never resolved but instead are 'constantly opened out and restaged' so that they 'can be tested, celebrated, and further complicated'.[77] *Doctor Who* is a myth that explores thresholds and discovers differences, sometimes reinforcing these but usually, in some way, challenging them. It is no coincidence that monsters have proved so fundamental to the series through the years, or that the most successful of these, from the Daleks, Cybermen, Sontarans and Ice Warriors to the Weeping Angels and the Silence, have been creatures of a hybrid, uncanny or otherwise anomalous identity. The following section will look at the depiction of threshold monstrosities, specifically two related varieties of creature that derive from established popular mythology: vampires and werewolves.

Vampires, werewolves and other universal monsters

In a mythology like *Doctor Who*, characterized by monsters, prone to borrowing, and inflected by the Gothic, it is to be expected that those stalwarts of the modern horror genre, vampires and werewolves, should have featured more than once, together with variants on Frankenstein's Monster, Jekyll and Hyde, and zombies. These are all, in different ways, spectral entities, haunting the thresholds between the human and non-human, life and death, nature and culture, and so on. The influence of Mary Shelley's novel *Frankenstein* (1818) and its cinematic/televisual adaptations is easy to locate, explicitly in 'The Brain of Morbius' (1976) and in Jonathan Morris's half-hour gem for Big Finish, 'Mary's Story' (2009), and thematically in the extended narratives of the Daleks and the Cybermen.[78] The archetype of the massed, mindless zombie scourge so beloved of horror films from Victor Halperin's *White Zombie* (1932) to Stefan Rozowitzky's *Patient Zero* (2018) – and, more recently, of TV serial dramas such as *The Walking Dead* (2010–present) – is also contained, to a degree, in those denizens of Skaro and Mondas/Telos. It is found, too, in *Doctor Who*'s many dehumanized collectives such as the Robomen of 'The Dalek Invasion of Earth' (1964), the infected specimen-humans of 'New Earth' (2006) and the spacesuit-stiffs of 'Oxygen' (2017). Here, though, the focus will be on reworkings of vampire and, especially, werewolf myths, with some reference to Robert Louis Stevenson's trope of mutant identity.

From the robot Dracula in 'The Chase' (1965) to the Plasmavore in 'Smith and Jones' (2007) and the Saturnyns of 'The Vampires of Venice' (2010), vampiric myth has been a frequent resource for writers of *Doctor Who* on television. It has, indeed, been a presence whenever themes of parasitism have been explored, most obviously in 'The Claws of Axos' (1972), an early title for which was 'The Vampire from Space'. Off screen, vampires have proliferated, featuring in several Virgin and BBC novels (including Terrance Dicks's *Blood Harvest* (1994), Paul Cornell's *Goth Opera* (1994) and Jonathan Blum and Kate Orman's *Vampire Science* (1996)) and across diverse series of Big Finish audio dramas, as well as in the anthology of Bernice Summerfield novellas, *The Vampire Curse* (2008). To date, however, only one all-out vampire story has been included in televised *Doctor Who*, this being Dicks's 1980 story 'State of Decay'.

I have written elsewhere of how this Hammer-inspired tale, an apparently clear-cut piece of Gothic melodrama, suggests a number of more complex attitudes towards the vampire as a creature of thresholds.[79] This has a significant bearing on wider themes of spectrality in *Doctor Who*, revealed in the Doctor and Romana's confrontation with the legends of their own race. The Great Vampire, escaping from 'the last great battle' with the Time Lords – 'vanished, even to his shadow, from Time and Space' – has been recovering on a remote planet in E-Space, a kind of nowhere between universes, a cosmic interface.[80] Vampire stories traditionally show them to be impatient of windows and doors, invisible to mirrors, but nevertheless discoverable wherever (to attempt a rough definition of the interface) one thing meets another. In this case, tellingly, the Great Vampire is represented only as an ominous trace on various interfaces. Most prominently, it is manifested through the avatarial presence of its servants King Zargo, Queen Camilla and Chancellor Aukon, the undead vestiges of the crew from a long-lost Earth colony ship. It also haunts the ritualized language of the faux-medieval community on the planet (The Great One, The Three Who Rule, The Wasting, The Selection, The Arising) and is glimpsed as a blurred image on a forbidden and antiquated hi-tech scanner and as a gigantic clawed hand breaking through the membrane of its subterranean resting place as it attempts resurrection. Like the ghosts discussed in the previous section, the Great Vampire, defined through its oppressively absent presence in the story, is a source of categorical unsettlement. Its threat is engendered through an uncanny confusion of living and dead, human and monstrous, magical and technological, atavistic and futuristic.

At first glance, werewolves seem to be thinner on the ground in *Doctor Who* than their blood-sucking cousins. In 1981, a year after 'State of Decay' and eighteen years after the television series began, John Nathan-Turner reported that he 'would love to see a werewolf story in the programme'.[81] Even so, it took another seven years for the punk lycanthrope Mags to menace Sylvester McCoy's Doctor in the ring of the Psychic Circus in Stephen Wyatt's 'The Greatest Show in the Galaxy' (1988–9). And for an out-and-out werewolf story, distinct from a story that happens to have a werewolf *in* it, viewers would need to wait until Russell T. Davies's 'Tooth and Claw' during the second season of the revived series in 2006.

Looking beyond televised stories, the *Doctor Who* werewolf pack swells to include creatures from the Eighth Doctor Adventures novel *Kursaal* (1998), the Past Doctor Adventures novel *Wolfsbane* (2003) and the Big Finish audio dramas *Loups-Garoux* (2001) and *Legend of the Cybermen* (2010). Then there are the Werelox, Wardog and the Windigo from the pages of *Doctor Who Weekly* and *Doctor Who Monthly*, and Flinthair, the prehistoric werewolf encountered by the Second Doctor in the story 'Loop the Loup' in the *Doctor Who Yearbook 1994*.[82] It would seem that the lupine contagion is heavy in the blood of the franchise after all, which might send us back to the small screen for a closer study. As werewolf lore tells us, we need to look for the fur beneath the skin; specifically, we need to look for the werewolf by any other name.[83]

If we approach the genus of werewolf in an inclusive spirit, allowing for complexity and ambiguity, Mags and the foundling host of 'Tooth and Claw' are soon joined by other contenders. Placing the emphasis on shapeshifting transformations between naked ape and hairy beast, or between other oppositional variations (cultural/natural, domesticated/feral, civilized/savage) reveals a number of monsters in the werewolf mould, none of them explicitly referred to as such but all of them drawing on the same mythology. There are the Primords of 'Inferno' (1970), for instance, the Anti-Man from 'The Planet of Evil' (1975), and Dorf, or the Lukoser, from the 'Mindwarp' episodes of 'The Trial of a Time Lord' (1986). These creatures are, if not strictly lycanthropic, at least lycanthrope-ish and they are certainly influenced by the long iconographic and mythopoeic traditions of the werewolf. This company might also, at a push, include the Tharils from 'Warriors' Gate' (1980), the Cheetah People from 'Survival' (1989) and even the Cybershades from 'The Next Doctor' (2008). The Tharils are distinctly leonine rather than lupine and they are a discrete race of alien beings, not transformed humans, but – with a design based closely on that of the Beast from Jean Cocteau's *La Belle et la Bête* (1946) – they have a lineage that connects them to myths of the accursed bestial hybrid. The Cheetah People, appearing in the final story of the classic series, are humans who have been mutated into a kind of savage nobility by the primal influence of an unnamed but dying planet. As their name suggests, they are human–cat rather than human–wolf hybrids, but they exhibit many of the physical and thematic attributes of the werewolf, including a sexual element, the 'lesbian subtext' identified by author Rona Munro.[84] The Cybershades, described by David Tennant's Doctor as 'some sort of primitive conversion, like they took the brain of a cat or a dog', are part animal and part Cyberman, which implies that in some aspects they might also be part human, so they can be located somewhere on the hybrid nexus between human, beast and machine.

In his transformation from obsessed Morestran geologist to flickering, hairy Anti-Man, Professor Sorenson of 'Planet of Evil' (1975) shares numerous features with the classic cinematic werewolf (burning eyes, coarse grey hair, fangs, claws, hunched back, loping walk), but he is also a version of the Id creature from Fred M. Wilcox's 1956 film *Forbidden Planet*, itself a version of Shakespeare's wild man, Caliban, from *The Tempest*. Clearly, the Sorenson/Anti-Man monster is most explicitly an adaptation of the Jekyll/Hyde character, especially as it has been realized in successive film adaptations of Stevenson's 1886 novella. Merging visual tropes from both John Barrymore's 1920 depiction of Hyde and that of Fredric March from Rouben Mamoulian's 1931 version, the Anti-Man is almost comically reliant on regular swigs from a smoking beaker of antimatter potion. Played with relish by Frederick Jaeger, he reminds us that *The Strange Case of Dr Jekyll and Mr Hyde* can, as Ken Gelder notes, be 'understood as a version of the werewolf myth'.[85] Infected, in effect possessed, by the planet Zeta Minor while leading a scientific expedition, Sorenson's condition is analogous to that of Henry Hull's botanist Wilfred Glendon in the earliest surviving werewolf film, *Werewolf of London* (1935).

What the Anti-Man shows, crucially, is an intensification of themes of possession and transformation within the series under Philip Hinchcliffe (producer) and Robert Holmes (script editor) between 1975 and 1977, frequently in conjunction with body horror. Figures of hybrid monstrousness dominated as never before or since in *Doctor Who*: not just the metallic hybridity of the Daleks and the Cybermen, but a more grisly organic variety epitomized by the Wirrn ('The Ark in Space' (1975)) and the Krynoid ('The Seeds of Doom' (1976)). Although not werewolves, such mutations occupy an equivalent imaginative territory where the limits of human beings are destabilized by an invading 'other', disclosing the state of abjection described by Julia Kristeva in *Powers of Horror*: 'These body fluids, this defilement, this shit are what life withstands, hardly and with difficulty, on the part of death. There, I am at the border of my condition as a living being.'[86] Where the physical boundaries of the human individual are seen, heard or simply *known* to be broken, it becomes impossible to refuse an awareness of those mortal realities that we 'permanently thrust aside in order to live'. This is dark matter for a teatime family audience, explaining (in part, at least) the constant moral attentions of Mary Whitehouse and the National Viewers' and Listeners' Association (NVLA) during the mid-1970s.[87] Both ontology and epistemology are implicated here and, linked (via Chantal Bourgault du Coudray) with Slavoj Žižek's reading of the modern monster as a 'spectral' challenge to Enlightenment rationality, these hybrids point to something intriguing about the wider use of Gothic motifs in the series.[88]

Given *Doctor Who's* ostensible status as science fiction, it is unsurprising that these motifs should be validated through scientific (or *pseudo*-scientific) narrative mechanisms rather than supernatural or metaphysical ones. The Anti-Man, the Krynoid and the Wirrn might well signify anxieties of the self and what it is to be human, unease about the things that take shape in the zone between society and the wilderness, but they do so in a specific context. With some similarities to George MacDonald's fairy tale of 1882, *The History of Photogen and Nycteris*, the hybrids of *Doctor Who* tell a mutable tale about our relationship with technology, one which can be mapped against the evolution of the programme itself. This is evident if we look from the Anti-Man to the monsters that he most closely resembles in the television series, the Primords (see Figure 3.3).

'Inferno' is a seven-part story that was broadcast in May and June of 1970, the final tale in Jon Pertwee's first season as the Doctor. A vital phase in the show's development, this had seen, among other significant changes, the transition from black-and-white to colour. James Chapman has argued, persuasively, that the shift to a full palette coincided with a shift in the paradigm of monstrosity within *Doctor Who*, the robotic giving way to the organic, silver-white to a greater variability of hue and texture.[89] This meant that those ubiquitous enemies of the 1960s, the Daleks and the Cybermen, were to be used far more sparingly in the 1970s. The Primords are emblematic in this respect.

Never actually named in the story on screen (instead they are identified in the closing credits), the Primords are humans who have suffered mutation as a result of the Inferno project, an attempt by the fanatical Professor Stahlman to mine the energy resources at the Earth's core. They have sometimes been referred to as ape-like in commentaries on the story and, as their name suggests, they seem to represent a regression to some primordial state of bestiality. Their realization on screen is wolfish rather than simian, however, and is clearly inspired

Figure 3.3 Platoon Under-Leader Benton (John Levene) comes over all Primord in the parallel fascist Britain of 'Inferno' (1970); ©BBC Worldwide.

by the classic werewolf designs of Jack Pierce and others.[90] Dicks's descriptions of the creatures in his novelization of the story tend to reinforce this impression: 'The face and hands were entirely covered with hair. The whole shape of the jaw had changed and the teeth were great yellow fangs. The eyes glared redly, bestial and savage.'[91] In a sense, ape-like or wolf-like is beside the point: the Primords are shape-shifting monsters, unlike anything seen previously in *Doctor Who*. Although Jon Pertwee is known to have been dismissive of them – 'these ridiculous werewolf things with great false teeth and fur-covered rubber gloves'[92] – they embody, as Graham Sleight suggests, a different and more complex approach to questions of human identity and technological ethics than had been conveyed by the mechanical hybrids of the first decade of the series.[93] A monstrous outcome of ecological meddling, the Primords are also a correlative of the fascist brutality that the Doctor encounters in the parallel version of Britain that features in the story, where they are literally harbingers of apocalypse.

Leslie Sconduto has written that 'werewolves, as a cultural product, have been and always will be a reflection of their time'.[94] This might seem self-evident but, as noted previously, the Gothic is easily oversimplified or misread. Its flirtation with modes of nostalgia is a defining aspect of its modernity and, regarded as a species of werewolf, the Primords are consistent with this, a brute atavism transposed to a *Doomwatch*-style science fiction environment. If, as technological determinists like Marshall McLuhan and Walter J. Ong have argued, the mythologies of an age are formed in response to the media that communicates them, it is possible to read something metafictional into the Primords: they embody not only familiar cultural narratives but also transformations in the format of *Doctor Who* itself. At a time of major change for the series, its audience and the wider culture, here are monsters that make both the possibilities and the anxieties manifest. Other creations from Pertwee's first season (a very 'grown-up' season) can also be read in this way – the plastic Autons, the prehistoric Silurians, the radioactive Martian ambassadors – but it is the Primords who most vividly contain the evolving moment.

This would seem an obscure point if it was restricted to the Primords, but forms of lycanthropic monstrosity seem to recur at points of strain or transformation in *Doctor Who*. Notably, the delayed appearance of werewolf creatures under Nathan-Turner – two in relatively quick succession, three if we count the Cheetah People – coincided with a period of decline and fall that would culminate in the indefinite suspension of the series. The Lukoser, the mutant product of genetic experimentation, featuring in the fourteen-episode 'Trial of a Time Lord' story arc which followed an ominous eighteen-month hiatus in the programme's production (a metafictional season if ever there was one), seems representative. Philip Martin, in the novelization of his own script, refers to the creature as 'the Wolfman' and describes it in unmistakable terms:

> Wild bloodshot eyes stared at them from out of a once-human face that had elongated into the muzzle of a wolf. On his bare torso large patches of fur grew at random. The slavering mouth opened, revealing long canine teeth, while from his throat came a rolling growl that made the hairs lift on Peri's neck. At the same time compassion made her somehow want to reach out to this hybrid creature, in chains and so obviously in torment.[95]

The pitiful but spirited and strangely noble creature, movingly performed on screen by Thomas Branch, reminds us of the association between horror and melancholy and looks compellingly like a metaphor of the series itself. The appearance of the exploited Mags two years later in 'The Greatest Show in the Galaxy' offers a return to werewolf mythology in conjunction with a similarly self-reflexive and anxiously ironic title. That Mags, unlike the Lukoser, survives the story, proposing to establish a new Psychic Circus (a new show on a new planet), seems to combine the newfound confidence of the show in the final two seasons of Sylvester McCoy's Doctor with a sense that it might somehow survive its own doom.

Just as the Primords, in their visual, physical and mythological presence, exhibit the progression from black-and-white to colour, so the werewolf of 'Tooth and Claw' reflects the evolving technological parameters of the day, being rendered in CGI but containing the essence of traditional lycanthropic folklore (see Figure 3.4). And just as the Primords incorporate the ecological concerns of 'Inferno', so the lycanthrope of the Torchwood Estate provides the basis for a degree of social satire at the expense of the Church (the belligerent monks

Figure 3.4 Queen Victoria (Pauline Collins) is menaced by the Lupine Wavelength Haemovariform in 'Tooth and Claw' (2006); ©BBC Worldwide.

of St Catherine's Glen) and the Royal Family ('So the royal family are werewolves?').

This was not, of course, Davies's first use of wolfish metaphors as a narrative vehicle for the new series. The Bad Wolf story arc of his debut season had been a more prolonged and less explicit manifestation of the wild dog allegory. First mentioned in the second episode of the revived series, 'The End of the World' ('This is the Bad Wolf scenario,' the Moxx of Balhoon tells the Face of Boe, enigmatically), the phrase recurs in various forms throughout the 2005 season, culminating in the revelation in 'The Parting of the Ways' that the Bad Wolf is actually Rose. Sent back to the safety of the Powell Estate in London in the twenty-first century by the Doctor, she is determined to return to support him in his battle, with Captain Jack, against the Daleks aboard the Game Station orbiting the Earth in the year 200000. Forcing the TARDIS console open, she stares into its heart, absorbing the lethal energies of the Time Vortex. Transmuted into an entity of god-like powers, a creature with acute consciousness of 'all that is, all that was, all that ever could be', and absolute power over life and death, she disperses the 'Bad Wolf' meme through time as a message to draw herself back to the Game Station as the Doctor's avenging angel: 'I am the Bad Wolf. I create myself.'

Rose as the Bad Wolf is a distinct and dangerous hybrid, a human merged with the uncontrollable forces of space and time. The inherent contradiction of this *sui generis* super-being, another version of the 'bootstrap paradox' (see the earlier discussion of 'Before the Flood'), has also been described by Hills as an effective reversal of the 'grandfather paradox'.[96] Rose does not destroy her own past, in other words; instead, she creates the future that will create a past that will create the future that will create a past … and so on. The causal loop encircling this story depends on an ontological uncertainty that is at least loosely analogous to the unsettled condition of lycanthropy. It also depends on the kind of narrative contrivance, *deus ex machina*, that some saw as unsatisfyingly prevalent under Davies's leadership, finding a more intricately developed counterpart in the shaggy-dog-story arcs of the Moffat era.[97] Hills has argued that this attraction to tales of temporal paradox in new *Who* is largely symbolic, representative of contemporary life. As well as being the matter of the particular mythology – a mythology 'about time', as Alec Charles notes, but also about 'timelessness' – it is a representation of the putatively postmodern condition of contemporary life.[98] This is true in terms of how *Doctor Who* is watched, and otherwise engaged with, in a culture of on-demand streaming services, transmedia proliferation, intensified nostalgia and encyclopaedic capacity. It also corresponds to the restlessness with which the mythology relates to its own past. Just as the modern werewolf wears its ancestry beneath the skin – Ovid's Lycaon lurks within the *Underworld* franchise (2003–present) as surely as it did within Henry MacRae's *The Werewolf* (1913) – so *Doctor Who* in the twenty-first century must always contain the rough, brilliant beast of its twentieth-century forerunner. It is not surprising, then, that the Doctor's werewolves might – in their many forms, and in a certain lunar light – present themselves as metaphors of the series itself.

Lucy Armitt, citing James B. Twitchell's privileging of the vampire over the werewolf, has noted the latter's tendency to 'fall into abeyance' while the former 'retains its currency'.[99] The werewolf, seen as unambiguous in its bestial monstrosity, lacks the uncanny elusiveness of the vampire, its more subtle questioning of cultural categories. Crucial to this reading is an assumption that the werewolf, because of its overt carnality, misses the erotic allure of the vampire, at least as it has been evident from Polidori's Lord Ruthven onwards. Many of the most successful werewolf tales subvert this pattern, notably Angela Carter's 'The

Company of Wolves' (1979) and John Landis's *An American Werewolf in London* (1982), but others seem to confirm it. After all, neither Henry Hull's stiff (in the non-priapic sense) Glendon in *Werewolf of London* nor Lon Chaney Jr's 'lumbering, affable' and 'repressed' Larry Talbot in *The Wolf Man* (1941) can be said to generate much sensual danger.[100]

Erotic allure and edginess, implied or explicit, have never been an issue for the lycanthropes of *Doctor Who*. There is nothing sexy about the Primords, the Anti-Man or even the Lupine Wavelength Haemovariform of *Tooth and Claw*. Not even Mags the Vulpanan is able to channel the libidinous energies of the Carterian werewolf, although it hardly requires a mind kinked by the prurient obsessions of tabloid journalism to read uncomfortable innuendo into her situation as the travelling companion of the old explorer Captain Cook:

> DOCTOR Do you often travel together?
> CAPTAIN Of late, yes. I found her on the planet Vulpana. Between you and me, old boy, she's rather an unusual little specimen.
> DOCTOR Of what?
> CAPTAIN Ah, that would be telling, old boy. What about yours?
> DOCTOR I never think of Ace as a specimen of anything.

The Captain is referring to Mags's condition as a werewolf, but the insinuation of sexual predation is clear.

It is intriguing to note that, where an overt eroticism was most likely to occur, during the span of the Virgin novels from 1991 to 1999, it never did. In the off-air years fans who had grown up with the series seized the opportunity to write out their fantasies of a more sophisticated, adult narrative. At a time of maximum unsettlement, with *Doctor Who* extinct as far as the wider world was concerned, the Virgin New Adventures and Virgin Missing Adventures introduced it to sex and drugs and rock 'n' roll. But there were no werewolves. When they did eventually reappear, it was within the generally less risqué context of BBC Books, although the darker, more adult tones of Big Finish meant that the werewolves of *Loups-Garoux*, at least, seemed to be stirred by libidinal energies. With the return of the series to television, such stirrings became sublimated: the kiss from the Doctor that saves Rose from her own raging godlike powers as the self-created Bad Wolf is clearly amatory, but also strangely innocent and conspicuously virtuous.

Little Rose Riding Hood, giving herself to the Big Bad Wolf in order to save her hero, is herself set free by the kiss that will kill him, or at least force him to regenerate.[101]

Suggestively, the most recent wolfish occurrence in TV *Doctor Who* alludes to the same fairy-tale sources but treats them rather differently. Frank Cottrell Boyce's 'In the Forest of the Night' (2014) is an eccentric and gentle tale about the vegetation of the Earth enveloping it overnight in order to protect it from solar flares. Lost in the sudden forests of London with a party of children from Coal Hill School and two of their teachers, Clara Oswald and her boyfriend Danny Pink, the Doctor is intrigued by the behaviour of the red-coated Maebh, a girl troubled by the recent disappearance of her older sister. At one point Maebh, the Doctor and Clara are chased by a small pack of wolves. In the event, the wolves are frightened by the arrival of an escaped tiger, a Blakean symbol that is itself mesmerized by Danny and driven away. Apart from perpetuating the myth of their threat to humans, the story is remarkable for featuring wolves rather than werewolves: not representations of unsettled hybridity, in other words, but agents of the natural world, set free from their cultural confinement by a vegetable love that seems almost supernatural. Maebh, whose medication for anxiety has been wearing off, is revealed to have a connection to 'the life that prevails', the spirit of the trees that appears as a busy cluster of lights in the air: 'We are here, here, always, since the beginning and until the end.'

The fleeting appearance of wolves in Cottrell Boyce's poetically understated parable of near-apocalypse says much about their wider meaning within the narratives of *Doctor Who*. 'Catastrophe is the metabolism of the universe,' the Doctor comments at one point. 'I can fight monsters. I can't fight physics.' The story has not proved popular with fans (it came last in the *Doctor Who Magazine* poll for 2014) and many have complained that it lacks a recognizable foe or threat, with no alien invasion, no monsters to fight. These memorably troubling words, however, expressing helplessness in the face of inexorable physical processes and imminent ecological disaster, contain a peril at least as potent as that signalled by 'Exterminate'.

Chapter 4
The hero and his worlds

World-building and the TARDIS: 'Home, the long way round'

Myths build worlds. That much is obvious. But myths are built *from* the world, too, not only from its anxieties and aspirations but also from its resources, expertise and imaginative improvisations. Perhaps this is obvious as well, although a theorist of world-building would be at pains to distinguish between the primary world of the audience and the secondary world of the mythology: in old money, the 'real world' and the 'fictional world'.[1] The fact remains that *Doctor Who*, as a TV series that spans over fifty years of transformation in the industry that produces it, is a unique case study in modern mythography. The revived series has evolved in parallel with new practices in transmedia storytelling, new models of consumption and participatory creation, and new critical understandings of world-building. At the same time, it retains strong taproots into the classic series that emerged into a pre-digital world of institutional aloofness, one-off broadcasts and a fan experience that was more local, more isolated and more obscure, even 'invisible'.[2]

In this section the intention is to explore aspects of the constructed universe of *Doctor Who*, both in terms of the mythological construction of a space within which stories can take place and in terms of the physical and digital realization of that space. There is insufficient room to carry out a thoroughgoing analysis of the world-building facet of the myth, nor is there scope to trace in detail its extension through transmedia channels. Some attention has been paid to this in the final section of Chapter 2, but the aim here is to focus specifically on the kinds of imagined location featured in *Doctor Who*'s text as it has unfolded. In part, the subject is the role of special effects (broadly understood) within the transportation of audiences to the worlds in which the Doctor's stories occur, both in-camera effects and those created post-production. The discussion will lead, at last, to a reflection on the qualitative myth of spectacle in the reception of *Doctor Who*. To what extent does 'the spirit of wobbliness' described by Brian Logan in his response to the announced return of the television series in 2003 still adhere to its cultural presence and reputation?[3]

Throughout these pages I have argued that *Doctor Who* is a distinctively reflexive mythology, one that (as Hills writes) 'circles back'[4] over itself even as it moves forward into new phases of production and personnel, new modes of storytelling. It is no coincidence, in this respect, that the TARDIS should be seen as its primary location, a metaphor for the text as a whole through its limitless capacity, its resilience, its kinetic flexibility, its conspicuous solidity that is nevertheless matched with a spectral intangibility. (These last qualities are combined in the title of Jodie Whittaker's second broadcast story, 'The Ghost Monument' (2018).) The TARDIS is the principal world built to support the *Doctor Who* mythos and it will provide the main focus of this section. However, it is worth making some general observations on the nature of world-building within the programme as a preface to this.

For Tolkien, the success of mythic world-building, or 'sub-creation' as he terms it, depends upon it being 'fully realized'.[5] The success of *Doctor Who*, though, has been dependent in many ways upon a refusal (or inability) to achieve such a state of final realization. Even as it forms a distinct accumulation of related texts, featuring the kinds of signature icon that Britton and Hills see as proxies for subcreated wholeness,[6] *Doctor Who* thrives on an awareness of its own incompleteness and relishes the inventive openness that this allows. The world being built is a world without edges, a world containing universes. Here *Doctor Who* has some kinship with classical mythologies which, however they might draw upon documented historical events, places and persons, are invariably situated outside any fixed or recognizable location in time or space. Beyond the TARDIS and various other recurrent locations, *Doctor Who* has essentially rebuilt its world with every story, although the urge to observe continuities has intensified over the years. Kim Newman notes how, in the early 1960s, 'each materialisation was also a reset',[7] but recurring non-Earth locations (Skaro, Gallifrey), characters (the UNIT family, the Master) and monsters, together with the emergence of a vocal fandom, led to an increasing pressure to establish finer details within the subcreation from the late 1970s onwards. Responses to this pressure were variable, but John Nathan-Turner took the task seriously (to a fault), seeing it as an opportunity to forge a more coherently branded programme. In the twenty-first-century context of new *Who*, creative and commercial pressures entail a more punctilious working through of the fictional details between stories and seasons. This has often been foregrounded through the use of intricate story arcs, both within and between seasons.

Story arcs are not a new invention, of course, and a self-contained experiment in extended episodic narrative can be found five stories into *Doctor Who*'s history. Terry Nation's 'The Keys of Marinus' (1964) has the imaginative ambition to construct a world of extreme cultural variety across which the TARDIS crew must quest. The physical task of this construction fell to Raymond Cusick and Daphne Dare, who were required, respectively, to furnish and dress discrete areas of the world across the six weeks of the story's broadcast. What is apparent in world-building terms is how diverse the planet of Marinus is, with each new location suggesting not simply another area of the planet but another planet altogether. As the Doctor and his companions strive to recover the scattered keys of the Conscience of Marinus, the powers of a supercomputer capable of maintaining global harmony in the heterogeneous contexts displayed on screen can only be wondered at, as can the creativity and resourcefulness of the production team within the confines of Lime Grove Studio D.

In a strange sense the Voord, the creatures whose attempts to seize control of the Conscience provide a frame for the quest narrative, can be seen as a shadowy, rubbery embodiment of the story itself, threatening to destroy the artificial harmony of Marinus just as the constantly shifting mise en scène threatens to disintegrate the world that Nation's script proposes. From this perspective, the scene during the first episode in which a member of the production crew can be seen on the other side of the pyramid wall as a Voord falls backwards through a revolving trapdoor becomes metaphorical. At the time of its initial transmission, no one was expecting that the story would ever be seen again. The incoherence of which it has often been accused and the production errors that can now be located, paused, captured and re-presented for discussion were entirely subordinate to the creation of a varied and entertaining one-off televisual experience. As an experiment in mythic creation, the significance of 'The Keys of Marinus' is indisputable, setting a formal precedent that would be refined and extended, with varying degrees of success, in stories such as 'The Chase' (1965) and 'The Daleks' Master Plan' (1965–6), and in the longer arcs of the UNIT years, the Peladon and Mara tales (two of each), the Key to Time season, the E-Space and Black Guardian trilogies, 'The Trial of a Time Lord' and the long narrative trajectories of Davies and Moffat. The arcing of a story is not the same as the building of a world, and most of the classic-series examples listed above are, like 'The Keys of Marinus', notable for their lack of a subcreated interconnectedness. The Peladon and Mara duologies are exceptions, and it might be argued that the E-Space trilogy is actually part of a more substantial arc marking the transition from Tom Baker to Peter Davison, a hexalogy running from 'Full Circle' (1980) to 'Castrovalva' (1982). By contrast, there is nothing to link the six stories of the Key to Time season (1978–9) beyond the quest narrative itself and the recurrent characters inhabiting it. Prominent among these characters is the TARDIS, the imaginative lodestone that binds together all other components of the developed *Doctor Who* world. It is notable that, even when it is *hors de combat*, as in the years of the Third Doctor's exile to Earth or for much of the Fourth Doctor's first season, the TARDIS remains a constant point of reference, something to be recovered, repaired or returned to.

Like the Doctor and the Daleks, the TARDIS is emblematic in that it has stayed the same whilst constantly changing (from subtle variations in the external blue to wholesale 'redecorations' of the interior). Apart from the nameless London bobby whose torch picks it out initially, it was – as Newman remarks[8] – the first 'character' to appear in *Doctor Who*, before Ian and Barbara, before Susan, and a good ten minutes before the Doctor himself. Indeed, the comparably evocative theme tune was still piping in the background when it made its initial appearance on screen. And it was the bright shock of entrance into the TARDIS that prompted the extraordinary conclusion to 'An Unearthly Child'. The mystery of the blue box framed the arrival of this modern myth within public consciousness and it has stayed there ever since. Not surprisingly, it offers a paradigm of location that is applicable to the worlds of *Doctor Who* in all their multiplicity.

The fixed and eccentric outward appearance of the TARDIS, the contrast in scale, materiality, aesthetic and functional expectation between this and the interior, is key to its iconographic power. Denoting a cultural object that was already entering its last decade at the time of *Doctor Who's* initial development and that is now known mostly through its association with that mythology, the permanent oddness of the TARDIS as a blue wooden box gives it tremendous connotative richness. It also, paradoxically, creates links between the secondary world of the mythology and the primary world of the audience. A child in thrall to the series can use a wardrobe, a garden shed or a public telephone kiosk (now also in decline) to take on the role of the Doctor, just as she can use a sink plunger and an egg whisk to become a Dalek. The potential for this kind of DIY play, immanent with a spirit of retro-futurist or steampunk nostalgia, is essential to both the enduringly intimate appeal and the boundless scope of *Doctor Who*. It is largely, of course, an accident of production constraints in the initial development of the series, where neither time nor budget allowed for the ambitions of metamorphic blending to be realized. The TARDIS's shape-shifting concealment function is mentioned in the second ever episode, 'The Cave of Skulls', named in 'The Time Meddler' (where reference is made to a 'camouflage unit') and attributed (via a phrase inherited from the Target novelizations) to the 'chameleon circuit' in 'Logopolis' (1981), at which point the Doctor finally attempts to repair it. The Sixth Doctor achieves a temporary fix of the chameleon circuit in 'Attack of the Cybermen', where it appears as an ornamental dresser and a pipe organ, but the idea of a permanently fluid external appearance is likely to remain just that.

The TARDIS exterior has remained a constant throughout the series, with only minor modifications, such as variations of blue (imperceptible for the first seven years of monochrome broadcast) and the return of the St John Ambulance logo (a feature of the original 1963 prop) for the 2010 series. These differences are rarely mentioned on screen, although Matt Smith's Doctor shows clear excitement in the refreshed look of the TARDIS as he walks towards it at the end of 'The Eleventh Hour'. In 'The Day of the Doctor', too, there is a witty recognition of difference in having three TARDISes side by side in the National Gallery as the Tenth, Eleventh and War Doctors (the latter played by John Hurt) prepare to go their separate ways, the latter recognizing his by its scarred appearance. By the time Jodie Whittaker's Doctor is reunited with the ship in her second story, 'The Ghost Monument' (2018), the St John's Ambulance logo has disappeared again. In general, though, there is an understanding that the outer shell of the TARDIS is in a fixed condition as part of the mythic furniture of the show. The interior is a different matter.

From 1963 until 1989 the interior architecture of the TARDIS was stable but not invariable. Indeed, within certain parameters, it changed constantly, the configuration of walls in the console room being especially prone to alteration. There were regular modifications in the number and position of walls featuring roundels, for example, as well as in the size and apparent depth of those distinctive features. Other walls, such as that containing the Fault Locator (used in 'The Edge of Destruction' and 'The Dalek Invasion of Earth'), were given greater or lesser prominence, depending on specific narrative requirements. For 'The Time Monster' (1972) the roundels were dramatically altered: larger, shinier, concave, with one of them acting as the ship's visual monitor ('Oh, just a spot of redecoration,' explains the Doctor). Previously, the location, size, shape and framing of the screen had been subject to frequent alteration, but never so overtly. A year later, in 'Planet of the Daleks', a set of fitted cupboards incorporating a medical unit, including a pull-out bed, were revealed to be part of the layout of the console room. The most radical change in the original run of *Doctor Who* was the wooden art deco secondary console room of Season Fourteen (1976–7), featuring glass-inlaid roundels, brass rails and very few moving parts. Interestingly, this anticipated the direction that the aesthetics of the TARDIS interior would take from the 1996 TV movie onwards – darker, less shiny and metallic, less obviously 'futuristic' and 'technological' – but it quickly disappeared, to be replaced by a variation on the original dazzling space. For the twentieth anniversary special of 1983, 'The Five Doctors', the TARDIS console was given an eye-catching makeover by designer Mike Kelt, the upgrade being referenced explicitly in the opening scene as the Fifth Doctor is seen polishing it admiringly. 'Finished?' asks Tegan. 'Yes. Looks rather splendid, doesn't it?'

Shifts in the interior design of the TARDIS have been dictated most often by the requirements of storyline or the exigencies of production, but they have nevertheless informed the mythic fabric of *Doctor Who*. From the earliest production an awareness of further rooms beyond the console room – beginning with a food machine area and an austere-looking communal bedroom in 'The Edge of Destruction' – has given the sense of an interior configuration that is extensive, possibly limitless. Although twenty-five per cent of the TARDIS is jettisoned in 'Castrovalva' to enable the ship to escape destruction in the hydrogen inrush of Event One, the notion that its dimensions are calculable and contained, or in any way stable, has become increasingly uncertain. In 'Journey to the Centre of the TARDIS' (2013), indeed, the Doctor asserts that 'this ship is infinite' and it has been shown in spin-off novels to be large enough to contain a city or an entire planet.[9] Since the mid-1970s, and especially during the Nathan-Turner era, considerable interior detail has been revealed. Individual bedrooms have been shown, as have walk-in wardrobes, a swimming pool, a library, an engine room, a sick bay, a workshop, the Cloister Room and oh-so-many corridors. Beyond its solitary on-screen appearance, the swimming pool has been referenced on several occasions, and there have also been mentions, across various media, of an art gallery, an observatory, a karaoke bar, a laundry room, a laboratory, a botanical house, several gardens, a rain forest, a cricket pitch, a garage and a zoo.

The conceptual brilliance of the TARDIS is that its simplicity generates its complexity. In its ostensible form, it is just a box, the most basic 3D geometric shape available. And yet, even before it is opened, entered and explored, this simple box suggests far more than the emergency phone kiosk that it denotes: it is a wardrobe or cupboard, a shed, a magician's cabinet, a coffin even. (In 'Warriors' Gate', Lane muses on the TARDIS being 'a coffin for a very large man', a grimly humorous foreshadowing of the Fourth Doctor's impending downfall at the end of the 1980–1 season.) Most of all, it is a miniature house, with windows and a door, and a light in place of a chimney. In this aspect, taking into account its ontological and mythic disruptions of scale, materiality and place, it recalls Gaston Bachelard's reflections on the home:

> This house, as I see it, is a sort of airy structure that moves about on the breath of time. It really is open to the wind of another time. It seems as though it could greet us every day of our lives in order to give us confidence in life.[10]

The TARDIS is at once the most homely component of the *Doctor Who* myth and the most fantastical. It *is* the Doctor's home, his supremely mobile abode, as close as he gets to a domestic environment or dwelling. This latter term is tinged, perhaps tainted, by association with Martin Heidegger and his notion of *Dasein*, formulated initially in *Being and Time* (1927). A permanent link to and reminder of Gallifrey, the TARDIS is also an emblem of the Doctor's revolt against the kind of romantic rootedness that has become entangled in appraisals of Heidegger's work with an awareness of his Nazi Party membership. As Tom Paulin argues, Heidegger's idea of home depends on an atavistic valorization of traditional dwellings, peasant cottages built from stone and wood, and a rejection of newer modes of residence: 'Technology designs buildings, not dwellings.'[11] Although this relies on a rather narrow definition of 'technology', it does open up an intriguing perspective on the TARDIS. This is especially apparent when it is recalled that the 'being-in-the-world' of *Dasein* (easily confined to the nostalgia described by Paulin) is predicated on an active, investigative, exploratory sense of futurity, the 'potentiality-of-being' or 'being-ahead-of-oneself'. It is 'grounded in having-been' but at the same time, like the best tales of time travel, '*its primary meaning is the future*' (emphasis in the original).[12]

From the outset the Doctor's ship has been characterized as impossibly advanced technology, designs from the classic series presenting it as an aggregation of SF conventions: clean lines and bright surfaces, levers, switches, buttons, flashing lights, hums and buzzes, bleeps and whirs. Nonetheless, the sense of something beyond the straightforwardly technological, something living and sentient, has been instilled from as early as the third story, 'The Edge of Destruction', reaching its apotheosis in 2011's 'The Doctor's Wife', in which our hero's long-standing appellation of his ship as 'she' is literalized in the body of a young woman. Frequent interior metamorphoses suggest that the TARDIS is a thing grown rather than made, most explicitly in the coral console room of the Ninth and Tenth Doctors. At the same time, the archaism of some elements of its appearance – the Cloister Room, for instance – stresses that it is a thing of the past as much as the future. The Time Lords are, in Earth terms, beings from the ancient past but also from the far-flung future: with the ability to transcend time, they are, literally, timeless, and this is manifested in their technology.

This might smack of the folksy, nostalgic rootedness of most right-wing (and much left-wing) philosophy, the pull away from history into trans-historical fantasizing that typifies many authoritarian political systems. The apparent mismatch between the barn-like structures of outer Gallifrey shown in 'The Day of the Doctor' (2013), 'Listen' (2014) and 'Hell Bent' (2015), and the dome-covered towering metropolis of the Capitol, exhibits a tension between rustic simplicity and extreme technological sophistication in the culture of the Doctor's home planet. More distinctly, it maps the territory between the Time Lords and the Outsiders (notably the Shobogans) depicted in 'The Invasion of Time' (1978). It therefore gives a larger context for the quirks of the TARDIS as a constructed world for the hero's journey. If, as implied, the barn shown in the three Moffat stories mentioned above is actually the *same* building, and is the Doctor's childhood home, then this would identify it – by association, at least – with Lungbarrow, the family dwelling that provides the setting for Marc Platt's Virgin New Adventures novel of the same name (1997).

In that tale, which supplies narrative links to the TV movie, it is indicated both how intricately Time Lord technology is interwoven with biological processes and how intimately these are reflected in the Doctor's relationship with his TARDIS. Lungbarrow is shown to be an organic structure as much as a built one and it is revealed that Time Lords (as a result of sterility) are born from Looms on which they are woven as full-grown adults. Although there is (inevitable) disputation about the canonical status of *Lungbarrow*, and there are (inevitably) many inconsistencies between the backstory it provides for the Doctor and the details that have been revealed on screen over the years, it casts interesting shadows across the mythos as it has developed on television. Whether or not it is possible to reconcile the creation myth of the Looms with the Third Doctor's remembrances of himself as 'a little boy' ('The Time Monster') or the inclusion in the post-2005 series of a woman who seems to be the Doctor's mother ('The End of Time') and of scenes that are indicative of an infancy for Gallifreyans (his cot in 'A Good Man Goes to War', the barn-like retreat in 'Day of the Doctor', 'Listen' and 'Hell Bent', the Master's childhood confrontation with the Untempered Schism in 'The Sound of Drums' and 'The End of Time'), *Lungbarrow* is a profoundly resonant text. Towards its conclusion the TARDIS transforms itself into the dark and cavernous structure that is introduced in the TV movie and, to an extent, inherited by new *Who*:

Wood and stone rose high in panels and buttresses, where once there had been the clean functionality of a white honeycomb.

'Home,' murmured the Doctor.

And it *was* like the Doctor's home. As if his ship understood the loss of the House [Lungbarrow] and had compensated to fill the emptiness. Shadowy corridors, alcoves and stairways, a secret at every turn. Like being in the Doctor's head. Like his life, for that matter, the details of which were strewn like flotsam across the floor.[13]

The Doctor in the TARDIS. And, it would seem, the TARDIS in the Doctor. The narrative function of the stolen or borrowed Type 40 is explicit.

The pastoral and monastic disposition of Gallifreyan society, its air of cloisters, hierarchies, ancient lore and half-remembered wisdom, its sense of the immense gravity of history but tendency to evade the pressures of the present, is given lethal expression in Rassilon's outburst to the War Council in the second part of 'The End of Time': 'I will not die! Do you hear me? A billion years of Time Lord history riding on our backs. I will not let this perish. I will not!' Combined with a paradigm of culture merged with nature, the built indistinguishable from the grown, science indistinguishable from magic, this constitutes a state of advanced decadence in which morality degenerates into instinct and technological progress into a condition of stagnation. Time Lord civilization begins to resemble Mervyn Peake's Gormenghast, J. K. Rowling's Ministry of Magic or Phillip Pullman's Magisterium.

There is something nastily brutish and long about Time Lord life as it has been depicted since the days of quietly dull autocracy in appearances spanning 'The War Games' (1969) to 'The Trial of a Time Lord' (1986). For all that Mark Gatiss has commented on the Doctor's people becoming 'too domesticated' through repeated appearances during the late 1970s and 1980s, analogous to 'a bunch of MPs',[14] the mythic expansion and complication of them through transmedia storytelling since the 1990s has brought to the foreground traits that were inherent in earlier portrayals. The Time Lords, even at their most bureaucratic (in 'The Five Doctors', for instance), are a troublingly despotic and inflexible group, as totalitarian in their own way as the Daleks. One of the reasons that Outsiders, such as the Shobogans, reject the life of the Capitol is boredom, but their motivation also seems to be political. Time Lords are shown to be isolationist, pacifist and rational, but not consistently, and it is noticeable how quickly they resort to dubious judicial processes, acts of banishment and capital punishment. Similarly, for a great power keeping itself to itself, they are remarkably prone to interference in the affairs of others. Their history from the Dark Times to the Last Great Time War is thick with abuses of power and violent excesses. To a degree, this superficially benign but tedious society of *Übermenschen* dramatizes Paulin's assertion of 'how easily Romantic ideas of authenticity, rootedness, traditional crafts, folklore, take on the stink of power politics and genocide'.[15] This connection should not be followed too comfortably or too far: *Doctor Who* is fiction and Paulin's assessment of Heideggerian pastoral is concerned with its connections to real historical atrocities. Even so, its focus on ideas of home, dwelling and belonging can be suggestive in relation to the mythic meaning of the Doctor's adventures, especially as these can be read through the home-from-home of the TARDIS.

During the early weeks of *Doctor Who* in 1963–4, much work was done to test the potential for the new drama to build multifarious worlds for its emergent audience. Directly after the secondary school, the junkyard, the TARDIS and primeval Earth came the 'dead planet', Skaro, so often revisited in the decades that followed, with Cusick's sets and model work being recreated in fine detail for the double bill that opened the 2015 season, 'The Magician's Apprentice' / 'The Witch's Familiar'. Rebuilding the first Dalek city, inside and out, was a remarkable act of homage reflected diegetically through the manifest *Daseinwillen* ('will-to-being') of Davros's children, linked troublingly to the Doctor: 'The Daleks remade it. Like you, they have a strong concept of home.' Davros means Gallifrey, but on a more general basis the Doctor's sense of home is represented most accurately by the location that contained the whole of the two-part story that followed 1963's introduction to the Dalek home-world. 'The Edge of Destruction' might have been an inexpensive makeweight, but in devoting almost an hour of paranoid and at times chaotic screen time to the Doctor's most intimate world, the TARDIS, it contributed greatly to the subcreation. If, as was threatened, *Doctor Who* had been discontinued after thirteen episodes, it would have formed a bookend to complement the series' opening episode, in which the TARDIS also plays a focal role. In the event, it concluded an extended introductory arc for the programme and it is therefore appropriate that it should have been issued in a DVD box set entitled *The Beginning* with the preceding two stories in 2006. This unofficial trilogy established from the outset that the Doctor's 'strong concept of home' was fundamentally itinerant, but not in an imperial or expansionist way. The Daleks, by contrast, in their first story, were shown to be essentially parochial: dangerously bellicose, yes, with genocidal designs on their Thal counterparts, but with no interest in (or, indeed, ability to) travel beyond their city. At this point they seemed to exhibit a belief in line with that of Heidegger that '*the basic character* of Being' is 'dwelling' (emphasis in the original).[16]

Heidegger, Paulin points out, only left his native Germany twice (and briefly), being buried in a graveyard that he passed as a schoolboy. His biography, in this respect, enacts the rootedness of his philosophy and is arguably the dense shadow of a lethal right-wing expansionism that he would appear to endorse. His adoration of vernacular folk architecture, seen as mythically permanent, is contiguous with this. The Doctor, by contrast, rejects roots and the false assurance of rootedness: he steals a TARDIS and leaves. The TARDIS becomes his home. Shed-like, simple-looking, no more (on the outside) than a blue wooden box, it looks superficially akin to one of the grounded dwellings beloved of Heidegger, but in its functions, its dimensions and its materiality, it is so much more. The TARDIS defies time, space and matter; it does not attempt to 'settle' them or turn them into monuments. In its apparently flimsy substance it resembles the wasps' nest in Elizabeth Bishop's poem 'Jerónimo's House', which Paulin describes as 'an ironic fairy palace made of perishable clapboards'.[17] Where the cottages of Heidegger are ephemeral edifices mythologized as eternal dwellings, the TARDIS – which looks so fragile – has the ability to survive almost anything. Fading in and out of being, a dwelling that does not dwell, it approximates the 'makeshift, temporary' buildings that Paulin finds venerated in Bishop's poetry of itinerancy and discovery.

Paulin declares 'Jerónimo's House' to be 'beautifully flimsy and deracinated and benign', comparing its style to 'the airiness of flowing script on airmail paper or voices singing on the airwaves'.[18] The ethereality of this, the insubstantial lightness, is not unlike the supposed quality of the 'rackety old TARDIS'[19] as it travels in a state of anomalous transit, between here and there, now and then, presence and absence, like the ghosts in the previous chapter. Recalling the magic carpets of Eliade and Suvin, this also recalls the awkward silences that exist between myth and science. These are the kinds of silence that mythographers debate (from E. B. Tylor to Robert Horton), that fictions relish and that extreme politics can appropriate. It is no coincidence that tyrants have often been drawn to distorted versions of the occult (Hitler, Himmler) or the ecclesiastical (Mussolini, Franco). In the third Virgin novel, Terrance Dicks's *Timewyrm: Exodus*, the Führer's documented fascination with occultism is dramatized through his mental occupation by the Timewyrm.[20] Significantly, the apocalyptic Timewyrm is a product of the Doctor's forced error in allowing a conjunction of the TARDIS's telepathic circuits with the mind of the alien criminal Qataka in the guise of the Mesopotamian goddess Ishtar. It is also via the TARDIS – specifically, the jettisoned secondary console room – that she is able to escape from the Vortex and emerge in 1930s Germany.

The TARDIS embodies *Doctor Who*'s erosion of the line between technology and magic, between science fiction and fantasy. In 'Battlefield' (1989), a Seventh Doctor story that attempts to short-circuit the distance between myth, magic and science, a discussion of the spaceship beneath the lake seems to reflect on the TARDIS and, by extension, on the culture of the Time Lords:

DOCTOR It wasn't built, it was grown.

ACE Who grows spaceships?

DOCTOR Very advanced bioengineers.

ACE Ask a stupid question. Well, if they're grown, how do they fly?

DOCTOR Magic.

ACE Oh, be feasible, Professor.

DOCTOR What is Clarke's Law?

ACE Any advanced form of technology is indistinguishable from magic.

DOCTOR Well, the reverse is true.

Here the Doctor and Ace engage in what is tantamount to Socratic dialogue, examining the traditional opposition of myth-magic-superstition and science-technology-rationality. As a 'world' constructed around a narrative distrust of this opposition, it would be hard to improve on the TARDIS. What is notable is that the more it is explored on television, the more problematic the representation of this world becomes, its sheer openness requiring that it remain unrealizable. Novels and audio plays can allow for the uncertainty and expansiveness necessary to communicate this. On screen, where the world is brought into view, the trick is harder to pull off. This is where the fantasy of *Doctor Who* begins, at times, to exceed itself, or at least to test the capacities of its originating medium.

While being pursued deep into the TARDIS by Sontarans in the final part of 'The Invasion of Time', the Doctor's old tutor Borusa rebukes him for the interior condition of his space-time vehicle: 'I wish you'd stabilize your pedestrian infrastructure, President!' Earlier in the episode, on first venturing into the inner corridors of the ship, Rodan suggests that it needs 'a lick of paint' to 'clean it up a bit': 'You know, redecoration.' Apart from a handful of scenes in rooms and corridors adjacent to the console room, this represents the first exploration of the TARDIS's internal architecture and certainly the first substantive expedition into its structure. A combination of BBC industrial action and budget limitations meant that filming of the scenes in the TARDIS interior took place not in studio sets, as planned, but on location at the British Oxygen building in Hammersmith and St Anne's Hospital in Redhill. As a result, viewers are shown concrete floors, brick walls, wheelchair ramps and a swimming pool rather than the gleaming white, roundel-studded corridors glimpsed in 'The Masque of Mandragora' (1976) at the start of the previous season. It is the inside of the TARDIS, but not as anyone expects it to be. And this, perhaps, is entirely appropriate: if the Doctor's ship is the floating signifier par excellence, then the drab solidity of corporate brickwork is as potent a representation as any other.

Inevitably, as a container for the ultimate fantastical space, the TARDIS is always likely to frustrate, if not disappoint. Some fans love Part Six of 'The Invasion of Time' because it shows them what they have never seen before; others hate it because it shows them what they have never wanted to see – or at least, *not like that*. The first few years of the Nathan-Turner era represent the most consistent period for showing the interior of the TARDIS, with a coherence (lots of roundels) that is the polar opposite of what is seen in the chase with Sontarans. For some, though, it is just too coherent, too clean and bright and conventional, to be a persuasive visualization of what a ship, a *world*, like the TARDIS must look like. In the final years of the classic series, less was seen of what lay beyond the console room and, in the McCoy years, the console room itself became, as it had during the Earth exile of the Third Doctor, a greatly diminished presence.

Since 2005, the visual emphasis has been on the console room, with many dialogue references to other areas of the ship but few actual visits. When there have been exceptions to this, tours have tended to be confined to generic metal corridors. One story, however, sets out with the specific and ambitious remit to reveal more of the TARDIS and, like 'The Invasion of Time', it struggles to meet expectations. 'Journey to the Centre of the TARDIS' was written by Stephen Thompson as a direct challenge from Steven Moffat, who nurses an ongoing disappointment about the chase scenes in 'The Invasion of Time'. In some ways the episode delivers well on its promise, with Michael Pickwoad's designs building convincingly from the renovated console room introduced in 'The Snowmen'. There are impressive set pieces in the TARDIS library (actually the library of Cardiff Castle, with some CGI embroidery) and at the Eye of Harmony (here an element *within* the TARDIS, as it was in the TV movie, rather than – or as well as – a power source housed on Gallifrey, as in 'The Deadly Assassin'). There is also a powerful scene at the edge of a precipice, with Clara and the Doctor being chased towards the abyss by scorched and twisted zombies that are future versions of themselves. Filmed at Argoed Isha Quarry, Llansannor, the Vale of Glamorgan, this outside-inside location turns out to be the ship's attempt to 'snarl' them away from the Engine Room. And then there is the Engine Room itself, a blazing white tableau of suspended debris, an explosion held in stasis, reminiscent of Cornelia Parker's installation *Cold Dark Matter: An Exploded View* (1991) and Robert Seidel's abstract computer animation *Grau* (2004). This is *Doctor Who* as modern art and it is, like the best modern art, beautifully unsettling. But is it enough?

Commentators on 'Journey to the Centre of the TARDIS' have been polarized in their responses to the world depicted: 'All we get is corridors that look like they're right outta every other science fiction spaceship,' complains one online reviewer; 'the production team seem to have squirreled away a sizeable chunk of the budget to do the ship proud,' writes another.[21] In the pages of *Doctor Who Magazine*, meanwhile, Graham Kibble-White lets slip the Freudian desire that haunts all fandoms, the desire to return to the mythic womb: 'What I'm trying to say is, I miss the roundels.'[22] This is a nostalgia that has been communicated to the Doctor himself, as shown in 'The Day of the Doctor' ('Hey, look! The round things!') and 'Deep Breath' ('I think there should be more round things on the walls'). A number of 'guest appearances' for classic console rooms from the fiftieth anniversary onwards – beginning with the recreated original set for Mark Gatiss's *An Adventure in Space and Time* (2013) and culminating in the departure of Clara and Ashildr in an 'all-white' set of 'new wheels' in 'Hell Bent' – have confirmed the potency of this particular gestalt fanwank.

If 'Journey to the Centre of the TARDIS' indicates one thing, it is that *Doctor Who*, on screen at least, is most likely to divide opinion when it pushes hardest to realize the conceptual extremes of its format. Quite simply, the world contained in the TARDIS is impossible to represent, even with the subtleties of modern material techniques and the facilities of digital post-production. How can an infinite environment be *shown*, and in a way that will satisfy the infinite expectations of an audience? This extreme challenge might suggest why other attempts to conjure impossible worlds and things have often met with subdued or negative reactions. Bill Strutton's 'The Web Planet' (1965) and Neil Cross's 'The Rings of Akhaten' (2013) come to mind here, from opposite ends of the series' history. Then there is Gallifrey, the home-world of god-like beings who too easily lapse into caricatures of fussy, bickering civil servants and whose citadel as presented during the 1980s has been described as looking like 'a sort of conference centre in space'.[23]

The challenge of realizing environmental otherness is thrown into relief by the fabled reliance on quarries in classic *Doctor Who*. The putative 'BBC sandpit' became an easy target for jokes about the show during these years and beyond, reaching an affectionate peak in Gatiss's 'The Web of Caves' sketches for BBC2's *Doctor Who Night* in 1999. At the height of Tom Baker's success as the Doctor, the production team deployed the joke self-reflexively, using a modern British quarry *as* a modern British quarry for the opening action of 1976's 'The Hand of Fear' (in this case, Slickstones Quarry in Gloucestershire). In fact, as an approach to building on-screen worlds, the use of quarries was both an effective way of signifying the 'cognitive estrangement' or 'ontological rupture' described by Darko Suvin and Katherine Fowkes in relation to science fiction and fantasy, respectively, and a signature strategy for establishing a mythic landscape.[24] It is a landscape that now epitomizes the comparably mythic territory of heritage, as seen in books by Nick

Griffiths and Richard Bignell, and on websites such as *Doctor Who: The Locations Guide*.[25]

Like those other stalwarts of classic *Who* – power stations, training camps and industrial complexes – quarries are parts of the quotidian landscape that tend to be either out-of-bounds danger areas or abandoned sites of damage and neglect. As embodiments of preternatural events they are especially powerful when presented in conjunction with other, more approachable everyday settings: so, in 'Survival', the contrast of Warmwell Quarry, Dorset, as the dying world of the Cheetah People, and the suburban streets of Ace's Perivale is stark. Not surprisingly, such settings have featured in new *Who*, as well as in *Torchwood*, *The Sarah Jane Adventures* and *Class*. Veynor Quarry, Merthyr Tydfil, for instance, hosted the climactic struggle between the Doctor and the Master in 'The Last of the Time Lords', echoing the famous contest from 'Survival' that was shot in the Dorset quarry.

Location filming in *Doctor Who* has never been restricted to quarries and similar 'wastelands'. Castles, churches, stately homes, schools and hospitals have been similarly important, sites that are neither off-limits nor the industrial-geological equivalent of scar-tissue but that are otherwise thick with connotations of liminal experience (childhood, illness, death) or of competing social and national histories (class, territory). The architectural iconography of the British landscape has been used extensively in the series since the first brief location scenes appeared in 'The Reign of Terror' (1964),[26] with historical buildings often forming a point of contrast with elements of the fantastical. Thus, in 'The Time Warrior' (1973–4), Peckforton Castle, Cheshire, is a mock-medieval castle (built 1844–50) acting as a medieval castle – actually, as *two* medieval castles – while forming a semiotic counterpoint to the medievalist futurism of the 'star warrior' Linx and his ship, the Gallifreyan wizard the Doctor and his magical cabinet, and the twentieth-century idiom of Sarah Jane Smith, UNIT and the 'top secret' Research Centre. More recently, the halls, passages and staircases of the castles of Cardiff and Caerphilly have supplemented studio sets to create the Otranto-ish labyrinth of 'Heaven Sent' (2015), a sinister clockwork stronghold that is the Doctor's own private hell.[27]

In its use of locations, *Doctor Who* has excelled in the often surrealistic collision of visual, material and topographical registers. The result is an atmosphere of custom unsettled and received views kinked into the comic, the uncomfortable, or both. Again, the TARDIS is the exemplar here, both in concept and design. It has acted as the threshold to visions and revisions ever since it transported two teachers from the contemporary environment of Coal Hill School and I. M. Foreman's scrapyard to the prehistoric landscape of the Tribe of Gum. Indeed, playing with perspectives is pretty much the TARDIS's *modus operandi*, of a piece with the figural emphasis on dimensionality that is its chief defining characteristic: bigger on the inside (or, in the lovely comic inversion from 'The Snowmen' (2012), 'smaller on the outside').

Conceptually, the TARDIS subverts the physical laws that define our everyday lives and taps into many of the ideas from post-Einsteinian physics that challenge this definition most radically. Because of this, some of the most remarkable stories to which it provides access are not those that feature a trip to exotic locations but those that force a shift in viewpoint on more mundane situations. It is significant that the story originally slated to open the series in 1963 was C. E. Webber's 'The Giants', a tale about the TARDIS and its crew becoming miniaturized. Although this particular adventure never transpired, there was an obsession to see its themes developed, with at least three different authors working on it at various points while it evolved into the three-part opener for the second season, 'Planet of Giants' (1964), written by Louis Marks. Drawing on Universal's 1957 film *The Incredible Shrinking Man* (dir. Jack Arnold), this story is generally reckoned to be rather dull, even reduced from its original four episodes. The dullness is due, largely, to the flat supporting characters, who – plodding through a potentially intriguing plot about industrial skullduggery and environmental threat – at no point interact with, or even become aware of, the shrunken TARDIS crew. In itself, this represents a bold experiment, the perspective of the protagonists being formalized in their separation from the world in which they find themselves, reduced, lost and voiceless in a landscape that threatens, literally, to overwhelm them. Here, due to Cusick's often astonishing set designs and some dexterous direction from Mervyn Pinfield, the commonplace territory of a suburban house and garden is shifted into the realms of the uncanny. This is not an alien landscape, it is not Skaro, Marinus or Vortis, but it is an *alienating* one. Watching 'Planet of Giants' is oddly Brechtian in the sense that attention is drawn almost completely away from the (minimal) plot to the mechanics of representation: the giant matchbox, the monster ant, worm and fly, the vast sink and plughole, the huge projected face of a cat with the regular cast dwarfed before it. The story is no *Gulliver's Travels* (1726), but the Brobdingnagian attitude that it shares with the second book of Swift's great novel does convey a spirit of absurdity that is tinged, at least, with the comic unease of a Kafka or a Beckett.

Howe and Walker are perplexed by the apparent determination of the initial *Doctor Who* production team to develop a story based around miniaturization, but such a scenario has a potential that has been exploited on a number of occasions in the show's on-screen history.[28] The adoption of Lilliputian scale is not without its practical hazards (examples in 'The Invisible Enemy' (1977) and 'The Armageddon Factor' (1979) have often been ridiculed), but as an approach to world-building it can effect a powerful inversion of the focused attention described by Lévi-Strauss in his meditation on the lace collar in François Clouet's 'Elisabeth of Austria' (1571).[29] In Tom Baker's swansong, 'Logopolis' (1981), it is used as a thematic intensifier, foreshadowing universal collapse as the Doctor and his TARDIS are (in the Master's words) 'cut down to size' at the end of the second episode. Elsewhere, a shift of the fantasy focus from the expansive to the claustrophobic has been at the core of a number of *Doctor Who*'s most powerfully original tales. These include 'Carnival of Monsters' (1973), in which the Doctor and Jo (apparently arriving on the SS *Bernice* in the Indian Ocean in the 1920s) discover that they are trapped in a Miniscope belonging to the galactic street entertainer Vorg, specimens in a mini-beast collection that also features Drashigs, Ogrons and Cybermen. More recently, in 'Into the Dalek' (2014), the Doctor and Clara are miniaturized as part of a military mission to repair a damaged Dalek from the inside. In both cases, it is possible to see the stories as metafictional, the Doctor exploring the interior of his own mythology. It is significant, in this respect, that the castle of 'Heaven Sent' should be revealed to be part of the bigger-on-the-inside mechanism of the Doctor's Confession Dial.

'Heaven Sent' transcends expected dimensions in several ways, not least in fitting its mythical quart into a narrative pint pot. A story with, in essence, only one location and two characters (only one of whom speaks), it succeeds nevertheless in achieving the feel of an epic. Its enclosed, oppressive setting suggests a corollary to the ways in which tropes of miniaturization have been employed in *Doctor Who* – namely that, unlike more intrinsically 'grand' science fiction or fantasy narratives, it works well, perhaps best, within confined and claustrophobic story environments. 'Horror of Fang Rock' (1977) and 'Midnight' (2008) are examples of this, the first set on a lighthouse, the second on a leisure shuttle. Budget is a factor here but mainly, as Moffat has reflected, to the extent that it encourages invention out of necessity:

> We're always trying to show audiences something they haven't seen elsewhere. If we do a dogfight in space, it's not going to look as good as *Star Wars – so don't do dogfights in space* … We don't look smaller than anything else, because no-one else is doing precisely what we do.[30] (Emphasis in the original)

The kind of 'brand-new visuals' that Moffat claims here as a unique selling point for *Doctor Who* are in startling evidence in 'Flatline' (2014), where writer Jamie Mathieson takes an innovative approach to the theme of miniaturization. Landing on the outskirts of Bristol, the Doctor realizes that the TARDIS is shrinking on the outside, while retaining its vast inner dimensions. Opting to stay trapped in the console room while Clara investigates the local area, eventually having a TARDIS that she can carry around in her handbag, the Doctor is able to monitor her discovery of a new dimensional instability. Habituated to the flexibility of scale and to the relativity of time and space, he is bewildered to discover that the three-dimensional universe is being invaded by creatures from a universe that has only two. 'I mean this is just embarrassing,' he says at one point. 'I'm from the race that built the TARDIS. Dimensions are kind of our thing. So why can't I understand this?' Fascinated and horrified by this challenge to his knowledge, the Doctor is ultimately frustrated to discover that the creatures are intent on being 'monsters' and, naming them the Boneless, he proceeds to send them back to their own dimension. There is clear reluctance in this, a sadness that the paradigm shift he is undergoing cannot be accompanied by a shift in his role. In part, the Boneless represent a challenge to the aesthetic of 3D realism that dominates contemporary media. At the same time, they reinforce – against the Doctor's evident aspirations – a particular way of telling stories. He finds that he is condemned to remain what he has always found himself to be: 'The man that stops the monsters.' This exquisitely disturbing tale, ostensibly 'Doctor-lite', reveals a tremendous amount about the affordances and constraints of his heroic character, partly through the way that Clara fulfils its mythic function. A prickly exchange at the end of the story exposes the Doctor's own views on this and refuses a two-dimensional conception of the hero:

> CLARA Come on, why can't you say it? I was the Doctor and I was good.
> DOCTOR You were an exceptional Doctor, Clara.
> CLARA Thank you.
> DOCTOR Goodness had nothing to do with it.

The conclusion of a novel piece of world-building, this takes us neatly to a point where we can begin, at last, to consider what kind of hero the Doctor is.

The Doctor as hero: A good man, an idiot, the destroyer of worlds

In a 1983 essay John Fiske argues that the form of heroism represented by the Doctor can best be 'defined according to … a post-romantic, individualistic, capitalist set of criteria'.[31] Recognizing that the character is 'essentially a healer, particularly of sick societies', Fiske associates him with an outlook that is liberal-humanist in temperament but fundamentally conservative in impact. Leaving aside the question of what it means to be a humanist when you are not human (or, perhaps, when you are only *half* human, depending on questions of canon), Fiske is surely right to argue that the Doctor's political and ethical identity, for all the variability of its production contexts, has been shaped from the outset by the dominant ideology of the culture that created it.[32]

Good, solid, decent: embodying the values of the BBC (here seen as implicitly and stably Reithian), the Doctor champions 'good' against 'evil', 'right' against 'wrong', in a universe that is, superficially at least, unambiguous in its morality. The most troubling aspect of this for Fiske, who bases his reading on a single story, David Fisher's 'The Creature from the Pit' (1979), is that it leads the Doctor into an unquestioning collusion with free trade economics, 'naturalised' as not only 'the obviously right system' but 'the only system possible'. As a piece of popular art, *Doctor Who* is trapped in a reactionary position, snagged in the wheels of mythic process *à la* Barthes: 'An art form which is radically opposed to dominant social discourses would not be popular, but would appeal largely to the converted ... It would lose the mass appeal necessary for effective social change.'[33] In other words, the Doctor cannot help being a hero fit for the age of late capitalism.

Fiske's analysis is neatly done, making its case via a steady extrapolation from an ever-so-close reading of the chosen object. It is reasonable in its tone, even-handed in its approach and very much of its time. It is also, for these reasons, extremely limited as a reading of a text as complex and extensive as *Doctor Who* (even as it was in 1983, before decline and fall, Virgin books, the TV movie, Big Finish, the RTD regeneration and Jodie Whittaker). The problem is that it represents only one way of evaluating the mythology, a perfectly serviceable and valid way, but one that is only ever going to yield one result: that the Doctor is a white, eccentric patriarch travelling in a universe constructed from British (often *English*) preoccupations and prejudices, in thrall to a more or less submerged imperial narrative, troubled by nostalgia, disrespectful of authority and any perceived Establishment, but ultimately compliant and reactionary. This is the character as he emerges from between the lines of Alec Charles's essay on *Doctor Who*'s 'ideology of anachronism'.[34] It is the character that can be discerned through Tulloch's exploration of national politics as represented in (again, a single story) 'The Monster of Peladon'.[35] It is the character that seems to niggle Chapman at various points in his history of the TV series, and that carries the burden of prolonged frustration in Lorna Jowett's forceful questioning of *Doctor Who*'s 'shit'.[36]

Britton, clarifying his preference for an ethics over a politics of *Doctor Who*, makes a fair observation about the predominantly 'leftist stance' of those cultural analyses that purport to adopt a political approach to popular artefacts. He notes a tendency to audit texts according to predetermined criteria of 'political correctness'. This checklist approach is not, in itself, a problem for the current study (in terms of the alleged leftist stance, I am guilty as charged), but it is problematic in terms of the predictability of its outcomes. As Britton writes, 'If the moralizing-by-another-name of political analysis is the sole basis for evaluation, then it is virtually a foregone conclusion that the *Doctor Who* texts will be found wanting, or worse.'[37]

Picking out the surface defects of the mythology – 'cultural imperialism, endorsement of violence (however ostensibly reluctant), sexism and heteronormativity, and a white patriarchal bias' – Britton reflects that any left-leaning, politically calibrated cultural analysis will inevitably prove 'terminally damning', and not only to *Doctor Who* but to the vast majority of other popular texts. He is right, surely, to suggest that such a critical enterprise is likely to prove both miserable and dull.[38] The aim here, then, is to avoid discursive redundancy and statements of the obvious and to propose, instead, a more nuanced reading. Far from intending to dodge the political trickiness of *Doctor Who*, the hope is to engage with it in a way that heeds Ricoeur's recommendation of liberating rather than destructive acts of interpretation. The ideological and the utopian exist, he argues, in a condition of permanent mutual challenge, the former's 'function of social integration' acting as a vehicle for the latter's 'function of social subversion'. Through a recognition of this dynamic, the mythological can be opened out to the 'horizon of the "possible"'.[39]

The nature of the Doctor's heroism has been pushed to the foreground since the revival of 2005. Reflecting at the end of the Davies era, Hills remarks that it has presented the Doctor as 'more conventionally heroic than ever before': 'Unlike all previous representations of the character – and hugely divergent from the show's beginnings in 1963 – this Doctor is an outright hero: a textually celebrated, mythicised figure.'[40] Noting that 'God-like status haunts the Ninth and Tenth Doctors', Hills speculates on a 'quasi-religious' dimension to the new *Who* format. His specific reference for this is 'The Doctor's Daughter' (2008), in which the Time Lord 'effectively founds a new social order in his own image' (as well as begetting an immaculately conceived daughter), but he undoubtedly also has in mind the local disciples of 'Love & Monsters' (2006) and 'The End of Time' (2009–10), the global following and resurrection of 'The Last of the Time Lords' (2007) and the elevation by angels in 'Voyage of the Damned' (2007). The fact that these are all Tenth Doctor stories is significant, of course: messianic tropes tend to be subject to fewer destabilizing ironies in the Tennant era than in that of Christopher Eccleston.

Through Eccleston's time as the Doctor, hints of superhuman capability are in tension with both the character's sullen, and at times angry, disposition and his vulnerability, even ineptitude, as a god. When he attempts to be a saviour, he is prone to errors of judgement that either require him to be rescued ('Rose') or lead to tragedy ('The Unquiet Dead'). In redeeming the human race from the stupefying influence of the Mighty Jagrafess during his first visit to Satellite 5, he unwittingly enables the Daleks to play a 'long game' through the total shutdown of news media. When faced with a decision between handing victory to the Daleks and wiping them out along with every living thing on Earth, he chooses the former, adopting a pose of resigned self-sacrifice, expecting extermination, only to be salvaged again by Rose, this time in the beatific guise of the Bad Wolf. Of course, in the end he *does* save his companion, drawing the lethal energy of the Time Vortex from her body via a kiss, triggering his own regeneration. He dies and is reborn. At other points in the season – giving himself to the Reapers in 'Father's Day', scattering nanogenes to ensure that 'everybody lives' in 'The Doctor Dances', giving Margaret Blaine her 'second chance' in 'Boom Town' – he takes on the role of divine interventionist, but the fear and fury he carries with him from the Time War makes this more problematic than it seems to be for the Tenth Doctor. This is not to suggest that the situation is entirely straightforward for Tennant's incarnation: his ascent with the Host in 'Voyage of the Damned' is only made possible through the self-sacrifice of Astrid Peth (Kylie Minogue).

Intimations of deific power are not new to the characterization of the Doctor. Fiske refers to his 'Christ-likeness' as early as 1983, describing him as 'an anomalous creature' who 'occupies the same space between Man and God as does Christ'.[41] Charles, too, recognizes the 'virtually divine' quality of the Doctor.[42] In particular, he examines the religious symbolism of the regeneration in the 1996 TV movie – Paul McGann, shrouded and wide-eyed, emerging from his 'tomb' – and points to the strikingly cruciform posture of regeneration in the revived series. The tableau that precedes the Fourth Doctor's regeneration might also come to mind, his young disciples gathered anxiously around his broken and dying body, sacrificed on the scaffold of the Pharos Project (see Figure 4.1). As the Watcher approaches to initiate the Doctor's rebirth, the scene resembles a Renaissance painting showing the removal of Christ's body from the Cross, such as that by Nicolas Tournier (see Figure 4.2). The Watcher, as both attending angel and Holy Ghost, seems to predict the aura of new *Who* regeneration, again suggesting what Charles describes as the character's 'provisional divinity'.[43]

Figure 4.1 The Doctor (Tom Baker) prepares for the end in 'Logopolis' (1981); ©BBC Worldwide.

Traces of Christian iconography are unsurprising given the provenance of *Doctor Who*, and yet the capriciousness of the leading character across all of his incarnations means that any intimations of the divine must be more closely aligned with the gods of classical mythologies, or at least with the God of the Old Testament and the Christ who raged against the moneylenders in the temple.[44] The Doctor's reputation as a hero who abhors violence, who is cerebral rather than physical in his approach to problems, who is (or was) asexual and prone to childlike rapture at the wonders of the universe, gives him a closer resemblance to traditional interpretations of Christ than to the brawnier action heroes of Babylonian, Graeco-Roman or Norse mythology. He is not a Marduk, a Heracles or a Thor. Even so, the divine associations of heroism within classical mythography, and the hero functions which can be deduced from these, are revealing when considering the Doctor as hero.

An idle précis of *Doctor Who* might describe it as the story of a humanoid alien who travels through space and time fighting Evil, the inference being that *he* represents Good. For those who have

Figure 4.2 Nicolas Tournier, *The Descent from the Cross* (*c.*1632), oil on canvas, 154cm x 305cm, Musée des Augustins, Toulouse, France; Public domain.

watched, read or listened to tales of the Doctor in any detail, however, this summation is inadequate because it occludes a moral complexity that is key to the endurance of the myth. This moral complexity is not always evident, especially in classic *Who*, where Good and Evil are often definitively inscribed. There is no room for ethical ambiguity in reading the conflict between the Moroks and the Xerons in 'The Space Museum' (1965), for instance, or between the Dominators and the Dulcians in 'The Dominators' (1968). An antagonist such as Sutekh, by contrast, for all that he is characterized as 'the Destroyer' in 'Pyramids of Mars' (1975), can invite readings of light and shade, in keeping with his basis in the Egyptian deity Seth. Like Milton's Satan in *Paradise Lost* (1667), this god of storms, violence and disorder has something of the heroic about him, a rebel at odds with received notions of goodness.

As a whole, the television series and its spin-offs have been more sophisticated in their approach to the moral dimensions of storytelling than has been credited. Even the Daleks, in their first outing, are shown to be as frightened as they are malignant, protective of their enclosed city, fearful of the otherness of the Thals, and there is no agent of evil in 'The Sensorites' (1964), just a number of humans and aliens who are deluded through anxiety. Across the years there has been a consistent concern for the kind of character the Doctor is, the kinds of situation he finds himself in and the kinds of action he takes in response. Two oft-cited scenes that act as coordinates in any review of this topic are the one from 'The Forest of Fear' (1963), the third ever episode of the series, in which the Doctor seems to contemplate smashing the skull of a wounded man with a rock, and that from Part Six of 'Genesis of the Daleks' (1975), in which he falters when given the opportunity to obliterate the Daleks at birth: 'Do I have the right? Simply touch one wire against the other and that's it. The Daleks cease to exist.'

It would be easy to dismiss the first of these as a piece of aberrant scripting at a time when neither the character nor the series had been established, or to accept at face value the Doctor's claim to Ian that he was simply planning to ask Za to use the rock to draw a map back to the TARDIS. There are, however, too many other awkward moments (often passed over without any awkwardness) for this to be overlooked in a survey of the mythology. In the final part of 'The Invasion of Time' (1978), for example, the Doctor seems strangely relaxed in his use of the Demat Gun to end the Sontaran threat to Gallifrey. There is also the infamous moment in 'Vengeance on Varos' (1985) when he watches impassively as two men die in an acid bath, then leaves with a casual, sub-Bond quip: 'You'll forgive me if I don't join you.' In the revived series an extraordinary piece of dialogue from

'A Good Man Goes to War' (2011) indicates the extent of the Doctor's own ethical fretfulness:

> DOCTOR Oh look, I'm angry. That's new. I'm really not sure what's going to happen now.
> KOVARIAN The anger of a good man is not a problem. Good men have too many rules.
> DOCTOR Good men don't need rules. Today is not the day to find out why I have so many.

Such lines seem troubled by the recollection of unrestrained fury and its effects. They show the disquiet of the hero who remained stone-faced while killing the Empress of Racnoss and her children in 'The Runaway Bride' (2006), and who is plagued by memories of a disavowed self.

A decisive scene in 'The Day of the Doctor' (2013) shows the War Doctor being joined by two of his successors in the derelict barn (perhaps his childhood home) where he has primed the Moment, ready for activation. The presiding moral spirit here is not the conscience of the Time Lord super-weapon, personified as Rose Tyler, but Terrance Dicks, the writer who surely added more to the accumulated mythology of *Doctor Who* than any other:

> He never gives in, and he never gives up, however overwhelming the odds against him.

> The doctor believes in good and fights evil. Though often caught up in violent situations, he is a man of peace. He is never cruel or cowardly.

> In fact, to put it simply, the Doctor is a hero.[45]

'Never cruel or cowardly.' 'Never give up, never give in.' At Clara's prompting, these are revealed as the 'promise' made by the Doctor when he chose his name. They point to a heroism that is, in fact, far from 'simple', since it is easy enough to find examples of cruelty, such as the acid bath incident mentioned above or the vengeance wreaked on the Family of Blood (2007). Depending on definitions, cowardice is harder to detect, despite the Ninth Doctor's protestation that he would choose 'coward [over killer], any day'. This is consistent with the Third

Doctor's pep talk from 'The Planet of the Daleks' (1973): 'Courage isn't just a matter of not being frightened, you know. It's being afraid and doing what you have to do anyway.'

The Doctor knows fear, it seems, but it is overridden in his philosophy by the force of knowing right from wrong (with no need for the inverted commas of relativism). This elucidates the dilemma of the War Doctor as he finds himself on the lonely verge of deploying the Moment to end the Time War: the wrong thing to do has become the right thing to do or, less reassuringly, the worst thing to do has become the only thing that can be done. It does not, however, explain the First Doctor chuckling while Rome burns or the Third Doctor blasting an Ogron into atoms without a second's hesitation. What is evident is that the second promise – never cowardly – is seriously compromised by the challenges of the first – never cruel. Can a hero who is prone to cruelty still be a hero? Then again, a flawless hero might be no hero at all. The 'excremental whiteness' disdained by Milton almost four hundred years ago – 'a blank virtue' – is no basis for defining the modern hero either.[46]

The Doctor, like the heroes of classical mythology, is a composite character, the work of many hands (albeit across a much shorter span of time), so the nature and appeal of his heroism is never going to be easy to resolve. In the case of the Doctor, the analysis is complicated by the fact that the character is not only authored by many but also performed by many, each actor playing the same character as a different character. There are comparable challenges, of course, with many different screen and audio versions of Sherlock Holmes, Batman and James Bond: comparable, but not the same. With the Doctor, the difference is crucial at the level of story, not simply at the level of the story's reception. Almost uniquely, character variance in the main role of *Doctor Who* registers as primarily a diegetic concern, with everything else being publicity.

Inescapably, the challenge and implications of an endlessly mutable hero have been taken directly into the developing storyworld. At various points this process has been intensified: throughout the Virgin novels of the 1990s, for instance, and in several of the subsequent BBC Books range, notably Terrance Dicks's *The Eight Doctors* (1997) and Lance Parkin's *The Infinity Doctors* (1998). The most radical engagement with the possibilities of the Doctor's heroic multiplicity is to be found, arguably, in the stories of the Big Finish *Doctor Who* Unbound series (2003, 2005, 2008), which – written by Marc Platt, Gary Russell, Eddie Robson and others – jettison continuity and canonical scruples to present 'alternate histories', with new actors presenting often startling interpretations of the Doctor. These have so far included Geoffrey Bayldon as an alternative First Doctor, Michael Jayston as a tangle of the Valeyard and the Sixth Doctor, and both David Warner and Arabella Weir as alternative Third Doctors.[47] More recently, the variable temperament of the Doctor as hero has become a focus within Moffat's production approach, reacting perhaps to what Hills identifies as the outright heroism and textual celebration of the Davies years.

Britton, too, notes the inflation of heroic tone during the Davies era, especially in the time of Tennant's Doctor, going further than Hills in his censure of this in relation to the character's acts of cruelty or ruthlessness: 'The texts became more rhapsodic in celebration of his messianic status, more saccharine in showing characters' adoration or gratitude, and more bombastic in trumpeting his "victories" than was ever true before.'[48] Even though he points to 'warnings' about the darker implications of the Doctor's heroism, Britton claims that these are too often 'drowned out by the ecstasies of praise' and, drawing on Wayne C. Booth, argues that the result is a reinforcement of simplistic moral messages, a reduction of complexity and bolstering of facile binaries that is the disappointing default position of popular narratives.[49] The point is well made but not entirely fair. Those periodic glimpses of an unexpectedly spiteful, capricious Doctor are more jolting because they punctuate a narrative of generally upbeat approval. His treatment of the Family of Blood is shocking because it is out of character and, even given the casual brutality of the aliens, uncomfortably extreme. It is as if the actions are serving not a form of cosmic justice in which we trust our hero's judgement but some kind of pitiless personal reprisal for a damaged ego (or for the heart that was broken while he was the human teacher John Smith). Taken with moments like this, taunts such as those from Davros in 'Journey's End' (2008) assume a gravity of knowledge equivalent to their articulacy:

How many more? Just think: how many have died in your name? The Doctor! The man who keeps on running, never looking back because he dare not, out of shame. This is my final victory, Doctor. I have shown you yourself.

Towards the end of this episode, as the Dalek Crucible burns around him and the Doctor offers the hand of deliverance to his old enemy, a fellow survivor of the Time War, Davros delivers the *coup de grâce* to any pretensions the Time Lord might have to being 'simply' heroic: 'Never forget, Doctor, *you* did this. I name you forever: *you* are the Destroyer of the Worlds!'

The accusation of self-delusion that Davros levels at the Doctor is, in effect, a continuation of discussions between the pair in previous encounters, most powerfully in 'Genesis of the Daleks' (1975) and 'Resurrection of the Daleks' (1984). Picked up again, with tremendous subtlety, in 'The Magician's Apprentice' / 'The Witch's Familiar' (2015), the dialogue provides not only a vital corrective to easy readings of the Doctor as hero but also a way of tracing ethical complexities through the extended narrative. These complexities are brought to a crescendo in the final two tales of the Davies–Tennant era, 'The Waters of Mars' (2009) and 'The End of Time' (2009–10). 'Rhapsodic' and 'bombastic' as these stories are, with the Tenth Doctor achieving the apotheosis of heroic self-sacrifice, they are also pervaded by a deep sense of the hero racked with uncertainties about the role he is expected to play.[50]

In the climax to 'The Waters of Mars', having resisted the urge to interfere with a fixed point in Earth history (the destruction of Bowie Base One, with the resultant deaths of Captain Adelaide Brookes (Lindsay Duncan) and her crew), the Doctor is driven to effect a rescue by the desperate sounds of their final moments. This should be business as usual for the Doctor: saving people is, after all, what he does. The tough, insistent teasing of the script, however, across the preceding forty-five minutes, its sudden ferocious energy at this point and the angry, arrogant force of Tennant's performance combine to make it clear that there is more at stake here than usual, that something is being exposed:

> There are Laws of Time. Once upon a time there were people in charge of those laws, but they died. They all died. Do you know who that leaves? Me! It's taken me all these years to realize the Laws of Time are mine, and they will obey me!

This is not the simple hero. The simple hero is always in control: there is no control here, only the attempt to be *in* control. In this scene the Doctor is simultaneously the bereaved family member, the tantruming child, the egomaniacal dictator. The local threat comes from the Flood, the staring, streaming, broken-mouthed zombies of the water-possessed crew, but the real antagonist is something else: 'We're not just fighting the Flood, we're fighting Time itself. And I'm going to win!' Tennant delivers this as 'gonna win', with the raging, spitting swagger of a street fighter. It is clear that 'Time itself' encompasses history, loss, his sense of his own limitations, ultimately his sense of self. For the viewer, there is something traumatic in seeing a hero at the limits of his heroism. The air of smugness once he has returned Adelaide, Yuri Kerenski (Aleksander Mikic) and Mia Bennett (Gemma Chan) to Earth is troubling: 'Isn't anyone going to thank me?' It is not nearly as troubling, though, as his dismissal of Yuri and Mia (and, by extension, of many others saved by him over the years) as 'little people'. What Davies and co-writer Phil Ford are indicating is a fundamental shift in the Doctor's understanding of himself: 'For a long time now, I thought I was just a survivor, but I'm not: I'm the winner. That's who I am: the Time Lord Victorious.' Adelaide challenges this new understanding – 'The Time Lord Victorious is wrong' – and refuses its benefaction by committing suicide, in effect resetting both history and the Doctor's sense of his role: 'I've gone too far.'

As the closing moments of 'The Waters of Mars' remind the viewer, there is an existential context for the Doctor's behaviour in the story, played out under the shadow of death following the prediction by Carmen (Ellen Thomas), in 'Planet of the Dead' (2009), that his 'song is ending' and will be marked by a sign: 'He will knock four times.' The Flood knock hard on the bulkhead door during the rescue on Bowie Base One but the Doctor makes sure that the count is limited – 'Three knocks is all you're getting!' – and it is evident that his conduct is affected by the prophecy. The Doctor is now acting in the pressurized confines of his own mortality.

When the prophesied knocks occur, of course, they come not from one of the Doctor's enemies but from one of his friends: Wilfred Mott (Bernard Cribbins), grandfather of Donna Noble, trapped in a booth that is about to flood with lethal radiation. This amplifies the pathos of the Tenth Doctor's ultimate predicament, the realization that his fate – his Fate, like a tragic hero of antiquity – is to sacrifice himself not for the sake of a world or a galaxy or a universe but for one tired and 'ordinary' old man, a war hero who has never fired a bullet in anger:

WILF Look, just leave me.

DOCTOR Okay, right then. I will. Because you had to go in there, didn't you? You had to go and get stuck. Oh yes. Because that's who you are, Wilfred. You were always this. Waiting for me, all this time.

WILF No, really, just leave me. I'm an old man, Doctor. I've had my time.

DOCTOR Well, exactly! Look at you: not remotely important. But me? I could do so much more. So much more! But this is what I get, my reward. And it's not fair! Oh. Oh, I've lived too long …

The Doctor's heroism in this scene is dependent upon his capacity to operate outside considerations of relative 'importance' and the distractions of ego. In Sartrean terms, Wilfred is just as important (and just as absurd) as the Doctor, just as much a hero in the narrative of his own life. In a moment of bad faith or *mauvaise foi* the Doctor is seen to work through conflicted emotions that are usually concealed or suppressed in his responses to deadly situations.[51] Is he mockingly sincere in his description of Wilfred as 'not remotely important' or is he rebuking the old man ironically for suggesting that this could ever really be his view? Either way, his words show a childish cruelty that is, again, at odds with the Dicks maxim. Tennant's wounded, destructive outburst – 'I could do so much more!' – is pitched beautifully to express both the pain of the character and the sadness of the departing actor, whose last words as the incumbent hero will be 'I don't want to go'.

Despite its caricature as a long-running adventure story structured around a hero engaged in the eternal conflict between Good and Evil, *Doctor Who* has never been a straightforwardly Manichean mythology and its cumulative body of texts does not, in the end, support a binary view of an ethical life untroubled by doubt. It is usually clear who the Doctor is fighting, and it is usually clear why, but an easy reliance on concepts of goodness and wickedness tends to be avoided. This is the case even in the classic series, where the appeal of a certain rhetorical effect led to the use of the word 'evil' in the titles of four stories from 1967 to 1977 ('The Evil of the Daleks', 'The Mind of Evil', 'Planet of Evil' and 'The Face of Evil'), as well as in the title of one episode from 1964 ('The Temple of Evil', the first part of the story now known as 'The Aztecs'). Leaving aside the last of these, in which the word is sprayed around liberally from the opening scene onwards through Barbara's yearning to end Aztec practices of human sacrifice, and 'The Mind of Evil' (1971), where it is repeatedly discussed as the primary appetite of the Keller Machine, these stories actually resist a simple conceptualization of evil. In 'The Evil of the Daleks' (1967) the term is used only twice, and in 'Planet of Evil' (1975) it is not used at all. Indeed, any suspicion of evil on the part of Zeta Minor is ultimately revealed to be the result of a misunderstanding between universes of matter and antimatter. 'The Face of Evil' (1977) makes profuse use of both the word and the idea in reference to Xoanon, the supercomputer left imprinted with a perverted version of the Doctor's personality, but it is evident that only Leela's tribe, the Sevateem, really *believe* in it. For the Doctor, Xoanon's megalomania is a programming issue, a fault in the 'data core', not a sign of spiritual malignancy. The Doctor's face is seen as evil, in other words, only by the descendants of a survey team who have degenerated to a condition of preliterate superstition, referred to as 'savages' by the rival tribe of the Tesh (technicians fallen into priesthood). The ethical conundrum of the tale, forty-plus years on at least, has less to do with evil than with the condescension shown towards pre-modern cultures.

Most stories in classic *Doctor Who* do not mention evil at all. When they do, any concerns about it as an explicit and named force are usually limited to characters who are implicitly understood to be either 'primitive' or irrational. So, the psychologically disturbed crewman John (Stephen Dartnell) in 1964's 'The Sensorites', the superstitious landlord Angus McRanald (Angus Lennie) in 1975's 'The Terror of the Zygons' and the Doctor himself in 1984's 'The Twin Dilemma' fit the latter category, while Bellal (Arnold Yarrow) in 1974's 'Death to the Daleks', Ranquin (John Abineri) in 1979's 'The Power of Kroll' and Yrcanos (Brian Blessed) in 1986's 'Mindwarp' fit the former. Other characters drawn to make appeal to the concept of evil tend to be those of a villainous or scheming disposition such as Maaga (Stephanie Bidmead) in 1965's 'Galaxy 4', Zentos (Inigo Jackson) in 1966's 'The Ark' and Hepesh (Geoffrey Toone) in 1972's 'The Curse of Peladon'. This has a disquieting resonance when considered alongside the Second Doctor's rhetorical manipulation of the black manservant Toberman (Roy Stewart) in the final episode of 'The Tomb of the Cybermen' (1967):

DOCTOR Toberman, you see what these creatures have done to you? They've tried to make you like them. Do you understand? They've tried to make you their slave. They just want to use you. They are evil. Think of Kaftan.

TOBERMAN Evil!

DOCTOR They must be destroyed, do you see? Evil must be destroyed. Now, come!

TOBERMAN Destroy!

DOCTOR Come! Come on! Come on!

Toberman learns his lesson well: he adopts the e-word in combat with the Cybermen and is clearly thinking of it when he gives his life to seal them in their tomb.

Of course, classic *Doctor Who* is no more consistent in its attribution of moral viewpoints than it is in any of its other properties. There are several examples of the Doctor voicing an uncomplicated belief in evil during the first twenty-six years of the series. 'This place is evil,' he remarks of the Cave of Skulls in the fourth ever episode, 'The Firemaker'. Eight weeks later, in 'The Edge of Destruction', he responds to a question from Ian – 'Good or evil?' – with a piece of textbook relativism: 'One man's law is another man's crime. Sleep on it, Chesterton.' Similarly, the Second Doctor's initial, even-handed estimation of Salamander's henchmen in 'The Enemy of the World' (1967–8) – 'Unpleasant, yes, destructive, but not necessarily evil' – is in stark contrast to his binary certitude in a well-known exchange from 'The Moonbase' in which he defends his use of language:

DOCTOR Evil is what I meant. There are some corners of the universe which have bred the most terrible things. Things which act against everything that we believe in. They must be fought.

Evil does not need to be named to be implied within a storyworld, but to name is to intensify and it seems significant that the Doctor's references to evil in the classic era, although few and far between, often feature within iconic moments. The above is one example; others include the ethical debate with Davros in 'Genesis of the Daleks' ('It's not the machines, it's the minds of the creatures inside them. Minds that you created. They are totally evil.' 'Evil? No. No, I will not accept that.') and the Doctor's outburst against his people in 'The Trial of a Time Lord':

In all my travellings throughout the universe I have battled against evil, against power-mad conspirators. I should have stayed here. The oldest civilisation, decadent, degenerate and rotten to the core.

Perhaps unsurprisingly it is in dialogue around his greatest enemies, and in reflection on his own first causes, that the hero's moral conceptions are distilled to an essence. The Doctor's earlier trial on home ground, at the end of 'The War Games' (1969), is an illustration of this.

Throughout the first nine episodes of Patrick Troughton's epic swansong, there is no mention of evil. Then, in the final twenty-five minutes, it becomes a moral tennis ball, hit back and forth between the Doctor and his accusers. It is the Time Lords who invoke it first ('to sort this evil matter out'), with the Doctor then referring to it three times in his defence, each time as a way of censuring his people's policy of non-intervention: 'All these evils I have fought while you have done nothing but observe.' In their summing-up the Time Lords return to it again: 'We have accepted your plea that there is evil in the universe that must be fought, and that you still have a part to play in that battle.' So, as the series reaches a momentous climax, poised to enter the era of colour and Earth exile, with a new Doctor, stylishly Bond-like in his approach to trouble, it seems to emphasize the starkness of its moral structure. It is interesting to observe, though, that this occurs in a script from Terrance Dicks and Malcolm Hulke. Dicks, as script editor during the Pertwee era, would combine with Barry Letts as producer and Hulke as a prominent writer, to shape five years of stories that, beneath the surface bluster of soldiers, gadgets and chases, would include some of the most disconcerting ethical scenarios in the history of the series. The Third Doctor's debut season of 1970 is exemplary in this respect, including as it does both 'The Silurians' and 'The Ambassadors of Death'. In later stories, including 'The Colony in Space' (1971), 'The Mutants' (1972), 'The Sea Devils' (1972), 'Frontier in Space' (1973) and 'Invasion of the Dinosaurs' (1974), a substantial complication of heroic and villainous perspectives is again presented. (Of the seven tales cited here, five have Hulke as their author, each being given a more fine-grained socio-political context in his novelizations.)

Both Russell T. Davies and Steven Moffat have commented unfavourably on the idea of using evil as a criterion against which to advance the Doctor's story. Hills quotes Davies's assertion that 'we have never used the word evil' (not quite true: it occurs in 'Fear Her' (2006), though only because one character rejects another's accusation of it) and also Moffat's statement on its limitations: 'I think it's boring to say that something is just "evil" – it's bad writing. "Evil" is just someone who has reasoning you don't understand.'[52] Moffat toys with this analysis in his first story as lead writer, 'The Eleventh Hour' (2010), when he has Matt Smith's debutant Doctor condemning food on moral grounds: 'Beans are evil. Bad, bad beans.' In fact, although direct reference to evil is a rarity in Moffat's era, it is not entirely absent and, when it does feature, it carries a weight of authority and seriousness. 'I know evil when I see it,' says the Eleventh Doctor, looking at Van Gogh's 1890 painting *The Church at Auvers* in 'Vincent and the Doctor' (2010), 'and I see it in that window.' By the close of the episode, however, the 'evil' of the creature glimpsed in the window, a Krafayis, has been converted to 'pathos', the true malignancy of the episode being mental illness. 'This is evil refined as engineering,' the Twelfth Doctor states with reference to a damaged arch-enemy in 'Into the Dalek', concluding at the end of that story that 'Daleks are evil. Irreversibly so.' The fact that this has been 'learned' in the previous forty minutes of screen time through an intimate attempt to either discover or create a 'good' Dalek suggests the gravity with which the issue is being approached: even with the metal devils of Skaro, it is not a case of fixed, clear, knowable categories.

The Twelfth Doctor's first season is haunted by a question he asks during the course of 'Into the Dalek': 'Clara, be my pal. Tell me: am I a good man?' Her response ('I don't know') is rebounded by the Doctor ('Neither do I'), but at the end of the story there is a codicil from Clara: 'I think you try to be and I think that's probably the point.' This is probably, in some ways, the point of *Doctor Who* as a whole, if it can be said to have one. Is the Doctor good and, if so, of what does his goodness consist, how is it to be defined? If not, can he still be considered a hero? And what have this hero and his heroism to do with us?

The Doctor is open to experience; he craves new knowledge. This is what keeps him travelling. 'My God,' he says in 2015's 'Under the Lake',

> every time I think it couldn't get more extraordinary, it surprises me. It's impossible. I hate it. It's evil. It's astonishing. I want to kiss it to death.

That word again, 'evil', but deployed here with ambiguity, with a tense positivity. Here the Doctor's aristocratic liberty to roam is highlighted so that he resembles one of those Europeans of the late 1700s and early 1800s whose Grand Tour became just a little *too* grand. This tallies with Tulloch and Alvarado's account of him as 'a quintessential Romantic hero', awkwardly Byronic, but it also provokes an awareness of the privileged and dilettante aspect of his eternal adventure and the attitudes it discloses, as picked up by Britton.[53] It is possible, and reasonable, to apply one of the many available models of the hero's journey to the adventures of the Doctor, perhaps Lord Raglan's twenty-two mythic stages or Northrop Frye's rhythmic, cyclical quest. There is every chance that these theoretical containers might be able to accommodate *Doctor Who*. The two most renowned templates, Vladimir Propp's morphology of the folk tale and Joseph Campbell's monomyth, seem especially promising.[54] Using a selection of Propp's thirty-one narrative functions to map out any of the Doctor's adventures would be relatively straightforward and it is easy enough to match his trajectory, untidy as it has often been, to Campbell's circular progress of departure, initiation and return. It seems likely, though, that more would be lost than gained by such an enterprise. There is an earnestness, a formulaic certainty, about these narrative models that our particular text would be unable to tolerate for long. Campbell's requirement, for instance, that heroes should act as 'the world's symbolic carriers of the destiny of Everyman' is surely both too restricting and too narrowly ambitious for the Doctor to fulfil, at least with any enthusiasm.[55] It reads like the mythographic equivalent of an exile to Earth.

Thomas Carlyle's categories of hero – Divinity, Prophet, Poet, Priest, Man of Letters, King – might be made to fit the case, since it is possible to find instances of the Doctor assuming, with lesser or greater unease, any one of these mantles.[56] Again, though, it is unclear what might be gained, especially as Carlyle's taxonomy of the hero does not include the category of Idiot. For this, strangely, is the label that most usefully fits the Doctor's heroic methodology (or lack of one), being the verdict that he delivers upon himself at the end of the season that began with the question 'Am I a good man?':

I am *not* a good man. I am not a bad man. I am not a hero. And I'm definitely not a president. And no, I'm not an officer. Do you know what I am? I am an idiot, with a box and a screwdriver, just passing through, helping out, learning.

A characteristically Moffatian moment of bathos, deflating to inflate, this is the kind of scripting that divides fans. It rehearses a categorization of the Doctor as a trickster, not in itself an original reading but one that chimes with the description of that character in Tulloch and Alvarado as both 'benefactor and buffoon'.[57]

The trickster of folklore is a shapeshifter, ageless, playful, volatile, disrespectful of rules and authority, capable of being both affectingly childlike and outrageously childish, but with access to immense knowledge, conveying an air of secret, withheld and potentially dangerous wisdom. The trickster can be arrogant and has an air of innate prerogative, a tendency to fool with power in frightening ways – he might frolic dangerously with the completed Key to Time or assume the role of Lord High President in order to invite the doom of his own people – but he also has difficulty in appreciating his own worth. In 'Amy's Choice' (2010) the Doctor is taunted and threatened by the Dream Lord (Toby Jones), an exaggeratedly tricksterish version of himself, a projection that confirms its own origins, exposing the Doctor's vulnerabilities in the process. 'No idea how you can be here,' the Doctor says at one point, 'but there's only one person in the universe who hates me as much as you do.' The poignancy of this is intensified later in the episode when Amy, having apparently seen Rory die, is told by the Doctor that he is unable to save him. 'Then what is the point of you?' she asks.

Moments of idiocy can be found in all eras of *Doctor Who*, in all incarnations, in all media. It is for this reason that no one should be troubled or irritated when the programme drifts into comedy or even farce, when it begins to look 'silly' or sends itself up. The Doctor is closer to the fools of Shakespeare and Rabelais or the tramps of Chaplin and Beckett than he is to Superman. Only, perhaps, in the battered figure of the War Doctor is this quality seen to decline, and only then because he represents a crucial inversion of the character's moral outlook, its collapse into terrible praxis rather than intuitive and brilliant improvisation. In a sense, his involvement with the Tenth and Eleventh Doctors is vital not only because it saves him from an act of terminal decisiveness but also because it revives his capacity for the 'uncertainties' of 'Negative Capability':[58]

TENTH DOCTOR There's always something we don't know, isn't there?
WAR DOCTOR One should certainly hope so.

His last line in 'The Day of the Doctor', as he echoes Hartnell ('wearing a bit thin') and begins to regenerate into Eccleston, is a joke: 'I hope the ears are a bit less conspicuous this time.'

Reading the Doctor as a wise fool, a brilliant idiot, means reading him as the kind of hero celebrated by Kenneth Burke and Edgell Rickword. In Burke's 'Definition of Man' he writes that 'mankind's only hope is a cult of comedy', remarking with grim historical awareness that 'the cult of tragedy is too eager to help out with the holocaust'.[59] Rickword's celebration of 'the fantastic and the comic' as the most appropriate modes for a modern hero is aligned with the traditions of the trickster and summarized sharply by Laurence Coupe:

> He has the centrality of a reviving god, but he has the sense of absurdity of a laughing animal. For above all, his universe will be 'humorous'; and he himself will emerge from the ranks of 'clowns' or 'loons'. He is, then, a force for endlessly productive imperfection rather than for arid and static perfection.[60]

This 'endlessly productive imperfection' is the universe as the Doctor leaves it. Too much in Fiske's identification of an innate conservatism within the mythology relies on a reading that grounds the Doctor's actions in an urge to restore the equilibrium of a status quo that is 'arid and static'. This is the popular text mirroring and endorsing the conditions of society rather than challenging them. It is myth as a version of T. S. Eliot's structure-to-live-within rather than Rickword's structure-to-live-beyond. In Coupe's words, it is 'tragic restraint' rather than 'comic release'.[61]

Doctor Who is not a comedy, but it does have a hero who is inherently absurd, heroically so, and this has led it, at times, to try too hard to be comical. Objections to '*Fawlty Towers* in space' are not unfounded, just inappropriately solemn. The Doctor's restlessness and rebelliousness, the heroism that derives from these qualities, is allied to an essentially comic vision of existence. This is a vision of unsettlement, expressed through the actions of a defiantly maverick and optimistic persona. Imbued with the spirit of elusiveness and paradox outlined by Julia Kristeva (after Bakhtin) in her account of the Menippean mode, *Doctor Who* is remarkable for what Tulloch and Alvarado call its 'constant displacement of the hermeneutic code by the proairetic'.[62]

Such displacement is a core element of Menippean satire, a notably eccentric *mythos*. Frye associates it with 'a loosejointed narrative form often confused with romance', arguing that 'it is not primarily concerned with the exploits of heroes', concentrating instead on 'the free play of intellectual fancy and the kind of humorous observation that produces caricature'.[63]

'The exploits of heroes' are very much the concern of *Doctor Who*: ironized they might be, but the ironization is heroic. In Campbell's distinction between popular heroism, which is primarily physical in its manifestation, and sacred heroism, which is primarily moral or intellectual, the Doctor discovers both his own anomaly and the limitations of the theoretical model. This is one key to the wider narrative universe. Another is offered in 'The Zygon Invasion' (2015), where the two versions of UNIT's Petronella Osgood (Ingrid Oliver) – one presumed human, the other presumed Zygon – present a dialectical view of ethics:

OSGOOD 1 Any race is capable of the best and the worst.
OSGOOD 2 Every race is peaceful and warlike.
OSGOOD 1 Good and evil.
OSGOOD 2 My race is no exception.
OSGOOD 1 And neither is mine.

This reiterates a formula of binary resolution (or disintegration) that has recurred at various points throughout the series, though most frequently since the 1970s. In 'The Time Monster' (1972), Kronos the Chronovore, having transformed from 'a raging monster' into 'a girl' (Jo Grant's designation), expresses a fundamental rejection of physical and principled constraints: 'I can be all things. A destroyer, a healer, a creator. I'm beyond good and evil as you know it.' The Nietzschean tenor of this last sentence is replicated in the situation of the Xeraphin in 1982's 'Time-Flight', 'infinitely divided' between good and evil by the Master's interference. Elsewhere, a sense of contingent morality is conveyed in mirroring statements from Sutekh (in 'Pyramids of Mars' (1975)) and the Black Guardian (in 'Mawdryn Undead' (1983)): 'Your evil is my good', 'The Doctor's good is my evil'. Both Sutekh the Destroyer and the Black Guardian are forces of chaos, forerunners of the Destroyer of 'Battlefield' (1989) and the Beast of 'The Satan Pit' (2006). They speak for disorder, defining their evil in antithesis to an ordered good, represented by the Doctor. There is no doubt that they are characters written as villains in relation to the Doctor's hero, and they lack the clear and largely sympathetic motivations of, say, Omega, Sharaz Jek or even (after the revelations of 'The End of Time') the Master. Even so, they present a more complicated moral understanding than might initially appear to be the case. In their madly heightened subjectivity, they point to the philosophical shortfall of the concept of evil, its imprecision and indeterminacy, as contended by Kevin S. Decker when he writes that 'evil wells up from an obscure nexus of metaphysics and ethics'.[64] For St Augustine, Decker reminds us, evil is not an absolute quality in itself but the absence of good. It is in this context, relativistic but in no sense neutral, that the nature of the Doctor's heroism begins to make sense. The equilibrium that it seeks to restore is, in most instances, not conservative at all but radically redemptive.

Redemption, in a mythology predicated on the idea of a hero who can live 'practically forever, barring accidents' ('The War Games' (1969)), is about endurance and what existentialist philosophy would think of as ontological authenticity. In plain terms, it is about bloody-mindedness ('never give up, never give in') and a genuine openness to experience. This is not just the authentic existence-towards-death of Heidegger but an authentic existence-towards-the-living-of-others, rejecting solipsism, striving for connection. The Doctor's anti-war speech from the climax of 'The Zygon Inversion' (2015), a *tour de force* of Capaldi's acting, is supremely representative here:

> DOCTOR Because it's always the same. When you fire that first shot, no matter how right you feel, you have no idea who's going to die. You don't know whose children are going to scream and burn. How many hearts will be broken! How many lives shattered! How much blood will spill until everybody does what they're always going to have to do from the very beginning – sit down and talk! Listen to me, listen, I just – I just want you to think. Do you know what thinking is? It's just a fancy word for changing your mind.
>
> BONNIE I will not change my mind.
>
> DOCTOR Then you will die stupid.

The emergence of the trope of waiting in new *Who* is similarly instructive, with Jack Harkness's frustrated and often agonized endurance of life following his eternal resurrection by Rose in 'The Parting of the Ways' (2005) being the archetype. Other examples are the stoicism of Rory as the Centurion guarding Amy in the Pandorica in 'The Big Bang' (2010), the patient resourcefulness of Amy herself as she waits to be rescued from an accelerated time stream in 'The Girl Who Waited' (2011) and the bitter survival of Ashildr as she outsits eternity in 2015's 'Hell Bent'.

The correlative for all of these, of course, is the Doctor himself, accepting the melancholy transience of human companionship throughout his adventures and, in 'Heaven Sent' (2015), suffering four and a half billion years of painful, repetitive death in order to punch his way through the Azbantium wall and fulfil his 'duty of care' to Clara. Ultimately, the heroism of the Doctor is defined in terms of bravery, self-sacrifice, persistence and – strangely, for a character who clearly finds it such an awkward concept – love. If this seems surprisingly conventional, if it returns us to the quasi-religious considerations with which this section began, it is perhaps because the conventions of heroism are always attuned to a handful of fundamental anxieties that are contained in the figure of the Doctor: anxieties about time, about vulnerability, loneliness, death. In being most alien, it seems, the Doctor is being most human.

Myths of representation / representations of myth

Performing at the Edinburgh Festival Fringe in 2006, Toby Hadoke asserted the limits of his suspension of disbelief: 'Funnily enough, *Doctor Who* fans notice when monsters are not terribly convincing. The thing is, we don't care. It's not like we're not aware they're not actually real. It's called using your imagination.'[65] Hadoke was responding to the ways in which *Doctor Who* had been disparaged in reports of Jon Pertwee's death a decade earlier, indicating that sometimes, contrary to popular stereotypes, it seems to be only the fans who treat it as a fiction. To an unusual extent, the show has been evaluated on the strength or otherwise of its special effects. Its reputation has suffered far more in this respect than those of its US science fiction television counterparts between the 1960s and 1980s, notably *Star Trek* (NBC, 1966–9) and *Battlestar Galactica* (ABC, 1978–9), and even more than contemporary UK productions which have retained cult followings but lack the longevity or widespread impact of *Who*, such as Roger Price's *The Tomorrow People* (ITV, 1973–9) or Gerry and Sylvia Anderson's *Space: 1999* (ITV/RAI, 1975–7). *Blake's 7* (BBC, 1978–81) comes close in its creaky repute but, running for only four series, is a smaller-scale artefact and at least has the weight of seriousness to balance against any criticism of its production values.

Doctor Who has often been *taken* seriously, but it has rarely been *seen* as 'serious'. There are several very good reasons for this. For starters, it is fun: those who watch it *enjoy* watching it and, for many of them, that is enough. This brings to mind the flexibility of its audience, which is an outcome of its ambiguous format: neither adult nor children's drama, never entirely respectable as 'pure' science fiction (against Suvinesque criteria) but clearly science fiction *of some kind*, a television programme, but one with a vivid and significant life beyond the small screen, it has effectively created the taste by which it is relished. The nervy prevalence of inverted commas, brackets and italics in these sentences speaks volumes: *Doctor Who*, almost as its *raison d'être* (the clue is in the title), raises questions of definition. In Barthesian terms, the myth that it does most to challenge is that of 'realism', and realism is a serious business. Arguably, since the emergence of CGI in the 1980s, it has become *too* serious or, at least, too narrowly defined and understood.

Realism is a code. The code changes. Unlike most screen-based science fiction (unlike most screen-based material of any genre) *Doctor Who* has recognized both the code and its variability. This might be necessity as the mother of invention, but there is more to the peculiar character of *Doctor Who* than budgetary constraints and their impact on verisimilitude. In other words, there is more to *Doctor Who* than the myth of wobbly sets. The Skarasen ('Terror of the Zygons' (1975)), the Myrka ('Warriors of the Deep' (1984)) and the Magma Creature ('The Caves of Androzani' (1984)) – and in new *Who*, the Slitheen ('Aliens of London' / 'World War Three' (2005)) and aspects of the Dalek Sec Hybrid ('Daleks in Manhattan' (2007)) – are noticeable for their artifice, but not necessarily because they detract from the illusion. The illusion is part of the format. How it is generated, and to what effect, is richly meaningful.

In the mid-1990s Lev Manovich speculated on the problems of realism in an age of computer-generated imagery, reflecting on the 'fake visual reality' achieved through digital techniques in *Terminator 2* (James Cameron, 1991) and *Jurassic Park* (Steven Spielberg, 1993).

> What is faked is, of course, not reality but photographic reality, reality as seen by the camera lens. In other words, what computer graphics has (almost) achieved is not realism, but only photorealism – the ability to fake not our perceptual and bodily experience of reality but only its photographic image.[66]

This is realism coded as a photographic way of looking. Refining the argument in *The Language of New Media*, Manovich outlined this version of the realist code as one adapted to a situation in which 'we have come to accept the image of photography and film as reality'.[67] In other words, what appears to the eye on screen, whether 'real' or 'not real' in an ontological sense, must *appear* to be as real as a real thing that has been filmed or photographed. So, against this criterion, a spaceship or a dinosaur or a cyborg or an explosion on screen must look like a real-life spaceship or dinosaur or cyborg or explosion, as captured on film. Or at least, these things must look like we *think* they would look if they were to be captured on film from real events. And while, as Manovich points out, the constant challenge for computer animators has been to degrade their imagery sufficiently for it to be integrated with live footage – 'their perfection [has] to be diluted to match the imperfection of film's graininess'[68] – for *Doctor Who* the problems of the shifting code are different, but no less complex or paradoxical.

The complexities and paradoxes begin, as complexities and paradoxes so often do, with oversimplification. It is a falsification, for example, to think of classic *Who* as an agglomeration of failed effects and admiration of its achievements as mere nostalgia for the charm of primitive times. As Chapman observes, 'the set design and visual effects of *Doctor Who* were state-of-the-art' during its first two decades, and Booy is surely right to assert that 'in the 1980s the programme was at a cutting edge nobody understood'.[69] The opening forty-five-second model shot for the first episode of 'The Mysterious Planet', the initial story within 'The Trial of a Time Lord' (1986), can be cited as an example of this technical edginess: depicting the captured TARDIS being hauled into the Time Lord space station, it was the most expensive single effect to date, costing £8,000, taking a week to film and involving the use of a motion-controlled camera and Mike Kelt's exquisitely detailed, six-foot-wide model. (That it was also, in narrative terms, entirely gratuitous and, in its impact on the season's budget, a damaging extravagance, should also be noted.) Attention might be drawn to the use of Quantel to depict the journey through Tegan's eyes and into her unconscious in 'Kinda' (1982), and to the 'bold and strangely beautiful' model work for the Eternals' space-racing ships in 'Enlightenment' (1983; Kelt again).[70] It is important to appreciate, in this respect, that the show was a consistent innovator in its experimentation with processes such as Chromakey (known in the BBC as Colour Separation Overlay or CSO), Scene-Sync, Paintbox and Ampex Digital Optics (ADO). Indeed, its pioneering of special effects technologies during the 1980s contributed towards the recoding of realist aesthetics that would arguably influence its own disappearance from screens and its unshakable reputation for dodgy production values. The ironies are plentiful.

In fact, *Doctor Who* had been technologically groundbreaking from the start. For evidence of this it is only necessary to consider the 'howlaround' effect used for the opening title sequence, achieved by pointing a camera into its own monitor and recording the resultant visual feedback. (Discovered by Norman Taylor, the method was subsequently refined by Bernard Lodge and Mervyn Pinfield.) Then, of course, there is Delia Derbyshire's treatment of Ron Grainer's theme music as part of her work for the BBC's Radiophonic Workshop. A vital element in the early creation of an atmosphere for *Doctor Who*, this was a prelude to some of the remarkable electronic incidental music produced for the series during the 1970s (notably Malcolm Clarke's score for 'The Sea Devils' (1972), created using the EMS Synthi 100). Pressures of budget and time were always – and, in real terms, continue to be – a restrictive factor for the makers of *Doctor Who*, but these were also a stimulus to creativity, experimentation and risk. The 1978 story 'Underworld' offers an extreme illustration, making unprecedented use of CSO to render the environment of the title. If the results have often been derided, the achievements should nevertheless be appreciated. Suffice it to say that the technical innovations of the 1980s were not so much a departure in the realization of the *Doctor Who* mythos as an intensification of its practical traditions. These traditions persist in the new series, evident in Moffat's advocacy of 'brand-new visuals' and in the latest adaptations of the theme music and title sequence for Jodie Whittaker's debut season (2018). The new music, composed by Segun Akinola and withheld until Whittaker's second episode, 'The Ghost Monument', wavers momentarily in its low, slow remembrance of the original 1963 theme, harmonizing with the darkly pulsing title sequence in an unnerving visual-sonic kink about five seconds in. Noticeably shorter than previous new *Who* title sequences, it speeds up towards the end as the swirling dark Rorschach blur of colours is pulled into streams of sudden light. The new sequence succeeds, like those before it, in both thematically consistent with the conventions of the series and technically wildly inventive.

In the context of this book, the mechanics of production – how *Doctor Who* and its stories are translated to the screen – are almost beside the point. The focus here is on the effects of the effects, not their processes. This is to do not only with the tales they help to tell, but also with the tales these tales can tell about our own myths of cultural reception. Does it matter if the use of silver-sprayed neoprene wetsuits to create the Cybermen costumes between 'The Wheel in Space' (1968) and 'Revenge of the Cybermen' (1975) is noticed by a viewer? If so, why? And what does it mean if the CGI scene in which Mickey Smith is attacked by a Nestene-possessed wheelie-bin in 'Rose' (2005) has aged as badly as, or perhaps worse than, the CSO scenes featuring a Nestene-possessed devil doll in 'Terror of the Autons' (1971)? The mythologies invoked here are not simply those of alien invasion and cyborgification but those of visual representation in narrative media. An analysis of realist codes in *Doctor Who* can offer a basis for challenging several mythic assumptions about spectacle, story and audiences. In particular, it can raise questions about the latest evolutionary phase of André Bazin's 'myth of total cinema', his prediction from the heart of the twentieth century of 'a perfect illusion'.[71] While debates begin to subside around claims that visual spectacle has overthrown narrative as the shaping spirit behind popular cinema, there is surely much to be learned from a text that has coincided perfectly with the rise of the digital age and that has incorporated within its own mythology a conviction that story is more important than visual realism.

It is a truism of *Doctor Who* fandom, expressed by Hadoke, that the appeal of the show is predominantly to do with 'stories and characters and ideas'.[72] This is, in part, a defensive strategy to deflect criticism of poor production outcomes. It is also, though, suggestive of a particular aesthetic, a mode of appreciation that is at odds with the dominant cultural narrative of realism and therefore in conflict with the naturalizing mode of representation that Fiske equates with the reactionary ideology of mass entertainment. If prevailing social discourses are directed at the incorporation of fantastical illusions, deploying them as a distraction from what Fiske (showing the influence of the Frankfurt School) identifies as the intrinsic historicity of texts, then it seems unlikely that a series which repeatedly draws attention to its own fictiveness will serve to reinforce the status quo with any reliability from within the 'culture industry' condemned by Theodor Adorno and Max Horkheimer.[73] It should be noted that Fiske has elsewhere challenged the pessimism of the Frankfurt School, arguing for 'the ability and freedom of the viewer to bring extra-textual experience and attitudes to bear' in their engagement with popular television, 'mak[ing] *their* culture out of the offerings of the culture industry'.[74] The viewers of *Doctor Who* – specifically, the fans – have modelled such processes of critical reimagining in many ways, and for many years.

Susceptibility to such apparently democratic reimagining is one of the reasons why it has been claimed that *Doctor Who* is a postmodern artefact.[75] In terms of narrative content this makes some sense but, as Susan Sontag pointed out around the time of the First Doctor's arrival on British television screens, the separation of content and form is a dubious basis for analysis.[76] It is also debatable whether there is any real critical value in trying to disentangle postmodernism from Modernism. If the former is seen as a largely tonal shift within the latter, a variation in attitude rather than a substantive change in formal qualities, then they need not be seen as mutually exclusive and chronologically plotted terms. There is much in the storytelling of *Doctor Who*, old and new, that can be considered postmodernist – allusive, parodic, disruptive and irreverent, happily inconsistent – but there is also much that is distinctively Modernist. As Britton and Barker contend, aspects of the core design of *Doctor Who* show clear signs of Modernist influence, most obviously the TARDIS console room and the Daleks.[77] It is even possible, as I have suggested elsewhere, to trace distinct lines of influence from the Vorticist movement in early-twentieth-century British art to the founding mythologies of *Doctor Who*, starting with the concept of the Vortex itself.[78]

The most obvious affinity with the procedures of Modernism can be seen in *Doctor Who*'s foregrounding of its own craft, its showing of its workings, typically to the detriment of the realist agenda. At the risk of stating the obvious, it should be acknowledged that this has usually been an unintended result of limitations in time or budget (rarely, if ever, in technical know-how). I have yet to meet a model designer or special effects practitioner whose desired outcome is not the perfect illusion described by Bazin. Even so, when a scuttling Zarbi collides with a camera ('The Web Planet' (1965)), when Kroll rises above the swampland with not so much as a splash or a ripple ('The Power of Kroll' (1978–9)), when the Mara uncoils to its full puppet height within the circle of mirrors ('Kinda' (1982)), when the glorious tableau of assembled Doctors at the climax of 'The Day of the Doctor' (2013) is haunted by spectres of the uncanny valley, this is *Doctor Who* exposing itself as fabulation, admitting the complicity of audience and producers in an act of playfulness and imagining. These moments of lapsed illusion place valuable emphasis on the aspects of Coleridge's famous formulation of representational narrative that are often ignored: the suspension of disbelief is 'willing' and 'for the moment', an enactment of 'poetic faith'.[79] More importantly, they result in an attentiveness to the mythological (in the traditional sense) at variance with the mythic (in the Barthesian sense): they constitute a form of resistance to the 'ideological work' that Fiske attributes to popular art forms generally and to *Doctor Who* specifically. It might seem preposterous to think of the Myrka in this way; even so, there is a case to be made, and it is a broadly political one.

Earlier in this chapter, and elsewhere in the book, attention is drawn to the problems inherent in attempting a political reading of *Doctor Who*. These stem mostly from its foundations as a BBC franchise, its multi-authored (and increasingly multi-platform and participatory) nature, and its sheer narrative vastness and mutability. To some, the Doctor will always be an anti-authoritarian, anarchistic, left-leaning pacifist agitator with pronounced revolutionary tendencies, unpredictable, confrontational, incendiary, yet somehow endlessly reassuring. The television stories alone, however, can furnish plentiful evidence to indicate that he is actually a conservative patriarch and defender of free-market economics, an aristocratic elitist who has defended countless dubious oligarchies, resorting to extreme violence whenever it suits his capricious instincts. And the less said about his sexual politics (until very recently, at least), the better.

For all that its first producer was female and its first director Asian, *Doctor Who* has tended to be written and produced (and the leading character played) by white men. Many of these men have been of a socially liberal cast of mind, often left-wing (and, in the case of Malcolm Hulke, actively Communist),[80] but this does not ensure a fixed political complexion for the series, still less for the extended mythology; nor does it justify an attempt to make the Doctor fit a predetermined ideological template. There are many, no doubt, for whom a consideration of *Doctor Who* as a political narrative would seem pointless or undesirable. Britton's relocation of the discursive base from the political to the ethical is important in this regard.[81] But formally, in its prolonged unfolding as a text, there remains a restlessness about this particular mythology that is manifestly, uniquely, political in its effects.

Doctor Who has always been, with the exception of the two mid-1960s Amicus films, televisual rather than cinematic. Even so, it has a striking aesthetic closeness to the 'cinema of attraction(s)' identified in the origins of moving-image media by Tom Gunning and linked directly to the avant-garde experimentation of Modernism.[82] Prior to the 'narrativization of cinema' by such film-makers as Edwin S. Porter and D. W. Griffith, Gunning contends that the medium was primarily magical and spectacular, a demonstration of (to borrow from Mr Jago) the 'dazzling display of lustrous legerdemain' and 'feats of superlative, supernatural skill'.[83] Before Porter's *The Great Train Robbery* (1903) and Griffith's *The Birth of a Nation* (1915), and before the splitting of cinema into traditions of 'live-action' and 'animation' during the same period (as discussed by Manovich),[84] the unsettled screen displayed the effects-based conjurations of Georges Méliès, Cecil Hepworth, J. Stuart Blackton and R. W. Paul. Dan North has shown the connections between this phase of film-making and prior traditions of theatrical illusion, and Gunning distinguishes between its 'exhibitionist' mode of entertainment and the 'voyeuristic' approach of subsequent realist narrative cinema.[85] The vital element for Gunning in early cinema's 'aesthetic of astonishment', whether in the phantasmagoric animations of Émile Cohl or the spectacular realities of pioneer documentary makers such as the Lumière Brothers, was the imaginative collaboration between producer and spectator. Early film-makers were less concerned with the transparency of realism than with its visible appearance as part of the 'act of showing and exhibition'.[86] As in the poetics of narrative defined by Coleridge less than a century before, the audience is invited to willingly suspend disbelief, the film-maker's 'harnessing of visibility' being a celebration of illusion rather than an attempt at its concealment.[87] To use the lexicon of new media theory established in Bolter and Grusin's *Remediation* (1999), the emphasis is on processes of hypermediacy (through which the medium draws attention to itself or 'shows off') rather than immediacy (through which it hides itself in plain sight).[88]

The first episode of *Doctor Who* aired twenty-five years after the death of Georges Méliès and forty years after the production of his final films. The BBC's new television serial, ostensibly science fiction, was developed in a very different media environment from Méliès's *Voyage à la Lune* (1902), also ostensibly science fiction and with claims to being the first film in that genre. There are, nonetheless, some intriguing aesthetic parallels between *Doctor Who* and early cinema that can offer both a perspective on the former's enduring appeal and an appreciation of its possible social meaning. In particular, I would argue that the role of special effects within *Doctor Who* has been akin to that of the improvised trickery in the films of Méliès and his contemporaries. This is most obvious in episodes of classic *Who* but, with important qualifications, it remains the case in the revived series. Gunning writes that 'the cinema of attractions solicits a highly conscious awareness of the film image engaging the viewer's curiosity. The spectator does not get lost in a fictional world and its drama, but remains aware of the act of looking, the excitement of curiosity and its fulfilment.'[89]

Story was, almost literally, the last thing on Méliès's mind when making his films and his intention was to create visible magic, not fake reality. Clearly this is different from the situation of *Doctor Who*, which has always been, first and foremost, about story and character. After all, fans have invariably appealed to the narrative quality of the show when redeeming it from accusations of wobbliness. And, as noted already, the aim of its visual effects teams has never been anything other than perfected illusion, whereas Méliès et al., with no standard of cinematic verisimilitude to judge themselves against, drew consciously on traditions of nineteenth-century stage illusion, which 'cannily exploited their unbelievable nature'.[90] The constant recoding of what audiences find realistic adds a further complication, recalling how *Doctor Who* suffered by comparison with George Lucas's *Star Wars* films in the late 1970s and early 1980s.

The poverty of the visual effects in classic *Who* has been grossly exaggerated, but the fact remains that sometimes, and sometimes in significant ways, they fail. Or, at least, they fail if the benchmark for evaluation is the ideal of the perfect illusion. But is it? When Hadoke says, partly in jest, that fans 'don't care', he implies that they actually care *differently*, that they appreciate *Doctor Who* as a story above all else, but also that they appreciate it *as an illusion*. Here is Gunning's Coleridgean account of the 'rationalist context' of the earliest cinema: 'The magic theatre laboured to make visual that which it was impossible to believe. Its visual power consisted of a trompe l'œil play of give-and-take, an obsessive desire to test the limits of an intellectual disavowal – I know, but yet I see.'[91] *Doctor Who* has also been appraised in a rationalist context. It is not, however, a rational thing: it is a fantasy, and an absurdist one at that. Through the original run of the series, it aspired towards realism as part of a celebration of televisual storytelling but always with an understanding, shared between producer and consumer, of its basis in ingenious illusion. In exploring narrative possibilities, it also explored technical possibilities, remaining compellingly visual and wonderfully estranging, even when it might be seen as deficient against the emergent Hollywood paradigm of hyperrealism.

A peculiar example of this, as indicated previously, is 'Underworld'. Written by Bob Baker and Dave Martin, the story adapts the Greek myth of Jason's quest for the Golden Fleece and takes place predominantly in the cave system of a newly formed planet, the domain of the Oracle (one of the many insane computers within *Doctor Who* mythology). Budgetary pressures meant that there were insufficient funds to construct the planned sets and so, rather than cancel the serial, designers Dick Coles, Richard Conway and A. J. Mitchell opted to produce the subterranean world through the use of CSO. Actors, performing within a blue-screen environment, were superimposed onto a single small-scale model shot from multiple angles and using varied lighting. In production terms this was ambitious, risky and desperate; as a technical enterprise, it was almost unique at the time, an exercise in improvisation that also required considerable innovation.

'Underworld' has a dismal reputation and, some excellent model work aside, it can hardly be denied that it looks cheap. It also, however, looks remarkable. The overlaying of the actors works well at times but their evident lack of a physical presence in the caves means that they never quite seem to belong, appearing to move above the environment rather than through it. This is a literal description of what they *are* doing, of course, and it has some fascinating consequences, with bodies lacking shadows (sufficient or accurate shadows, at least), limbs ghosting into transparency, and approaching groups of the pursued and the pursuing seeming to float towards the audience like rapid cartoon phantoms. These are obvious defects, flaws in the process, but they are, in a strange way, visually enthralling, creating a dreamlike, otherwordly aesthetic that is – as Howe and Walker have noted – entirely appropriate.[92]

The technical achievement of 'Underworld', its messy, hard-won brilliance, is a correlative for that of the Minyan crew of the *R1C* in their centuries-long search for the *P7E* and the missing race-banks of their people. It is reported that the serial's cast and crew adopted the Minyan motto, 'The quest is the quest', for satiric uplift during difficult times in the production, and it is interesting to note how the different mythic aspects of the story have become interwoven. The unsubtle flaunting of source material in the script has often been criticized (for *R1C* read *Argosy*, for *P7E* read Persephone, for Jackson read Jason), but this intentional exposure of the story's epic framework is mirrored by the unintentional conspicuousness of its visual effects. Both aspects can be seen as weaknesses, and yet they are characteristic of the exhibitionist manner of *Doctor Who*, its celebration of illusion even when 'the simple reality effect' is not accomplished. Manovich urges that 'we should not be too impressed' by landmark CGI films, hinting that the mechanics of digital realism are actually less complex (and less novel) than the requirement to roughen them into coherence with live-action footage.[93] He argues, with playful provocation, that such effects 'exemplify the triviality of what at first may appear to be an outstanding technical achievement'.[94] Ironically, in the case of the CSO environment of 'Underworld', the reverse might be said to be true: it exemplifies the significance of what at first may appear to be a crude technical achievement.

Whatever the shortcomings of 'Underworld' (the sluggishness of its narrative, for one), the bloody-minded resourcefulness of its production and the uniquely eerie results should be commemorated. These begin to approximate a formal politics at odds with Fiske's reading of 'The Creature from the Pit' (1979) and consistent with an awareness of the design and realization of *Doctor Who* as singularly unsettled throughout its history, including the post-2005 version. This tallies with Gunning's account of how early cinema refused the 'deadly temptation' of slickness: 'Shock becomes not only a mode of modern experience, but a strategy of a modern aesthetics of astonishment. Hence the exploitation of new technological thrills that flirt with disaster.'[95] Gunning aligns this analysis with those political accounts of cinema by Siegfried Kracauer and Walter Benjamin that asserted its expressive power as a medium of cultural estrangement and breakdown, akin to Bertolt Brecht's Epic Theatre. Even though the Doctor is playing the role of a reluctant god in 'Underworld', flourishing his superior knowledge of events, he nevertheless embodies a disruptive force in keeping with the restless aesthetic of the production and subversive of his superficially aristocractic function. He atones for the errors of the Time Lords, assisting the Minyans in the completion of their quest, at the same time rousing their enslaved descendants, the Trogs, into rebellion against the tyranny of the Oracle and its Seers. Ultimately he destroys this regime or, rather, he tricks it into destroying itself.

In making the case for finding a politics of form in *Doctor Who*, this book echoes an observation made by Tulloch and Alvarado:

Even at the most simplistic level – of recognition of references to Greek myth, Shakespeare, the Bible, history, Lang's *Metropolis*, 'specialised' sciences, etc. – the programme seeks to establish a 'complicit' relationship with its audience, which is much closer to the conventions of theatrical vaudeville than to those of dramatic 'realism'.[96]

This non-realist, exhibitionist mode is implied from a different viewpoint by Tom Baker when, in his autobiography, he jokes about his attitude to sets and realism as the incumbent Doctor: 'It was often impossible to enter into our sets and close the door "naturally" without the whole set shaking: it was the producers who called for retakes. I could never persuade them that on other planets the architecture was a bit different.'[97] Baker's relaxed view, mischievous as it is, shows an understanding of *Doctor Who* as a show beyond realism. To the irritation of many (but the delight of many more), his portrayal of the Fourth Doctor came to enact, literally, the elaborate performativity and extreme representational self-consciousness that has been outlined in this section. A notorious moment in 'The Invasion of Time' (1978) sees him turning to the camera and addressing the audience directly: 'Even the sonic screwdriver won't get me out of this one!' Such a flagrant breach of the fourth wall is indicative of a confidence – an *over*-confidence, arguably – that belongs not just to Baker but to the mythology he inhabits, its audience and its cultural place. It is the lead actor of *Doctor Who*, four years into his time in the role, not only conceding the staginess of the series but also revelling in it. Although some fans might never forgive him for this, seeing the excesses of his Williams-produced seasons as symptomatic of a decline into decadence, it is important to recognize that the revel is not (or not merely) the narcissistic self-indulgence that is sometimes alleged. Rather, it evinces a degree of sensitivity to the producer– consumer connection described a few years later by Tulloch and Alvarado. This reciprocal understanding has been stressed by Baker more recently in an interview for *Doctor Who Magazine*, during which he makes several references to the playful, mutually knowing relationship that he has always sought to maintain with audiences.[98]

Such a relationship is comparable to that attributed by Sontag to the cognoscenti of 'Camp' in an essay first published in 1964: 'esoteric – something of a private code, a badge of identity even'.[99] As with the similarly curious attribution 'cult', it is difficult to consider something with the global brand presence of *Doctor Who* as 'esoteric'. Even so, it might be that fandom inevitably partakes of a camp sensibility, not least because it 'nourishes itself on the love that has gone into certain objects and personal styles'.[100] Performance, too, can be camp and even the most determinedly naturalistic actor is only ever in denial. The world of cosplay, in this sense, is where the relationship between fans and the objects of their fandom achieves its most honest synthesis. The tenets of realism, however, insist that the highest goal of any cultural production is to conceal its roots and resist signs of artifice. When the Fourth Doctor addresses the audience directly from the screen, he breaks the surface tension that surrounds any attempt to fake reality and gives in to camp's 'love of the unnatural: of artifice and exaggeration'.[101] This is not just a Tom Baker thing, as his detractors would argue; nor is it confined to classic *Who*. After all, the Adipose could have been shown as irregular, gristly and repulsive monstrosities of fat rather than smiling and waving epitomes of uniformly merchandisable cuteness. And the sustained and intricate to-camera soliloquies of Peter Capaldi in 'Listen' (2014) and 'Before the Flood' (2015) go far beyond Tom Baker's moments of provocative whimsy.

The truth is that *Doctor Who* has a propensity towards campness written into its mythic DNA. Sontag's notes are replete with applicable phrases, describing camp's 'glorification of "character"' and 'spirit of extravagance', its 'state of continual incandescence' and desire 'to dethrone the serious'. Camp 'sees everything in quotation marks', has an affinity for 'the old-fashioned, out-of-date, *démodé*' and is 'a feat goaded on, in the last analysis, by the threat of boredom'. It is 'Dandyism in the age of mass culture'.[102] In so many ways this is a critical model fitted to the personality of *Doctor Who*. Tales from the earliest days have played up the camp qualities inherent in the format, from 'The Romans' (1965) and 'The Celestial Toymaker' (1966) during the Hartnell era to 'Robot of Sherwood' (2014) and 'The Woman Who Lived' (2015) in Capaldi's first two seasons. It is clear that some forays into out-and-out camp have been received more appreciatively than others: so, while 'The Mind Robber' (1968), 'Carnival of Monsters' (1973) and 'City of Death' (1979) are generally well regarded within fandom, 'The Creature from the Pit' (1979), 'Delta and the Bannermen' (1987) and 'Love & Monsters' (2006) are not. Significantly, the use of camp as a critical term in connection with *Doctor Who* has usually been disparaging, a way of drawing attention to perceived inadequacies in production or problems in reception. Hills, for instance, recognizes the challenge encountered by the developers of new *Who* in positioning the series as 'quality television' in contrast with popular recollections of classic *Who* as 'camp, frivolous fare, marked by silly, dated special effects'. Newman, similarly, laments the capitulation of the classic series to 'the curse of campery'.[103]

There is a limit to how much camp any audience can tolerate and it is hardly likely that *Doctor Who* would have lasted so long or reproduced itself so successfully if it was camp in any straightforward sense. I have argued, after all, that there is a political dimension to the mythology, manifested explicitly but variably in its content, and more consistently in its formal restlessness. Camp, Sontag tells us, is 'disengaged, depoliticized – or, at least, apolitical'.[104] Some would argue that this is true of *Doctor Who*, and yet several of the most ostentatiously camp stories in the television series are also among the most overtly political. Those scrutinized by Tulloch and Fiske, 'The Monster of Peladon' and 'The Creature from the Pit', are fair examples, and 'The Sun Makers' (1977), as well as being one of Robert Holmes's satirical masterworks, is also an exercise in camp impudence. Sontag sets camp in opposition to the ironical and the satirical but many of Holmes's scripts – 'Carnival of Monsters' again comes to mind – seem to contradict this. Eric Saward's 'Revelation of the Daleks' and Philip Martin's 'Vengeance on Varos' (both 1985), seen as the outstanding stories of the Colin Baker era, are also fusions of the camp and the satirical-political. These are stories in which the camp and Menippean modes coincide. Within new *Who* we might think of Davies's 'Bad Wolf' (2005) and 'The Sound of Drums' (2007), both the opening episodes for two-part, end-of-season stories, the first of which sees the camp carnival toned down for a darker finale, the second allowing the grim (the Toclafane as the sadistic apotheosis of humanity) and the outrageous (the Doctor-Dobby) to coexist.

Of course, camp needs to be taken seriously – it is 'a seriousness that fails' – and in a well-known comment towards the end of her life, Verity Lambert accused later classic-era production teams of not being serious enough about the mythology she had set in motion.[105] It was hardly an original allegation and it continues to be levelled at the stories of the Williams and Nathan-Turner years (and sometimes those of the new series). Leaving aside issues of budget, BBC politics and public taste, it is reasonable to suggest that it was not so much that the producers of *Doctor Who* between 1977 and 1989 stopped taking it seriously but that their fusing of camp with other elements became more heavy-handed. This is partly because, after more than a decade of relative innocence, as its original audience grew into adulthood, the series had become too self-aware, too conscious of its own character. 'Camp which knows itself to be Camp ("camping") is usually less satisfying,' Sontag writes.[106] When the naive mode becomes too knowing it loses much of its power. Stories such as 'Paradise Towers' (1987) and 'The

Happiness Patrol' (1988) from the era of the Seventh Doctor attempt the same mix of camp aesthetics and socio-political satire as 'The Sun Makers'. If they are generally less esteemed, it is because the elements fail to combine convincingly. A similar criticism might be made of 'Love & Monsters' and *has* been made (by Moffat himself) of 'The Beast Below (2010).[107] In the most respected tales of the McCoy years, such as 'The Greatest Show in the Galaxy' (1988–9) and 'Ghost Light' (1989), the combination is more successful, although it remains far from subtle. Interestingly, there is a contrast here with the first season of Nathan-Turner's producership. The hard science fiction promoted by Christopher H. Bidmead as script editor is not accompanied by a reduction in camp but by a more discreet merging of elements: it allows, after all, for a sentient, megalomaniacal cactus ('Meglos'), a pastiche of Cocteau's *La Belle et La Bête* ('Warriors' Gate') and a diabolically chuckling, black-clad, goatee-bearded villain (Anthony Ainley's Master, who first appears in the final moments of 'The Keeper of Traken'). There is no shortage of camp in Tom Baker's swansong season, epitomized by the horror melodramatics of 'State of Decay'.

Horror is a notoriously camp genre and *Doctor Who* can be frightening and camp at the same time. The fear that attends horror, though, is often mingled with a humane consciousness of the tragic and, for Sontag, tragedy is the opposite of camp; her notes allow for 'seriousness' and 'pathos' but 'never, never tragedy'.[108] Again, if the *Doctor Who* mythos asserts anything with consistency, it is that such categories are never stable, always contingent. Between the scripted, broadcast and published versions of 'The Happiness Patrol', for example, a separation into extremes of horror and camp can be discovered in variant conceptions of the Kandy Man. The script describes the character as being

COMPOSED OF SWEET SUBSTANCES (WITH A ROBOTIC SKELETON, COMPLETELY UNSEEN, DEEP INSIDE HIS SYNTHETIC BODY). HE IS CHUBBY AND JOLLY LOOKING, BUT AT THE SAME TIME ELEGANT AND SINISTER. THE COLOUR OF HIS SKIN, LIPS, ETC. SHOULD SUGGEST SWEETS AND SUGAR CONFECTIONS RATHER THAN HUMAN FLESH.[109]

The character as seen on TV, however, designed initially by make-up artist Dorka Nieradzik and constructed by Robert Allsopp, with additional components developed by Artem, is a less grotesque, more camply robotic figure, played by David John Pope and notoriously evocative of the Liquorice Allsorts mascot Bertie Bassett. When Graeme Curry came to adapt his tale for Target, he restored the sticky gothic phantom of his original script, with white lab coat, red bow tie and glasses, pale sugary skin and blackened teeth.[110] Similarly, when Bidmead novelized his 1984 story 'Frontios', he took the opportunity to reinstate elements of physical horror that had been both ethically and technically problematic on screen. The return of the human colonists' lost leader, Captain Revere, incorporated into the Tractators' excavating machine is a vivid case in point:

> It was a repellent sight: a huge and hideous assembly of human bodies … White bones tipped with metal cutters scraped against the rock, white rotting hands polished the surface smooth. Through illuminated windows in the body Tegan glimpsed more mechanically gesticulating human arms and legs in an advanced state of decay. It was a machine built from the dead.[111]

Representing the kind of technological body horror more often associated with the films of David Cronenberg or Shinya Tsukamoto, the emergence of Revere as the still-living but 'fearfully wasted' pilot of an alien corpse-machine achieves a degree of grisly tragedy in the book that could only be implied on family television. These are graphic instances of how the camp and the tragic can slip across each other in *Doctor Who*. There are, of course, quieter examples. The explosive demise of the boy-genius Adric, played by Matthew Waterhouse, in the final moments of 'Earthshock' (1982), remains a stunning breach of convention, a trauma intensified by the use of silent closing credits, but it in no way reduces the silliness of the character.[112]

Tragedy has been brought to the fore in new *Who*, both as part of a drive towards greater emotional complexity in the characters and as a result of placing writers in the position of showrunners. If this has led to a degree of 'soapification', welcomed by some, bemoaned by others, it has also modified the underlying equation of camp, horror and tragedy. The death of the Doctor's daughter, Jenny (Georgia Moffett), is horrific and tragic but it is also, because of Davies's refusal to show blood on screen, strangely camp. (Then again, the buckets-of-blood approach to violence during Saward's time as script editor was camp in a different way.) Similarly, the repeated deaths of Rory Williams are a contrived absurdity tinged with pathos. The surprise appearance of an elderly Tom Baker as the Curator at the end of 'The Day of the Doctor' can also be seen as a camp folly, but one enacted with reflexive and humane wit, haunted by mortal frailty in a way that Waterhouse's sacrificial leave-taking could not be.

Sontag insists that 'not all seriousness that fails can be redeemed as Camp'.[113] In connection with *Doctor Who*, this is seen most sharply when the explicit importation of classical mythology is considered. When the Doctor and his story are brought into deliberate conjunction with the well-known tales of ancient civilizations, the outcomes are often regarded as less than the sum of their parts. Graham Kibble-White, reviewing the 2010 *Myths and Legends* box set, appraises its contents – 'The Time Monster' (1972), 'Underworld' (1978) and 'The Horns of Nimon' (1979–80) – as 'three of the heaviest thuds in *Doctor Who* history'.[114] This is not a controversial ruling: in the *Doctor Who Magazine* readers' poll of 2014 they rank at 222, 236 and 223 of 241, respectively.[115]

Revered as stories, exploited repeatedly as raw material for popular narratives, classical myths are taken seriously as objects of often contested cultural inheritance, but they are not (and cannot be) experienced as they were by the civilizations that gave rise to them. They can be understood as narrative traces, as archaeological remains, as the fetishized relics of a putative heritage, but they cannot be felt or lived or really comprehended as they once were. The secular, materialist democracies that provide most of the audiences for *Doctor Who* are too far removed from the worlds of ancient Greece and Rome; they are too far removed, even, from the worlds that yielded the Arthurian and Norse mythologies behind 'Battlefield' and 'The Curse of Fenric' (both 1989). Early mythographers such as Tylor and Frazer recognized this distancing of modernity from the founding contexts of ancient myths and argued that it marked a shift from 'primitive' to 'scientific' world views.[116] Later commentators, notably Lucien Lévy-Bruhl and Bronisław Malinowski, offered more nuanced readings but still held that a fundamental break had occurred between the cultures that created the mythologies and the cultures that now attempted to interpret them, whether through scholarship or fictional adaptation.[117]

One consequence of this is that ancient mythologies retain an irresistible allure for us moderns; another is that, no matter how sophisticated our representational technologies, they can only ever appear camp when adapted as narratives for contemporary audiences. State-of-the-art adaptations of classical material for cinema can be spectacular, exciting and even (on their own terms) mimetically convincing, accomplishing the photorealistic illusion described by Manovich, but they can never avoid looking and sounding theatrical. If we consider the 1981 version of *Clash of the Titans* (dir. Desmond Davis), it is an extraordinarily camp film, but no more so than the ostensibly more realistic CGI-heavy remake of 2010 (dir. Louis Leterrier). In the same way, each major screen depiction of the Hercules myth has pushed hard at the available technical resources, but it would be difficult to make a convincing case that Brett Ratner's 2014 version, starring wrestler Dwayne 'The Rock' Johnson, is any less of a burlesque than Pietro Francisci's 1957 version, starring bodybuilder Steve Reeves. For the ancients, a myth means what it says, it is what it is, with no room for interpretation or symbolism. For the moderns, a myth is what we make it: it is what it is made to be. The classical world, recreated in the modern world, can only ever be a display of elaborate artifice, a piece of extreme theatre. This does not prevent the stories from being enjoyable ('Camp taste is, above all, a mode of enjoyment'),[118] but it does suggest a need to enjoy them on different terms. These are terms that can offer a revised perspective on *Doctor Who*'s supposed mythological let-downs.

The most powerful modern adaptations of classical mythology are those that demonstrate a formal incorporation of the source material rather than a literal representation of it. In such cases, mythic elements are acknowledged as part of the fabricated artefact, their creative illusion and shift of cultural context highlighted rather than downplayed. This equates, in part, to the 'mythological method' that Eliot attributes to *Ulysses*, and Joyce's great novel is the prime exemplar here. Another is to be found in Picasso's integration of the minotaur myth within successive artworks, from *Le Minotaure* (1928) to *Le roi des Minotaures* (1958). *Guernica*, his vast canvas responding to the fascist bombing of Basque civilians in April 1937, features a bull rather than a minotaur but it is notable that the creature's shocked white head seems to float free of its lost black body, as if trying to find a kind of hybrid wholeness among all the screaming, broken forms in the tableau. Both Joyce and Picasso integrate ancient, non-indigenous mythologies within work that goes beyond the depressive snobbery of Eliot's formalism in confronting historical and political trauma. Their mythological methods are closer to the imaginatively liberated and transformational ideal espoused by Ricoeur than they are to the reactionary gloom of Eliot.

Television, self-evidently, is a younger medium than either the novel or the oil painting, and its traditions are still emergent, evolving rapidly. This means that when its relatively brief history furnishes instances of mythic adaptation, the formal effects are likely to be less refined, less calculated, than in the experimentation of older media.

'The Time Monster' plays its mythic sources straight, with the result that it seems more artlessly camp than either 'Underworld' or 'The Horns of Nimon'. This, thrown into relief by moments of laboured comedy in the modern-day sections (John Levine's Sergeant Benton in a nappy), is not to its advantage, putting it on a par with an earlier depiction of doomed Atlantis, 'The Underwater Menace' (1967). The snow-white birdman costume for Kronos has been much criticized and yet, glimpsed in flapping, ominous smudges of light, the creature is impressively unsettling, hinting in formal terms at its amoral, androgynous otherness. A similarly epicene embodiment of power is to be found in the design for the Nimon costumes. Whatever can be said about these boulder-headed, world-hopping parasites, they are not – as Newman claims[119] – 'baggy', and with their sleek, slim torsos they represent a more intriguing and threatening variant of the Minotaur than is seen in the hybrid's previous brief appearances in 'The Mind Robber' and 'The Time Monster'. The Nimons are absurd as they totter on their platform hooves, the actors' necks becoming visible at times as their massive heads rise up awkwardly, but they are also fascinating in their strangeness, genuinely threatening. As a design, they succeed despite their snags, largely because of the contradictions between bulk and slenderness, litheness of form and growling animalism of voice.

The original conception of the Nimons' outsized heads as masks or helmets, concealing their true horrific appearance, was dropped at a relatively late stage in production, leading to an accidentally exaggerated theatricality in the presentation. Acting as a material metaphor for the story itself, darkly ridiculous, grim but silly, these monsters set the tone for the overall realization, giving Graham Crowden the dramatic license for his camped-up display as Soldeed, at the same time providing a context for Lalla Ward's imposing performance as Romana and Tom Baker's puckish exhibition as the Doctor. In contrast with 'The Time Monster', and in defiance of Sontag's denigration of self-aware camp, 'The Horns of Nimon' knows itself to be a pantomime, but a pantomime presented with conviction and an ominous edge. It takes a playful, transformative approach to the mythology that it draws on, and the outcome is a greatly underestimated tale.

In the end, the realist code is a myth about myths, about how we receive the stories we tell, and it is as theological in its concerns as it is aesthetic. Realism relies on belief, which is another way of saying that it relies on faith. The grounds of faith change constantly but, by definition, they can never rest on certainty, faith being the opposite of knowledge. It is not the job of this book to speculate on the state and status of religion in the modern world, but the growth in popularity of fantasy genres over recent years – and the proliferation of papers, articles and books discussing these – seems to suggest that when religion comes under strain, when it begins to sicken and die, or turns toxic and aggressive, there is an instinct to look elsewhere for the stories we can have faith in. This is the key theme in Toby Whithouse's Eleventh Doctor story 'The God Complex' (2011), which name-checks the Nimons as part of a further mutation of the Minotaur myth. Noted as the distant cousins of a fierce bull-headed creature which prowls a drifting space-prison, itself a labyrinthine and hallucinatory rendering of a 1980s Earth hotel, the Nimons appear here to be both commemorated and superseded.

Ostensibly, the Minotaur of 'The God Complex' confirms the victory of the realist code of contemporary production, its costume a triumph of material realization. In containing the myth of its earlier and 'cheaper' relative, however, it also bolsters the continuity between the classic and the new. The luridly nostalgic setting, nightmarish in its disturbed sense of familiarity and its recall of the Overlook Hotel in Stanley Kubrick's *The Shining* (1980), adds to this suggestion of merged paradigms. Most powerfully, because the Minotaur is imprisoned as the last survivor of a race that dominated others by assuming the function of deity, relying on their belief to maintain control, it suggests a symbolic parallel with the Doctor as a character. The Doctor recognizes this and denies it immediately ('I wasn't talking about myself') but, for both his companions and the audience, the connection is reinforced even as it is rejected. His strategy for defeating, or bringing peace to, the Minotaur is especially poignant in this respect: he destroys Amy's faith in him. The echo of the Seventh Doctor's desperate triumph over Fenric through the corrosion of Ace's belief is unmistakable.

If companions are the audience's avatars within the storyworld, then the implications of such plot points for *Doctor Who*'s fandom, with its size, variety, devotion and unpredictability, are worth considering. In 1989, when the faith of the casual viewer was lost and the faith of the BBC was put to the test and found wanting, it was the faith of the fans that not only sustained the myth but also transformed it, preparing the ground for the regeneration of 2005. It is, after all, axiomatic of *Doctor Who* that even the bleakest situation, the most unlikely idea, the least convincing effect, can become a thing of wonder. Faith is one thing. Hope is something else again.

Chapter 5
Conclusion: 'The universe will surprise you'

When these closing pages were first drafted, it was in a spirit of some apprehension, invoking the Fourth Doctor's typically Panglossian observation from 'Warriors' Gate' (1981) that 'One good solid hope's worth a cartload of certainties'. With the final season of the Capaldi era about to begin, *Doctor Who* seemed to be caught between an eager anticipation of new adventures and unease brought about by rumours of a crisis. In the run-up to the 2016 Christmas Special, 'The Return of Doctor Mysterio', the first new story for sixteen months, there had been reports of institutional frustration with both the recent decline in ratings and a concurrent deterioration in merchandise sales. It was claimed that, to stop the perceived rot, incoming showrunner Chris Chibnall had been directed to institute a radical overhaul in order to produce 'a brand new show' for 2018.[1] In advance of Capaldi making public his decision to quit the role of the Doctor, there was an insinuation that his departure alongside Steven Moffat and new companion Pearl Mackie (who had yet to even make her full debut as Bill Potts) might be welcomed by the BBC.[2]

Regardless of whether the BBC itself might be culpable for any waning of the show's popularity, with questions being asked around scheduling and promotion in particular, the apparent decline stirred inevitable anxieties in fans of a certain age, who recalled the hiatus of 1985. This was when, following Colin Baker's first season as the Sixth Doctor, the series was suspended for eighteen months, returning at last with the forlornly titled portmanteau tale 'The Trial of a Time Lord'. It was also when the original *Doctor Who* exhibition closed its doors on Blackpool's Golden Mile. Fatalistic fans of the revived series could hardly fail to notice that reports of degeneration had coincided with news that the Doctor Who Experience in Cardiff would be closing in 2017.[3] Capaldi's notice of resignation – notwithstanding that three full seasons seems to be the default tenure for a twenty-first-century Doctor – meant that 'The Pilot' was broadcast in an atmosphere of some trepidation. Although the title of the opener for Moffat's valedictory series placed a wry emphasis on beginnings, the conjectural rhythm in the background resembled the Cloister Bell tolling the End of Days.

Thirteen weeks later, a fortnight after the conclusion of the two-part season finale and only minutes after the 2017 Wimbledon Men's Singles Final, Jodie Whittaker was revealed as Capaldi's successor, the first woman to be cast in the role of the Doctor (excepting Joanna Lumley's comic turn in 'The Curse of Fatal Death', scripted by Moffat for the Red Nose Day telethon of 1999). Suddenly, the discourse around the series changed. There had been much speculation about the possibility of a female Doctor – of course, there has been much speculation prior to every regeneration since at least 1980, when Tom Baker stoked rumours about his own heir – but on this occasion there seemed to be a steadier impetus to the narrative than previously. Although adherents of the repeated meme maintained that Kris Marshall was the prime candidate, actors such as Tilda Swinton, Olivia Colman and Thandie Newton were also said to be in the frame. Alec Charles argued online that the casting of the Thirteenth Doctor 'may signal the BBC's confidence as a bold trendsetter – or not', suggesting that 'the casting of this particular role may offer a gauge as to its confidence (and dexterity) in negotiating a route towards a post-Brexit Britain'.[4] Then *Fleabag* creator Phoebe Waller-Bridge showed an apparently revelatory awkwardness when dodging the Doctor question during a vlog interview, her inadvertent 'spoiler' – with added regeneration effect – becoming the closing item on *Newsnight*.[5]

In the event, the unveiling of Whittaker – who had been mentioned in relation to the role, but not very often and not very loudly – was performed through an atmospheric one-minute scene featuring no dialogue but rich in visual and sonic signs. Unlike the clumsy and uncomfortable talk-show format that announced Capaldi's casting in 2013, this was a presentation that showed a first-rate actor emerging from within the mythic fabric of the show. Unsurprisingly, confirmation of a shift from spear to distaff was met with considerable excitement, the overall reaction being enthusiastic. Most fans welcomed what they saw as either a sharply appropriate piece of casting, a long-overdue redressing of the balance or a necessarily dramatic shake-up of the format.[6] Nervousness among some, however, escalated into toxic fury among a minority. At the limits of negative opinion, there were *ad hominem* attacks, plangent howls of disbelief and a TARDIS-load of bad old-fashioned chauvinism, reinforced by tabloid 'revelations' about sex scenes in Whittaker's acting career and the ripped jeans that she wore to go shopping. Similarly unedifying was the spectacle of Peter Davison being deployed by the media in opposition to Colin Baker, before being trolled off Twitter by those who objected to some moderate reservations quoted out of context.[7]

Predictably, the most vitriolic resistance to Whittaker as the Doctor could be traced to those with a culturally conservative agenda, whether professional media goblin Katie Hopkins – who jibed on Twitter about the Doctor going on maternity leave – or US evangelicals like James Huckabee, whose tweet read, '#DoctorWho died today. He didn't die nobly as you might expect. He was murdered by Political Correctness.' At times, the ferocity of those reacting against the news was terrifying in its misogyny. 'Not really a DW fan,' raved one voice, again on Twitter, 'but female DW can suck my D ffs – stupid ideology bullshit infesting everything.' Reading this, it is hard not to agree with Jonn Elledge's declaration that Whittaker's casting had 'annoy[ed] exactly the right people'.[8]

For all the furore around Whittaker's casting, both pro and con, the most shocking thing about it might well be that, like Bill Potts's lesbianism, it should have been viewed as a news story at all. Indeed, as Matt Hills argued, citing examples of 'regendering' in other popular fantasy franchises, the radicalism of the moment was liable to be overstated if viewed in isolation: 'It could even be argued that the new team is following the market rather than enacting bold public service programming. The real risk would have been to cast yet another white male, consigning Doctor Who to a sense of being yesterday's brand.'[9] From a different perspective, Lorna Jowett also played down the degree of change heralded by the arrival of Whittaker, stressing the need for continuity in the character:

[Whittaker] needs to be the Doctor, not the (or, hopefully, a) 'female Doctor'. My hope is that the thirteenth Doctor will be doing all the things the Doctor usually does – getting into trouble, saving worlds, showing off, and wielding a sonic screwdriver with aplomb – without gender being an issue.[10]

Just as successive male Doctors had retained aspects of their predecessors while evolving a necessary distinctness, so Whittaker's Doctor would be recognizably the same character. Crucially, for Jowett, the mere act of casting a woman in the lead role would not, in itself, constitute a redress of the gender balance. Whittaker's performance in front of the camera would mean little if the culture behind it remained frozen, if she was somehow 'expected to make up for the lack of women driving the series creatively'.[11]

Although Jowett was acerbic in her criticism of Moffat's efforts at laying the foundations for a female Doctor, the fact that the foundations were put in place should be acknowledged. Both the good intentions and the dubious deeds were apparent in the first lines given to the Doctor by Moffat during his time as showrunner – 'Hair. I'm a girl! No. No, I'm not a girl' – and also in a rejoinder to John Simm's Master towards the end of his tenure:

> MASTER Is the future going to be all 'girl'?
> DOCTOR We can only hope.

Jowett was not disposed to give the benefit of any doubt to such well-meaning but misjudged efforts – 'Girls, ladies and Missy. Could the future possibly just be *female* [my italics]? We can only hope' – but the range and extensiveness of the efforts is noticeable. From the presentation of the feminine soul of the TARDIS, Idris, in Neil Gaiman's 'The Doctor's Wife' (2011) via Clara's 'performance' as the Doctor in Jamie Mathieson's 'Flatline' (2014) – 'Does this mean I'm you now?' – to Michelle Gomez's glorious reign as Missy, from 'Deep Breath' (2014) to 'The Doctor Falls' (2017), it was clear that Moffat's agenda included the destabilization of Gallifreyan gender and sexuality. That there was a self-reflexive irony to this destabilization (after all, the writers listed here are all male) is suggested in an exchange between the Doctor and Bill in 'World Enough and Time' (2017):

> DOCTOR Yeah, I think she [Missy] was a man back then. I'm fairly sure that I was too. It was a long time ago though.

BILL So, the Time Lords – a bit flexible on the whole man–woman thing then, yeah?

DOCTOR We're the most civilized civilization in the universe. We're billions of years beyond your petty human obsession with gender and its associated stereotypes.

BILL But you still call yourselves Time *Lords*?

DOCTOR Yeah. Shut up.

In the light of this, the Doctor's shooting of the General in 'Hell Bent' (2015), triggering his regeneration from a white man into a black woman, begins to have a significance beyond the vexed question of the hero's supposed repudiation of violence. If nothing else, it makes clear Moffat's conviction that the Doctor represents an unusually indefinite form of definite article.

The degree to which *Doctor Who* might become a different show, a different narrative, a different myth, with a female Doctor at the TARDIS controls, can be assessed through a review of Whittaker's first season, the eleventh of the returned series. This began with the airing of 'The Woman Who Fell to Earth' on 7 October 2018 and ended nine weeks later with the catchily titled 'The Battle of Ranskoor Av Kolos' – or, arguably, with the festive coda of 'Resolution' which followed on New Year's Day 2019. The slightly shorter season (previous years of the revived series had lasted twelve or thirteen weeks) was formed from slightly longer episodes (fifty rather than forty-five minutes, with the opener running to sixty-five minutes and the festive special to sixty), and Chibnall was clear from the start that there would be no multi-part stories, no dominant story arcs and no returning monsters. Whittaker was joined in her adventures by Ryan Sinclair (Tosin Cole), a young black warehouse worker with dyspraxia, Yasmin Khan (Mandip Gill), a probationary police officer of Punjabi-Muslim background and Graham O'Brien (Bradley Walsh), Ryan's step-grandfather, a middle-aged former bus driver in recovery from cancer. The recurrent locus for the season was modern-day Sheffield, in South Yorkshire, England, less than an hour from Whittaker's birthplace of Skelmanthorpe, and also where Chibnall studied for his master's degree.

The cultural diversity evident in the new *dramatis personae* was mirrored in that of the creative team that Chibnall had assembled for the series. The writers of the five episodes not scripted by Chibnall himself were all new to the series, two of them being women (Malorie Blackman, Joy Wilkinson) and two from black or Asian backgrounds (Blackman, Vinay Patel). Blackman and Patel were, in fact, the first writers in the history of the programme to come from such backgrounds, with Blackman and Wilkinson being only the seventh and eighth women. Two of the five directors for the season were women (Sallie Aprahamian, Jennifer Perrott), script editing was split between Fiona McAllister and Nina Métivier, and the bulk of the production was by Nikki Wilson. Stepping into the symphonic breach left by Murray Gold, musical director since the return of the show in 2005, was British-Nigerian composer Segun Akinola. For a serial drama that had seemed, in its first four weeks at least, to offer the promise of an inclusive vision of creativity – a female producer in Verity Lambert, an Asian director in Waris Hussein, both eye-catching appointments in 1963 – *Doctor Who* had settled quickly into a familiar pattern of hegemony. The approach taken by Chibnall and his executive producers, Matt Strevens and Sam Hoyle, picking up the markers set down (with scant recognition from his critics) in the later years of the Moffat era, was determinedly reformist in this sense. Whether it was sufficient in scale and impact to unsettle, with any long-term effect, the foundations of an obdurately white, male mythos remains to be seen. That it responded in the only reasonable way to a creative context buffeted by the shockwaves of social justice movements such as Black Lives Matter and Me Too, not to mention the divisiveness of local and global politics in the age of Donald Trump, Brexit and the Islamic State, is hard to deny. That it was always going to encounter some resistance and hostility is equally so. The Doctor regenerating into a woman was never going to happen quietly.

As with the initial announcement of Whittaker's casting, responses to her first season have been generally positive. The prominence of some extreme negative viewpoints across social media and video sharing platforms has tended, however, to distort surface readings at times, with opposition invariably focusing on the agenda for, and the perceived effects of, cultural diversification within the production team and the TARDIS crew. From Bowlestrek, whose anti-SJW ('social justice warrior') fulminations on YouTube and Twitter seem measured and progressive compared with the ventings of many of his followers, to Facebook groups such as 'We Hate Jodie Whittaker As DR WHO' and '#NotOurDoctor', the malcontented voices within fandom have been raucous if not, on closer inspection, particularly numerous. Although Bowlestrek currently has 28,505 subscribers to his YouTube channel and can receive 30,000 views for his videos, these are not particularly large figures by the standards of the website. Similarly, his Twitter account, started in 2008, has only a fraction of the followers (1,361) that the accounts 'Whovian Feminism' (9,182), 'The Time Ladies' (6,805) and 'The Women of Who' (9,880) have attracted in much less time (started in 2013, 2017 and 2017, respectively). Meanwhile, the #NotMyDoctor Official Page on Twitter has secured only 269 followers. Over on Facebook, a similar pattern can be discerned. We Hate Jodie Whittaker As DR WHO (created in July 2017) has 544 members and #NotOurDoctor (created in March 2018) has 272. In contrast, Progressive Doctor Who Fans (also created in July 2017) has 3,065 members and Doctor Who Fans Who Actually Like The Show (created in November 2018) has 5,669.[12]

Beyond social media, some mainstream journalistic coverage of the first Whittaker–Chibnall season appears to validate the discourse of extreme fan division, representing a narrative in which the common people revolt against the sacrifice of a national treasure to the whims of the 'metropolitan liberal elite'. After only three episodes, for instance, *The Mail on Sunday*'s Chris Hastings declared a crisis: 'Exterminate! Fans' Backlash over Doctor Who's Latest Transformation – into TV's Most PC Show'.[13] A week later, Rod McPhee repeated the rhetoric in *The Sun*: 'EXTERMINATING VIEWERS: Doctor Who Ratings Plunge after Jodie Whittaker Takes Over with PC Plots'.[14] Notwithstanding the ambiguity of the initial verb – is 'exterminating' active or passive here? – it is intriguing that both newspapers seemed to endorse fan disapproval by equating them with the Daleks. More straightforwardly, their hyperbole around the 'backlash' effectively agitated against Whittaker's *Doctor Who* (and, by association, the *bête noire* of the BBC) through a substantive misrepresentation of the series' reception. The political subtext was surely as much about perceived institutional bias as it was about a female Doctor – or, rather, it was about the ways in which a female Doctor might be used as evidence of that perceived institutional bias. Whittaker's arrival had, the *Mail* suggested, transformed the escapism of *Doctor Who* into 'a tiresome ordeal of political correctness', 'a platform for social justice issues, complete with a racially diverse cast'.[15] Noticeably, these allegations were expressed at a journalistic distance – 'for some viewers', 'they say', '[a] viewer tweeted' – and supported by little or no evidence, or else by evidence presented out of context. This was nowhere clearer than in Jeremy Clarkson's response in *The Sun* to McPhee's previous response in *The Sun*, a third order simulation of reportage that would have made the most hardcore Baudrillardian blush:

> HAVEN'T watched Dr Who since I was a small boy and I didn't understand it even then, but I'm told the current series is in trouble – with viewing figures in freefall.
>
> Angry fans say it's littered with ham-fisted attempts to ram Lefty dogma down our throats, and if you look at the storylines, it seems they do have a point.[16]

This bizarrely hollow ramble makes a rhetorical virtue of its own ignorance but, in the spirit of the age, aspires to a plangent condition of reactionary irritation. It is a protest of such lazy, entitled complacency that it is tempting to invoke the Doctor's observation from 'The Witchfinders': 'These *are* hard times for women! If we're not being drowned, we're being patronized to death!' Back on Twitter, Alec Charles took the annoyance of Clarkson as a measure of the new era's achievement to date: 'To provoke such a bitter rant from such a nasty piece of work, you know you must be doing something very right.'[17]

As the season progressed, a lot was made by those declaring a sense of crisis in *Doctor Who* of the decline in overnight ratings from the 8.2 million who tuned in for 'The Woman Who Fell to Earth' to the 5.07 million who watched 'It Takes You Away'. As Tom Spilsbury has pointed out, however, the overall average television-only viewing figure of 7.7 million 'compares very favourably' with those from previous debut seasons of new *Who*, which range from 7.26 million for Capaldi to 7.95 million for Eccleston.[18]

Considered dispassionately, the socially inflected criticism levelled at Season Eleven of the revived series looks, for the most part, like the confirmation of a pre-existing bias among a certain minority of the audience. Fans and casual viewers who objected (and continue to object) to the casting of a woman in the role of the Doctor have found their suspicions validated and their prejudices borne out by stories that engage with sensitive historical subject matter and 'big issues' of race, gender, family, sexuality and violence. The simple equation seems to be that the regeneration from man to woman (or from biologically male body to biologically female body) has resulted in an emotional softening of the show and a concurrent ethical oversensitivity. VanMan on Twitter seems representative of this outlook: 'What the bloody hell is the world coming to, even #DoctorWho has gone completely PC. That's the last episode I'll be watching, I don't watch this type of TV show to get subliminal PC lectures, it's supposed to be entertainment.'[19] The catch-all insult *de nos jours*, 'PC', is almost redundant here, since its intended effect is to appeal to a putative 'common sense' and thus to close down discussion. The 'even', on the other hand, seems significant: *'even* #DoctorWho', as if there is an absurdity in the very notion of the series being 'correct' in its politics, or perhaps of having a politics at all. It is telling that VanMan's Twitter profile reads, 'All politicians Muted ... I'm sick of your BS', as it asserts a detachment that, whatever its motivations and frustrations, is aligned with the mythic view of popular art forms that Fiske sees as essentially ideological.[20] If it is 'supposed to be entertainment', then it follows, in this Barthesian view, that *Doctor Who* is *not* supposed to challenge the way things are or ask awkward questions about the way things have been or might be. The 'naturalizing force' of a supposedly entertaining popular narrative is to conceal, or distract from, politics and to deny the contingency of historical processes.[21]

Superficially, the objection of some fans to what they see as the overt political conscience of Whittaker's first season might seem to substantiate Fiske's contention that 'an art form which is radically opposed to dominant social discourses would not be popular, but would appeal largely to the converted'.[22] Then again, those irritated by what they characterize as a pandering to political correctness would doubtless see this as entirely consistent with 'dominant social discourses' rather than opposed to them. For *Doctor Who* to celebrate the defiance of Rosa Parks in refusing to give up her seat on a racially segregated bus in Montgomery, Alabama, in December 1955 ('Rosa'), or to commemorate the internecine trauma of Indian partition eight years earlier ('Demons of the Punjab'), simply corresponds with a view of the series as having been absorbed into the prevailing narratives of twenty-first-century liberalism. Such absorption is seen, of course, to be wholly incompatible with the kind of 'entertainment' that *Doctor Who* is 'supposed' to represent and detrimental to its imaginative integrity. This integrity, never defined but apparently utopian in its ability to float free of the mess of history and politics, suspended in some fantastical realm where fiction never needs to get its hands dirty, is similarly corrupted by visions of a future in which men can become pregnant ('The Tsuranga Conundrum') and Amazonian e-commerce spans galaxies ('Kerblam!'). It also struggles, it seems, with satires on pathologically narcissistic and aggressive American businessmen with political pretensions ('Arachnids in the UK').

Disdainful views of a perceived moral wetness in Season Eleven (a sneering scorn for so-called 'Generation Snowflake' has never been far away) are hard to square with an unease among some viewers about the elements of political *incorrectness* in several stories. For all the reactionary objections to, say, the portrayal of dubious fathering in 'It Takes You Away', there have been counter-accusations levelled at the corporate politics of 'Kerblam!' (it is a disaffected worker who is the 'villain' of the piece, after all, not the galactic mega-corporation) and the cartoon queering of King James I in 'The Witchfinders'. It would be reasonable to argue, in fact, that the constantly reversing polarities of the discursive flow around Chibnall's first season are an intensified version of those which have operated around *Doctor Who* since at least the late 1970s and, in some ways, since its very inception. Questions raised by Fiske, Chapman, Britton, Charles, Jowett and others about its apparently conservative bias have alternated with those at odds with its inappropriately libertarian spirit, whether in the form of parents on *Talkback* in 1967 bemoaning the violence of 'The Tomb of Cybermen' or the handful of viewers who complained to Ofcom and the BBC about the 'promotion' of homosexuality in 2014's 'Deep Breath'. Typically, this polarization reveals a pattern of difference between academic critics and those from more popular, or populist, areas of discourse. Where the former are often motivated by concerns about cultural representation or ideological subtext, the latter tend to be exercised by matters of moral appropriateness or franchise fidelity; where the former are apt to evince an essentially left-liberal viewpoint, the latter show a more reactionary disposition. While this debatable generalization is neither surprising nor newsworthy, it is worth acknowledging as evidence that there is nothing new under the Gallifreyan suns.

Those opposed to Whittaker have been predisposed towards narratives of a tradition betrayed, depicting *Doctor Who* as a grand old treasure despoiled by the clumsy, overeager and ignorant attentions of social do-gooders. Those who have ruined the show, the story goes, do not understand the thing they have ruined: they lack sympathy with its essence and have therefore corrupted it. Notwithstanding that this is a curious accusation to level at life-long fan Chibnall (and it needs to be remembered that comparable accusations were levelled at life-long fan Moffat and, to a lesser extent, life-long fan Davies), it seems even more curious when it is considered how much Season Eleven has either continued or revived the conventions of the series. Indeed, it could be argued that, in significant ways, Chibnall has taken *Doctor Who* even further back towards its origins than Moffat did, and certainly than Davies did. He has, for instance, increased the size of the TARDIS crew, constituting it as the Doctor-plus-three for the first time since 1983 (Doctor, Nyssa, Tegan and Turlough) and bringing it in line with the original conception of the series (Doctor, Susan, Barbara and Ian). Obviously, the constitution of the current foursome is distinct from those earlier versions, and not only in its ethnic mix. Where the original TARDIS crew featured a heroic young man to counterbalance the anti-heroic old Doctor, and an intelligent earthly woman to counterbalance the intelligent unearthly child, and where the early 1980s iterations placed an emphasis on youth and gender balance, there is now a young(-looking) female Doctor, a younger female companion, an equivalently young man (Yaz and Ryan were at school together) and an older man as counterbalance. The founding familial dynamic of grandparent and grandchild has been replicated, with the peculiarity of the Doctor and Susan's relationship (there have been far more questions raised by her nominal status as his 'granddaughter' than have ever been answered) being replaced by the more quotidian peculiarity of that between Graham and Ryan (a white step-grandfather and a black step-grandson who are initially uneasy with each other following the death of Grace, the woman who – as wife to the former and grandmother to the latter – brought them together). Concentration on the easy target of a diverse TARDIS crew has, it seems, distracted some commentators from its mirroring of character configurations from the classic era of the show. That the composition of a regular cast reflecting the culture out of which *Doctor Who* is actually produced should be seen by some as radical, shocking or even offensive is a sign not only of the programme's ethnographical belatedness but also of a worryingly belligerent lack of domestic confidence on the part of some sections of its audience.

Other aspects of maintained or revived tradition under Chibnall have also been overlooked in an apparent readiness, or eagerness, to be outraged by the new. Even if the key structuring icon of the Doctor herself has been transformed beyond precedents, others – most obviously, the TARDIS and the sonic screwdriver – remain the same, albeit modified through small-scale redesigns. More strikingly, Chibnall's structuring of his inaugural season implements a pattern of storytelling that is reminiscent of that favoured by Verity Lambert in the earliest days of *Doctor Who*. Where the original producer preferred a binary rhythm, through which historical tales and science fiction tales would alternate, Chibnall has opted for a ternary sequence, stories on present-day Earth alternating with those set in the planet's past and others set in its future and/or on an extraterrestrial elsewhere. The sequence has not been entirely regular (nor was it for Lambert) but it has been noticeable, demonstrating a concern to achieve a balanced variety of scenarios.

The historical stories in Whittaker's first season have all contained science fiction elements. In this sense, they do not quite replicate the 'pure' historical format of the Hartnell era, being closer to the spirit of 'The Time Meddler' (1965) than that of 'The Aztecs' or 'The Reign of Terror' (both 1964). Even so, the historical contexts are foregrounded in ways that they have not been in previous history-based stories within new *Who*. 'Rosa', 'Demons of the Punjab' and, to a lesser extent, 'The Witchfinders' are historical tales with science fiction embellishments rather than the other way around. Indeed, it could be argued that 'Rosa' and 'Demons of the Punjab' are primarily about the histories that they inhabit and that the elements of science fiction are secondary concerns, even superfluous. The real monster of 'Rosa' is the racism of 1950s USA, not the rather bland villain Krasko (Joshua Bowman), a narcissistic über-criminal from the future who is defeated far more easily than human bigotry will ever be. Krasko is, without doubt, a nasty piece of work, a fascistic mass murderer and unapologetic racist. His malevolence, though, seems strangely trivial alongside the casual sociological viciousness which leads a white man to slap Ryan across the face for picking up and returning a dropped glove: 'Get your filthy black hands off my wife!' This is arguably the most shocking moment in

Doctor Who's television history, compounded moments later when the man warns Graham that his grandson 'will be swinging from a tree with a noose for a neckerchief if he touches a white woman in Montgomery'.

A similar inhibition of the science-fictional mode can be seen in 'Demons of the Punjab', where the planned marriage of Yaz's grandmother, Umbreen (Leena Dhingra / Amita Suman), a Muslim, to her Hindu sweetheart, Prem (Shane Zaza), is subject to the violent ethnic pressures of Indian partition. When a final and startling act of murderous conflict takes place, signalled through the explosive jolt of an off-screen gunshot as the Doctor and her friends escape with Umbreen and her mother, Hasna (Shaheen Khan), it seems almost incidental that the alien Thijarians should appear to observe and ensure the dignity of lonely death. A reformed race of ancient galactic assassins, the last of their kind, this potentially interesting new species of *Who* monster becomes little more than a narrative red herring or, perhaps worse, a redundant marker of 'correct' sentiment. To subtract the Thijarians from Vinay Patel's story would do little to diminish its power, just as the removal of Krasko from 'Rosa' would amount to the loss of a plot device but not, in any real sense, a reduction of impact. The broader theme of 'The Witchfinders', the persecution of women (of old, poor or unconventional women in particular) in early modern Europe, means that the alien presence can be given a more distinct and integrated role within the storyline. That said, the Morax, the mud monsters imprisoned beneath Pendle Hill, Lancashire, are more eerily compelling in their guise of lumbering resurrected corpses than they are in the manifested form of the Morax Queen, crinkled and booming beneath the ostentatious curls of the local magistrate, Becka Savage (Siobhan Finneran).

It is noticeable that the historical stories have been among the most popular of Whittaker's first season, with an average Audience Appreciation Index (AI) score of 81. ('Rosa' achieved the joint-highest figure of 83 and went on to win 'Television Show of the Year' in BAFTA's inaugural Visionary Arts Organisation Awards in February 2019.)[23] It is equally noticeable that the least popular stories seem to be those set in the future, with 'The Tsuranga Conundrum' and 'The Battle of Ranskoor Av Kolos' achieving the joint-lowest scores of 79. There is not a huge difference here, of course, and the sample is small. Moreover, Pete McTighe's futuristic satire 'Kerblam!' has an impressive AI of 81. Nevertheless, it might be significant that those stories in which the role of monsters is marginal are also those about which the audience has been most enthusiastic. Chibnall was insistent from an early stage in the development process that Whittaker's first season would include no returning monsters and, inevitably, this meant that an unusually high level of expectation was placed on *new* monsters. In keeping with his remit to make a clean break with the Moffat years, Chibnall's *carte blanche* with regard to monsters seemed entirely reasonable, repeating the approach taken for Jon Pertwee's first season. Given the centrality of monsters within the public consciousness of *Doctor Who*, however, it was always going to be a risky enterprise. In the absence of old monsters, the new monsters had better be good. Pertwee's debuting Doctor was confronted with full-colour Autons, Silurians, radioactive Martian ambassadors and Primords as substitutes for the Troughton era's proliferation of monochrome Daleks, Cybermen, Yeti and Ice Warriors. How did Whittaker fare in comparison?

On the face of it, there is nothing substantively *wrong* with the monsters encountered during Season Eleven. The Stenza warrior, Tzim-Sha, the SniperBots, the Remnants, the Thijarians and the TeamMates are soundly designed and well realized, not especially original but effective enough within the constraints of the stories they occupy. These constraints are significant, however, and they mean that none of the new monsters demand attention in the way that the most successful of the old monsters, from the Daleks to the Weeping Angels, have done. Tzim-Sha (Samuel Oatley), positioned as the season's 'big bad',[24] is somehow neither big enough nor bad enough (or, in fairness, established enough) to justify the Doctor's breathy anxious utterance in the teaser-trailer for the season finale: 'I know that voice!' He is ruthless and sadistic in his *modus operandi*, with an appearance that merges hi-tech armoured sleekness and ritual savagery, his face studded with the teeth of his victims, but the sense of threat is oddly muted. The decision to construct his identity around a joke name, 'Tim Shaw', means that his menace is diminished, from the start, through mockery. It is true that Daleks, Cybermen and Sontarans have all been subjected to facetious taunts from the Doctor across the years but not in the first moments of their first encounter, and not before the peril they represent has been unequivocally demonstrated. As a lone wolf, Tzim-Sha is shown to be an indiscriminate killer from the moment he is introduced in 'The Woman Who Fell to Earth', but his agenda of terrorization is never entirely convincing, not even when he is shrinking down entire planets for his private collection (à la Pirate Captain) in 'The Battle of Ranskoor Av Kolos'. The issue is, in part, that his martial support, the SniperBots, are seen, in both the series finale and 'The Ghost Monument', to be incapable of hitting a barn door at two paces with a fair wind behind them. He is also, in the end, defeated too easily.

The limitations that afflict Tzim-Sha, or variations of them, are evident in other creatures from the season. As mentioned already, the Thijarians have too peripheral and passive a role to rise above the events that they observe and, by the time the Doctor encounters them, their worst is long behind them. The Gollum-ish Ribbons of the Seven Stomachs who lurks in the Antizone in 'It Takes You Away' is a promisingly repellent but similarly underused character, played with relish by Kevin Eldon. Reminiscent of Sil (Nabil Shaban), the Sixth Doctor's Thoros Betan sparring partner in 'Vengeance on Varos' (1985), 'Mindwarp (1986)' and several off-screen spin-offs, he is killed half-way through the episode by the inconsistently voracious Flesh Moths. The Remnants, from 'The Ghost Monument', are a comparably rushed opportunity. Sentient rags and patches that rise at night from the sands of Desolation to suffocate the unwary, they are on screen for a frustratingly brief time. The giant mutant spiders of 'Arachnids in the UK' have more air time and are rendered in more impressive CGI than the Remnants, but they seem a fairly hoary idea and are, in any case, brushed aside in a hasty denouement that has little logic or clarity. The TeamMates who make up the bulk of the workforce on the retail moon of Kerblam! are the stuff of technological nightmares, square-jawed Postman Pats with fixed Colgate grins and staring, lidless, blue-blazing eyes. They are close in design and concept, though, to previous robotic monster-servants, most obviously the Dums, Vocs and Super-Vocs of 'The Robots of Death' (1977) and the Host of 'Voyage of the Damned' (2007), and – because they remain sinister rather than aggressive in any sustained and self-directed way – they do not benefit by the comparison.

The most remarkable monsters of the season are those that are likely to prove most divisive among fans, specifically the Pting of 'The Tsuranga Conundrum' and the Solitract of 'It Takes You Away'. Inhabiting the vacuum of deep space, the first of these (with another comedy name) are creatures that live by absorbing energy sources and consuming enormous quantities of inorganic material. Apparently indestructible, they have poisonous skin and a 'fatally violent nature', capable of destroying an entire space fleet: 'Risk to life, ultimate,' announces the computer on board the spaceship *Tsuranga*. The potential for inventive and terrifying monstrousness in the Pting's design is considerable but, ultimately, the creature discovered in a corridor munching its way through the metalwork is a computer-generated cutie that looks as though it has stumbled in from the latest instalment of Illumination's *Despicable Me* franchise (2010, 2013, 2017). The descriptions and behaviours of the Pting suggest an extreme form of alienness, an entity as far removed from bipedal humanoid life as it is possible to be, inexorable and corrosive in its instinct to consume. What is presented on the screen, though, is a small, peevish imp with two stubby legs, two stubby arms, big doe eyes and a smirking, unfeasibly flexible mouth. The closest kinship in *Doctor Who* terms is with the Adipose, from 2008's 'Partners in Crime', another potentially grisly and disturbing concept for a monster that was realized with a cartoon lovability that clearly targeted young children and the potential for merchandise.

Even more than the Pting, the Solitract constitutes a challenge to paradigms of monstrousness and, thus, to the ways in which monstrousness is designed, produced and understood. Defined as '[a] consciousness, an energy' from 'pre-Time, pre-everything', the Solitract is 'a theory, a myth, a bedtime story' from the Doctor's childhood, an entity that craves integration with the universe but is literally unable to coexist with it. The Solitract, simply by existing, prevented the universe from forming, even though 'all the laws and elements and nuts and bolts' were in place. Only when the universe, through some powerful existential imperative, 'managed to exile the Solitract to a separate, unreachable existence' did 'everything make sense' as a created reality: 'The universe could finally work because the Solitract had been removed.' A cosmogonic myth, almost pandeistic in its implications, this posits a life form that is arguably one of the most conceptually interesting and imaginative in the show's history. Whether this is enough to make it a successful *Doctor Who* monster is another matter.

There are a number of analogous precursors for the Solitract, including the Animus, the Great Intelligence and the Chronovores, although – in its disembodied and unwilled opposition to the material reality of the universe – it also resembles Omega, trapped in his domain of antimatter. The conspicuous difference between the Solitract and these forerunners is its basically innocent character: the threat that it poses, formidable thought it is, derives not from motives of malice or vengeance but from the accident of incompatibility. The Solitract, as its name suggests, is lonely, isolated, bored: its desire is not to destroy but to make friends. Its monstrousness, then, is devastating in its effects but sympathetic in its causes, like that of Mary Shelley's Creature or Gaston Leroux's Phantom. The problem is that both the Creature and the Phantom are memorably embodied in their originating fictions and have become, through successive stage and screen adaptations, visually iconic. The Solitract, on the other hand, is intrinsically bodiless – 'My own form is endless' – and takes delight in manifesting itself to the Doctor as a small frog, one that talks with the voice of Graham's late wife, Grace, complete with her pronounced Yorkshire accent. This is surprising, quirky, funny, evocative and (given that the inspiration comes from Grace's frog pendant and her own predilection for the amphibious creatures) touching, but it is also wide open to ridicule and unlikely to earn the Solitract an assured place in the pantheon of great *Doctor Who* monsters.

Even the most cursory exploration of reviews will show the extreme polarization of opinion around the appearance of the lonely, voluble, all-powerful-but-sadly-helpless frog in 'It Takes You Away'. For Darren on *the m0vie blog* it 'is perhaps the most *Doctor Who* beat within the entire eleventh season', and Ed Power, for *The Independent*, agrees, writing that it 'mark[s] the point at which the new Tardis chief achieves "Peak Who" '.[25] Alternatively, *Den of Geek*'s Chris Allcock identifies it as 'ammunition for anyone who wants to chronicle 2018 as the year *Doctor Who* seriously messed up', while Morgan Jeffery, for *Digital Spy*, simply asks, 'Who thought a *talking frog* was a good idea?'[26] Paul Kirkley, for *Doctor Who Magazine*, also 'address[es] the amphibian in the room' through the interrogative mode, but allows things to remain rhetorical: 'Is it a daringly inventive flight of surrealist fantasy worthy of Lewis Carroll? Or just utterly ridiculous?'[27] It is both, no doubt, and possibly neither at the same time. It very much depends on who is watching, and when, and why. What is clear from the comment threads on social media is that few are neutral on the subject of the cosmic frog and much fun is had in making links to such counterparts as Kermit, Crazy Frog, Gabriel the Toad from *Bagpuss* (BBC, 1974) and, more pertinently, Monarch the Urbankan from the 1982 story 'Four to Doomsday', as well as frog themes in NBC's *The Good Place* (2016–present). The fact that the Solitract frog now has several Twitter accounts of its own does not, of course, mean that it has filled the gap left by Chibnall's decision to feature no old monsters.

As events transpired, an old monster – the *oldest* – did in fact return for the end of the season, appearing in the New Year's Day episode, 'Resolution'. Here a lone Dalek, defeated on Earth by ancient tribes and hidden across the planet in three buried segments, is resurrected as the result of an archaeological dig in modern-day Sheffield. Separated from its travel machine, the Dalek is able to possess one of the archaeologists, Lin (Charlotte Ritchie), using her to collect the materials needed to build a new one. Bringing back an old monster, Chibnall nevertheless does so in a way that emphasizes novelty, showing the destructive power and obsessive malice of a Dalek outside its shell (this is a long way from the feeble, dependent creature hauled from its casing in David Whitaker's novelization of the first Dalek story).[28] The scene in which the possessed archaeologist constructs a Dalek travel machine in an isolated warehouse reprises the equivalent (and equivalently far-fetched) scene in 'The Woman Who Fell to Earth' in which the Doctor creates her new sonic screwdriver. Motifs of improvised renewal are seen to link the Doctor and her greatest enemy – 'So that's what you've been doing: reconstructing yourself from memory, and remnants, and spare parts' – and this becomes, in an important sense, a keynote for both the new era of *Doctor Who* and its extended mythology.

The title of 'Resolution' refers to both the relationship between Ryan and his errant father, Aaron, and the long-postponed culmination of the Dalek's mission. Identified by the Doctor as a 'reconnaissance scout', among 'the first to leave Skaro, possibly the first to reach Earth', it is targeted in her own seasonal vow: 'Here's my New Year's resolution: I'm coming for you, Dalek.' The resolution is also, perhaps, that of the Thirteenth Doctor's era, because it is in this story that the tone and temperament of the season finally seem to settle. Previous stories, even the very best of them, had struggled to retain narrative coherence or to resolve themselves successfully, to avoid the sense that they were trying too hard at times. In 'Resolution' there is a general confidence and air of relaxed intent – of sheer *enjoyment* – that earlier tales achieved more intermittently. This is not to say that 'Resolution' is the best or most original or most interesting story in Whittaker's first season, but it is the most consistently assured. This means that the irksomely convenient absurdity of the Doctor blocking the Dalek's death ray with her sonic screwdriver when she encounters it in the warehouse does not prevent this scene (and the subsequent one, in which a British army patrol is massacred by the 'unknown drone') from being among the most memorable of recent years. It may be that it takes the presence of an old monster to warrant such conviction at a time when the series is undergoing a vital recoding of its mythic DNA.

Beyond the predictable gripes and grumbles about the presence of a female Doctor, the diversity of the TARDIS crew and the foregrounding of what has been seen as a 'social justice' agenda, the bulk of complaints about Season Eleven have tended to be in relation to the perceived quality of the storytelling: there are too many companions, the endings have been rushed or lacking in clarity, it has all felt too fragmented, inconsistent in tone, uncertain in pace, and so on. Writing for *The Atlantic*, Kelly Connolly asserts that 'taken as a whole, the season felt directionless',[29] a view consistent with a pervasive sense that the varied and often impressive components never quite cohered, that it was somehow less than the sum of its parts.

Notwithstanding that there is some justification for these criticisms, it needs to be recognized that *Doctor Who* 2018 was produced and broadcast under conditions of singular scrutiny and expectation. The intensity of interest, unprecedented in the history of the show, meant that a period of acclimatization was going to be more important than for any previous iteration, and it is hardly a shock that there was significant variance in the reception. Looking at the characterization of Whittaker's Doctor, for instance, Connolly praises what she calls her 'radical helplessness', while Katherine Cross, writing for *Polygon*, offers a view that is almost diametrically opposed, arguing that she presents 'no doubt, no trauma and no overwhelming sense of having to prove something'.[30] Cross overstates the case, surely, when she writes of Whittaker 'put[ting] everything into a role that's holding her back', but the idea that her acting – and that of Walsh as Graham – has outshone the writing is not an unusual one. Although some online fan criticism suggests that Whittaker is 'chewing the scenery', it is hard to see how such an assessment could be reasonably sustained without conceding similar tendencies in many, if not most, previous portrayals of the Doctor. Tom Baker and David Tennant could both be accused of overacting at times, but they are also, arguably, the two most popular and successful Doctors across classic and new *Who*. The indication here (and it is surely self-evident) is that the character is intrinsically excessive, with an alien allure that is reliant on an often manic energy and an intimidating degree of unstable charisma. The notion of a restrained portrayal of the Doctor is almost unthinkable and, indeed, it might be argued that Whittaker's depiction (so far) has been quieter than those of the majority of her predecessors.

As with other incarnations, Whittaker's Doctor shows the unsettlement of new identity, literally the ecstasy – the self-transcendence – of regeneration:

> Right now, I'm a stranger to myself. There's echoes of who I was and a sort of call towards who I am. And I have to hold my nerve and trust all these new instincts. Shape myself towards them.

The excited unease of these lines, from 'The Woman Who Fell to Earth', is diminished by the glibness of those that follow – 'when people need help, I never refuse' – but Whittaker's delivery remains compelling. Tonally, her Doctor is perhaps closest to that of Peter Davison, with a comparable mix of wide-eyed enthusiasm and compassionate vulnerability. Energized by the possibilities of renewal – 'This is going to be fun!' – she is, at times, almost ponderously conscientious in offering up reassurance:

> We're all capable of the most incredible change. We can evolve while still staying true to who we are. We can honour who we've been and choose who we want to be next.

This is spoken to Tzim Sha in the climactic moments of the episode, high up on the crane jib above Sheffield, but it could be aimed equally at the anticipated resistance among the audience. The appeal to change is not unusual in confrontations between heroes and villains, of course, but the implicit equation here of conservative viewers with the malicious egotism of an alien enemy is extraordinary. It suggests both an eloquent confidence and a degree of sublimated paranoia, a fear that the Remnants identify, or attempt to provoke, in 'The Ghost Monument', when they accuse the Doctor of being 'afraid of [her] own newness'. Her furious response – 'Get out of my head!' – seems to channel an exasperation with the Remnants' mansplaining (their voice is distinctly and jeeringly male) which goes beyond the single episode. The fact that they are burnt up in a gas explosion ignited by one of the most conventionally masculine status symbols, a cigar, wrested from the boorish, patronizing Etzo (Shaun Dooley), is telling. What could be lost in an analysis such as this – and it does seem to have been lost in many analyses of Whittaker's first season – is that there is a wit and comic lightness to her performance. If some have taken this as a sign of overstraining, it is surely no more so than in the cases of, at different times, Matt Smith, Tom Baker or even Patrick Troughton. The spotlight on Whittaker is, undeniably, a harsher one than that turned on her predecessors, but the doubts and prejudices that inflame it should not detract from a wider appreciation that the change she represents – 'all this fizzing inside' – is, indeed, fun.

In time, perhaps, the impact of *Doctor Who*'s shift to a female leading actor will be seen as less problematic than some of the smaller adjustments made to the show's format. Reducing from twelve (formerly thirteen) episodes per season to ten, albeit episodes of fifty minutes rather than forty-five, presents a challenge both to narrative structure and character development, especially when a decision has been taken to eschew complex story arcs. In the earliest years of *Doctor Who*, a large TARDIS crew could be sustained because stories composed of several twenty-five-minute episodes allowed multiple characters to be active across a gradually unfolding narrative.[31] Sometimes, indeed, entire episodes would be focused on the progress of companions, with the Doctor (in other words, Hartnell) being given 'a week off', and vice versa. The preference for self-contained tales in new *Who* – especially in Chibnall's first season which, like Moffat's in 2012–13 (Season Seven), consists of discrete episodes – means that there is a busy compression of action to ensure weekly closure. This gives precedence to pace, appeals to the casual viewer and follows the formula of those serials which most directly influenced the *Who* revival of 2005 (notably Joss Whedon's *Buffy the Vampire Slayer*), but it also risks incoherence and a congestion of characters. A TARDIS crew of four requires not only space but also time, and some have suggested that the individual members of the ensemble seemed far too confined during Season Eleven. Yaz, in particular, has been perceived as an under-utilized character, but even the Doctor has seemed, at times, to be in need of more to do.

Fifteen years on from 'Rose', patterns of media consumption have changed dramatically and a range of current television series demonstrate that the episodic short-form can be highly successful in the age of on-demand streaming. *The Good Place* (NBC, 2016–present), *The End of the F***ing World* (Channel 4/All 4, 2017–present) and *Russian Doll* (Netflix, 2019–present) are all structured around episodes of thirty minutes or fewer, while the vampiric web series *Carmilla* (2014–17), based loosely on Sheridan Le Fanu's 1872 novella, comprises YouTube episodes of between two and eight minutes' duration. Although none of these shows are directly analogous to *Doctor Who*, they share a generic ambiguity and eccentricity of tone, and their interlacing of self-contained and continuing diegesis is an example that might be followed. It would require a more thoroughgoing break with the format established so successfully by Russell T. Davies, but perhaps the time has come for the BBC's adventure in space and time to return to episodes of twenty-five minutes in length, with the 'suspended enigma'[32] of good old-fashioned cliffhangers to pull the viewers through to the next instalment.

Whittaker is surely right to have stated, on accepting the role of the Time Lord, that '*Doctor Who* represents everything that's exciting about change'.[33] It thrives on transformation, even as it flourishes on a basis of continuity. This is, in Ted Hughes's terms, its 'mythic equation'.[34] The story is always about to be renewed and extended, and never more thrillingly than when it seems to be coming to an end. This was apparent from the moment a new Doctor clambered to his feet in the opening scenes of 'The Power of the Daleks' on 5 November 1966, a week after his predecessor fell.[35] Over thirty years later, in the supposed wilderness of the classic series' aftermath, Lance Parkin published a novel that includes a line redolent of the Fourth Doctor's 'good solid hope': 'The Rutan had cracked a joke and the Sontarans had laughed. There was hope for them all yet.'[36] Based around the convening of a peace conference on Gallifrey, *The Infinity Doctors* (1998) is a useful text from which to move towards a conclusion for this book. Manifesting a delight in the mythic possibilities of the *Doctor Who* narrative, a desire to play with its continuities and discontinuities, it was published to mark the thirty-fifth anniversary of the TV series and is deliberately anomalous in terms of the canon. Conspicuously, it does not even specify which

Figure 5.1 The Doctor (Jodie Whittaker) in 'The Woman Who Fell to Earth' (2018); ©BBC Worldwide.

incarnation of the Doctor it features, although there is a strong hint in its conclusion that it might be a young version of the First Doctor, about to take flight from his home planet. It is both a gift and a provocation to the critical fandom of which its author is a part, a story of ends and beginnings, wit and horror, absurdity and brilliance, told with imagination, gusto, hope. What else, through all the changes in personnel, technology and cultural economy, has *Doctor Who* ever been? As Whittaker's Doctor advises at the end of 'The Battle of Ranskoor Av Kolos', 'None of us know for sure what's out there. That's why we keep looking. Keep your faith. Travel hopefully. The universe will surprise you, constantly.' The spirit of this exhortation is captured in a remarkable scene from the first episode of the season in which Whittaker's Doctor, still wearing the tattered remnants of her predecessor's costume, stands on a hillside with her back to the viewer, gazing out over Sheffield (see Figure 5.1). Evoking Caspar David Friedrich's *Wanderer above the Sea of Fog* (Figure 5.2), painted two centuries earlier, the image shows the Doctor

Figure 5.2 Caspar David Friedrich, *Wanderer above the Sea of Fog* (c.1817), oil on canvas, 95cm × 75cm, Kunsthalle, Hamburg, Germany; Photo by Heritage Images/Getty Images.

alone at the edge of possibility, paused in a moment of stillness, eternal but renewed, ancient and forever.

Even if the BBC were to lose faith again in the 'Exciting Adventure' that it devised to bridge the gap between *Grandstand* and *Juke Box Jury*,[37] if that adventure fades from the television as it did in 1989, the story will continue. The quiet revolution that took place then, off-screen, among fans, with most of the world looking the other way, enabled *Doctor Who* to change form, survive, regenerate, just as it did in the final moments of 'The Tenth Planet'. It will do so again, in big and small ways, always different but essentially the same, long after Chibnall and Whittaker have filmed their final episodes. There are no certainties in this, but there is hope in cartloads. 'Meanwhile,' as C. E. Webber urged in his notes back in 1963, 'proliferate stories.'[38]

Notes

Introduction

1   Robert Graves, *The Greek Myths: Complete Edition* (Harmondsworth: Penguin, 1992), 12.

2   T. S. Eliot, *'Ulysses*, Order, and Myth', in *Selected Prose*, ed. Frank Kermode (London: Faber and Faber, 1975), 177–8.

3   Joseph Campbell, *The Hero with a Thousand Faces* (London: Fontana, 1993; orig. 1948), 255.

4   Neil Clarke, 'Holy Terror and Fallen Demigod: The Doctor as Myth', in *The Mythological Dimensions of Doctor Who*, ed. Anthony Burdge, Jessica Burke and Kristine Larsen (Crawfordville, FL: Kitsune Books, 2010), 37.

5   Laurence Coupe, *Myth* (London: Routledge, 1997), 5.

6   Piers D. Britton, *TARDISbound: Navigating the Universes of Doctor Who* (London: I.B. Tauris, 2011), 12. The term is borrowed from *Third Person: Authoring and Exploring Vast Narratives*, ed. Pat Harrigan and Noah Wardrip-Fruin (Cambridge, MA: MIT Press, 2009).

7   Gayatri Spivak, 'Translator's Introduction', in Jacques Derrida, Of Grammatology (Baltimore, MD: John Hopkins University Press, 1976), xiv. *Sous rature* is usually rendered in English as 'under erasure'.

8   Robert A. Segal, *Myth: A Very Short Introduction* (Oxford: Oxford University Press, 2004), 2.

9   Ivan Strenski, *Four Theories of Myth in Twentieth-Century History: Cassirer, Eliade, Lévi-Strauss and Malinowski* (Basingstoke: Macmillan, 1987), 1.

10 Ibid., 1.

11 G. S. Kirk, *Myth: Its Meaning and Function in Ancient and Other Cultures* (Cambridge: Cambridge University Press, 1970), 2.

12 Matt Hills, '"Mythology Makes You Feel Something": The Russell T. Davies Era as Sentimental Journey', in Burdge, Burke and Larsen (eds), *Mythological Dimensions*, 197–213. Other academic texts have brought concepts from the study of myth to bear on *Doctor Who*, of course, notably Matt Hills, *Triumph of a Time Lord: Regenerating Doctor Who for the Twenty-First Century* (London: I.B. Tauris, 2010); David

Layton, *The Humanism of Doctor Who: A Critical Study in Science Fiction and Philosophy* (Jefferson, NC: McFarland, 2012); Marcus K. Harmes, *Doctor Who and the Art of Adaptation: Fifty Years of Storytelling* (New York: Rowman & Littlefield, 2014); Ross P. Garner, Melissa Beattie and Una McCormack (eds), *Impossible Worlds, Impossible Things: Cultural Perspectives on Doctor Who, Torchwood and the Sarah Jane Adventures* (Newcastle-upon-Tyne: Cambridge Scholars, 2010).

13   Hills, ' "Mythology Makes You Feel Something" ', 198.

14   Matt Hills (ed.), *New Dimensions of Doctor Who: Adventures in Space, Time and Television* (London: I.B. Tauris, 2013), 1–16. The phrase '*Doctor Who* studies' was coined by Paul Magrs, in his 'Afterword: My Adventures', in David Butler (ed.), *Time and Relative Dissertations in Space: Critical Perspectives on Doctor Who* (Manchester: Manchester University Press, 2007), 308.

15   John Tulloch and Manuel Alvarado, *Doctor Who: The Unfolding Text* (Basingstoke: Macmillan, 1983); James Chapman, *Inside the TARDIS: The Worlds of Doctor Who* (London: I.B. Tauris, 2013; orig. 2006), viii.

16   Bruce Lincoln, 'An Early Moment in the Discourse of "Terrorism": Reflections on a Tale from Marco Polo', *Comparative Studies in Society and History*, 48:2 (April 2006), 242.

17   Paul Ricoeur, *Lectures on Ideology and Utopia* (New York: Columbia University Press, 1986), 266.

18   Roland Barthes, *Mythologies*, trans. Annette Lavers (London: Vintage, 1993), 129; Paul Ricoeur, *A Ricoeur Reader: Reflection & Imagination*, ed. M. J. Valdés (New York: Harvester, 1991), 489.

19   John Fiske, '*Doctor Who*, Ideology and the Reading of a Popular Narrative', *Australian Journal of Screen Theory*, 14–15 (1983), 96.

20   Ibid.

21   Ibid., 99.

22   Tulloch and Alvarado, *Unfolding Text*, 16–17.

23   Miles Booy, *Love and Monsters: The Doctor Who Experience, 1979 to the Present* (London: I.B. Tauris, 2012), 126.

24   Chapman, *Inside the TARDIS*, 168; Kim Newman, *Doctor Who* (London: BFI, 2005), 78–9, 106; Jim Leach, *Doctor Who* (Detroit, MI: Wayne State University Press, 2009), 82; Booy, *Love and Monsters*, 129.

25   David Rafer, 'Mythic Identity in *Doctor Who*', in Butler (ed.), *Time and Relative*, 123–37.

26   Booy, *Love and Monsters*, 130.

27   Kevin S. Decker, *Who Is Who? The Philosophy of Doctor Who* (London: I.B. Tauris, 2012).

28   Coupe, *Myth*, 88.

29   Lance Parkin and Lars Pearson, *Ahistory: An Unauthorized History of the Doctor Who Universe* (Des Moines, IA: Mad Norwegian Press, 2012), 28.

30   Tulloch and Alvarado, *Unfolding Text*, 85.

31   Ibid., 303.
32   Hills, *Triumph*, 68–72.
33   Ibid., 4.
34   Andrew O'Day (ed.), *Doctor Who: The Eleventh Hour – A Critical Celebration of the Matt Smith and Steven Moffat Era* (London: I.B. Tauris, 2014), 6.
35   Newman, *Doctor Who*, 21.
36   Parkin and Pearson, *Ahistory*, 23.
37   Lance Parkin, 'Canonicity Matters: Defining the *Doctor Who* Canon', in Butler (ed.), *Time and Relative*, 257.
38   Ibid., 259.
39   Britton, *TARDISbound*, x; Decker, *Who Is Who?*, x.
40   Walter J. Ong, *Orality and Literacy: The Technologizing of the Word* (New York: Routledge, 2002), 20–7.
41   Benjamin Cook, interview with Frank Skinner, *Doctor Who Magazine*, 478 (November 2014), 27–8.
42   Ian Bogost, 'Against Aca-Fandom: On Jason Mittell on *Mad Men*', *bogost.com* (2010), available at http://bogost.com/writing/blog/against_aca-fandom/ (accessed 3 March 2017).
43   Matt Hills, 'Afterword: Scholar-Fandom's Different Incarnations', in Garner, Beattie and McCormack (eds), *Impossible Worlds*, 210.
44   1milescarf, 'DS Forums' (16 May 2014), *Digital Spy*. Available at www.cookdandbombd.co.uk/forums/index.php?topic=39943.1420;wap2 (accessed 3 March 2017); Kyle Anderson, 'Comedian Frank Skinner to Guest on *Doctor Who*', *The Nerdist* (26 May 2014), available at http://archive.nerdist.com/comedian-frank-skinner-to-guest-on-doctor-who/ (accessed 3 March 2017).
45   Fanwank: 'a continuity reference thrown into a story and having little relevance to the plot, but there purely as a device to please fans' (Craig Hinton, quoted in Hills, *Triumph*, 58).
46   See n. 12, above.
47   Harmes, *Doctor Who and the Art of Adaptation*, 186.

Chapter 1

1   Malcolm Hulke and Terrance Dicks, *The Making of Doctor Who* (London: Pan, 1972); revised second edition: Terrance Dicks and Malcolm Hulke, *The Making of Doctor Who* (London: Target, 1976). For the various Howe et al. *Handbooks*, see the Bibliography.
2   The clone race usually have three fingers, of course, except in 'The Sontaran Experiment' (1975), where Styre is seen to have five.
3   John Tulloch and Henry Jenkins, *Science Fiction Audiences: Watching Star Trek and Doctor Who* (London: Routledge, 1995); Piers D. Britton

and Simon J. Barker, *Reading between Designs: Visual Imagery and the Generation of Meaning in The Avengers, The Prisoner, and Doctor Who* (Austin: University of Texas Press, 2003).

4   Mr. Steve Bryant. 'Thought Provoking Book', *Amazon.co.uk* (18 August 2010), available at www.amazon.co.uk/Triumph-Time-Lord-Regenerating-Twenty-first/dp/1848850328/ref=sr_1_1?s=books&ie=UTF8&qid=143 3890717&sr=1-1&keywords=triumph+of+a+time+lord+hills (accessed 9 June 2015).

5   Robin Pierce, review of Decker, *Who Is Who?*, *Starburst* (21 December 2013), available at www.starburstmagazine.com/reviews/book-reviews-latest-literary-releases/7544-book-review-who-is-who-the-philosophy-of-doctor-who (accessed 3 March 2017).

6   Hywel Evans, review of Hills, *New Dimensions of Doctor Who*, in *Doctor Who Magazine*, 470 (March 2014), 73.

7   Ian Briggs, *Doctor Who: Dragonfire* (London: W. H. Allen, 1989), 59.

8   James Chapman, *Inside the TARDIS: The Worlds of Doctor Who* (London: I.B. Tauris, 2013; orig. 2006), vii; Matt Hills, *Triumph of a Time Lord: Regenerating Doctor Who for the Twenty-First Century* (London: I.B. Tauris, 2010), 3.

9   Hills, *Triumph*, 3.

10 Matthew Sweet, review of Chapman, *Inside the TARDIS*, in *The Independent* (27 May 2006), available at www.independent.co.uk/arts-entertainment/books/reviews/inside-the-tardis-by-james-chapman-480122.html (accessed 3 March 2017).

11 Paul Magrs, 'Afterword: My Adventures', in David Butler (ed.), *Time and Relative Dissertations in Space: Critical Perspectives on Doctor Who* (Manchester: Manchester University Press, 2007), 306.

12 Hills, *Triumph*, ix–x.

13 Matt Hills, *Fan Cultures* (London: Routledge, 2002), 20.

14 Roland Barthes, *Mythologies*, trans. Annette Lavers (London: Vintage, 1993), 109.

15 Roland Barthes, *Image-Music-Text*, trans. Stephen Heath (London: Fontana, 1984), 156, 164.

16 Ibid., 164.

17 Ibid., 155.

18 Matt Hills (ed.), *New Dimensions of Doctor Who: Adventures in Space, Time and Television* (London: I.B. Tauris, 2013), 3–4.

19 Christopher H. Bidmead's 'Castrovalva', Peter Davison's debut story, was broadcast in January 1982. It was the M. C. Escher-influenced sequel to his 'Logopolis', Tom Baker's swansong of the previous year (February–March 1981).

20 Joe Ford, 'Absorbatrix???' (20 July 2006), and Ron Mallet, 'A Review', both in 'Love & Monsters', *The Doctor Who Ratings Guide* (12 January 2007), available at www.pagefillers.com/dwrg/lovemonsters.htm (accessed 17 July 2015).

21 Steve Cassidy, 'Elton! Fetch a Spade!!', in 'Love & Monsters', *The Doctor Who Ratings Guide* (18 October 2006), available at www.pagefillers.com/dwrg/lovemonsters.htm (accessed 28 October 2017).

22 Finn Clark, 'A Review', in 'Love & Monsters', *The Doctor Who Ratings Guide* (20 April 2007), available at www.pagefillers.com/dwrg/lovemonsters.htm (accessed 28 October 2017).

23 See *Doctor Who Magazine*, 413 (14 October 2009), 19; and *Doctor Who Magazine*, 474 (July 2014), 62–3.

24 James Castle, 'Love & Benny! (Benny Hill & Doctor Who)', *YouTube* (1 August 2006), available at www.youtube.com/watch?v=PLOrL_-odvl (accessed 19 July 2015).

25 In John Tulloch and Manuel Alvarado, *Doctor Who: The Unfolding Text* (Basingstoke: Macmillan, 1983), 151.

26 '*Blue Peter* design to be turned into *Doctor Who* monster', *BBC Press Office* (17 August 2005), available at www.bbc.co.uk/pressoffice/pressreleases/stories/2005/08_august/17/who.shtml (accessed 3 March 2017).

27 Russell T. Davies and Phil Collinson, 'Love & Monsters' episode commentary (17 June 2006), *Doctor Who Official Website*. Available at www.bbc.co.uk/doctorwho/s4/episodes/S2_10 (accessed 21 July 2015; content now archived, podcast unavailable); 'The New World of *Doctor Who*', *Doctor Who Confidential*, Series 2, Episode 10, BBC3 (17 June 2006); James Rampton, 'Peter Kay: I Still Go to the Co-op for a Tizer', *Daily Express* (13 November 2011), available at www.express.co.uk/expressyourself/283358/Peter-Kay-I-still-go-to-the-Co-op-for-a-Tizer (accessed 21 July 2015).

28 UNIT (originally the United Nations Intelligence Taskforce but, from 2005, the Unified Intelligence Taskforce) is a paramilitary organization established with a view to defending the Earth against threats from extraterrestrial or other preternatural forces. Conceived by producer Peter Bryant and script editor Derrick Sherwin, it first featured in the Second Doctor story 'The Invasion' (1968), building on the potential for military action developed in two previous tales, 'The War Machines' (1966) and 'The Web of Fear' (1968). Its British operation, led by Brigadier Alistair Gordon Lethbridge-Stewart (Nicholas Courtney), provided the primary setting for *Doctor Who* during the era of Jon Pertwee's Third Doctor (1970–4), when he was exiled by the Time Lords to twentieth-century Earth. From 1974 until 1989, UNIT featured only intermittently on screen, although its narrative was later extended into other media, notably the Virgin and BBC novels and Big Finish audio dramas. Included in a number of post-2005 episodes, as well as in stories from the spin-off series *The Sarah Jane Adventures* and *Torchwood*, UNIT remains a prominent element within the *Doctor Who* mythos. In 'Resolution', however, the New Year's Day episode of 2019, it was revealed that 'UNIT operations have been suspended pending review', implicitly as a result of Brexit.

The chronology of the UNIT stories is riddled with contradictions, although Parkin and Pearson make a lucid attempt in *Ahistory* to resolve what they describe as 'probably the most contentious *Doctor Who* continuity issue' (pp. 233–61). It is not, they argue, that there is 'no right answer'; it is 'that there are several, mutually incompatible, right answers' (p. 233).

29 Russell T. Davies, quoted in Hills, *Triumph*, 55; Terrance Dicks, quoted in Tulloch and Alvarado, *Unfolding Text*, 263.

30 Britton and Barker, *Reading between Designs*, 132; Russell T. Davies, quoted in Hills, *Triumph*, 55.

31 Toby Hadoke, *Moths Ate My Doctor Who Scarf*, produced by Paul Hardy (London: BBC Audio, 2007); Miles Booy, *Love and Monsters: The Doctor Who Experience, 1979 to the Present* (London: I.B. Tauris, 2012), 188.

32 Booy, *Love and Monsters*, 188.

33 Hills, *Fan Cultures*, 83.

34 Bertolt Brecht, *Brecht on Theatre: The Development of an Aesthetic* (London: Methuen, 1978), 91–2.

35 Hills, *Triumph*, 216; Booy, *Love and Monsters*, 186.

36 Booy, *Love and Monsters*, 2.

37 Mark Campbell, *Doctor Who: The Complete Guide* (London: Constable & Robinson, 2013), 9; Britton and Barker, *Reading between Designs*, 132.

38 Piers D. Britton, *TARDISbound: Navigating the Universes of Doctor Who* (London: I.B. Tauris, 2011), 148.

39 Ibid., 190.

40 Hills, *Triumph*, 5.

41 Jonathan Swift, letter to Alexander Pope, 29 September 1725, in Carol Fabricant (ed.), *A Modest Proposal and Other Writings* (Harmondsworth: Penguin, 2009), 189–90.

42 Booy, *Love and Monsters*, 7.

43 Hills, *Triumph*, 6.

44 Especially the two 'missing' episodes, animated in fairly basic 2D by Qrios Entertainment for the 2014 DVD release.

45 Hills, *Triumph*, 5.

46 Tulloch and Jenkins, *Science Fiction Audiences*, 108.

47 Tulloch and Alvarado, *Unfolding Text*, 83.

48 Tulloch and Jenkins, *Science Fiction Audiences*, 142.

49 Kim Newman, *Doctor Who* (London: BFI, 2005), 125.

50 Robert A. Segal, *Myth: A Very Short Introduction* (Oxford: Oxford University Press, 2004), 6.

51 Samuel Taylor Coleridge, *Biographia Literaria, or, Biographical Sketches of My Literary Life and Opinions* (London: Dent, 1957; orig. 1816), 168–9.

52 Steven Moffat, interviewed in *Doctor Who: Earth Conquest – The World Tour*, first broadcast BBC3, Friday 17 January 2015, 7 pm.

53 John Keats, letter to George and Thomas Keats, 21 December 1817, in Maurice Buxton Foreman (ed.), *The Letters of John Keats* (London: Oxford University Press, 1947), 72.

54 Tulloch and Jenkins, *Science Fiction Audiences*, 147.

55   Alan McKee, 'How to Tell the Difference between Production and Consumption: A Case Study in Doctor Who Fandom', in S. Gwenllian-Jones and R. E. Pearson (eds), *Cult Television* (Minneapolis: University of Minnesota Press, 2004), 169, 172, 176–7; Hills, *Fan Cultures*, 51–7; Hills, *Triumph*, 203, 213.

56   Tulloch and Jenkins, *Science Fiction Audiences*, 147.

57   Brigid Cherry, 'Squee, Retcon, Fanwank and the Not-We: Computer-Mediated Discourse and the Online Audience for NuWho', in Chris Hansen (ed.), *Ruminations, Peregrinations, and Regenerations: A Critical Approach to Doctor Who* (Newcastle-upon-Tyne: Cambridge Scholars, 2010), 217.

58   In the *Doctor Who Magazine* fiftieth-anniversary poll, 'Kinda' came 63rd out of 241 stories overall and was the seventh-most popular story of the 1980s. See *Doctor Who Magazine*, 474 (July 2014), 62–3.

59   John Fiske, '*Doctor Who*, Ideology and the Reading of a Popular Narrative', *Australian Journal of Screen Theory* (1983), 69–100.

60   Lucien Lévy-Bruhl, *How Natives Think* (New York: Washington Square Press, 1966; orig. 1926), and *Primitive Mythology: The Mythic World of the Australian and Papuan Natives* (Queensland: University of Queensland Press, 1984; orig. 1935); Ernst Cassirer, *The Myth of the State* (New Haven, CT: Yale University Press, 1946), and *Symbol, Myth and Culture: Essays and Lectures of Ernst Cassirer, 1935–45*, ed. Donald Philip Verene (New Haven, CT: Yale University Press, 1979).

61   Marshall McLuhan, 'Catholic Humanism & Modern Letters', *Christian Humanism in Letters* (Hartford, CT: St. Joseph's College, 1954), 80; Walter J. Ong, *Orality and Literacy: The Technologizing of the Word* (New York: Routledge, 2002), 18–27.

62   McLuhan, 'Catholic Humanism & Modern Letters', 75.

63   Kenneth Burke, *Language as Symbolic Action: Essays on Life, Literature, and Method* (Berkeley: University of California Press, 1978).

64   T. S. Eliot, '*Ulysses*, Order, and Myth', in *Selected Prose*, ed. Frank Kermode (London: Faber and Faber, 1975), 177–8.

65   Eliot, 'Tradition and the Individual Talent', in *Selected Prose*, 37–44.

66   Ibid.

67   Ibid.

68   Tulloch and Jenkins, *Science Fiction Audiences*, 169.

69   Ibid., 141.

70   Fredric Jameson, *Postmodernism, or, the Cultural Logic of Late Capitalism* (London: Verso, 1992), 68, 78, 169, 346, 354.

71   Mircea Eliade, *Myth and Reality* (London: Allen and Unwin, 1964), 45.

72   Segal, *Myth*, 55.

Chapter 2

1   Marina Warner, *Managing Monsters: Six Myths of Our Time* (London: Vintage, 1994), 8.

2   Frederic Jameson, *The Political Unconscious: Narrative as a Socially Symbolic Act* (Ithaca, NY: Cornell University Press, 1981), 31, 20.

3   Ibid., 20.

4   Laurence Sterne, *The Life and Opinions of Tristram Shandy, Gentleman* (Harmondsworth: Penguin, 1967), 615; Nicholas Cull, '"Bigger on the Inside …" *Doctor Who* as British Cultural History', in Graham Roberts and Philip M. Taylor (eds), *The Historian, Television and Television History* (Luton: University of Luton Press, 2001), 95.

5   James Boswell, *The Life of Samuel Johnson* (Harmondsworth: Penguin, 2008; orig. 1791), 504.

6   David Butler (ed.), *Time and Relative Dissertations in Space: Critical Perspectives on Doctor Who* (Manchester: Manchester University Press, 2007), 21.

7   James Chapman, *Inside the TARDIS: The Worlds of Doctor Who* (London: I.B. Tauris, 2013; orig. 2006), 4.

8   Warner, *Managing Monsters*, xiv, xiii; John Tulloch and Manuel Alvarado, *Doctor Who: The Unfolding Text* (Basingstoke: Macmillan, 1983), 4.

9   Piers D. Britton, *TARDISbound: Navigating the Universes of Doctor Who* (London: I.B. Tauris, 2011), 26.

10 Butler, *Time and Relative*, 20.

11 Ibid., 19.

12 Darko Suvin, *Metamorphoses of Science Fiction: On the Poetics and History of a Literary Genre* (New Haven, CT: Yale University Press, 1979), 8.

13 Ibid.

14 Butler, *Time and Relative*, 20.

15 Chapman, *Inside the TARDIS*, 15–16.

16 Suvin, *Metamorphoses*, 36, 7.

17 Tulloch and Alvarado, *Unfolding Text*, 120–1.

18 Alan McKee, 'Is *Doctor Who* Political?', *European Journal of Cultural Studies*, 7:2 (2004), 214.

19 Ibid.

20 Claude Lévi-Strauss, *The Raw and the Cooked: Introduction to a Science of Mythology, vol. 1* (London: Jonathan Cape, 1970; orig. 1964), and *Myth and Meaning* (London: Routledge and Kegan Paul, 1978).

21 Matt Hills, '"Mythology Makes You Feel Something": The Russell T. Davies Era as Sentimental Journey', in *The Mythological Dimensions of Doctor Who*, ed. Anthony Burdge, Jessica Burke and Kristine Larsen (Crawfordville, FL: Kitsune Books, 2010), 197–213.

22 'Doctor Who Returns to TV', *BBC News* (26 September 2003), available at http://news.bbc.co.uk/1/hi/entertainment/3140786.stm (accessed 30 October 2015).

23 Rachel Cooke, 'What's Up Doc?', *The Observer* (Sunday 6 March 2005), available at www.theguardian.com/theobserver/2005/mar/06/features.review17 (accessed 30 October 2015).

24 Paul Ricoeur, interviewed by Richard Kearney, in Paul Ricoeur, *A Ricoeur Reader: Reflection & Imagination*, ed. M. J. Valdés (New York: Harvester, 1991), 484.

25 Ibid., 488.

26 Marcus Hearn, *The Vault: Treasures from the First 50 Years* (London: BBC Books, 2013), 245.

27 Ibid., 246.

28 Steven Moffat, San Diego Comic-Con 2008, http://news.bbc.co.uk/1/hi/entertainment/7531310.stm (accessed 7 November 2015).

29 Matt Hills, *Triumph of a Time Lord: Regenerating Doctor Who for the Twenty-First Century* (London: I.B. Tauris, 2010), 13, 116–44.

30 See Piers Britton, 'Making "A Superior Brand of Alien Mastermind": *Doctor Who* Monsters and the Rhetoric of (Re)design', in *New Dimensions of Doctor Who: Adventures in Space, Time and Television*, ed. Matt Hills (London: I.B. Tauris, 2013), 30.

31 Tulloch and Alvarado, *Unfolding Text*, 151.

32 Linda Hutcheon, *The Politics of Postmodernism* (London: Routledge, 1989), 117.

33 Quoted in Cooke, 'What's Up Doc?'

34 Moffat, San Diego Comic-Con 2008.

35 Paul Cornell, 'Canonicity in Doctor Who', *Paul Cornell: Novelist, Screenwriter, Comics Writer* (10 February 2007), available at www.paulcornell.com/2007/02/canonicity-in-doctor-who/ (accessed 7 November 2015).

36 Neil Gaiman, interviewed by Nick Setchfield, *SFX* (7 May 2013), available at www.gamesradar.com/exclusive-neil-gaiman-talks-doctor-who-and-cybermen/ (accessed 8 November 2015).

37 David Lewis, '"Doctor Who" Finale: A Look at the Brigadier's Last Bow in "Death in Heaven"', *CULTBOX* (8 November 2014), available at www.cultbox.co.uk/features/opinion/doctor-who-finale-a-look-at-the-brigadiers-last-bow (accessed 11 November 2015).

38 Moffat, San Diego Comic-Con 2008.

39 Ricoeur, *Ricoeur Reader*, 486.

40 Ibid.

41 Davies was almost 7 years old when 'Spearhead from Space' was broadcast, coming up to the perceived optimum age for 'hooking' new *Doctor Who* fans.

42 Steven Hancock and Brian DiPaolo, reviews of 'Rose', *DoctorWhoNews.net* (17 October 2006, 24 March 2006), available at http://guide.doctorwhonews.net/story.php?story=Rose&detail=reviews#1624 (accessed 3 March 2017).

43 Peter Huntley, review of 'Rose', *DoctorWhoNews.net* (4 April 2005).

44 Dwight E. Sora, review of 'Rose', *DoctorWhoNews.net* (4 April 2005).

45 Andrew Roberts and Jonathan Hili, reviews of 'Rose', *DoctorWhoNews.net* (both 4 April 2005); Nick, *Riftwatch: Examining the Worlds of Doctor*

Who and Torchwood (23 July 2009), available at https://riftwatch. wordpress.com/tag/doctor-who/ (accessed 3 March 2017).

46   James Castelli, review of 'Rose', *DoctorWhoNews.net* (15 November 2005).

47   Terrance Dicks, *Doctor Who and the Auton Invasion* (London: W. H. Allen, 1974), 148; Terrance Dicks, *Doctor Who and the Terror of the Autons* (London: W. H. Allen, 1975), 120.

48   Craig Hinton, *Synthespians™* (London: BBC Books, 2004), 221.

49   John Bensalhia, review of 'Rose', *Shadowlocked.com* (19 April 2011), available at https://web.archive.org/web/20160414153433/www. shadowlocked.com/201104191741/reviews/doctor-who-complete-reviews-rose.html (accessed 13 September 2019).

50   Alan McKee, 'How to Tell the Difference between Production and Consumption: A Case Study in Doctor Who Fandom', in S. Gwenllian-Jones and R. E. Pearson (eds), *Cult Television* (Minneapolis: University of Minnesota Press, 2004), 182–3.

51   Robert Holmes, from an unspecified 1980s interview, *Doctor Who Interview Archive* (posted 24 October 2009), available at https:// drwhointerviews.wordpress.com/2009/10/24/robert-holmes-1980s/ (accessed 3 March 2017).

52   Steve West, 'The Yeti Set to Return to Doctor Who', *Giant Freakin Robot* (10 January 2012), available at www.giantfreakinrobot.com/scifi/the-yeti-set-to-return-to-doctor-who.html (accessed 3 March 2017).

53   Interviewed for *Doctor Who: Thirty Years in the TARDIS* (Kevin Davies, 1993), available as part of *The Legacy Collection* box set (BBC 2013).

54   Interestingly, only a year after young Walter Simeon encounters the Intelligence in 'The Snowmen', Marc Brunel's Thames Tunnel, the beginnings of the London Underground, would open to pedestrians, with the City of London solicitor Charles Pearson promoting the idea of an underground train system shortly afterwards. See 'Timeline: History of the Tube', *Evening Standard* (2013), available at www.standard.co.uk/ news/transport/timeline-history-of-the-tube-8443521.html (accessed 3 March 2017).

55   Steven Cooper and Kevin Mahoney, *Steven Moffat's Doctor Who 2012– 2013: The Critical Fan's Guide to Matt Smith's Final Series (Unauthorized)* (Cambridge: Punked Books, 2014), 182.

56   Elton Townend Jones, '"The Web of Fear" DVD – Reviewed!', *Kasterborous* (12 February 2014), available at https://web.archive.org/ web/20150906020845/www.kasterborous.com/2014/02/web-fear-dvd-reviewed/ (accessed 13 September 2019).

57   James Hoare, '*Doctor Who*'s Steven Moffat on "Rubbish" Ice Warriors Return', *SciFiNow* (21 February 2013), available at www.scifinow.co.uk/ news/doctor-whos-steven-moffat-on-rubbish-ice-warriors-return/ (accessed 20 November 2015).

58   Britton, *TARDISbound*, 80.

59 Paul Virilio, *Speed and Politics: An Essay on Dromology* (New York: Semiotext(e), 1977).

60 Graham Kibble-White, review of 'Cold War', *Doctor Who Magazine*, 460 (June 2013), 65.

61 Brian Hayles, *Doctor Who and the Ice Warriors* (London: Target, 1976), 30.

62 The Watcher, 'A History of *Doctor Who* in 100 Objects, #53: Varga's Implants', *Doctor Who Magazine*, 482 (February 2015), 82.

63 Ibid.

64 Hayles, *Doctor Who and the Ice Warriors*, 54.

65 Tulloch and Alvarado, *Unfolding Text*, 31.

66 Stephen Kelly, '*Doctor Who* boss Steven Moffat Admits the Colourful New Paradigm Daleks "Were a Mistake"', *Radio Times* (15 November 2015), available at www.radiotimes.com/news/2015-11-15/doctor-who-boss-steven-moffat-admits-the-colourful-new-paradigm-daleks-were-a-mistake (accessed 4 December 2015).

67 Henry Jenkins, *Convergence Culture: Where Old and New Media Collide* (New York: New York University Press, 2006).

68 Tulloch and Alvarado, *Unfolding Text*, 21.

69 Dale Smith, 'Broader and Deeper: The Lineage and Impact of the *Timewyrm* Series', in Butler (ed.), *Time and Relative*, 272.

70 Henry Jenkins, 'Transmedia 202: Further Reflections', *Confessions of an Aca-Fan: The Official Weblog of Henry Jenkins* (1 August 2011), available at http://henryjenkins.org/2011/08/defining_transmedia_further_re.html (accessed 5 December 2015); J. R. R. Tolkien, 'On Fairy Stories' (1939), in Tolkien, *Tree and Leaf* (New York: HarperCollins, 1964). Tolkien originally indicated the idea of subcreation in his poem 'Mythopoeia' of 1931, referring to 'Man, Sub-creator'.

71 Henry Jenkins, 'Transmedia Storytelling 101', *Confessions of an Aca-Fan* (22 March 2007), available at http://henryjenkins.org/2007/03/transmedia_storytelling_101.html (accessed 5 December 2015).

72 Jenkins, 'Transmedia 202'.

73 Matt Hills, *Fan Cultures* (London: Routledge, 2002), 137.

74 Benjamin Cook, *The New Audio Adventures: The Inside Story* (Maidenhead: Big Finish, 2003), 3.

75 Dan Tostevin, 'Davies' Debut', interview with Russell T. Davies, *Doctor Who Magazine*, 486 (June 2015), 17.

76 Paul Clarke, review of Russell T. Davies, *Damaged Goods*, in 'Discontinuity Guide', *The Whoniverse* (n.d.), available at www.whoniverse.net/discontinuity/na55 (accessed 5 December 2015).

77 Russell T. Davies, audio commentary, *Queer as Folk: Definitive Collector's Edition* (4 DVD, 2003).

78 Cornell, 'Canonicity in Doctor Who'.

79 First mentioned in 'Day of the Daleks' (1972), the Blinovitch Limitation Effect is a catastrophic discharge of energy brought about when two

versions of the same person come into contact with each other at the same point in time. The effect has become a recurrent feature of *Doctor Who* lore.

80 *Doctor Who and the Zarbi* was published by Frederick Muller in September 1965, the same month as the first *Dr Who Annual*.

81 'On the Web Planet', *TV Comic*, issues 693–8 (27 March–1 May 1965).

82 *The Prisoners of Time* was published in twelve parts by IDW Publishing between 29 January and 20 November 2013.

83 David J. Howe, *Doctor Who: A Book of Monsters* (London: BBC Books, 1997), 12; Anon., 'DR. WHO: A New Adventure on a Strange Planet Begins Today', *Radio Times*, 9 April 1964, included on the DVD release *Doctor Who: The Keys of Marinus* (BBC/2 Entertain, 2009).

84 Philip Hinchcliffe, *Doctor Who and the Keys of Marinus* (London: Target, 1980), 11–12; Terrance Dicks and Malcolm Hulke, The Making of Doctor Who (London: Target, 1976), 55; Jean-Marc Lofficier, *The Doctor Who Programme Guide: Volume 2: What's What and Who's Who* (London: Target, 1981), 91; Lesley Standring, *The Doctor Who Illustrated A–Z* (London: W. H. Allen, 1985), 111.

85 *Doctor Who and the Daleks* (Slough: Cadet Sweets, 1964); Terry Nation and David Whitaker, *The Dalek Book* (London: Souvenir Press, 1964).

86 Pat Harrigan and Noah Wardrip-Fruin (eds), Third Person: *Authoring and Exploring Vast Narratives* (Cambridge, MA: MIT Press, 2009), 2; Britton, *TARDISbound*, 5, 12, 22.

87 Matt Hills, 'Televisuality without Television? The Big Finish Audios and Discourses of "Tele-centric" *Doctor Who*', in Butler (ed.), *Time and Relative*, 292, 286.

88 For a detailed overview of 'the Doctor's inconsistent gaming history' (57), beginning with the Atari code published in *Computer & Videogames* magazine in March 1983, see Chris Dring, 'The Long Game', *Doctor Who Magazine*, 496 (March 2016), 50–7.

89 Lev Manovich, *The Language of New Media* (Cambridge, MA: MIT Press, 2001), 222–5.

90 Lance Parkin, 'Canonicity Matters: Defining the *Doctor Who* Canon', in Butler (ed.), *Time and Relative*, 249.

91 Miles Booy, *Love and Monsters: The Doctor Who Experience, 1979 to the Present* (London: I.B. Tauris, 2012), 55.

92 Ibid., 161.

93 Jonathan Morris, 'The TV Movie: Twenty Years On', *Doctor Who Magazine*, 497 (April 2016), 14.

94 Cornell, 'Canonicity in Doctor Who'.

95 McKee, 'How to Tell the Difference', 182–3.

96 Ibid., 182.

97 G. S. Kirk, *Myth: Its Meaning and Function in Ancient and Other Cultures* (Cambridge: Cambridge University Press, 1970), 74.

98 Nymphadorax Lestrange, 'Don't Tell Amy', *FanFiction.Net* (6 September 2011), available at www.fanfiction.net/s/7357784/1/Don-t-Tell-Amy (accessed 21 February 2017).

99 Nearly thirty years later, when evidence of Jimmy Savile's paedophile career came to light, Colin Baker would recall his unease during the recording of the *Jim'll Fix It* sketch, describing the presenter as 'creepy and patronising'. Alex Ward, 'His Eyes Were Cold ...', *Mail Online* (9 November 2012), available at www.dailymail.co.uk/news/article-2230497/Colin-Bakers-verdict-Jimmy-Savile-His-eyes-cold-behaved-like-child-indulged.html (accessed 21 April 2016).

Chapter 3

1 John Ainsworth (ed.), *Doctor Who: The Complete History: Stories 14–17*, vol. 5 (London: Hachette/BBC Worldwide, 2016), 79.

2 John Peel, *Doctor Who – The Chase* (London: Target, 1989), 87.

3 Tsvetan Todorov, *The Fantastic: A Structural Approach to a Literary Genre*, trans. Richard Howard (Ithaca, NY: Cornell University Press, 1975).

4 Rosemary Jackson, *Fantasy: The Literature of Subversion* (London: Routledge, 1998), 45.

5 Daniel O'Mahony, '"Now How Is That Wolf Able to Impersonate a Grandmother?" History, Pseudo-History and Genre in *Doctor Who*', in David Butler (ed.), *Time and Relative Dissertations in Space: Critical Perspectives on Doctor Who* (Manchester: Manchester University Press, 2007), 57.

6 C. E. Webber and Sydney Newman, '"Doctor Who" – General Notes on Background and Approach for an Exciting Adventure-Science Fiction Serial for Children's Saturday Viewing', with handwritten notes by Sydney Newman (1963). See 'The Genesis of Doctor Who: Creating a Science Fiction Hero', *BBC Archive*, available at https://web.archive.org/web/20190509154410/www.bbc.co.uk/archive/doctorwho/6403.shtml?page=txt (accessed 13 September 2019).

7 James Chapman, *Inside the TARDIS: The Worlds of Doctor Who* (London: I.B. Tauris, 2013; orig. 2006), 29.

8 David Whitaker, letter to R. Adams Quinton of Birmingham, May 1964. See Butler, *Time and Relative*, 80; and Alan Kistler, *Doctor Who: A History* (London: Rowman & Littlefield, 2013), 58.

9 Jean Baudrillard, *Selected Writings*, ed. Mark Poster (Cambridge: Polity Press, 1988), 170.

10 Umberto Eco, *Travels in Hyperreality: Essays*, trans. William Weaver (London: Picador, 2003), 67.

11 Ibid., 65.

12 O'Mahony, 'History, Pseudo-History and Genre', 57.

13 Ibid.

14 Chapman, *Inside the TARDIS*, 44.

15 Webber and Newman, ' "Doctor Who" – General Notes'.

16 Matthew Kilburn, 'Bargains of Necessity? *Doctor Who*, *Culloden* and Fictionalising History at the BBC in the 1960s', in Butler (ed.), *Time and Relative*, 75.

17 Robert A. Rosenstone, 'History in Images/History in Words: Reflections on the Possibility of Really Putting History onto Film', *American Historical Review*, 93:5 (December, 1988), 1185.

18 Fred Botting, *Gothic* (London: Routledge, 1996), 169; Jim Leach, *Doctor Who* (Detroit, MI: Wayne State University Press, 2009), 50.

19 Alec Charles, 'The Ideology of Anachronism: Television, History and the Nature of Time', in Butler (ed.), *Time and Relative*, 119–20. See Fredric Jameson, *Postmodernism, or, the Cultural Logic of Late Capitalism* (London: Verso, 1992), and The Ancients and the Postmoderns (London: Verso, 2015); Terry Eagleton, *The Illusions of Postmodernism* (Oxford: Blackwell, 1996); Alex Callinicos, *Against Postmodernism: A Marxist Critique* (Cambridge: Polity, 1990).

20 Mircea Eliade, *The Myth of the Eternal Return, or, Cosmos and History* (Princeton NJ: Princeton University Press, 1971) 86; Jameson, *Postmodernism*, 78, 169.

21 Clifford Geertz, *The Interpretation of Cultures: Selected Essays* (London: Fontana, 1993), 29.

22 Charles, 'Ideology of Anachronism', 121; John Fiske, '*Doctor Who*, Ideology and the Reading of a Popular Narrative', *Australian Journal of Screen Theory* (1983), 69–100; Lorna Jowett, *Dancing with the Doctor: Dimensions of Gender in the Doctor Who Universe* (London: I.B. Tauris, 2017).

23 Written by Malorie Blackman and Chris Chibnall, 'Rosa' won the BAFTA Visionary Arts Organisation Award for Television Show of the Year in February 2019. It has also been nominated for a 2019 Hugo Award (Best Dramatic Presentation, Short Form), with the climactic arrest scene being nominated in the Must-See Moment category of the BAFTA Television Awards 2019.

24 'Demons of the Punjab' has been nominated in the same Hugo Award 2019 category as 'Rosa'.

25 Richard Kearney, *The Wake of Imagination: Toward a Postmodern Culture* (London: Routledge, 1988), 19.

26 David Harvey, *The Condition of Postmodernity* (Oxford: Blackwell, 1991), 54.

27 Kearney, *Wake of Imagination*, 20.

28 Charles, 'Ideology of Anachronism', 112.

29 Matt Hills, *Triumph of a Time Lord: Regenerating Doctor Who for the Twenty-First Century* (London: I.B. Tauris, 2010), 87.

30 Charles, 'Ideology of Anachronism', 119.
31 Hayden White, 'Introduction: Historical Fiction, Fictional History, and Historical Reality', *Rethinking History*, 9:2/3 (June/September 2005), 147.
32 Samuel Taylor Coleridge, *Biographia Literaria, or, Biographical Sketches of My Literary Life and Opinions* (London: Dent, 1957; orig. 1816), 167, 91, 160.
33 Jean-François Lyotard, *The Postmodern Condition: A Report on Knowledge* (Manchester: Manchester University Press, 1979), 76; Kearney, *Wake of Imagination*, 181.
34 Coleridge, *Biographia Literaria*, 174.
35 Ibid.
36 Ibid., 174, 167.
37 Todorov, *The Fantastic*, 24–32, 41–4. See also Jackson, *Fantasy*, 24–33, 37–42; Butler, *Time and Relative*, 27–8.
38 Siegfried Kracauer, *Theory of Film: The Redemption of Physical Reality* (New York: Oxford University Press, 1960), 77.
39 Ibid., 78.
40 W. H. Auden and Christopher Isherwood, *The Ascent of F6 / On the Frontier* (London: Faber and Faber, 1958), 92.
41 Benjamin Cook, interview with Steven Moffat, *Doctor Who Magazine*, 500 (July 2016), 62.
42 White, 'Historical Fiction', 147. See Michel de Certeau, *The Writing of History* (New York: Columbia University Press, 1988).
43 White, 'Historical Fiction', 154.
44 Ibid., 152.
45 Jacques Derrida, *Specters of Marx: The State of the Debt, the Work of Mourning and the New International*, trans. Peggy Kamuf (New York: Routledge, 2006).
46 Rosenstone, 'History in Images/History in Words', 1175.
47 Ibid.
48 See the following televised stories: 'The Dæmons' (1971), 'Image of the Fendhal' (1977), 'The Impossible Astronaut' / 'Day of the Moon' (2011) and 'Ghost Light' (1989).
49 Rosenstone, 'History in Images/History in Words', 1175.
50 Claude Lévi-Strauss, *The Savage Mind* (London: Weidenfeld and Nicolson, 1966), 16–19.
51 Webber and Newman, ' "Doctor Who" – General Notes'.
52 Mark Fisher, 'What Is Hauntology?', *Film Quarterly*, 66:1 (Fall 2012), 19.
53 Pamela McCallum, 'Questions of Haunting: Jacques Derrida's *Specters of Marx* and Raymond Williams's *Modern Tragedy*', *Mosaic*, 40:2 (June 2007), 240.
54 Derrida, *Specters of Marx*, 40.
55 Marc Platt, *Doctor Who – Ghost Light* (London: Target, 1990), 121.
56 Ibid., 7–10, 70.

57 Roger Poole, 'The Real Plot Line of Ford Madox Ford's *The Good Soldier*: An Essay in Applied Deconstruction', *Textual Practice*, 4:3 (December 1990), 390–427.

58 Fisher, 'What Is Hauntology?', 19.

59 See, for instance, Fred Botting, *Limits of Horror: Technology, Bodies, Gothic* (Manchester: Manchester University Press, 2011); Nick Groom, *The Gothic: A Very Short Introduction* (Oxford: Oxford University Press, 2012); and Catherine Spooner, *Contemporary Gothic* (London: Reaktion, 2006).

60 Jessie Weston, *From Ritual to Romance* (London: Doubleday, 1957; orig. 1920).

61 Derrida, *Specters of Marx*, 6.

62 Gas-lighting was provided in Cardiff from the 1820s. See 'The Aberdare Gas Undertaking', *Glamorgan Archives*, available at https://glamarchives.wordpress.com/tag/wales-gas-board/ (accessed 13 September 2019).

63 Hills, *Triumph*, 47.

64 Ibid.

65 The most prominently hauntological episode of Season Eleven, Joy Wilkinson's 'The Witchfinders' (2018), with its superstitious persecutions and alien-possessed corpses, saw the focus moving away from twenty-first-century Yorkshire to seventeenth-century Lancashire. Filming of the fictitious Pendle village of Bilehurst Cragg took place, however, back in the new *Who* homeland of Wales and in the Hampshire town of Gosport.

66 The location is actually St Paul's Church in Grangetown, south Cardiff, built between 1889 and 1902.

67 Phil Collinson, Paul Cornell and Billie Piper, audio commentary, 'Father's Day', *Doctor Who: The Complete First Series* DVD box-set (BBC Worldwide/2 Entertain, 2005).

68 Rory Carroll, 'Bell Did Not Invent Telephone, US Rules' (17 June 2002), available at www.theguardian.com/world/2002/jun/17/humanities.internationaleducationnews (accessed 5 March 2017).

69 Erik Davis, *Techgnosis: Myth, Magic and Mysticism in the Age of Information* (London: Serpent's Tail, 1999), 66.

70 Ibid., 66, 67.

71 Ibid., 66–7.

72 John Tulloch and Manuel Alvarado, *Doctor Who: The Unfolding Text* (Basingstoke: Macmillan, 1983), x–xi.

73 Heinlein's story was originally published in the October 1941 edition of *Astounding Science Fiction* magazine, under the pseudonym Anson MacDonald. It was subsequently included in his 1959 collection *The Menace from Earth* (Riverdale, NY: Baen Books, 1987).

74 Northrop Frye, *Anatomy of Criticism: Four Essays* (Princeton, NJ: Princeton University Press, 1971), 76.

75 Thomas Kuhn, *The Structure of Scientific Revolutions* (London: University of Chicago Press, 1962); Michel Foucault, *The Order of Things* (London: Routledge, 1989).

76 John William Polidori, *'The Vampyre' and Other Writings*, ed. Franklin Charles Bishop (Manchester: Carcanet Press, 2005).

77 Matt Hills, '"Mythology Makes You Feel Something": The Russell T. Davies Era as Sentimental Journey', in *The Mythological Dimensions of Doctor Who*, ed. Anthony Burdge, Jessica Burke and Kristine (Crawfordville, FL: Kitsune Books, 2010), 206, 203.

78 The authorship of 'The Brain of Morbius' has, in itself, a Frankensteinian hybridity: credited to 'Robin Bland', it was scripted initially by Terrance Dicks, then revised by Robert Holmes. Dicks, irked by the changes, insisted on the 'bland pseudonym' concocted by Holmes. See David J. Howe, Mark Stammers and Stephen James Walker, *Doctor Who: The Handbook – The Fourth Doctor* (London: Virgin, 1992), 175–6.

79 Ivan Phillips, 'The Vampire in the Machine: Exploring the Undead Interface', in Sam George and Bill Hughes (eds), *Open Graves, Open Minds: Representations of Vampires and the Undead from the Enlightenment to the Present Day* (Manchester: Manchester University Press, 2013), 228–9.

80 Terrance Dicks, *Doctor Who and the State of Decay* (London: Target Books, 1981), 90–1.

81 Jeremy Bentham, 'Interview with John Nathan-Turner', *Doctor Who Monthly*, 51 (April 1981), 33.

82 Peter Anghelides, *Doctor Who – Kursaal* (London: BBC Books, 1998); Jacqueline Rayner, *Doctor Who – Wolfsbane* (London: BBC Books, 2003); Marc Platt, *Doctor Who – Loups-Garoux* (London: Big Finish, 2001); Mike Maddox, *Doctor Who – Legend of the Cybermen* (London: Big Finish, 2010); Pat Mills, John Wagner and Alan Gibbons, 'The Dogs of Doom', *Doctor Who Weekly* (16 April–5 June 1980), 27–34; Scott Gray, Martin Geraghty and David A. Roach, 'Bad Blood', *Doctor Who Magazine* (7 January–28 April 2004), 338–42; Marc Platt and Paul Vyse, 'Loop the Loup', *Doctor Who Yearbook 1994* (Marvel, 1994).

83 In the folklore of werewolves, it is often believed that the fur of the wolf remains hidden beneath the skin between transformations. The metamorphosis from human to werewolf therefore involves a process of turning inside-out. Angela Carter refers to this literalization of the concept of 'the beast within' in her story 'The Company of Wolves' – included in *The Bloody Chamber and Other Stories* (London: Gollancz, 1979) – as well as in its subsequent film adaptation (Neil Jordan, 1984).

84 David Darlington, 'You're Killing My Lesbian Subtext …!!', interview with Rona Munro, *Deejsaint* (25 November 2007), available at http://web.archive.org/web/20110604155734/http://www.btinternet.com/~david.darlington/rona2007.html (accessed 28 August 2015).

85 Ken Gelder, *Reading the Vampire* (London: Routledge, 1994), 127.

86   Julia Kristeva, *Powers of Horror: An Essay in Abjection*
     (New York: Columbia University Press, 1982), 3.
87   See Tulloch and Alvarado, *Unfolding Text*, 11, 159–60, 190; Chapman,
     Inside the TARDIS, 113–15, 146.
88   Chantal Bourgault du Coudray, *The Curse of the Werewolf: Fantasy,
     Horror and the Beast Within* (London: I.B. Tauris, 2006), 4. See also
     Slavoj Žižek, *Enjoy Your Symptom! Jacques Lacan in Hollywood and
     Out* (London: Routledge, 2001), 136.
89   Chapman, *Inside the TARDIS*, 76.
90   Pierce (1889–1968) was the pioneering head of make-up design
     at Universal Studios during the 1930s and 1940s, responsible for
     creations including Boris Karloff as Frankenstein's creature (1931, 1935,
     1939) and the werewolf make-up of Henry Hull (Werewolf of London,
     1935) and Lon Chaney Jr. (The Wolf Man, 1941).
91   Terrance Dicks, *Doctor Who – Inferno* (London: Target, 1984), 86.
92   'Posts tagged "Jon Pertwee"', *Dr Who Interviews* blog (4 October
     2009), available at https://drwhointerviews.wordpress.com/tag/jon-
     pertwee/ (accessed 30 January 2016).
93   Graham Sleight, *The Doctor's Monsters: Meanings of the Monstrous in
     Doctor Who* (London: I.B. Tauris, 2012), 34–8.
94   Leslie A. Sconduto, *Metamorphoses of the Werewolf: A Literary Study
     from Antiquity through the Renaissance* (Jefferson, NC: McFarland,
     2008), 200.
95   Philip Martin, *Doctor Who – Mindwarp* (London: Target, 1989), 17–18.
96   Hills, *Triumph*, 87.
97   Chapman, *Inside the TARDIS*, 207, 278.
98   Alec Charles, *Out of Time: The Deaths and Resurrections of Doctor
     Who* (Oxford: Peter Lang, 2015), 8–9, 70–2, 101–30, 139–54, 167–71;
     Hills, *Triumph*, 87.
99   Lucy Armitt, 'Twentieth-Century Gothic', in *Terror and Wonder: The
     Gothic Imagination*, ed. Dale Townshend (London: British Library,
     2014), 170–1. See also James B. Twitchell, *The Living Dead: A Study
     of the Vampire in Romantic Literature* (Durham, NC: Duke University
     Press, 1981).
100 Dave Kehr, review of *The Wolf Man* (1941), *Chicago Reader* (8 October
     2008), available at www.chicagoreader.com/chicago/the-wolf-man/
     Film?oid=1056197 (accessed 22 February 2016); Darren Mooney,
     'Non-Review Review: *The Wolf Man* (1941)', *the m0vie blog* (31 October
     2012), available at http://them0vieblog.com/2012/10/31/non-review-
     review-the-wolf-man-1941 (accessed 22 February 2016).
101 'Little Rose Riding Hood' is one of the stories in Justin Richards's
     Time Lord Fairy Tales (London: BBC Books, 2015), 123–37, where the
     märchen of so many human childhoods are reworked as fables from
     Gallifrey.

Chapter 4

1 Mark J. P. Wolf, *Building Imaginary Worlds: The Theory and History of Subcreation* (New York: Routledge, 2012), 14.

2 Miles Booy, *Love and Monsters: The Doctor Who Experience, 1979 to the Present* (London: I.B. Tauris, 2012), 5.

3 Brian Logan, 'The Spirit of Wobbliness', *The Guardian* (29 September 2003), available at www.theguardian.com/media/2003/sep/29/broadcasting.bbc (accessed 5 July 2016).

4 Matt Hills, '"Mythology Makes You Feel Something": The Russell T. Davies Era as Sentimental Journey', in *The Mythological Dimensions of Doctor Who*, ed. Anthony Burdge, Jessica Burke and Kristine Larsen (Crawfordville, FL: Kitsune Books, 2010), 206.

5 J. R. R. Tolkien, quoted in Wolf, *Building Imaginary Worlds*, 191.

6 Piers D. Britton, *TARDISbound: Navigating the Universes of Doctor Who* (London: I.B. Tauris, 2011), 26; Matt Hills, *Triumph of a Time Lord: Regenerating Doctor Who for the Twenty-First Century* (London: I.B. Tauris, 2010), 58–62.

7 Kim Newman, *Doctor Who* (London: BFI, 2005), 21.

8 Ibid., 11.

9 Marc Platt, *Cat's Cradle: Time's Crucible* (London: Virgin, 1992); Jim Mortimore, *Doctor Who – Blood Heat* (London: Virgin, 1993); Peter Anghelides and Stephen Cole, *Doctor Who – The Ancestor Cell* (London: BBC Books, 2000).

10 Gaston Bachelard, *The Poetics of Space* (Boston, MA: Beacon Press, 1994), 54.

11 Tom Paulin, *Minotaur: Poetry and the Nation State* (London: Faber and Faber, 1992), 190.

12 Martin Heidegger, *Being and Time: A Translation of* Sein und Zeit, trans. Joan Stambaugh (New York: State University of New York Press, 1996), 153, 180, 301.

13 Marc Platt, *Lungbarrow* (London: Virgin, 1997), 215–16.

14 Stephen Kelly, '*Doctor Who*: Mark Gatiss on Why the Time Lords Shouldn't "Become Like a Bunch of MPs"', *Radio Times* (24 March 2014), available at www.radiotimes.com/news/2014-03-24/doctor-who-mark-gatiss-on-why-the-time-lords-shouldnt-become-like-a-bunch-of-mps (accessed 5 March 2017).

15 Paulin, *Minotaur*, 190.

16 Martin Heidegger, 'Building Dwelling Thinking' (1951), in *Poetry, Language, Thought*, trans. Albert Hofstadter (New York: Harper Perennial, 2001), 156.

17 Paulin, *Minotaur*, 193.

18 Ibid., 194.

19 Tegan's description of the TARDIS at the end of 'The Five Doctors' (1983).

20 See, for instance, Hermann Rauschning's *Hitler Speaks: A Series of Political Conversations with Hitler on His Real Aims* (Whitefish, MT: Kessinger, 2010); and Alice A. Bailey, *The Externalisation of the Hierarchy* (New York: Lucis, 1957).

21 Mary Ann Johanson, 'Doctor Who Blogging: "Journey to the Centre of the TARDIS"', *flickfilosopher.com* (30 April 2013), available at www.flickfilosopher.com/2013/04/doctor-who-blogging-journey-to-the-centre-of-the-tardis.html (accessed 5 March 2017); Kate Kulzick, 'Doctor Who Ep. 7.11, "Journey to the Centre of the TARDIS": Creative, Fun Ep Marred by Series' Biggest Flaw', *PopOptiq.com* (27 April 2013), available at www.popoptiq.com/doctor-who-ep-7-11-journey-to-the-centre-of-the-tardis-creative-fun-ep-marred-by-series-biggest-flaw/ (accessed 5 March 2017).

22 Graham Kibble-White, review of 'Journey to the Centre of the TARDIS', *Doctor Who Magazine*, 460 (June 2013), 68.

23 Alan Barnes, in 'Out of Time', DVD extra (Disc 2), *The Invasion of Time* (BBC/2 Entertain).

24 Darko Suvin, *Metamorphoses of Science Fiction: On the Poetics and History of a Literary Genre* (New Haven, CT: Yale University Press, 1979), 15; Katherine A. Fowkes, *The Fantasy Film* (Chichester: Wiley-Blackwell, 2010), 2.

25 Nick Griffiths, *Who Goes There: Travels through Strangest Britain in Search of the Doctor* (London: Legend Press, 2009); Richard Bignell, *Doctor Who: On Location* (London: Reynolds & Hearn, 2000); *Doctor Who: The Locations Guide*, available at www.doctorwholocations.net (accessed 10 May 2019).

26 The two earliest location scenes, filmed in Buckinghamshire on 15 June 1964, both show the Doctor supposedly walking in France, once in the countryside (Isle of Wight Farm, Gerrards Cross) and once up a boulevard (White Plains Retirement Home, Denham).

27 See Rachel Talahay, 'Notes on Heaven Sent, Part 1', *RachelTalahay* (16 December 2014), available at http://racheltalalay.tumblr.com/post/135339295759/notes-on-heaven-sent-part-1 (accessed 22 July 2016).

28 David J. Howe and Stephen James Walker, *Doctor Who: The Television Companion* (London: BBC Worldwide, 1998), 36.

29 Claude Lévi-Strauss, *The Savage Mind* (London: Weidenfeld and Nicolson, 1966), 22–30.

30 Benjamin Cook, interview with Steven Moffat, *Doctor Who Magazine*, 500 (July 2016), 58–9.

31 John Fiske, '*Doctor Who*, Ideology and the Reading of a Popular Narrative', *Australian Journal of Screen Theory* (1983), 75.

32 Ibid., 77.

33 Ibid., 99.

34 Alec Charles, 'The Ideology of Anachronism: Television, History and the Nature of Time', in David Butler (ed.), *Time and Relative Dissertations in*

Space: Critical Perspectives on Doctor Who (Manchester: Manchester University Press, 2007), 108–22.

35   John Tulloch, 'Dr Who: Similarity and Difference', *Australian Journal of Screen Theory*, 11–12 (1982), 8–24.

36   Chapman, *Inside the TARDIS*, 7, 56, 79–82, 115–16, 220, 247–8; Lorna Jowett, 'The Girls Who Waited? Female Companions and Gender in *Doctor Who*', *Critical Studies in Television: The International Journal of Television Studies*, 9:1 (Spring 2014), 77–94; Lorna Jowett, *Dancing with the Doctor: Dimensions of Gender in the Doctor Who Universe* (London: I.B. Tauris, 2017).

37   Britton, *TARDISbound*, 192.

38   Ibid.

39   Paul Ricoeur, *From Text to Action: Essays in Hermeneutics, II* (Evanston, IL: Northwestern University Press, 1991), 320; Paul Ricoeur, *A Ricoeur Reader: Reflection & Imagination*, ed. M.J. Valdés (New York: Harvester, 1991), 485, 489.

40   Hills, *Triumph of a Time Lord*, 65.

41   Fiske, '*Doctor Who*, Ideology and the Reading', 81.

42   Alec Charles, *Out of Time: The Deaths and Resurrections of Doctor Who* (Oxford: Peter Lang, 2015), 131–8.

43   Ibid., 138.

44   The religious connotations of the show have been explored in several volumes over the last decade, notably Andrew Crome and James McGrath (eds), *Time and Relative Dimensions in Faith: Religion and Doctor Who* (London: Darton, Longman and Todd, 2013).

45   Terrance Dicks and Malcolm Hulke, *The Making of Doctor Who* (London: Target, 1976), 23.

46   John Milton, *Prose Writings* (London: J. M. Dent, 1958), 158.

47   See Karen Hellekson, '"Doctor Who Unbound", the Alternate History and the Fannish Text', in *Fan Phenomena: Doctor Who*, ed. Paul Booth (London: Intellect, 2013), 136–47.

48   Britton, *TARDISbound*, 205.

49   Ibid., 205. See also Wayne C. Booth, *The Company We Keep: An Ethics of Fiction* (Berkeley: University of California Press, 1988).

50   Britton, *TARDISbound*, 205.

51   See Jean-Paul Sartre, *Being and Nothingness: A Phenomenological Essay on Ontology* (1943) (Abingdon: Routledge, 2003), 70–94, and *Essays in Existentialism* (New York: Citadel Press, 1993), 160–9.

52   Hills, *Triumph*, 134–5.

53   Britton, *TARDISbound*, 29–54.

54   Lord Raglan, *The Hero: A Study in Tradition, Myth and Drama* (New York: Vintage, 1956); Northrop Frye, *Anatomy of Criticism: Four Essays* (Princeton, NJ: Princeton University Press, 1971); Vladimir Propp, *Morphology of the Folk Tale* (Austin: University of Texas Press, 1968);

Joseph Campbell, *The Hero with a Thousand Faces* (London: Fontana, 1993; orig. 1948).

55   Campbell, *Hero with a Thousand Faces*, 36.

56   Thomas Carlyle, *On Heroes, Hero-Worship and the Heroic in History* (London: Chapman and Hall, 1840).

57   John Tulloch and Manuel Alvarado, *Doctor Who: The Unfolding Text* (Basingstoke: Macmillan, 1983), 278.

58   Maurice Buxton Foreman (ed.), *The Letters of John Keats* (London: Oxford University Press, 1947), 72.

59   Kenneth Burke, *Language as Symbolic Action: Essays on Life, Literature, and Method* (Berkeley: University of California Press, 1978), 20.

60   Laurence Coupe, *Myth* (London: Routledge, 1997), 46. See Edgell Rickword, *The Calendar of Modern Letters, March 1925–July 1927*, ed. Douglas Garman (London: Routledge, 1966), and *Essays and Opinions, 1921–1931*, ed. Alan Young (Manchester: Carcanet, 1974).

61   Rickword, *Essays and Opinions*, 118.

62   Julia Kristeva, *The Kristeva Reader*, ed. Toril Moi (Oxford: Blackwell, 1986), 49–55; Newman, *Doctor Who*, 21; Tulloch and Alvarado, *Unfolding Text*, 28.

63   Frye, *Anatomy of Criticism*, 309–10.

64   Kevin S. Decker, *Who Is Who? The Philosophy of Doctor Who* (London: I.B. Tauris, 2012), 59.

65   Toby Hadoke, *Moths Ate My Doctor Who Scarf*, produced by Paul Hardy (London: BBC Audio, 2007).

66   Lev Manovich, 'The Paradoxes of Digital Photography', *Photography after Photography: Memory and Representation in the Digital Age* (G&B Arts, 1995), 14, available at http://manovich.net/content/04-projects/004-paradoxes-of-digital-photography/02_article_1994.pdf (accessed 16 August 2016).

67   Lev Manovich, *The Language of New Media* (Cambridge, MA: MIT Press, 2001), 200.

68   Ibid., 202.

69   Chapman, *Inside the TARDIS*, 8; Booy, *Love and Monsters*, 88.

70   Howe and Walker, *Television Companion*, 436.

71   André Bazin, *What Is Cinema?*, vol. 1 (Berkeley: University of California Press, 1967), 17–22.

72   Hadoke, *Moths Ate My Doctor Who Scarf*.

73   Fiske, '*Doctor Who*, Ideology and the Reading', 89; Theodor Adorno and Max Horkheimer, *Dialectic of Enlightenment* (London: Verso, 1986).

74   John Fiske, *Television Culture* (London: Routledge, 1989), 39, 93.

75   See, for instance, Chapman, *Inside the TARDIS*, 225, 281; Jim Leach, *Doctor Who* (Detroit, MI: Wayne State University Press, 2009), 50, 70; Hills, *Triumph*, 87–8, and ' "Gothic" Body Parts in a "Postmodern" Body of Work? The Hinchcliffe/Holmes Era of *Doctor Who* (1975–77)',

Intensities: The Journal of Cult Media, 4 (2007), available at https://intensitiescultmedia.files.wordpress.com/2012/12/hills-gothic-body-parts-in-postmodern-body-of-work.pdf (accessed 13 June 2017); Paul Booth, 'Effecting the Cause: Time Travel Narratives', in *Doctor Who in Time and Space: Essays on Themes, Characters, History and Fandom, 1963–2012*, ed. Gillian I. Leitch (Jefferson, NC: McFarland, 2013), 101–8.

76 Susan Sontag, *Against Interpretation and Other Essays* (New York: Delta, 1967), 15.

77 Piers D. Britton and Simon J. Barker, *Reading between Designs: Visual Imagery and the Generation of Meaning in The Avengers, The Prisoner, and Doctor Who* (Austin: University of Texas Press, 2003), 168.

78 Ivan Phillips, '*Doctor Who* and the Terror of the Vorticists: Popular Fantasy and the Cultural Inheritance of *BLAST*', BLAST 2014 Conference, Bath Spa University, 24–26 July, 2014.

79 Samuel Taylor Coleridge, *Biographia Literaria, or, Biographical Sketches of My Literary Life and Opinions* (London: Dent, 1957; orig. 1816), 168–9.

80 Michael Herbert, *Doctor Who and the Communist: Malcolm Hulke and his Career in Television* (Nottingham: Five Leaves, 2015).

81 Britton, *TARDISbound*, 194.

82 Tom Gunning, 'The Cinema of Attraction[s]: Early Film, Its Spectator, and the Avant-Garde', in *The Cinema of Attractions Reloaded*, ed. Wanda Strauven (Amsterdam: Amsterdam University Press, 2006), 381–8.

83 In Robert Holmes's rightly celebrated (but also rightly controversial) 1977 story 'The Talons of Weng-Chiang'.

84 Manovich, *Language of New Media*, 200–1, 296–308.

85 Dan North, 'Magic and Illusion in Early Cinema', *Studies in French Cinema*, 1:2 (2001), 70–9; Gunning, 'Cinema of Attraction[s]', 382.

86 Gunning, 'Cinema of Attraction[s]', 381.

87 Ibid.

88 Jay David Bolter and Richard Grusin, *Remediation: Understanding New Media* (Cambridge, MA: MIT Press, 1999), 5–6, 21–50.

89 Tom Gunning, 'An Aesthetic of Astonishment: Early Film and the (In)Credulous Spectator', in *Film Theory and Criticism: Introductory Readings*, 7th edition, ed. Leo Braudy and Marshall Cohen (Oxford: Oxford University Press, 2009), 743.

90 Ibid., 739.

91 Ibid., 739.

92 Howe and Walker, *Television Companion*, 337.

93 Manovich, *Language of New Media*, 200.

94 Manovich, 'The Paradoxes of Digital Photography', 14.

95 Gunning, 'An Aesthetic of Astonishment', 749.

96 Tulloch and Alvarado, *Unfolding Text*, 151.

97 Tom Baker, *Who on Earth Is Tom Baker? An Autobiography* (London: Harper Collins, 1997), 218.

98 Benjamin Cook, 'The Ultimate Interview', *Doctor Who Magazine*, 501 (August 2016), 4–68.

99 Sontag, *Against Interpretation*, 275.

100 Ibid., 292.

101 Ibid., 275.

102 Ibid., 285, 283, 286, 288, 285, 289.

103 Hills, *Triumph*, 150; Newman, *Doctor Who*, 88.

104 Sontag, *Against Interpretation*, 277.

105 Interviewed for *Doctor Who: Thirty Years in the TARDIS* (Kevin Davies, 1993), available as part of *The Legacy Collection* box set (BBC 2013).

106 Sontag, *Against Interpretation*, 282.

107 Ed Stradling, interview with Steven Moffat, *YouTube* (20 February 2013), available at www.youtube.com/watch?v=h7VQrnMzjrU&feature=pla yer_embedded (accessed 6 March 2017).

108 Sontag, *Against Interpretation*, 287.

109 David J. Howe, *Doctor Who: A Book of Monsters* (London: BBC Books, 1997), 66–8.

110 Graeme Curry, *Doctor Who – The Happiness Patrol* (London: Target, 1985), 16.

111 Christopher H. Bidmead, *Doctor Who – Frontios* (London: Target, 1985), 107.

112 Only two companions had been killed in the television series prior to Adric's departure, both in the twelve-part Hartnell story 'The Dalek's Master Plan' (1965–6). However, both the Trojan handmaiden Katarina (Adrienne Hill) and the space agent Sara Kingdom (Jean Marsh) were relatively short-term presences in the TARDIS, the former appearing in only one other story and the latter in this one alone.

113 Sontag, *Against Interpretation*, 283.

114 Graham Kibble-White, review of *Myths and Legends* box set, *Doctor Who Magazine*, 421 (11 May 2011), 60–1.

115 'The First Fifty Years', *Doctor Who Magazine*, 474 (July 2014), 62–3.

116 See E. B. Tylor, *Primitive Culture: Researches into the Development of Mythology, Philosophy, Religion, Language, Art and Custom*, 2 vols (London: Murray, 1871); J. G. Frazer, *The Golden Bough: A Study in Magic and Religion*, 12 vols (London: Macmillan, 1890–1911).

117 Lévy-Bruhl, *How Natives Think* and *Primitive Mythology*; Bronisław Malinowski, *Myth in Primitive Psychology* (London: Norton, 1926), and *Magic, Science and Religion and Other Essays* (Glencoe, IL: Free Press, 1948).

118 Sontag, *Against Interpretation*, 291.

119 Newman, *Doctor Who*, 96.

Chapter 5

1 Mark Jefferies and Nicola Methven, 'Doctor Who Due a Major Shake-up as Bosses Aim for "Brand New Show" in 2018', *Mirror* (14 November 2016), available at www.mirror.co.uk/tv/tv-news/doctor-who-due-major-shake-9254797 (accessed 3 January 2017). See also Ivan Phillips, 'Is the End of Time in Sight for *Doctor Who*?', *The Conversation* (22 December 2016), available at https://theconversation.com/is-the-end-of-time-in-sight-for-doctor-who-70353 (accessed 3 January 2017).
2 Capaldi announced his decision to leave the series during an interview on Jo Whiley's show on BBC Radio 2 on 30 January 2017. An excerpt is available at www.bbc.co.uk/programmes/p04rcql8 (accessed 31 July 2017).
3 Huw Fullerton, 'Doctor Who Experience to Close Next Year', *Radio Times* (7 November 2016), available at www.radiotimes.com/news/2016-11-07/doctor-who-experience-to-close-next-year (accessed 3 January 2017).
4 Alec Charles, 'What the Casting of the Next Doctor Who Will Tell Us about the BBC', *The Conversation* (13 April 2017), available at https://theconversation.com/what-the-casting-of-the-next-doctor-who-will-tell-us-about-the-bbc-76162 (accessed 2 August 2017).
5 Stuart Heritage, 'Is Phoebe Waller-Bridge Really the New Face of Doctor Who?' *The Guardian* (5 July 2017), available at www.theguardian.com/tv-and-radio/2017/jul/05/is-this-the-new-face-of-doctor-who-phoebe-waller-bridge (accessed 2 August 2017).
6 Matt Hills, 'Casting a Female Doctor Who Wasn't so Bold – Choosing Another White Male Would Have Been Really Risky', *The Conversation* (26 July 2017), available at https://theconversation.com/casting-a-female-doctor-who-wasnt-so-bold-choosing-another-white-male-would-have-been-really-risky-81410 (accessed 2 August 2017).
7 See Ivan Phillips, 'Reversing the Polarity of the Gender Flow: On Reactions to Jodie Whittaker as the Doctor', *TVAD: Theorising Visual Art and Design* (28 July 2017), available at http://tvad-uh.blogspot.co.uk/2017/07/reversingthe-polarity-of-gender-flow-on.html (accessed 13 May 2019).
8 Jonn Elledge, '"This Will Annoy Exactly the Right People": Why Casting Jodie Whittaker as Doctor Who Is a Brilliant Decision', *New Statesman* (16 July 2017), available at www.newstatesman.com/culture/tv-radio/2017/07/will-annoy-exactly-right-people-why-casting-jodie-whittaker-doctor-who (accessed 4 August 2017).
9 Hills, 'Casting a Female Doctor Who Wasn't so Bold'.
10 Lorna Jowett, 'The Thirteenth Doctor: Lucky for Some?' *Medium* (21 July 2017), available at https://medium.com/@UniNorthants/the-thirteenth-doctor-lucky-for-some-215e53940caa (accessed 13 May 2019).
11 Lorna Jowett, '"Is the Future Going to Be All Girl?" *Doctor Who* and the Frustrations of a Feminist', *CST online* (23 March 2018), available at

https://cstonline.net/is-the-future-going-to-be-all-girl-doctor-who-and-the-frustrations-of-a-feminist-by-lorna-jowett/ (accessed 13 May 2019).

12   Figures correct as of 13 May 2019.

13   Chris Hastings, 'Exterminate! Fans' Backlash over Doctor Who's Latest Transformation – into TV's Most PC Show', *Mail Online* (28 October 2018), available at https://www.dailymail.co.uk/news/article-6324799/Doctor-sparks-fan-backlash-Time-Lord-branded-TVs-politically-correct-show.html (accessed 13 May 2019).

14   Rod McPhee, 'EXTERMINATING VIEWERS: Doctor Who Ratings Plunge after Jodie Whittaker Takes Over with PC Plots', *The Sun* (5 November 2018), available at https://www.thesun.co.uk/tvandshowbiz/7666311/doctor-who-ratings-fall-pc-plots/ (accessed 13 May 2019).

15   Hastings, 'Exterminate!'

16   Jeremy Clarkson, 'BBC Is Now Only Giving Front-Line Jobs to Women Just Like Doctor Who – and They've Totally Lost the Plot', *The Sun* (10 November 2018). Available at https://www.thesun.co.uk/news/7705458/bbc-giving-jobs-to-women-jeremy-clarkson/ (accessed 16 May 2019).

17   Alec, @AlecRCharles, Twitter (7.06 am, 11 Nov. 2018), available at https://twitter.com/AlecRCharles/status/1061515376075382784 (accessed 16 May 2019).

18   Tom Spilsbury, 'Public Image', *Doctor Who Magazine*, 534 (February 2019), 7.

19   VanMan, @T5VanMan, Twitter (8.49 am, 5 Nov. 2018), available at https://twitter.com/T5VanMan/status/1059367161737568256 (accessed 16 May 2019). Quoted in McPhee, 'EXTERMINATING VIEWERS'. The tweet is also quoted in many other online articles. Interestingly, it is a more extreme version of a tweet from 29 October (8.15 am), which read, 'Afraid #DoctorWho has lost me. Jodie Whittaker is great as the Doctor but the writing is not. I don't watch the Doctor to have subliminal PC social correct messages pushed down my throat in the guise of science fiction fantasy,' available at https://twitter.com/T5VanMan/status/1056821846937546752 (accessed 16 May 2019). It is significant, of course, that those intending negative coverage of the series should have selected the later tweet for dissemination.

20   John Fiske, '*Doctor Who*, Ideology and the Reading of a Popular Narrative', *Australian Journal of Screen Theory* (1983), 96.

21   Ibid.

22   Ibid., 99.

23   Huw Fullerton, 'Doctor Who Picks Up Special Award for Malorie Blackman Episode "Rosa"', *Radio Times* (9 February 2019), available at https://www.radiotimes.com/news/tv/2019-02-09/doctor-who-picks-up-special-award-for-malorie-blackman-episode-rosa/ (accessed 17 May 2019).

24   The concept of the 'Big Bad' originates in Joss Whedon's television series *Buffy the Vampire Slayer* (WB, 1997–2001; UPN, 2003), first featuring in

the episode 'Bewitched, Bothered and Bewildered' from Season Two, written by Marti Noxon and initially broadcast on 10 February 1998.

25 Darren, 'Doctor Who: It Takes You Away (Review)', *the m0vie blog* (2 December 2018), available at https://them0vieblog.com/2018/12/02/doctor-who-it-takes-you-away-review/ (accessed 17 May 2019); Ed Power, 'Doctor Who Review, "It Takes You Away": Jodie Whittaker's Best Outing Yet', *The Independent* (2 December 2018), available at https://www.independent.co.uk/arts-entertainment/tv/reviews/doctor-who-series-11-episode-9-it-takes-you-away-review-jodie-whittaker-bradley-walsh-a8663501.html (accessed 17 May 2019).

26 Chris Allcock, 'Doctor Who Season 11 Review: It Takes You Away', *Den of Geek* (2 December 2018), available at https://www.denofgeek.com/uk/tv/doctor-who/62104/doctor-who-series-11-review-it-takes-you-away (accessed 17 May 2019); Morgan Jeffery, 'Doctor Who Series 11, Episode 9 Review: "It Takes You Away" Is Both Brilliant and Baffling', *Digital Spy* (2 December 2018), available at https://www.digitalspy.com/tv/a871637/doctor-who-series-11-episode-9-review/ (accessed 17 May 2019).

27 Paul Kirkley, 'Reviews ["It Takes You Away"]', *Doctor Who Magazine*, 534 (February 2019), 59.

28 David Whitaker, *Doctor Who and the Daleks* (London: Target, 1973), 80–2.

29 Kelly Connolly, 'The Radical Helplessness of the New *Doctor Who*', *The Atlantic* (10 December 2018), available at https://www.theatlantic.com/entertainment/archive/2018/12/doctor-who-radical-helplessness-jodie-whittaker-season-11/577741/ (accessed 25 January 2019).

30 Katherine Cross, 'Doctor Who Has Given Us a Doctor without Inner Conflict', *Polygon* [Online], 1 January 2019, available at https://www.polygon.com/2019/1/1/18152028/doctor-who-whitaker-season-review (accessed 3 January 2019).

31 Stories were usually between two and seven, although the number expanded to twelve for 'The Daleks' Master Plan' of 1965–6.

32 John Tulloch and Manuel Alvarado, *Doctor Who: The Unfolding Text* (Basingstoke: Macmillan, 1983), x–xi.

33 The Doctor Who Team, '13 Questions for the Thirteenth Doctor' (16 July 2017), available at www.bbc.co.uk/blogs/doctorwho/entries/633b5583-f0b1-4917-baf5-eb02ca44552a (accessed 7 August 2017).

34 Ted Hughes, *Shakespeare and the Goddess of Complete Being* (London: Faber and Faber, 1992), 1 *et passim*.

35 This landmark and long-missing story has recently become available to view again (in 2D animated form) through the efforts of Charles Norton, Martin Geraghty and Adrian Salmon. The achievement is metaphorical: loss, change, renewal, continuity, expansion.

36 Lance Parkin, *The Infinity Doctors* (London: BBC Books, 1998), 75.

37   C. E. Webber and Sydney Newman, '"Doctor Who" – General Notes
     on Background and Approach for an Exciting Adventure-Science
     Fiction Serial for Children's Saturday Viewing', with handwritten notes
     by Sydney Newman (1963). See 'The Genesis of Doctor Who: Creating
     a Science Fiction Hero', *BBC Archive*, available at https://web.archive.
     org/web/20190509154410/www.bbc.co.uk/archive/doctorwho/6403.
     shtml?page=txt (accessed 13 September 2019).
38   Ibid.

Bibliography

Adorno, Theodor, and Max Horkheimer, *Dialectic of Enlightenment* (London: Verso, 1986).

Ainsworth, John (ed.), *Doctor Who: The Complete History: Stories 14–17*, vol. 5 (London: Hachette/BBC Worldwide, 2016).

Anghelides, Peter, *Doctor Who – Kursaal* (London: BBC Books, 1998).

Anghelides, Peter, and Stephen Cole, *Doctor Who – The Ancestor Cell* (London: BBC Books, 2000).

Armitt, Lucy, 'Twentieth-Century Gothic', in Dale Townshend (ed.), *Terror and Wonder: The Gothic Imagination* (London: British Library, 2014), pp. 170–1.

Auden, W. H., and Christopher Isherwood, *The Ascent of F6 / On the Frontier* (London: Faber and Faber, 1958).

Bachelard, Gaston, *The Poetics of Space* (Boston, MA: Beacon Press, 1994).

Baker, Tom, *Who on Earth Is Tom Baker? An Autobiography* (London: HarperCollins, 1997).

Barthes, Roland, *Image-Music-Text*, trans. Stephen Heath (London: Fontana, 1984).

Barthes, Roland, *Mythologies*, trans. Annette Lavers (London: Vintage, 1993).

Baudrillard, Jean, *Selected Writings*, ed. Mark Poster (Cambridge: Polity Press, 1988).

Bazin, André, *What Is Cinema?*, vol. 1 (Berkeley: University of California Press, 1967).

Bentham, Jeremy, 'Interview with John Nathan-Turner', *Doctor Who Monthly*, 51 (April 1981), pp. 32–3.

Bidmead, Christopher H., *Doctor Who – Frontios* (London: Target, 1985).

Bignell, Richard, *Doctor Who: On Location* (London: Reynolds & Hearn, 2000).

Blum, Jonathan, and Kate Orman, *Vampire Science* (London: Virgin, 1997).

Bogost, Ian, 'Against Aca-Fandom: On Jason Mittell on *Mad Men*' (2010), *bogost.com*. Available at http://bogost.com/writing/blog/against_aca-fandom/ (accessed 3 March 2017).

Bolter, Jay David, and Richard Grusin, *Remediation: Understanding New Media* (Cambridge, MA: MIT Press, 1999).

Booth, Paul (ed.), 'Effecting the Cause: Time Travel Narratives', in Gillian I. Leitch (ed.), *Doctor Who in Time and Space: Essays on Themes,*

Characters, History and Fandom, 1963–2012 (Jefferson, NC: McFarland, 2013), pp. 101–8.

Booth, Paul, *Fan Phenomena: Doctor Who* (Bristol: Intellect, 2013).

Booth, Wayne C., *The Company We Keep: An Ethics of Fiction* (Berkeley: University of California Press, 1988).

Booy, Miles, *Love and Monsters: The Doctor Who Experience, 1979 to the Present* (London: I.B. Tauris, 2012).

Botting, Fred, *Gothic* (London: Routledge, 1996).

Botting, Fred, *Limits of Horror: Technology, Bodies, Gothic* (Manchester: Manchester University Press, 2011).

Brecht, Bertolt, *Brecht on Theatre: The Development of an Aesthetic* (London: Methuen, 1978).

Briggs, Ian, *Doctor Who: Dragonfire* (London: W. H. Allen, 1989).

Briggs, Nicholas, *Doctor Who – Beachhead* (London: Big Finish, 2017).

Britton, Piers D., *TARDISbound: Navigating the Universes of Doctor Who* (London: I.B. Tauris, 2011).

Britton, Piers D., 'Making "A Superior Brand of Alien Mastermind": *Doctor Who* Monsters and the Rhetoric of (Re)design', in Matt Hills (ed.), *New Dimensions of Doctor Who: Adventures in Space, Time and Television* (London: I.B. Tauris, 2013), pp. 39–53.

Britton, Piers D., and Simon J. Barker, *Reading between Designs: Visual Imagery and the Generation of Meaning in The Avengers, The Prisoner, and Doctor Who* (Austin: University of Texas Press, 2003).

Bulis, Christopher, *Twilight of the Gods* (London: Virgin, 1996).

Burdge, Anthony, Jessica Burke and Kristine Larsen (eds), *The Mythological Dimensions of Doctor Who* (Crawfordville, FL: Kitsune Books, 2010).

Burke, Kenneth, *Language as Symbolic Action: Essays on Life, Literature, and Method* (Berkeley: University of California Press, 1978).

Butler, David (ed.), *Time and Relative Dissertations in Space: Critical Perspectives on Doctor Who* (Manchester: Manchester University Press, 2007).

Callinicos, Alex, *Against Postmodernism: A Marxist Critique* (Cambridge: Polity, 1990).

Campbell, Joseph, *The Hero with a Thousand Faces* (London: Fontana, 1993; orig. 1948).

Campbell, Joseph, *Myths to Live By* (London: Souvenir Press, 2000).

Campbell, Mark, *Doctor Who: The Complete Guide* (London: Constable & Robinson, 2013).

Carlyle, Thomas, *On Heroes, Hero-Worship and the Heroic in History* (London: Chapman and Hall, 1840).

Cassirer, Ernst, *The Myth of the State* (New Haven, CT: Yale University Press, 1946).

Cassirer, Ernst, *Symbol, Myth and Culture: Essays and Lectures of Ernst Cassirer, 1935–45*, ed. Donald Philip Verene (New Haven, CT: Yale University Press, 1979).

Chapman, James, *Inside the TARDIS: The Worlds of Doctor Who* (London: I.B. Tauris, 2013; orig. 2006).

Charles, Alec, 'The Ideology of Anachronism: Television, History and the Nature of Time', in David Butler (ed.), *Time and Relative Dissertations in Space* (Manchester: Manchester University Press, 2007), pp. 108–22.

Charles, Alec, *Out of Time: The Deaths and Resurrections of Doctor Who* (Oxford: Peter Lang, 2015).

Charles, Alec, 'What the Casting of the Next Doctor Who Will Tell Us about the BBC', *The Conversation* (13 April 2017). Available at https://theconversation.com/what-the-casting-of-the-next-doctor-who-will-tell-us-about-the-bbc-76162 (accessed 2 August 2017).

Cherry, Brigid, 'Squee, Retcon, Fanwank and the Not-We: Computer-Mediated Discourse and the Online Audience for NuWho', in Chris Hansen (ed.), *Ruminations, Peregrinations, and Regenerations: A Critical Approach to Doctor Who* (Newcastle-upon-Tyne: Cambridge Scholars, 2010), pp. 209–32.

Clarke, Neil, 'Holy Terror and Fallen Demigod: The Doctor as Myth', in Anthony Burdge, Jessica Burke and Kristine Larsen (eds), *The Mythological Dimensions of Doctor Who* (Crawfordville, FL: Kitsune Books, 2010), pp. 37–51.

Coleridge, Samuel Taylor, *Biographia Literaria, or, Biographical Sketches of My Literary Life and Opinions* (London: Dent, 1957; orig. 1816).

Collinson, Phil, Paul Cornell and Billie Piper, audio commentary, 'Father's Day', *Doctor Who: The Complete First Series* DVD box-set (BBC Worldwide/2 Entertain, 2005).

Connolly, Kelly, 'The Radical Helplessness of the New *Doctor Who*', *The Atlantic* (10 December 2018). Available at https://www.theatlantic.com/entertainment/archive/2018/12/doctor-who-radical-helplessness-jodie-whittaker-season-11/577741/ (accessed 25 January 2019).

Cook, Benjamin, *The New Audio Adventures: The Inside Story* (Maidenhead: Big Finish, 2003).

Cook, Benjamin, Interview with Frank Skinner, *Doctor Who Magazine*, 478 (November 2014), pp. 27–28.

Cook, Benjamin, Interview with Steven Moffat, *Doctor Who Magazine*, 500 (July 2016), pp. 58–9.

Cook, Benjamin, 'The Ultimate Interview', interview with Tom Baker, *Doctor Who Magazine*, 501 (August 2016), pp. 4–68.

Cooke, Rachel, 'What's Up Doc?', *The Observer* (Sunday 6 March 2005). Available at www.theguardian.com/theobserver/2005/mar/06/features.review17 (accessed 30 October 2015).

Cooper, Steven, and Kevin Mahoney, *Steven Moffat's Doctor Who 2012–2013: The Critical Fan's Guide to Matt Smith's Final Series (Unauthorized)* (Punked Books, 2014).

Cornell, Paul, *Timewyrm: Revelation* (London: Virgin, 1991).

Cornell, Paul, *Goth Opera* (London: Virgin, 1994).

Cornell, Paul, *No Future* (London: Virgin, 1994).

Cornell, Paul, *Human Nature* (London: Virgin, 1995).

Cornell, Paul, 'Canonicity in Doctor Who', *Paul Cornell: Novelist, Screenwriter, Comics Writer* (10 February 2007). Available at www.paulcornell.com/2007/02/canonicity-in-doctor-who/ (accessed 7 November 2015).

Cornell, Paul, *Four Doctors* (London: Titan, 2015).

Coupe, Laurence, *Myth* (London: Routledge, 1997).

Crome, Andrew, and James McGrath (eds), *Time and Relative Dimensions in Faith: Religion and Doctor Who* (London: Darton, Longman and Todd, 2013).

Cross, Katherine, 'Doctor Who Has Given Us a Doctor without Inner Conflict', *Polygon* (1 January 2019). Available at https://www.polygon.com/2019/1/1/18152028/doctor-who-whitaker-season-review (accessed 3 January 2019).

Cull, Nicholas, '"Bigger on the Inside …" *Doctor Who* as British Cultural History', in Graham Roberts and Philip M. Taylor (eds), *The Historian, Television and Television History* (Luton: University of Luton Press, 2001), pp. 95–111.

Curry, Graeme, *Doctor Who – The Happiness Patrol* (London: Target, 1985).

Darlington, David, 'You're Killing My Lesbian Subtext …!!', interview with Rona Munro, Deejsaint (25 November 2007). Available at http://web.archive.org/web/20110604155734/http://www.btinternet.com/~david.darlington/rona2007.html (accessed 28 August 2015).

Davies, Russell T., *Dark Season* (London: BBC Consumer, 1991).

Davies, Russell T., *Doctor Who – Damaged Goods* (London: Virgin, 1996).

Davies, Russell T., *Doctor Who – Rose* (London: BBC Books, 2018).

Davis, Erik, *Techgnosis: Myth, Magic and Mysticism in the Age of Information* (London: Serpent's Tail, 1999).

de Certeau, Michel, *The Writing of History* (New York: Columbia University Press, 1988).

Decker, Kevin S., *Who Is Who? The Philosophy of Doctor Who* (London: I.B. Tauris, 2012).

Derrida, Jacques, *Specters of Marx: The State of the Debt, the Work of Mourning and the New International*, trans. Peggy Kamuf (New York: Routledge, 2006).

Dicks, Terrance, *Doctor Who and the Auton Invasion* (London: W.H. Allen, 1974).

Dicks, Terrance, *Doctor Who and the Terror of the Autons* (London: W.H. Allen, 1975).

Dicks, Terrance, *Doctor Who and the State of Decay* (London: Target, 1981).

Dicks, Terrance, *Doctor Who – Inferno* (London: Target, 1984).

Dicks, Terrance, *Timewyrm: Exodus* (London: Virgin, 1991).

Dicks, Terrance, *Blood Harvest* (London: Virgin, 1994).

Dicks, Terrance, *Doctor Who – The Eight Doctors* (London: BBC Books, 1997).

Dicks, Terrance, and Malcolm Hulke, *The Making of Doctor Who*, revised second edition (London: Target, 1976).

The Dr Who Annual (Manchester: World Distributors, 1965).

Doctor Who and the Daleks (Slough: Cadet Sweets, 1964).

Dorney, John, *Doctor Who – The Lords of the Red Planet* (London: Big Finish, 2013).

Dring, Chris, 'The Long Game', *Doctor Who Magazine*, 496 (March 2016), pp. 50–57.

du Coudray, Chantal Bourgault, *The Curse of the Werewolf: Fantasy, Horror and the Beast Within* (London: I.B. Tauris, 2006).

Eagleton, Terry, *The Illusions of Postmodernism* (Oxford: Blackwell, 1996).

Eco, Umberto, *Travels in Hyperreality: Essays*, trans. William Weaver (London: Picador, 2003).

Eliade, Mircea, *Myth and Reality* (London: Allen and Unwin, 1964).

Eliade, Mircea, *The Myth of the Eternal Return, or, Cosmos and History* (Princeton, NJ: Princeton University Press, 1971).

Eliot, T. S., *Selected Prose*, ed. Frank Kermode (London: Faber and Faber, 1975).

Elledge, Jonn, '"This Will Annoy Exactly the Right People": Why Casting Jodie Whittaker as Doctor Who Is a Brilliant Decision', *New Statesman* (16 July 2017). Available at www.newstatesman.com/culture/tv-radio/2017/07/will-annoy-exactly-right-people-why-casting-jodie-whittaker-doctor-who (accessed 4 August 2017).

Evans, Hywel, Review of Matt Hills (ed.), *New Dimensions of Doctor Who: Adventures in Space, Time and Television*, in *Doctor Who Magazine*, 470 (March 2014), p. 73.

Evans, Hywel, Review of James Chapman, *Inside the TARDIS: The Worlds of Doctor Who*, in *Doctor Who Magazine*, 477 (October 2014), p. 89.

Fisher, Mark, 'What Is Hauntology?', *Film Quarterly*, 66:1 (Fall 2012), pp. 16–24.

Fiske, John, '*Doctor Who*, Ideology and the Reading of a Popular Narrative', *Australian Journal of Screen Theory*, 14–15 (1983), pp. 69–100.

Fiske, John, *Television Culture* (London: Routledge, 1989).

Foucault, Michel, *The Order of Things* (London: Routledge, 1989).

Fowkes, Katherine A., *The Fantasy Film* (Chichester: Wiley-Blackwell, 2010).

Frazer, James George, *The Golden Bough: A Study in Magic and Religion*, 12 vols (London: Macmillan, 1890–1911).

Frye, Northrop, *Anatomy of Criticism: Four Essays* (Princeton, NJ: Princeton University Press, 1971).

Gaiman, Neil, interviewed by Nick Setchfield, *SFX* (7 May 2013). Available at www.gamesradar.com/exclusive-neil-gaiman-talks-doctor-who-and-cybermen/ (accessed 8 November 2015).

Garner, Ross P., Melissa Beattie and Una McCormack (eds), *Impossible Worlds, Impossible Things: Cultural Perspectives on Doctor Who,*

Torchwood and the Sarah Jane Adventures (Newcastle-upon-Tyne: Cambridge Scholars, 2010).

Gelder, Ken, *Reading the Vampire* (London: Routledge, 1994).

Geertz, Clifford, *The Interpretation of Cultures: Selected Essays* (London: Fontana, 1993).

Goss, James, Douglas Adams and David Fisher, *Doctor Who – City of Death* (London: BBC Books, 2015).

Graves, Robert, *The Greek Myths: Complete Edition* (Harmondsworth: Penguin, 1992).

Gray, Scott, Martin Geraghty and David A. Roach, 'Bad Blood', *Doctor Who Magazine*, 338–42 (7 January–28 April 2004).

Gray, Warwick, 'The Naked Flame', *Doctor Who Yearbook 1995* (London: Marvel, 1994).

Griffiths, Nick, *Who Goes There: Travels through Strangest Britain in Search of the Doctor* (London: Legend Press, 2009).

Groom, Nick, *The Gothic: A Very Short Introduction* (Oxford: Oxford University Press, 2012).

Gunning, Tom, 'The Cinema of Attraction[s]: Early Film, Its Spectator, and the Avant-Garde', in Wanda Strauven (ed.), *The Cinema of Attractions Reloaded* (Amsterdam: Amsterdam University Press, 2006), pp. 381–8.

Gunning, Tom, 'An Aesthetic of Astonishment: Early Film and the (In)Credulous Spectator', in Leo Braudy and Marshall Cohen (eds), *Film Theory and Criticism: Introductory Readings*, 7th edition (Oxford: Oxford University Press, 2009), pp. 736–50.

Hadoke, Toby, *Moths Ate My Doctor Who Scarf*, produced by Paul Hardy (London: BBC Audio, 2007).

Halliday, Mags L., Kelly Hale, and Philip Purser-Hallard, *Bernice Summerfield – The Vampire Curse* (London: Big Finish, 2008).

Hansen, Chris (ed.), *Ruminations, Peregrinations, and Regenerations: A Critical Approach to Doctor Who* (Newcastle-upon-Tyne: Cambridge Scholars, 2010).

Harmes, Marcus K., *Doctor Who and the Art of Adaptation: Fifty Years of Storytelling* (New York: Rowman & Littlefield, 2014).

Harrigan, Pat, and Noah Wardrip-Fruin (eds), *Third Person: Authoring and Exploring Vast Narratives* (Cambridge, MA: MIT Press, 2009).

Harvey, David, *The Condition of Postmodernity* (Oxford: Blackwell, 1991).

Hayles, Brian, *Doctor Who and the Ice Warriors* (London: Target, 1976).

Hearn, Marcus, *The Vault: Treasures from the First 50 Years* (London: BBC Books, 2013).

Heidegger, Martin, *Being and Time: A Translation of* Sein und Zeit, trans. Joan Stambaugh (New York: State University of New York Press, 1996).

Heidegger, Martin, 'Building Dwelling Thinking' (1951), in *Poetry, Language, Thought*, trans. Albert Hofstadter (New York: Harper Perennial, 2001).

Heinlein, Robert A., *The Menace from Earth* (Riverdale, NY: Baen Books, 1987; orig. 1959).

Hellekson, Karen, '"Doctor Who Unbound", the Alternate History and the Fannish Text', in Paul Booth (ed.), *Fan Phenomena: Doctor Who* (London: Intellect, 2013), pp. 136–47.

Herbert, Michael, *Doctor Who and the Communist: Malcolm Hulke and His Career in Television* (Nottingham: Five Leaves, 2015).

Hills, Matt, *Fan Cultures* (London: Routledge, 2002).

Hills, Matt, '"Gothic" Body Parts in a "Postmodern" Body of Work? The Hinchcliffe/Holmes Era of *Doctor Who* (1975–77)', *Intensities: The Journal of Cult Media*, 4 (2007). Available at https://intensitiescultmedia.files. wordpress.com/2012/12/hills-gothic-body-parts-in-postmodern-body-of-work.pdf (accessed 13 June 2017).

Hills, Matt, 'Televisuality without Television? The Big Finish Audios and Discourses of "Tele-centric" *Doctor Who*' in David Butler (ed.), *Time and Relative Dissertations in Space* (Manchester: Manchester University Press, 2007), pp. 280–95.

Hills, Matt, 'Afterword: Scholar-Fandom's Different Incarnations', in Ross P. Garner, Melissa Beattie and Una McCormack (eds), *Impossible Worlds, Impossible Things: Cultural Perspectives on Doctor Who, Torchwood and the Sarah Jane Adventures* (Newcastle-upon-Tyne: Cambridge Scholars, 2010), pp. 210–17.

Hills, Matt, '"Mythology Makes You Feel Something": The Russell T. Davies Era as Sentimental Journey', in Anthony Burdge, Jessica Burke and Kristine Nilsen (eds) *The Mythological Dimensions of Doctor Who* (Crawfordville, FL: Kitsune Books, 2010), pp. 197–213.

Hills, Matt, *Triumph of a Time Lord: Regenerating Doctor Who for the Twenty-First Century* (London: I.B. Tauris, 2010).

Hills, Matt (ed.), *New Dimensions of Doctor Who: Adventures in Space, Time and Television* (London: I.B. Tauris, 2013).

Hills, Matt, 'Casting a Female Doctor Who Wasn't So Bold – Choosing Another White Male Would Have Been Really Risky', *The Conversation* (26 July 2017). Available at https://theconversation.com/casting-a-female-doctor-who-wasnt-so-bold-choosing-another-white-male-would-have-been-really-risky-81410 (accessed 2 August 2017).

Hinchcliffe, Philip, *Doctor Who and the Keys of Marinus* (London: Target, 1980).

Hinton, Craig, *GodEngine* (London: Virgin, 1996).

Hinton, Craig, *The Quantum Archangel* (London: BBC Books, 2001).

Hinton, Craig, *Synthespians™* (London: BBC Books, 2004).

Hoare, James, '*Doctor Who*'s Steven Moffat on "Rubbish" Ice Warriors Return', *SciFiNow* (21 February 2013). Available at www.scifinow. co.uk/news/doctor-whos-steven-moffat-on-rubbish-ice-warriors-return/ (accessed 20 November 2015).

Howe, David J., *Doctor Who: A Book of Monsters* (London: BBC Books, 1997).

Howe, David J., and Stephen J. Walker, *Doctor Who – The Handbook: The Fifth Doctor: The Peter Davison Years 1982–1984* (London: Virgin, 1995).

Howe, David J., and Stephen J. Walker, *Doctor Who – The Handbook: The Third Doctor: The Jon Pertwee Years 1970–1974* (London: Virgin, 1996).

Howe, David J., and Stephen J. Walker, *Doctor Who – The Handbook: The Sylvester McCoy Years 1987–1996* (London: Virgin, 1998).

Howe, David J., and Stephen J. Walker, *Doctor Who: The Television Companion* (London: BBC Worldwide, 1998).

Howe, David J., Mark Stammers and Stephen J. Walker, *Doctor Who – The Handbook: The Fourth Doctor: The Tom Baker Years 1974–1981* (London: Virgin, 1992).

Howe, David J., Mark Stammers and Stephen J. Walker, *Doctor Who – The Handbook: The Sixth Doctor: The Colin Baker Years 1984–1986* (London: Virgin, 1993).

Howe, David J., Mark Stammers and Stephen J. Walker, *Doctor Who – The Handbook: The First Doctor: The William Hartnell Years 1963–1966* (London: Virgin, 1994).

Howe, David J., Mark Stammers and Stephen J. Walker, *Doctor Who – The Handbook: The Second Doctor: The Patrick Troughton Years 1966–1969* (London: Virgin, 1997).

Hughes, Ted, *Shakespeare and the Goddess of Complete Being* (London: Faber and Faber, 1992).

Hulke, Malcolm, and Terrance Dicks, *The Making of Doctor Who* (London: Pan, 1972).

Hutcheon, Linda, *The Politics of Postmodernism* (London: Routledge, 1989).

Jackson, Rosemary, *Fantasy: The Literature of Subversion* (London: Routledge, 1998).

Jameson, Frederic, *The Political Unconscious: Narrative as a Socially Symbolic Act* (Ithaca, NY: Cornell University Press, 1981).

Jameson, Frederic, *Postmodernism, or, the Cultural Logic of Late Capitalism* (London: Verso, 1992).

Jameson, Frederic, *The Ancients and the Postmoderns* (London: Verso, 2015).

Jenkins, Henry, *Convergence Culture: Where Old and New Media Collide* (New York: New York University Press, 2006).

Jenkins, Henry, 'Transmedia Storytelling 101', *Confessions of an Aca-Fan* (22 March 2007). Available at http://henryjenkins.org/2007/03/transmedia_storytelling_101.html (accessed 5 December 2015).

Jenkins, Henry, 'Transmedia 202: Further Reflections', *Confessions of an Aca-Fan: The Official Weblog of Henry Jenkins* (1 August 2011). Available at http://henryjenkins.org/2011/08/defining_transmedia_further_re.html (accessed 5 December 2015).

Jowett, Lorna, 'The Girls Who Waited? Female Companions and Gender in *Doctor Who*', *Critical Studies in Television: The International Journal of Television Studies*, 9:1 (Spring 2014), pp. 77–94.

Jowett, Lorna, *Dancing with the Doctor: Dimensions of Gender in the Doctor Who Universe* (London: I.B. Tauris, 2017).

Jowett, Lorna, 'The Thirteenth Doctor: Lucky for Some?', *Medium* (21 July 2017). Available at https://medium.com/@UniNorthants/the-thirteenth-doctor-lucky-for-some-215e53940caa (accessed 2 August 2017).

Kearney, Richard, *The Wake of Imagination: Toward a Postmodern Culture* (London: Routledge, 1988).

Keats, John, *The Letters of John Keats*, ed. Maurice Buxton Foreman (London: Oxford University Press, 1947).

Kelly, Stephen, '*Doctor Who*: Mark Gatiss on Why the Time Lords Shouldn't "Become Like a Bunch of MPs"', *Radio Times* (24 March 2014). Available at www.radiotimes.com/news/2014-03-24/doctor-who-mark-gatiss-on-why-the-time-lords-shouldnt-become-like-a-bunch-of-mps (accessed 5 March 2017).

Kelly, Stephen, '*Doctor Who* Boss Steven Moffat Admits the Colourful New Paradigm Daleks "Were a Mistake"', *Radio Times* (15 November 2015). Available at www.radiotimes.com/news/2015-11-15/doctor-who-boss-steven-moffat-admits-the-colourful-new-paradigm-daleks-were-a-mistake (accessed 4 December 2015).

Kibble-White, Graham, Review of *Myths and Legends* box-set, *Doctor Who Magazine*, 421 (11 May 2011), pp. 60–1.

Kibble-White, Graham, Review of 'Cold War', *Doctor Who Magazine*, 460 (June 2013), p. 65.

Kibble-White, Graham, Review of 'Journey to the Centre of the TARDIS', *Doctor Who Magazine*, 460 (June 2013), p. 68.

Kilburn, Matthew, 'Bargains of Necessity? *Doctor Who*, *Culloden* and Fictionalising History at the BBC in the 1960s', in David Butler (ed.), *Time and Relative Dissertations in Space* (Manchester: Manchester University Press, 2007), pp. 68–85.

Kirk, G. S., *Myth: Its Meaning and Function in Ancient and Other Cultures* (Cambridge: Cambridge University Press, 1970).

Kirkley, Paul, Review of 'It Takes You Away', *Doctor Who Magazine*, 534 (February 2019), pp. 58–9.

Kistler, Alan, *Doctor Who: A History* (London: Rowman & Littlefield, 2013).

Kracauer, Siegfried, *Theory of Film: The Redemption of Physical Reality* (New York: Oxford University Press, 1960).

Kristeva, Julia, *Powers of Horror: An Essay in Abjection* (New York: Columbia University Press, 1982).

Kristeva, Julia, *The Kristeva Reader*, ed. Toril Moi (Oxford: Blackwell, 1986).

Kuhn, Thomas, *The Structure of Scientific Revolutions* (London: University of Chicago Press, 1962).

Layton, David, *The Humanism of Doctor Who: A Critical Study in Science Fiction and Philosophy* (Jefferson, NC: McFarland, 2012).

Leach, Jim, *Doctor Who* (Detroit, MI: Wayne State University Press, 2009).

Leitch, Gillian I. (ed.), *Doctor Who in Time and Space: Essays on Themes, Characters, History and Fandom, 1963–2012* (Jefferson, NC: McFarland, 2013).

Lévi-Strauss, Claude, *The Savage Mind* (London: Weidenfeld and Nicolson, 1966).

Lévi-Strauss, Claude, *The Raw and the Cooked: Introduction to a Science of Mythology*, vol. 1 (London: Jonathan Cape, 1970; orig. 1964).

Lévi-Strauss, Claude, *Myth and Meaning* (London: Routledge and Kegan Paul, 1978).

Lévy-Bruhl, Lucien, *How Natives Think* (1926) (New York: Washington Square Press, 1966).

Lévy-Bruhl, Lucien, *Primitive Mythology: The Mythic World of the Australian and Papuan Natives* (1935) (Queensland: University of Queensland Press, 1984).

Lincoln, Bruce, 'An Early Moment in the Discourse of "Terrorism": Reflections on a Tale from Marco Polo', *Comparative Studies in Society and History*, 48:2 (April 2006), pp. 242–59.

Lofficier, Jean-Marc, *The Doctor Who Programme Guide: Volume 1: The Programmes* (London: Target, 1981).

Lofficier, Jean-Marc, *The Doctor Who Programme Guide: Volume 2: What's What and Who's Who* (London: Target, 1981).

Logan, Brian, 'The Spirit of Wobbliness', *The Guardian* (29 September 2003). Available at www.theguardian.com/media/2003/sep/29/broadcasting.bbc (accessed 5 July 2016).

Lyotard, Jean-François, *The Postmodern Condition: A Report on Knowledge* (Manchester: Manchester University Press, 1979).

McCallum, Pamela, 'Questions of Haunting: Jacques Derrida's *Specters of Marx* and Raymond Williams's *Modern Tragedy*', *Mosaic*, 40:2 (June 2007), pp. 231–44.

MacDonald, Anson (pseud. Robert A. Heinlein), 'By His Bootstraps', *Astounding Science Fiction* (October 1941), pp. 9–47.

McKee, Alan, 'How to Tell the Difference between Production and Consumption: A Case Study in *Doctor Who* Fandom', in Sara Gwenllian-Jones and Roberta E. Pearson (eds), *Cult Television* (Minneapolis: University of Minnesota Press, 2004), pp. 167–85.

McKee, Alan, 'Is *Doctor Who* Political?' *European Journal of Cultural Studies*, 7:2 (2004), pp. 201–17.

McLuhan, Marshall, 'Catholic Humanism & Modern Letters', *Christian Humanism in Letters* (Hartford, CT: St. Joseph's College, 1954), pp. 78–80.

McLuhan, Marshall, *Understanding Media: The Extensions of Man* (London: Routledge and Kegan Paul, 1964).

Maddox, Mike, *Doctor Who – Legend of the Cybermen* (London: Big Finish, 2010).

Magrs, Paul, 'Afterword: My Adventures', in David Butler (ed.), *Time and Relative Dissertations in Space* (Manchester: Manchester University Press, 2007), pp. 296–309.

Magrs, Paul, *The Diary of a Doctor Who Addict* (London: Simon & Schuster, 2010).

Malinowski, Bronisław, *Myth in Primitive Psychology* (London: Norton, 1926).

Malinowski, Bronisław, *Magic, Science and Religion and Other Essays* (Glencoe, IL: Free Press, 1948).

Manovich, Lev, 'The Paradoxes of Digital Photography', *Photography after Photography: Memory and Representation in the Digital Age* (G&B Arts, 1995). Available at http://manovich.net/content/04-projects/004-paradoxes-of-digital-photography/02_article_1994.pdf (accessed 16 August 2016).

Manovich, Lev, *The Language of New Media* (Cambridge, MA: MIT Press, 2001).

Martin, Philip, *Doctor Who – Mindwarp* (London: Target, 1989).

Miles, Lawrence and Tat Wood, *About Time 3: The Unauthorized Guide to Doctor Who 1970–1974: Seasons 7 to 11* (Des Moines, IA: Mad Norwegian Press, 2004).

Miles, Lawrence and Tat Wood, *About Time 4: The Unauthorized Guide to Doctor Who 1975–1979: Seasons 12 to 17* (Des Moines, IA: Mad Norwegian Press, 2004).

Miles, Lawrence and Tat Wood, *About Time 5: The Unauthorized Guide to Doctor Who 1980–1984: Seasons 18 to 21* (Des Moines, IA: Mad Norwegian Press, 2005).

Mills, Pat, John Wagner and Alan Gibbons, 'The Dogs of Doom', *Doctor Who Weekly* (16 April–5 June 1980), pp. 27–34.

Milton, John, *Prose Writings* (London: J. M. Dent, 1958).

Moffat, Steven, '"What I Did On My Christmas Holidays" by Sally Sparrow', *Doctor Who Annual 2006* (Tunbridge Wells: Panini, 2005).

Morris, Jonathan, 'Mary's Story', *The Company of Friends* (London: Big Finish, 2009).

Morris, Jonathan, 'The TV Movie: Twenty Years On', *Doctor Who Magazine*, 497 (April 2016), pp. 12–18.

Morrison, Grant, 'The World Shapers', *Doctor Who Magazine* (August–October 1987), pp. 127–9.

Mortimore, Jim, *Blood Heat* (London: Virgin, 1993).

Nation, Terry, and David Whitaker, *The Dalek Book* (London: Souvenir Press, 1964).

Newman, Kim, *Doctor Who* (London: BFI, 2005).

North, Dan, 'Magic and Illusion in Early Cinema', *Studies in French Cinema*, 1:2 (2001), pp. 70–9.

O'Day, Andrew (ed.), *Doctor Who: The Eleventh Hour – A Critical Celebration of the Matt Smith and Steven Moffat Era* (London: I.B. Tauris, 2014).

O'Mahony, Daniel, *Doctor Who – Return to the Web Planet* (London: Big Finish, 2007).

O'Mahony, Daniel, '"Now How Is That Wolf Able to Impersonate a Grandmother?" History, Pseudo-History and Genre in *Doctor Who*', in David Butler (ed.), *Time and Relative Dissertations in Space* (Manchester: Manchester University Press, 2007), pp. 56–67.

Ong, Walter J., *Orality and Literacy: The Technologizing of the Word* (New York: Routledge, 2002).

'On the Web Planet', *TV Comic*, 693–8 (27 March–1 May 1965).

Orthia, Lindy (ed.), *Doctor Who and Race* (Bristol: Intellect, 2013).

'Out of Time', DVD extra (Disc 2), *The Invasion of Time* (BBC/2 Entertain).

Parkin, Lance, *The Infinity Doctors* (London: BBC Books, 1998).

Parkin, Lance, 'Canonicity Matters: Defining the *Doctor Who* Canon', in David Butler (ed.), *Time and Relative Dissertations in Space* (Manchester: Manchester University Press, 2007), pp. 246–62.

Parkin, Lance, and Lars Pearson, *Ahistory: An Unauthorized History of the Doctor Who Universe* (Des Moines, IA: Mad Norwegian Press, 2012).

Paulin, Tom, *Minotaur: Poetry and the Nation State* (London: Faber and Faber, 1992).

Peel, John, *Doctor Who – The Chase* (London: Target, 1989).

Peel, John, *Timewyrm: Genesys* (London: Virgin, 1991).

Peel, John, *Doctor Who – War of the Daleks* (London: BBC, 1997).

Phillips, Ivan, 'Frock Coats, Yo-Yos and a Chair with a Panda on It: Nostalgia for the Future in the Life of a *Doctor Who* Fan', in Paul Booth (ed.), *Fan Phenomena: Doctor Who* (Bristol: Intellect, 2013), pp. 16–27.

Phillips, Ivan, 'The Vampire in the Machine: Exploring the Undead Interface', in Sam George and Bill Hughes (eds), *Open Graves, Open Minds: Representations of Vampires and the Undead from the Enlightenment to the Present Day* (Manchester: Manchester University Press, 2013), pp. 225–44.

Phillips, Ivan, '*Doctor Who* and the Terror of the Vorticists: Popular Fantasy and the Cultural Inheritance of *BLAST*', BLAST 2014 Conference, Bath Spa University, 24–6 July 2014.

Phillips, Ivan, 'Is the End of Time in Sight for *Doctor Who*', *The Conversation* (22 December 2016). Available at https://theconversation.com/is-the-end-of-time-in-sight-for-doctor-who-70353 (accessed 3 January 2017).

Phillips, Ivan, 'Reversing the Polarity of the Gender Flow: On Reactions to Jodie Whittaker as the Doctor', *TVAD: Theorising Visual Art and Design* (28 July 2017). Available at http://tvad-uh.blogspot.co.uk/2017/07/reversingthe-polarity-of-gender-flow-on.html (accessed 2 August 2017).

Phillips, Ivan, '"All This Fizzing Inside": Watching the Return of *Doctor Who*', *CST online* (12 October 2018). Available at https://cstonline.net/all-this-fizzing-inside-watching-the-return-of-doctor-who-by-ivan-phillips/ (accessed 18 May 2019).

Phillips, Ivan, ' "I Am the Bad Wolf. I Create Myself": The Metafictional Meanings of Lycanthropic Transformations in *Doctor Who*', in Sam George and Bill Hughes (eds), *In the Company of Wolves: Werewolves, Wolves and Wild Children* (Manchester: Manchester University Press, 2020), pp. 178–89.

Platt, Marc, *Doctor Who – Ghost Light* (London: Target, 1990).

Platt, Marc, *Cat's Cradle: Time's Crucible* (London: Virgin, 1992).

Platt, Marc, *Lungbarrow* (London: Virgin, 1997).

Platt, Marc, *Doctor Who – Loups-Garoux* (London: Big Finish, 2001).

Platt, Marc, *Doctor Who – Spare Parts* (London: Big Finish, 2002).

Platt, Marc, and Paul Vyse, 'Loop the Loup', *Doctor Who Yearbook 1994* (Marvel, 1994).

Poole, Roger, 'The Real Plot Line of Ford Madox Ford's *The Good Soldier*: An Essay in Applied Deconstruction', *Textual Practice*, 4:3 (December 1990), pp. 390–427.

Propp, Vladimir, *Morphology of the Folk Tale* (Austin: University of Texas Press, 1968).

Rafer, David, 'Mythic Identity in *Doctor Who*', in David Butler (ed.), *Time and Relative Dissertations in Space* (Manchester: Manchester University Press, 2007), pp. 123–37.

Raglan, Lord, *The Hero: A Study in Tradition, Myth and Drama* (New York: Vintage, 1956).

Rayner, Jacqueline, *Doctor Who – Wolfsbane* (London: BBC Books, 2003).

Richards, Justin, *Time Lord Fairy Tales* (London: BBC Books, 2015).

Rickword, Edgell, *The Calendar of Modern Letters, March 1925–July 1927*, ed. Douglas Garman (London: Routledge, 1966).

Rickword, Edgell, *Essays and Opinions, 1921–1931*, ed. Alan Young (Manchester: Carcanet, 1974).

Ricoeur, Paul, *Lectures on Ideology and Utopia* (New York: Columbia University Press, 1986).

Ricoeur, Paul, *From Text to Action: Essays in Hermeneutics, II* (Evanston, IL: Northwestern University Press, 1991).

Ricoeur, Paul, *A Ricoeur Reader: Reflection & Imagination*, ed. Mario J. Valdés (London: Harvester Wheatsheaf, 1991).

Robinson, Nigel, *Timewyrm: Apocalypse* (London: Virgin, 1991).

Rosenstone, Robert A., 'History in Images/History in Words: Reflections on the Possibility of Really Putting History onto Film', *The American Historical Review*, 93:5 (December 1988), p. 1185.

Russell, Gary, *Doctor Who – Placebo Effect* (London: BBC Books, 1998).

Russell, Gary, *Doctor Who: The Inside Story* (London: BBC Books, 2006).

Sartre, Jean-Paul, *Being and Nothingness: A Phenomenological Essay on Ontology* (1943) (Abingdon: Routledge, 2003).

Sartre, Jean-Paul, *Essays in Existentialism* (New York: Citadel Press, 1993).

Sconduto, Leslie A., *Metamorphoses of the Werewolf: A Literary Study from Antiquity through the Renaissance* (Jefferson, NC: McFarland, 2008).

Segal, Robert A., *Myth: A Very Short Introduction* (Oxford: Oxford University Press, 2004).

Shearman, Rob, *Doctor Who – Jubilee* (London: Big Finish, 2003).

Sleight, Graham, *The Doctor's Monsters: Meanings of the Monstrous in Doctor Who* (London: I.B. Tauris, 2012).

Smith, Andrew, *Doctor Who – Domain of the Voord* (London: Big Finish, 2014).

Smith, Dale, 'Broader and Deeper: The Lineage and Impact of the *Timewyrm* Series', in David Butler (ed.), *Time and Relative Dissertations in Space* (Manchester: Manchester University Press, 2007), pp. 263–79.

Sontag, Susan, *Against Interpretation and Other Essays* (New York: Delta, 1967).

Spilsbury, Tom, 'Public Image', *Doctor Who Magazine*, 534 (February 2019), p. 7.

Spivak, Gayatri, 'Translator's Introduction', in Jacques Derrida (ed.), *Of Grammatology* (Baltimore, MD: John Hopkins University Press, 1976).

Spooner, Catherine, *Contemporary Gothic* (London: Reaktion, 2006).

Standring, Lesley, *The Doctor Who Illustrated A–Z* (London: W.H. Allen, 1985).

Sterne, Laurence, *The Life and Opinions of Tristram Shandy, Gentleman* (Harmondsworth: Penguin, 1967; orig. 1759–67).

Strenski, Ivan, *Four Theories of Myth in Twentieth-Century History: Cassirer, Eliade, Lévi-Strauss and Malinowski* (Basingstoke: Macmillan, 1987).

Strutton, Bill, *Doctor Who and the Zarbi* (London: Fredrick Muller, 1965).

Suvin, Darko, *Metamorphoses of Science Fiction: On the Poetics and History of a Literary Genre* (New Haven, CT: Yale University Press, 1979).

Sweet, Matthew, Review of James Chapman, *Inside the TARDIS*, in *The Independent* (27 May 2006). Available at www.independent.co.uk/arts-entertainment/books/reviews/inside-the-tardis-by-james-chapman-480122.html (accessed 3 March 2017).

Swift, Jonathan, *A Modest Proposal and Other Writings*, ed. Carole Fabricant (Harmondsworth: Penguin, 2009).

Talahay, Rachel, 'Notes on Heaven Sent, Part 1', *RachelTalahay* (16 December 2014). Available at http://racheltalalay.tumblr.com/post/135339295759/notes-on-heaven-sent-part-1 (accessed 22 July 2016).

Tipton, Scott, and David Tipton, *Doctor Who – Prisoners of Time* (San Diego, CA: IDW).

Todorov, Tsvetan, *The Fantastic: A Structural Approach to a Literary Genre*, trans. Richard Howard (Ithaca, NY: Cornell University Press, 1975).

Tolkien, J. R. R., *Tree and Leaf* (New York: HarperCollins, 1964).

Tulloch, John, 'Dr Who: Similarity and Difference', *Australian Journal of Screen Theory*, 11–12 (1982), pp. 8–24.

Tulloch, John, and Manuel Alvarado, *Doctor Who: The Unfolding Text* (Basingstoke: Macmillan, 1983).

Tulloch, John, and Henry Jenkins, *Science Fiction Audiences: Watching Star Trek and Doctor Who* (London: Routledge, 1995).

Twitchell, James B., *The Living Dead: A Study of the Vampire in Romantic Literature* (Durham, NC: Duke University Press, 1981).

Tylor, E. B., *Primitive Culture: Researches into the Development of Mythology, Philosophy, Religion, Language, Art and Custom*, 2 vols (London: Murray, 1871).

Virilio, Paul, *Speed and Politics: An Essay on Dromology* (New York: Semiotext(e), 1977).

Walker, Stephen James, David J. Howe and Mark Stammers, *Doctor Who: The Handbook – The Fourth Doctor* (London: Virgin, 1992).

Warner, Marina, *From the Beast to the Blonde: On Fairy Tales and Their Tellers* (London: Chatto and Windus, 1994).

Warner, Marina, *Managing Monsters: Six Myths of Our Time* (London: Vintage, 1994).

Watcher, The, 'A History of *Doctor Who* in 100 Objects, #53: Varga's Implants', *Doctor Who Magazine*, 482 (February 2015), p. 82.

Webber, C. E., and Sydney Newman, '"Doctor Who" – General Notes on Background and Approach for an Exciting Adventure-Science Fiction Serial for Children's Saturday Viewing', with handwritten notes by Sydney Newman (1963). Available at https://web.archive.org/web/20190509154410/www.bbc.co.uk/archive/doctorwho/6403.shtml?page=txt (accessed 13 September 2019).

Weston, Jessie, *From Ritual to Romance* (London: Doubleday, 1957; orig. 1920).

Whitaker, David, 'The Lair of Zarbi Supremo', *The Dr Who Annual* (Manchester: World Distributors, 1965).

Whitaker, David, *Doctor Who and the Daleks* (London: Target, 1973). Originally published as *Doctor Who in an Exciting Adventure with the Daleks* (London: Frederick Muller, 1964).

White, Hayden, 'Introduction: Historical Fiction, Fictional History, and Historical Reality', *Rethinking History*, 9:2/3 (June/September 2005), pp. 147–57.

Wolf, Mark J. P., *Building Imaginary Worlds: The Theory and History of Subcreation* (New York: Routledge, 2012).

Wood, Tat, and Lawrence Miles, *About Time 1: The Unauthorized Guide to Doctor Who 1963–1966* (Des Moines, IA: Mad Norwegian Press, 2006).

Wood, Tat, and Lawrence Miles, *About Time 2: The Unauthorized Guide to Doctor Who 1966–1969: Seasons 4 to 6* (Des Moines, IA: Mad Norwegian Press, 2006).

Wood, Tat, and Lawrence Miles, *About Time 6: The Unauthorized Guide to Doctor Who 1985–1989: Seasons 24 to 26 / TV Movie* (Des Moines, IA: Mad Norwegian Press, 2007).

Wood, Tat, and Lawrence Miles, *About Time 7: The Unauthorized Guide to Doctor Who 2005–2006: Series 1 & 2* (Des Moines, IA: Mad Norwegian Press, 2013).

Žižek, Slavoj, *Enjoy Your Symptom! Jacques Lacan in Hollywood and Out* (London: Routledge, 2001).

Internet Sources

A Teaspoon and an Open Mind: A Doctor Who Fan Fiction Archive. Available
    at www.whofic.com/ (accessed 22 November 2017).
BBC Writersroom. Available at www.bbc.co.uk/writersroom/scripts (accessed
    21 November 2017).
Blogtor Who. Available at https://blogtorwho.com/ (accessed 21
    November 2017).
'Doctor Who'. *Chrissie's Transcript Site*. Available at www.chakoteya.net/
    DoctorWho/ (accessed 21 November 2017).
Doctor Who Fandom Newsletter. Available at https://who-daily.livejournal.com/
    (accessed 21 November 2017).
'Doctor Who'. *FanFiction*. Available at www.fanfiction.net/tv/Doctor-Who/
    (accessed 22 November 2017).
Doctor Who Guide. Available at http://guide.doctorwhonews.net/ (accessed
    21 November 2017).
Doctor Who Interview Archive. Available at https://drwhointerviews.wordpress.
    com/ (accessed 21 November 2017).
Doctor Who – Official BBC Website. Available at www.bbc.co.uk/blogs/
    doctorwho/ (accessed 21 November 2017).
The Doctor Who Ratings Guide. Available at www.pagefillers.com/dwrg/
    (accessed 21 November 2017).
Doctor Who: The Locations Guide. Available at www.doctorwholocations.net
    (accessed 10 May 2019).
Kasterborous: Doctor Who News and Reviews. Available at http://
    kasterborous.com/ (accessed 21 November 2017).
The Whoniverse. Available at www.whoniverse.net (accessed 21
    November 2017).

Index